1989

Rural society
and the search for order in
early modern Germany

Rural society
and the search for order in
early modern Germany

THOMAS ROBISHEAUX

Duke University

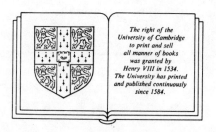

The right of the
University of Cambridge
to print and sell
all manner of books
was granted by
Henry VIII in 1534.
The University has printed
and published continuously
since 1584.

CAMBRIDGE UNIVERSITY PRESS

Cambridge

New York   New Rochelle   Melbourne   Sydney

Published by the Press Syndicate of the University of Cambridge
The Pitt Building, Trumpington Street, Cambridge CB2 1RP
32 East 57th Street, New York, NY 10022, USA
10 Stamford Road, Oakleigh, Melbourne 3166, Australia

First published 1989

Printed in the United States of America

Library of Congress Cataloging-in-Publication Data
Robisheaux, Thomas Willard.
Rural society and the search for order in eary modern Germany / Thomas
Robisheaux.
p. cm.
Bibliography: p.
Includes index.
ISBN 0 521 35626 1
1. Württemberg (Germany) – Social conditions. 2. Württemberg (Germany) – Rural
conditions. I. Title
HN458.W85R63 1989   88–27450
307.7'2'094347 – dc 19   CIP

British Library Cataloguing in Publication Data
Robisheaux, Thomas
Rural society and the search for order in early modern Germany.
1. Germany. Rural regions, Social conditions, history I. Title
943'.009'734
ISBN 0 521 35626 1

Contents

v

Contents

Part Two: Search for order

Part Three: Crisis and recovery

Contents

vii

Illustrations and tables

Graphs

Acknowledgments

As I reflected on how this book came to be written I remembered the words of an English poet who left the bustling world of London and discovered the meaning of his work and life living close to the earth in a small and remote Suffolk village. "So much of poetry is oblation and the putting of the seed into the ground is also a religious rite – perhaps the oldest religious rite that there is," he told Ronald Blythe. "Like the rest of the villagers, I grow not only for myself but to give away. This is important. All country gardeners do this."[1] Words and poetry, like apples, squashes, and corn, are made in order to be given away. It is not enough simply to tend a garden for one's own subsistence, to write poetry alone in a stone cottage, or to write history books that no one will read. One must also give them all up, pass on what has been grown or made; one must share what one knows or has learned. I would add to his observation two others about farmers and historians gathered from my own experiences: All of us, like laborers everywhere, borrow seeds, tools, labor, inspiration, and ideas from each other. All of us talk to each other, and make and remake the world with our words and gossip. History, like farming and poetry writing, is a social activity.

I should therefore like to thank a number of institutions and individuals who made possible the research, the thought, the social activity, that went into this book. The archival research for this book was first undertaken during two lengthy stays in the Federal Republic of Germany in 1977 and 1978–9. On both occasions the German Academic Exchange Service provided me with support for my work. It is fair to say that this work, like many others sponsored by them, would never have been possible without their generous financial and institutional support. They also showed flexibility for the unusual requests I made for help in living in Neuenstein, a small town far from the traditional centers of university life in Baden-Württemberg. To Duke University and the Department of History I am thankful for a junior faculty leave and other support

---

[1] Ronald Blythe, *Akenfield: Portrait of an English Village* (New York: Pantheon, 1969), 295.

xi

in 1986–7. They made it possible for me to take time off from the demands of teaching to finish writing the manuscript.

Some of the seeds for this work were first passed on to me during a year or so of research in West Germany. I should never have discovered the remarkable collection of manuscript sources for the old County of Hohenlohe had Peter Blickle, Rudolf Endres, and David Sabean not put me on the right track. Thanks to their advice, I ventured out from the well-used archives of Stuttgart, Karlsruhe, Würzburg, and other cities into an obscure castle archive in the small town of Neuenstein. At that time the Hohenlohe-Zentralarchiv (Neuenstein) was rumored to house an untapped and rich collection of sources for the sixteenth and seventeenth centuries. The rumors were right. Peter Blickle in particular imparted to me his contagious enthusiasm and interest in the political history of Germany as seen from the village up. Rudolf Endres and Gerd Wunder, two masters of Franconian history, impressed me with the possibilities of doing the history of this region of Germany, and encouraged me from the start. From the beginning Heide Wunder also took a keen interest in the project. I learned a great deal from her about the uses of anthropology in helping to unlock some of the secrets of the early modern village.

Any North American scholar who works periodically in Tübingen will almost inevitably come to know Hans-Christoph Rublack. I benefited not only from the opportunities to discuss my work in its raw early stages, but also from the hospitality that he extends so routinely and graciously to Anglo-American Reformation historians. Franz Irsigler kindly gave me the opportunity to present some of the first results of my work at Trier University.

Other ideas came to me later as seedlings, and to these individuals I am particularly indebted. Erik Midelfort advised me as I wrote up my first ideas as a dissertation at the University of Virginia in 1981. He showed me the human side of the venture and the importance of thinking big and writing well. From him I learned and experienced compassion and understanding. I can now say that his influence was always much stronger than I realized at the time. Joe Miller read every word of the dissertation and offered detailed and insightful commentaries on almost every point I made. Duane Osheim shared with me his own ideas about late medieval and early modern rural life, and from him I felt encouragement in venturing out into new and uncharted areas. As I took the scary step of leaving the dissertation behind, and began to write a new book – this book – from scratch, my colleagues at Duke took the time to read drafts and offer cogent comments. Jack Cell, Bill Reddy, and Ronald Witt read portions of the early drafts of the manuscript and offered comments and criticisms that helped me at several turns. I have been fortunate to have them as colleagues. Mason Barnett, Sarah Blanshei, John Bohstedt, Calvin Davis, Ted Dix, Jan Ewald, Jack Goody, Arthur Haas, Mary Ellen Isaacs, Kristen Neuschel, Bob and Laine Rosin, Anne Scott, and Jörn and Bärbel Sieglerschmidt either responded to my ideas or gave me encouragement at key points. I am grateful to Karen Wysocki for the cartography.

I have accumulated a set of special debts to a small handful of individuals. Without them this work would not have taken the shape it finally did. No scholar can work on German peasants and not be deeply impressed by the work of David Sabean. Many of my ideas about village life in early modern Germany took shape in response to his work. He also advised me long ago about the importance of finding a solid and deep run of archival materials for this study, put me on the track of the Hohenlohe archives, and read every word of the final manuscript. His comments have improved the argument in a number of places. Winfried Schulze not only influenced my thinking about German peasants, he also extended his hospitality to me during a long stay at the Ruhr University at Bochum in 1987. He too read the manuscript from cover to cover. Tom Brady read the final manuscript and offered the kind of support and encouragement I needed at key moments to overcome a writing block. His influence runs deeper than he suspects. Miriam Chrisman also urged me on, and showed faith in me in the ways which only she can.

I also owe a special debt of gratitude to the staff of the Hohenlohe-Zentralarchiv (Neuenstein). During the year or so that I worked in Neuenstein they had only begun the massive task of cataloguing one of the finest private archival collections available for the early modern period. They showed the professional and personal interest in this work that only happens at a small archive. They made it possible for me to look at German village life in ways not achievable before. Then Oberarchivrat Dr. G. Thaddey made available to me a whole series of uncatalogued manuscripts from the Langenburg collection, and always took time to discuss the troublesome problems I encountered in my research. Archivist W. Beuter patiently guided me through the collection, kept a keen eye out for documents that would interest me, expertly advised me in reading and interpreting difficult passages, and provided cheerful companionship during my long year in residence in Neuenstein. Frau Schumm unfortunately never lived to see this work completed, but she always supported my interest in the history of this land and introduced me to contemporary Hohenlohe in a way most outsiders can never experience. Every novice in the archives should be as fortunate as I was in working with such dedicated individuals.

Finally, I am grateful for all of the support that Earl, Jane, Ed, and Lonnie Robisheaux gave me from start to finish. From them I have learned more than they will ever know, and have come to understand that a scholarly adventure is also a long journey of the soul. With my daughter, Anna, I have discovered the joy and grace that one finds unexpectedly in this journey. I have also learned from her not only the pleasure of telling stories, but the importance of telling them the right way and looking for the truth they contain. To her this book is dedicated.

A note on usages

Wherever possible I have employed English translations or their closest equivalents for many technical German terms. Those terms for which a translation was not possible or would have been misleading I have left in German. Readers will find these terms briefly defined in the glossary. The names of political units have been anglicized; for example, "empire," not *Reich*, "County," not *Grafschaft*. Village names, however, have been rendered according to current German usage; for example, Binselberg, not Binzelberg. The names of individuals have been left as they appear in the documents. Dates have not been modernized; they have been left in the old style.

I have left land areas, measures, and currencies for Hohenlohe as they appear in the records. They can be rendered into the following modern equivalents:

Land area
  1 *morgen* = 0.564 hectares = 1.392 acres

Grain measure
  1 *malter* = 184.5 liters

Currency equivalents
  1 *gulden* (fl.) = 15 *batzen*
  1 *batzen* = 4 *kreuzer*
  1 *kreuzer* = 4 *pfennigs*
  1 *pfennig* = 2 *heller*

Glossary

Assecuration: Treaty of 1609
Bauer: tenant farmer; holder of a *Hof*
Bürgermeister: chief officer of a village or town
Centgericht: district court
Dienstgeld: yearly tax in lieu of labor services
Einkindschaft: adoption; children made legally equal for purposes of inheritance
Gerichtsherrschaft: lordship over court jurisdiction
Grundherrschaft: lordship over land; landlordship
Gut: indivisible smallholding
Herrschaft: lordship; authority; domination; state
Hof: indivisible compact farm
Köbler: smallholder; holder of a *Gut*
Kontribution: war levy during Thirty Years' War
Landsteuer: yearly tax levied on assessed wealth
Leibherrschaft: lordship over serfs
Römermonat: unit of imperial taxes
Schultheiss: chief administrative officer of a village
Schutz und Schirm: protection
Sendgericht: itinerant bishop's court
Spital: ecclesiastical institution for charitable purposes
Türkensteuer: imperial war tax levied to fight the Ottoman Empire
Ungeld: consumer tax
Vogt: steward; chief administrative officer of a district

Abbreviations

In the notes and in the table and graph sources I have employed the following abbreviations to designate manuscript holdings from the Hohenlohe-Zentralarchiv (Neuenstein):

Archiv Kirchberg	AK
Kanzlei	AKK
Archiv Langenburg	AL
Amt Langenburg	ALAL
Almosenrechnungen Amt Langenburg	ALAlmAL
Amtsrechnungen Amt Langenburg	ALARL
Contributionsrechnungen Amt Langenburg	ALCRAL
Gemeinschaftliches Archiv Langenburg	ALGAL
Kanzlei I	ALKI
Ältere Kammer Langenburg (before 1700)	ALKL
Supplikenprotokolle Amt Langenburg	ALSPL
Gemeinschaftliches Hausarchiv	GHA
Hohenlohe-Zentralarchiv	HZAN
Linienarchiv Neuenstein	LAN
Lager-, Gült-, and Schatzungsbücher	L/L
Particulararchiv Öhringen	PAÖ

Introduction

Problems

This study began ten years ago as a history of rural society in the age of the German Reformation. At that time scholars knew that the majority of the population lived and worked in the countryside, that the village formed the foundation, the cornerstone, of ecclesiastical and secular power, and that the Peasants' War had played a decisive role in shaping the course of the early Reformation. The old view of Leopold von Ranke no longer rang true. To him German villagers exploded onto the scene of the Reformation with the fury of a storm; but they then vanished, as does every storm, within a short time. What had vanished from the history of the Reformation was not the peasantry, however, but Ranke's interest in it. Yet, despite the attention paid the Peasants' War in the mid-1970s and the earlier pioneering work of Wilhelm Abel on the agrarian cycle, little was known of how villagers came to terms with the wrenching changes of the "long sixteenth century" in the German countryside. And these changes had only just begun to be felt in 1525.

This strange neglect of the history of the German peasantry after 1525 was a symptom of a deeper problem. Astonishingly little attention had been paid to German social history as a whole in the early modern period. The historical literature on early modern German history at that time resembled a painting of Caravaggio, Titian, or even Goya. Much that one would have liked to see, much that was essential to grasp the meaning of the whole picture, remained hidden in the shadows or only hinted at in a strained manner. Robert Scribner could argue, in fact, in the late 1970s that the outlines of a social history of the most thoroughly studied subject of early modern German history, the Reformation, remained poorly understood, the major trends hardly yet grasped.[1] The state of research for the period after the Reformation was even more poorly developed. Only a few beams of light had been cast into some of the darkest

[1] Bob Scribner, "Is There a Social History of the Reformation?" *Social History* 4 (1977), 483–505.

corners. Scholars had concentrated their attention on the two great events of the sixteenth and seventeenth centuries – the Protestant Reformation and the Thirty Years' War – and, while never leaving the period between them entirely blank, they had more often than not filled the gap with a narrow kind of political and religious history. The outlines of early modern German history – Reformation (1517–55), Confessional Age (1555–1618), Thirty Years' War (1618–48), the Age of Absolutism (1648–1789) – were, and still are, conceived in strictly political and religious terms. The idea that the social history of this period demands a different conceptual framework has not had wide acceptance.

The canvas has never been entirely dark, of course, and a few masters have recently let in more light here and there. The social history of the late sixteenth and early seventeenth centuries, as a result, now appears far more complex, far richer and more fascinating, than it did ten years ago. From a number of recent studies one now knows that peasant revolts did not come to an end in 1525: They continued to threaten the stability of large areas of Central Europe right to the end of the Old Regime.[2] And when villagers did not actually go over into rebellion, they showed a disturbing aggressiveness – disturbing to their masters, that is – in carrying out their disputes in the courts and before imperial commissions of arbitration.[3] Yet these studies, welcome and important contributions though they may be, raise more questions than they answer. What conditions led some villagers to stride to open defiance of their lords and rulers, and what kept others obedient, loyal, and compliant? How did this chronic instability, this pervasive fear of unrest, disobedience, and revolt, shape lord–peasant relationships and villagers' relations with the state? Above all, in a time when the administrative structures of the state still proved weak and fragile, when they all too easily broke down altogether, how were social order and hierarchy imposed and maintained and then reproduced?

A number of historians point out now how religion remained inseparable from the problems of social order, political control, and state building in the decades after the Reformation. In the confessional cultures of Germany religion became more than a sparring field for theologians carrying out their bitter doctrinal debates. Religion remained, perhaps more so than in England or France, the language of community, the language of politics and social orga-

---

[2] See Helga Schultz, "Bäuerliche Klassenkämpfe zwischen frühbürgerliche Revolution und Dreissigjährigen Krieg," *Zeitschrift für Geschichtswissenschaft* 20 (1972), 156–73; Peter Blickle, Peter Bierbauer, Renate Blickle, and Claudia Ulbrich, *Aufruhr und Empörung? Studien zum bäuerlichen Widerstand im Alten Reich* (Munich: C. H. Beck, 1980); and Winfried Schulze, ed., *Aufstände, Revolten, Prozesse: Beiträge zu bäuerlichen Widerstandsbewegungen im frühneuzeitlichen Europa*, Geschichte und Gesellschaft: Bochumer Historische Studien, vol. 27 (Stuttgart: Klett-Cotta, 1983). See also Thomas Barnett-Robisheaux, "Peasant Revolts in Germany and Central Europe after the Peasants' War: Comments on the Literature," *Central European History* 17 (1984), 384–403.

[3] Winfried Schulze, *Bäuerlicher Widerstand und feudale Herrschaft in der frühen Neuzeit*, Neuzeit im Aufbau, vol. 6 (Stuttgart–Bad Cannstatt: Frommann-Holzboog, 1980).

nization, of power in all its complex forms. One cannot simply set "religion" aside as one category of analysis, as some historians do, separating out the "social" and the "political" from the "purely religious."[4] Yet these recent studies, focused as they are on the elites, the state, and the cities, still leave many questions about the relationship of church, state, and society in the village unanswered. How did villagers respond to the relentless efforts of elites to establish new confessional cultures? From other studies about popular culture in early modern Europe one would expect villagers to reinterpret cultural ideas and symbols in light of their own needs. But what forms did this take? How *did* villagers reinterpret village culture to explain, to tame, to bring under control, if that was at all possible, the rapidly changing social world of the late sixteenth and early seventeenth centuries?

This study therefore focuses on one central problem: the search for social order, discipline, and hierarchy in a time of disturbing change and disorder. But this complex problem must be approached on several levels and with more careful attention to the interconnectedness of social, cultural, and political history than has yet been paid. Anyone familiar with social anthropology, for example, understands that kin relations, inheritance practices, and property-holding play dominant roles in shaping a peasant society, and so a careful treatment of these themes naturally represents the core of this work. This focus is important, for an extraordinary amount of attention focused on the patriarchal family, on family roles, marriage rituals, and inheritance practices, in the sixteenth and seventeenth centuries. Yet this portion of the study makes little sense when treated in isolation from the most fundamental social and economic changes of this period: the steady growth in population, the growing shortage of arable land, the erosion of wages, and the inflation of food prices. How did rural communities deal with the massive threat to social order created by poverty, landlessness, and chronic famine by the 1570s? What role did market relationships, everywhere far more important at the end of the sixteenth century than at its beginning, play in fostering social order in the countryside? Or did these economic ties also undermine order and help spread chaos and confusion in years of famine?

This study also looks at the problem of social order as a part of another problem, a timeless and disturbing one: the exercise of power. Religious discipline, social order, the control of wealth and property, obedience, and loyalty

---

[4] Almost all of such studies have built on the original insights of Ernst Walter Zeeden, *Die Enstehung der Konfessionen: Grundlagen und Formen der Konfessionsbildung im Zeitalter der Glaubenskämpfe* (Munich: Oldenbourg, 1965). See, for example, Heinz Schilling, *Konfessionskonflikt und Staatsbildung: Eine Fallstudie über das Verhältnis von religiösem und sozialem Wandel in der Frühneuzeit am Beispiel der Grafschaft Lippe*, Quellen und Forschungen zur Reformationsgeschichte, vol. 48 (Gütersloh: Gerd Mohn, 1981); and, more recently, Jane Abray, *The People's Reformation: Magistrates, Clergy and Commons in Strasbourg, 1500–1598* (Ithaca, N.Y.: Cornell University Press, 1986).

were all variations on this theme. This naturally leads to an exploration of the exercise of state power in the village.[5] But in order to answer those ancient and always relevant questions about power – who exercised it? how? at whose expense? – one must penetrate the village itself. Once that is done, once documents are found that reveal the byzantine complexity of social life in the village, the old questions about the building of the early modern state must be cast in new forms. For it involves understanding not simply the growth of state power as it shaped the social order, but also discerning the limits to state domination, the subtle use and ironic consequences of paternalism and deference, and the ways, fascinating in their implications for the whole agrarian order, in which villagers shared in the fruits of their own domination. Power was widely and diffusely spread within the village, its exercise very often tentative and conditional. For villagers themselves knew where the power lay in their communities, and they understood how to lay their hands on a share of it. This study stresses the fact that villagers, then, and not simply their masters, played a more central role in creating and maintaining order, discipline, and hierarchy than many scholars commonly assume.

Methods, sources, and limits

One cannot examine a problem as complex as this for all of Germany, of course, not even for one whole region. The best approach remains the tightly focused local study, one preferably carried out with a comparative perspective. No doubt some scholars will argue that one cannot generalize about the social history of early modern Germany, that a study of this type runs the risk of interpreting Central European history through the narrow experiences of one small land. The argument is still made that the territories of the Holy Roman Empire differed so thoroughly from each other, that localism weighed so heavily on the history of early modern Germany, that any effort to seek out common patterns of social change is doomed to failure. One cannot deny that villagers and, yes, most German princes too, played out their everyday lives in small local worlds before 1800. But this argument for the peculiarity of German history has often undermined the effort to write its modern social history. Scholars of early modern France and England have long noted the pervasive regionalism of these countries. Yet the social history of these countries has made rapid progress because attempts have been made to see patterns in the diversity, to identify problems and themes that cut across narrow regional and political boundaries.

---

[5] I am particularly indebted to David Sabean for helping me see this problem. See his *Power in the Blood: Popular Culture and Village Discourse in Early Modern Germany* (Cambridge: Cambridge University Press, 1984).

Introduction

For only in this way can truly comparative history be written. Only in this way can one understand, more clearly than ever before, just how peculiar or unusual certain lands or case studies indeed are.

This study is therefore meant as a contribution, and a spur, to a comparative social history of Germany in the sixteenth and seventeenth centuries. As such it aims to rise above the narrow objectives of local history to pay careful attention to the broader historical patterns and trends of which this one small land was, or was not, a part. Any scholar who sets sail on the wind-tossed sea of this period of history, with only a few poor and outdated maps to guide him, comes upon a new and strange land. The central focus of this work, the major point of reference, is the land of Hohenlohe, a lonely land of rolling plains, picturesque river valleys, and imposing Renaissance castles in the German Southwest. The search for social order in this rural society is examined at several levels. In places comparisons with other areas of South Germany or the German West point up essential similarities and differences. In other places attention shifts back and forth among the Holy Roman Empire, the region of which this land was a part – Franconia or South Germany as a whole – and Hohenlohe itself. Only in this way can one see the interconnectedness of the agrarian order in a handful of small, seemingly remote villages with conditions in the territories around them, indeed with the structure of the Holy Roman Empire as a whole. In a venture such as this, one should never mistake a barren island in the Caribbean as an outpost of civilization off the coast of Cathay, to claim more for one small corner of the world than is right and due. The success of this enterprise the reader will have to judge.

Most social historians today build their work from the ground up by first identifying a well-defined region and then exhaustively analyzing its social, political, and economic institutions from several angles. This method provides the foundation of this study as well. But how large an area can one examine meaningfully? The whole Hohenlohe? That proved impossible from the start, for the records are far more voluminous than any individual could possibly handle in a reasonable amount of time. A single village? The village study, though quite popular today and an important undertaking in its own right, would have restricted the broad view that is the goal of the work.[6] Social patterns vary from village to village, from group to group, even from family to family, and the best social histories take the rich variation of experience into account. That old question "How typical could one village be?" can never be satisfactorily answered. Yet the advantage, indeed the necessity, of having a detailed understanding of at least some villages

---

[6] See the excellent recent example of this type of study for a Hessian village by Arthur Imhof, *Die verlorenen Welten: Alltagsbewältigung durch unsere Vorfahren – und weshalb wir uns heute so schwer damit tun* (Munich: C. H. Beck, 1984).

seemed undeniable. How else could one precisely plot population movements, the distribution of wealth, the rise and fall of debts, or land-use patterns? The questions that guided this work from the start demanded quantitative answers to some questions. Still, the goals of the work required moving beyond the limits of the village study.

The statistical foundations of this work therefore rest on an exhaustive study of one district in the County of Hohenlohe, the district of Langenburg, one of ten or twelve districts in the principality as a whole. This solution to the methodological problem represents a compromise. In this way the strengths of the village study can be combined with the broader and comparative perspective of a regional study. The one offers methodological rigor – crucial when dealing with questions that demand statistical analysis – while the other adds the necessary comparative perspective. In this way one can begin to develop a sense of what was typical and what was not. One finds in this district, for example, a variety of different types of communities, twelve in all, not at all unlike the others in the region as a whole: a small market town (Langenburg), site of one of the castles and an administrative center of the territory; seven compact villages, all of them densely populated; and four small hamlets, each one settled by two to seven households. These communities were also scattered across the two major ecological niches of the region. Some, dating back to the old Alemannic settlements in the region, were to be found along the floor of the Jagst River valley. Others, carved out of the dense forest, the Ohrnwald, which once covered the area, were founded in the great wave of land clearing in the eleventh and twelfth centuries; these settlements were on the flat, now open, plain above the river valley. The names of these villages are therefore the ones that fill the pages of this book.

Other methods the reader will find employed, less systematically, at various points in this study. Given the wide variety of questions essential to answer, some having to do with lordship (*Herrschaft*) and power, others with kinship and inheritance, and still others with economic history, this study draws on the insights of sociologists and social anthropologists in an eclectic way. Some of the insights about the exercise of state power in the village, about domination in its various forms, and about the ways in which power pervaded social relations in the village rest on ideas drawn from Max Weber and Pierre Bourdieu.[7] The sections dealing with the meaning of marriage in village society and the social consequences of certain inheritance practices rest, to a great extent, upon insights gained from the work

---

[7] Max Weber, *Wirtschaft und Gesellschaft: Grundriss der verstehenden Soziologie*, 5th ed. (Tübingen: J. C. B. Mohr, 1985); and Pierre Bourdieu, *Outline of a Theory of Practice* (Cambridge: Cambridge University Press, 1977).

of Jack Goody.[8] This work also benefited from the work of other anthropologists, too many to name, who have shown how land and various types of movable goods circulate in separate spheres of exchange and carry far more than a strictly economic meaning.[9]

In none of these cases, however, does this work follow blindly any single theory at the expense of the data. Some scholars will find shortcomings in this eclecticism and the controlled use of sociological and anthropological theory, and will wish for a more rigorous theoretical interpretation of the material. But this study rests, as most good social histories do, more on the principles of Occamism than on those of Thomism. Theories, processes, or even discussions of abstract legal rights have little meaning except insofar as they can actually explain social behavior. Throughout this work the focus therefore remains on individuals and groups acting in specific historical circumstances. What is always foremost, what keeps the use of theory in check, is this question: Does the theory help explain the emergence of a new sense of order, hierarchy, and social discipline in the village?

Most historians of early modern Europe who write history "from the bottom up" lament the limits of the sources and complain about the sparseness of archival records before 1650. The problems with the sources for Hohenlohe, however, are of a different order. They are the problems of working through mountains of records, sources that illuminate village life in astonishing, at times overwhelming, detail, and this from a remarkably early period at that, from roughly 1580 on. For when it came to cleaning out the cellars of their castles, bundling up and throwing away all those everyday records from the local courts, district officials, and, yes, from peasants themselves, the counts of Hohenlohe never seem to have made much headway. From Langenburg district complete series of rent books, tax registers, and surveys of assessed taxable wealth survive for much of the the sixteenth and seventeenth centuries. Other records are available as well: chancellery records, petitions, the marriage-court records of Hohenlohe-Neuenstein, visitation records, and district reports. In addition, a virtually complete set of district account books illuminate the everyday practice

[8] Jack Goody, *Production and Reproduction: A Comparative Study of the Domestic Domain*, Cambridge Studies in Social Anthropology, no. 17 (Cambridge: Cambridge University Press, 1976).
[9] See, to name only a few recent theoretical works of importance, Paul Bohannan, "Some Principles of Exchange and Investment Among the Tiv," *American Anthropologist* 57 (1955), 60–70; Mary Douglas and Baron Isherwood, *The World of Goods* (New York: Basic Books, 1979); Mary Douglas, "Primitive Rationing: A Study in Controlled Exchange," in Raymond Firth, ed., *Themes in Economic Anthropology* (London: Tavistock, 1967), 119–47; Marcel Maus, *The Gift: Forms and Functions of Exchange in Archaic Societies*, trans. Ian Cunnison (New York: Norton, 1967); Claude Meillassoux, "From Reproduction to Production: A Marxist Approach to Economic Anthropology," *Economy and Society* 1 (1972), 93–105; and Marshall Sahlins, *Stone Age Economics* (Chicago: Aldine, 1972).

of domination in the village for almost every year after 1600. These last records are essential for understanding population trends, the distribution of land and wealth, and economic change. But they also reveal, in surprising detail, how paternalism and deference worked on an everyday basis. Together these records allow a detailed reconstruction of village life.

Even with the advantages of the exceptional archival records for this territory, several limitations of this study must be kept in mind. The weight of the evidence, for one, comes from the period between 1550 and 1700. Few records illuminate village life for the decades around 1500 and for the Peasants' War. The early sixteenth century is therefore not as thoroughly and soundly documented as the later period. Second, the attention of this study tends to fall primarily, though not exclusively, on the peasantry. Writing a social history of Germany's rural elites – the petty princes, nobles, state officials, Lutheran reformers, and pastors – would require a separate undertaking altogether. That does not mean that this work underestimates the central role these elites played in imposing order, hierarchy, and social discipline in the village. But all too little is known about the social histories of these groups in early modern Germany. Indeed, readers familiar with the history of other European countries may be surprised to note the complete absence from this study of one of these groups: a landed nobility. In most of the small states of the German Southwest the nobility had long since retreated into their own small enclaves independent from the princes. Hohenlohe, and a number of other states as well, therefore had by the sixteenth century no landed nobility to mediate peasants' relationships with the state.

The focus of this study falls on a small patrimonial state. This choice was a deliberate one. Historians have paid too little attention to developments in these small states, although more careful studies of the social structures that supported them would help illuminate a sorely neglected problem: the limits to state building in early modern Germany. What this work says about the exercise of power at the village level therefore will not necessarily illuminate the patterns one may find in the larger states of Germany. That is, however, by no means always the case.

Any discussion of a small early modern German state can easily run into conceptual and terminological problems. Chapters 1, 7, and 9 make it clear that one should not confuse the personalized and concrete relationships of authority and power in this territory with the more abstract and impersonal structures of domination in a modern state. The German term *Herrschaft* can convey more precisely the meaning of these relationships. *Herrschaft* always referred to specific relationships of power, all of them rooted in law and entailing personal relationships with reciprocal obligations. One can understand the term abstractly, of course, but throughout most of the period covered here the term was always understood concretely, that is, inseparable from the exercise of specific types of power over villagers: *Herrschaft* over the land (*Grundherrschaft*), serfs (*Leibherrschaft*), or the courts (*Gerichtsherrschaft*), to name only a few examples. With each of these authorities came the right to extract certain surpluses (rents, dues, labor services, and so forth) or the right to command obedience and loyalty from those under a jurisdiction. But lords had always to provide protection (*Schutz und Schirm*) in exchange for these rights, or their authority could be called into question.[10] In the chapters that follow, various English terms are employed – "authority," "dominion," "lordship," "rule," "domination," "small state" – but none of them can capture the full range of meaning of *Herrschaft*.

This small territory also became Protestant, and one cannot doubt the importance of Lutheranism in shaping its social history. But this study makes no systematic effort to compare the changes in this land with changes in a Catholic territory. Some important differences, but also many similarities, would have become apparent. But such comparisons can also be misleading, for they implicitly ascribe to the confessional cultures of Germany a causal role in shaping social change that they did not necessarily have. Whether patterns of social change can be traced to a particular confessional culture is a problem far more difficult to solve than is commonly supposed, and one that will require a number of other studies before firm answers present themselves.

Arguments

The chronology and overall framework of this study are not set by the history of state building or by the events of the Reformation. In order to understand the search for order, hierarchy, and discipline in the countryside in this period, one must begin by looking at social change in the light of one inexorable movement: the long cycle of population expansion, contraction, and recovery between 1500 and 1720. State making, the drive for religious discipline, the reform of the family, and economic expansion: Each of these changes was decisively influenced by agrarian conditions created by this cycle. The study that follows therefore falls into three parts. Part One introduces the reader to rural Hohenlohe at the beginning of the sixteenth century and then examines the upheavals that came with agrarian expansion in the first three quarters of the sixteenth century. In Part Two attention shifts to the attempts to impose order, hierarchy, and social discipline between 1550 and 1620 as the agrarian cycle reached its peak, as land became scarce and the demands of the state and the marketplace began to place village society under additional stress. Part Three

[10] For a short discussion of the terminological and conceptual problems involved here see Sabean, *Power in the Blood*, 20–7. See also "Herrschaft," in Otto Brunner, Werner Conze, and Reinhart Kosseleck, eds., *Geschichtliche Grundbegriffe: Historisches Lexikon zur politisch-sozialen Sprache in Deutschland* (Stuttgart: Klett-Cotta, 1982), vol. 3, 1–102.

Introduction

then examines the agrarian crisis that set in between 1620 and 1640, its profound consequences for village society, and how, after 1640, order was slowly restored.

One cannot escape the conclusion that the first half of the sixteenth century was a time of massive upheaval in rural Germany. The beginnings of sustained population growth, the making of the territorial state, market expansion, the Peasants' War, the appalling end of Christian unity, and the perceived erosion of the family all contributed to a sense of unease, and at times desperation, that reached into every princely and peasant household. But from the vantage point developed here, with all of these changes understood, as much as is possible, from the perspective of the village, some familiar problems and themes take on a slightly different appearance. The authority and power of the princes, for one, appear less secure, less certain, than is sometimes supposed. This followed not simply from the poorly developed structures of princely authority and domination in the countryside, but also from the fact that power rested, to a degree still not fully understood, on villagers sharing in the process of their domination. When that obedience vanished, as it did in 1525, the power of lords and princes withered away with breathtaking speed.

One other conclusion from this section may seem surprising, but it is nonetheless inescapable. When placed within the context of the agrarian cycle, the Peasants' War appears less important as a watershed in lord–peasant relations than is often assumed. The evidence supports a view of the Peasants' War as an extension of the early evangelical movements; it also suggests that the suppression of the rising marked the end of popular support in the countryside for the early reformation.[11] This certainly left the masters of the countryside – the princes, the lords, and the nobles – largely in control of religious reform when it was eventually introduced. But the rising, and its suppression, left most of the problems in the agrarian order unsolved. Of far more importance in this first half of the sixteenth century was the gradual erosion of the social foundations of the village commune. This problem deserves more study than it receives here, and one hopes that others will explore the transformation of communal life after 1525 with greater care.[12] For, from the vantage point developed here, the growth of massive rural poverty, the polarization of the village between wealthy tenant farmers and smallholders, between propertyholders and the propertyless, had more lasting consequences for agrarian society that did the events of 1525.

Part Two focuses on the foundations for renewed social order and stability

[11] In this regard, my study confirms the major view put forward by Peter Blickle in *Gemeindereformation: Die Menschen des 16. Jahrhunderts auf dem Weg zum Heil* (Munich: Oldenbourg, 1985).
[12] The recent work by Heide Wunder is therefore welcome, and an important contribution to this problem. See *Die bäuerliche Gemeinde in Deutschland* (Göttingen: Vandenhoeck & Ruprecht, 1986), especially pp. 80–113.

by 1600 or 1610. Here careful attention is given four major problems: the reform of the patriarchal family, property and inheritance, market and class relationships, and the relationships of villagers to the state. Several themes appear repeatedly in these chapters, but two of them become particularly important clues to our understanding of rural society in these decades.

Social relationships, first of all, appear to have been in an almost continuous state of flux by 1560. In some ways the princes set the pace in trying to bring order in the midst of this change, to reinforce the structures of hierarchy. The princely reformation, the reform of the peasant family, the development of broader and more complex market relationships, a heavier burden of taxes, all allowed the princes to penetrate village society more thoroughly than was possible early in the sixteenth century. The erosion of communal loyalty played a crucial part at this time in allowing the state a firmer control over village life than ever before. Yet this flux, and the flexibility in many key social and political institutions, made it possible for villagers to turn reforms to their own advantage, to refashion old relationships in new ways, to carve out new ones, even to set strict limits to the power of the state. For in none of these areas did any single group, the German princes and their servants included, have the power to refashion rural society in the image it wanted. The order that emerged came out of conflict, compromise, and, at times, cooperation. A village elite of tenant farmers secured their domination of the village through the patriarchal family, their landholdings, their place in the market economy, and their power to resist some of the incursions of the state. And other groups carved out places of power at times as well: widows, even on occasion youths, craftsmen, and the village poor. By 1600 the places of all of these groups began, slowly, to become more certain and secure.

But this search for social order, laced as it was with a heavy emphasis on patriarchal authority, a rigid sense of hierarchy and status, and calls for obedience and discipline at every turn, created new tensions in the village. One of the features of this society on the eve of the Thirty Years' War was therefore the continual alternation between order and disorder, stability and instability, harmony and security, and unbearable tensions and uncertainty. In this way the striving for order in the village mirrored the political and religious climate in the territorial state and the Holy Roman Empire as a whole on the eve of the Thirty Years' War. The search for order took place on three levels, each linked up with the others. That princes and peasants concerned themselves with bringing order out of a world understood as dangerously unstable should come as no real surprise. Yet too often the focus in this period falls on the sources of instability: the peasant revolts, the wage–price scissors, overpopulation, land hunger, famine, and the destructive cycles of war. In this section the argument is made that a measure of stability was also achieved, but that it came at a terrible price.

Introduction

In the final section of this book the consequences of this desperate and intensive search for order are examined for the seventeenth century. The two theses here seem paradoxical when put side by side, but they are nonetheless true. For the unresolved tensions led, almost inexorably, to a wrenching crisis. But, at the same time, the social, political, and economic relationships that fueled those tensions also became the keys to the relative stability that settled over rural Germany once the crisis passed.

With this argument in mind, the Thirty Years' War looms as both more and less important than is commonly portrayed. The war becomes more important because it was part of a crisis of the whole society, a crisis that shook the agrarian order to its very foundations. The violence and incredible chaos in many parts of Germany between 1620 and 1650 came from the fact that many of the cornerstones of social order, so carefully built up over the last century, began to give way. The war, the levying of a crushing burden of taxes in particular, played a crucial role in helping destroy village society as contemporaries understood it. But the war alone could not have caused a crisis as deep and profound as this. One must keep in mind that its origins lay in other conditions as well: overpopulation, plague and the catastrophic fall in population after 1630; the sharp inflation of food prices in the 1620s and chronic famine in the 1630s and 1640s; the dramatic increase in rural poverty; intensified social conflict within the village; the unprecedented rise in taxes and the harsh measures used to drive them in; and the erosion of customary relations of paternalism and deference. J. V. Polišenský argues that the Thirty Years' War represented a clash of two social systems, one feudal and Catholic, one capitalist and Protestant. While not supporting that argument as a whole, this section does show how the underpinnings of the whole agrarian hierarchy, from the power of the prince right down to the place of the tenant farmer and the village poor in village society, were violently challenged between 1620 and 1660.[13]

In the end, however, this crisis did little to alter the fundamental social, political, and economic structures of village life in the German West. For the late seventeenth century one must draw a careful balance between continuity and change. Much of the social stability of the decades between 1660 and 1700 can be ascribed to the weight of social institutions and relationships established in the late sixteenth century. But the foundations of a new cycle of agrarian expansion were also laid at this time, and the study concludes with some thoughts on the surprising flexibility of what seems, by the eighteenth century, to be an archaic social system.

If the French *annalistes* inspired some of the guiding ideas of this work, it should become clear by this point where it differs with them. The view de-

[13] J. V. Polišenský, *The Thirty Years' War*, trans. Robert Evans (Berkeley and Los Angeles: University of California Press, 1971).

12

veloped here shows villagers living out their lives in social relationships difficult but not impossible to change. They also never became the helpless victims of a merciless and exploitive state, the experience of certain years during the Thirty Years' War aside. From the tumults of 1525 to the stress and anxiety in the village in the decades around 1600 and the crisis of the seventeenth century, the reader will certainly find described here a harsh, brutal, and alien world. But from the first to the last villagers showed almost endless imagination and tenacity to shape and reshape the harsh world that was given them.

Part One

Agrarian expansion, revolt, and the decay
of community

I

~~~~~~

Anatomy of a rural society

Setting

Two days after leaving the imperial city of Frankfurt am Main, just south of
the town of Mergentheim a traveler on his way to Augsburg entered one of
the most remote rural areas of Renaissance Germany. The important waterways
and heavily traveled roads that linked Frankfurt with South Germany's rapidly
growing, wealthy, and powerful imperial cities largely bypassed the tiny towns
and villages of the Hohenlohe plain in 1500 (see Map 1.1). To reach Öhringen,
the largest and most important town in Hohenlohe in 1500, one had first to
travel either overland or by boat on the Main River to Wertheim. From there
the road to Öhringen led overland on the major north–south axis of South
Germany, the Emperor's Highway, up the winding valley of the Tauber River
to Mergentheim. But here one had to branch off the main thoroughfare and
head south on a smaller road to the tiny market town of Künzelsau on the
Kocher River (see Map 1.2). Only then did a road lead on to the small town
of Öhringen. Travelers heading east from the imperial city of Wimpfen to
Schwäbisch Hall might take the older and more direct route to Öhringen. But
in 1500 none of the major roads would take the traveler quickly and easily to
this remote part of the German Southwest. Most merchants and travelers would
simply bypass Hohenlohe to the east on the main stretch of the Emperor's
Highway that led directly to the great commercial cities of South Germany and
northern Italy.

The striking openness and flatness of the Hohenlohe plain would immediately impress any traveler then as it still does today. The plain was a world
unto itself in the early modern period. To the north and west one finds
most towns and trade routes stretched along the relatively densely populated Main and Neckar river valleys. Farther to the south the steep hills
and ridges of the Swabian Alb confined towns and villages, and the winding roads that linked them, into even more narrow valleys. But just south
of the Tauber valley a traveler would cross a strikingly different landscape:

Map 1.1. Southern Germany, ca. 1500.

an expansive plain stretching for twenty or thirty miles to a line of foothills that rise sharply three or four hundred feet to the heights of the Mainhardt Forest near Waldenburg. To the east this broad plain comes to an end in the hilly country near the Tauber River. To the west the plain narrows where the Kocher and Jagst rivers, the two waterways that cut through the plain, flow into the Neckar River. Johann Friedrich Mayer, who knew this part of Germany not as a traveler but as a resident long familiar with the landscape, captured the impression of surprising spaciousness many visitors have when they first come to Hohenlohe: "The whole region is completely open, where the sun shines directly, the wind blows unhindered and never does one miss fresh air; the wind never blows too strong because in the south from east to west the plain is protected by a chain of hills".[1] The

[1] Johann Friedrich Mayer, *Lehrbuch für die Land- und Hauswirthe in der pragmatischen Geschichte*

18

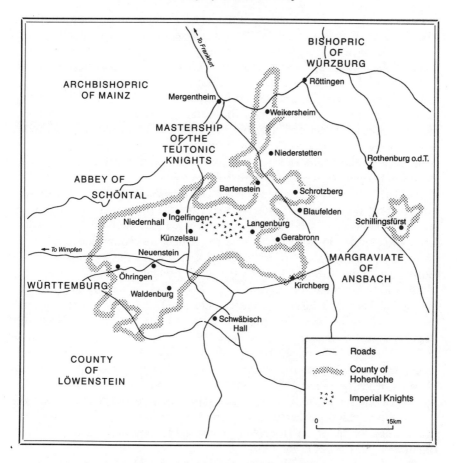

Map 1.2. The old County of Hohenlohe.

parapets of the castle at Waldenburg, perched on one of the prominent ridges to the south several hundred feet above the plain, offer the best view of this land. From this elevation one can see the plain stretching north in the direction of Würzburg as far as the eye can see.

From that vantage point at Waldenburg an observer might have the impression that no rivers flowed through this expansive plain. Traveling south from Mergentheim to Öhringen, one might share this impression until the road suddenly descends into the deep and very narrow valley of the Jagst River. This valley, much like the ones cut in the plain by the Tauber,

der gesamten Land- und Hauswirtschaft des Hohenlohe Schillingsfürstischen Amtes Kupferzell (Nuremberg: Johann Eberhard Zeh, 1773), 3.

19

Brettach, Vorbach, and Kocher rivers, appears more like a canyon than many other river valleys of Southwest Germany. Looking up the Jagst River from the small castle at Langenburg, for example, one sees that the walls of the valley slope gently down to the river flowing past the village of Bächlingen. On the north and west of the castle at Langenburg, however, the valley walls drop precipitously to the valley floor below (see Map 1.3). Descending the winding road into the valley, an observer might also note that the climate changes, slightly but perceptibly. The winds, for one, subside and the air becomes calm. And in those places in the valley where the walls face to the south and are warmed by the sun, the temperature becomes noticeably warmer than on the plain above.

The castles that come into view at several locations on or near every important road reminded travelers that they were far from the protection of South Germany's wealthy and powerful Renaissance cities. From these castles the powerful lords of the House of Hohenlohe dominated the countryside, controlled trade and travel, and ruled over the local population. Three such castles were positioned on the east–west highway through Öhringen: one in the town itself, another in Neuenstein, and, farther in the direction of Schwäbisch Hall, a third on the heights above the road. Others would come into view near the clusters of communities on each of the rivers: Künzelsau on the Kocher; Langenburg, Jagstberg, and Kirchberg on the Jagst; Weikersheim on the Tauber; and Schrotzberg on the Vorbach. None of these castles yet had the luxurious and decorative look of Renaissance palaces. They had their origins in the glorious decades of the twelfth and thirteenth centuries when the nobles of the House of Hohenlohe served the Hohenstaufen emperors as loyal followers. Though continually rebuilt since that time, they remained heavy, stone, fortified positions from which the House of Hohenlohe continued to exercise its dominion over the towns and villages of the territory.

The town of Öhringen, the main market town of Hohenlohe, is situated on the southern edge of the plain. The impression one might have of this walled town would be typical of many small market towns of South Germany in 1500. These towns lived not from long-distance trade, manufactures, or finance – the keys to the prosperity of the large imperial cities such as Nuremberg and Schwäbisch Hall – but from local and regional trade in grain, wine, and other agricultural products. And they bore testimony not to traditions of urban autonomy and self-government, the key feature of the imperial and free cities of the Holy Roman Empire in the late Middle Ages, but to the power of the rural nobility who continued to dominate them.

Öhringen itself, for all its importance as the center of communications and trade in this remote area, was first and foremost the prized center of power for the House of Hohenlohe. That fact had shaped the layout of the town from the time the ambitious Gottfried of Hohenlohe acquired the powers of lordship

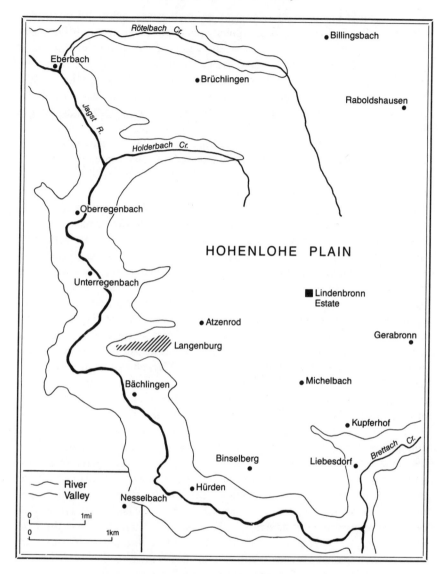

Map 1.3. Langenburg district and nearby villages.

over it in 1253.[2] From the west one entered Öhringen through a gate that led along the winding main street to the marketplace at the center of the town.

[2] Heinz Stoob, "Zur Städtebildung im Lande Hohenlohe," *Zeitschrift für bäyerische Landesgeschichte* 36 (1973), 547.

Here one could see some modest signs of small-town wealth and urban development that had come with the commercial expansion in South Germany in the fifteenth century. Rows of well-kept houses of merchants lined the main street and bordered the marketplace itself. Off to the side of the marketplace, down the narrow side streets, craftsmen, bakers, and butchers kept their shops. And, in the middle of the marketplace, the *Spital* church dominated the heart of the town. What would most impress a visitor, however, would be the heavily fortified castle and the whole quarter near the marketplace given over to stewards of the House of Hohenlohe. From this quarter the officials of the lords supervised the market and completely dominated the town's government. Here too they had their residences and storehouses for the supplies of grain and wine that came from the countryside.

Öhringen, as the administrative, religious, and economic center of the territory, was not typical of Hohenlohe's towns. Most towns remained largely isolated from the currents of trade animating the economies of South Germany's larger and more prosperous cities and towns. The roads from Öhringen to other parts of Hohenlohe in fact discouraged travel and trade even within the region itself. Merchants from Öhringen could reach Wimpfen, Heilbronn, and Schwäbisch Hall much more easily than they could travel to most of the small towns and villages of Hohenlohe that lay north and east of the town. Here there were not even secondary roads, only small and winding local tracks. The tiny town of Langenburg on the Jagst River, for example, lay nine miles from even the poor secondary highway that ran from Mergentheim south to Crailsheim. These parts of Hohenlohe were therefore not just isolated from the major cities of South Germany, they also had poor communication links with each other and with the one major town of the region as well.

Most of these towns probably looked more like walled villages than proud and independent towns. Many were nothing more than tiny settlements nestled just outside the gates of one of the castles. In contrast to Öhringen, these towns had very few merchant houses, no complex urban neighborhoods or towering cathedrals to compete with the castle as the dominant structure in the community. The town of Langenburg was typical in this regard. The castle stood on a rock promontory jutting out over the Jagst valley. Immediately to the west, just outside the castle gate and on the other side of the moat, the tiny town developed on the narrow road that led to the east in the direction of Gerabronn and, eventually, Rot am See on the Emperor's Highway. How this community actually looked in 1500 is difficult to say. But in 1578, when the population was certainly larger, Heinrich Schweickher, a cartographer, sketched the town and the surrounding villages. Looking at the castle and town from the south, the buildings of the town appear, as they do today, crammed together behind the town wall along the one main street. At the end of the town, bearing the symbol of two leopards, the coat of arms of the House of Hohenlohe, were the town gates. The whole complex of houses and shops appears to have been only as large as the castle and its attached buildings.[3]

The overwhelming majority of Hohenlohers, however, lived in the country-side. In this part of the German Southwest one does not find the large and sprawling villages typical of Franconia and parts of Swabia. Nor does one see many examples of scattered individual homesteads such as the ones that dot the landscape of the Black Forest. The small nucleated village dominated the settlement pattern of Hohenlohe. This was the case in the district of Langenburg (see Map 1.3). In 1528, the first year for which we have reliable records of the numbers of households in this district, the majority of the population of this district was concentrated in four compact villages: Atzenrod, Bächlingen, Billingsbach, and Nesselbach. The rest of the population, excepting those who lived in the town of Langenburg, lived in the slightly smaller compact villages of Oberregenbach, Raboldshausen, and Unterregenbach. There were a few small hamlets – Brüchlingen, Kupferhof, and Hürden – but these settlements were home to at most two to five households each. Scattered across the district one would find some isolated properties: one mill near Bächlingen, another across the Jagst from Oberregenbach, the brickworks outside Langenburg, and the House of Hohenlohe's estate at Lindenbronn just east of Atzenrod. On each of these properties, however, the account books describe buildings for only one household each. The compact village of Hohenlohe, Johann Mayer thought, had its distinct advantages, since "the country people are so distributed, the fields narrow, the work for men and cattle much easier and less than in other territories where there are large villages and hamlets."[4] In those unfortunate villages, he complained, peasants lost a great deal of time simply walking back and forth to fields far from their homes.

Farmers and winegrowers

Even in a region seemingly removed from the dynamic centers of change in South Germany, a careful observer would have found signs of disturbing stress and social change around 1500. Part of the uncertainty was the consequence of the limits of agricultural technology and the dependence of the harvests on unpredictable cycles of weather and natural conditions. Modern meteorologists and geologists have confirmed what villagers in Hohenlohe have long understood about the land and the environment of this corner of South Germany. Hohenlohe lies in a transitional climatic zone between the warmer Southwest and the colder parts of Central Germany that begin in Franconia.[5] Within this

[3] HZAN, "Atlas von Heinrich Schweickher, 1578."
[4] Mayer, *Lehrbuch für die Land- und Hauswirthe*, 5.
[5] For a description of the climate of this region see R. Nestle, "Witterung und Klima," in *Der*

zone it made a great deal of difference whether farmers settled on the open and exposed plain or in the narrow but sheltered valleys. The plain offered the best land for the production of cereal crops; the valleys offered shelter from the harsh winter winds and gentle slopes of land suitable for viticulture.[6] In neither of the region's two microenvironments could villagers count on a secure subsistence from the soil. They might minimize the risk of crop failure, but they had still to reckon with the fact that their yields were always uncertain and varied sharply from year to year.

The origins of the classic division between farmers and winegrowers are almost as ancient as agriculture itself in this part of Central Europe. The land of Hohenlohe on the whole was fertile, more so than the lands around it. But the fertile soils were unequally distributed between the river valleys and the open plains. The farmland of Langenburg district was again typical of this general pattern in Hohenlohe. Peasants in early modern Hohenlohe, like the early Germanic settlers, still found some of the best soils in the rich and well-watered valley of the Jagst River. The valley certainly flooded on occasion. But because the valley, like the Kocher and Tauber valleys, lay fifty to a hundred meters below the plain, cut into the soft bedrock of limestone, its farmlands and pasture were easily sheltered from the harsh winter winds that sweep across the plain in October. The second belt of fertile soils lay on the plain itself. Here the rich, loamy topsoils proved particularly suitable for the planting of grain crops and fruit orchards. But farmers had long found the land along the slopes of the river valleys, as well as those near the rims, the most difficult to plough. On these slopes soils eroded easily, exposing rocks and calcium deposits.[7] By clearing these lands of rocks some farmers could transform them into vineyards, especially if the field had a favorable southern exposure. But, in general, the land along the slope and near the valley rims tended to be marginal, the last to be cleared when population grew. It was the land to be claimed by winegrowers in the sixteenth century.

Peasants who worked the marginal soils were the most vulnerable to crop failures, to famines, and of course to the seigneurial levies that created short-term crises in household incomes. Even in the best of years these marginal producers had seed–yield ratios significantly below those of tenant farmers on the plains. The evidence comes from the seed–yield ratios in Langenburg district in 1623, admittedly a century after the Peasants' War, but still typical

---

Landkreis Öhringen: Ämtliche Kreisbeschreibung, Die Stadt- und Landkreise in Baden-Württemberg, vol. 3 (Öhringen: H. Wolf, 1961), 41–123.

[6] For a discussion of the two microenvironments of Hohenlohe see *Der Landkreis Öhringen*, 4–152, and *Der Landkreis Crailsheim: Kreisbeschreibung*, Die Stadt- und Landkreise in Baden-Württemberg, vol. 1 (Gerabronn: M. Rückert, 1953), 1–31.

[7] For a study of the soils of this area see Georg Wagner, *Geologische Heimatskunde von Württembergisch-Franken* (Öhringen: Hohenlohische Buchhandlung Ferdinand Rau, 1921).

Table 1.1. *Seed-yield ratios in Langenburg district, 1623*

Village	No. of households	Median seed-yield ratio
Atzenrod	9	3.4
Kupferhof	2	4.2
Raboldshausen	17	4.9
Billingsbach	18	5.4
Brüchlingen	5	5.7
Total	51	Median 4.9

Source: ALKL II/6/13, September 26-27, 1623.

of the productivity in the early modern period, since agricultural technology remained the same (see Table 1.1). Peasants who farmed the land on the plain, in the villages of Brüchlingen, Billingsbach, and Raboldshausen, had seed–yield ratios of 1:4.9 or more, all significantly above the average of 1:4.5 for German farmers as a whole in the seventeenth century.[8] But peasants with land on the rim of the Jagst valley, in Atzenrod and Kupferhof, had ratios of only 1:3.4 and 1:4.2 respectively; both were lower than the average for Germany. All peasants minimized the chances of crop failure by planting two hardy strains of cereals, spelt and rye, both of which could grow on poor soils and resist crop damages from frost or excessive rainfall.[9] But these low levels of agri-

---

[8] The average seed–yield ratio of Germany of 1:4.5 between 1600 and 1649 was calculated by B. H. Slicher van Bath, "Agriculture in the Vital Revolution," in *The Cambridge Economic History of Europe*, vol. 5: *The Economic Organization of Early Modern Europe*, ed. E. E. Rich and C. H. Wilson (Cambridge: Cambridge University Press, 1977), 81.

[9] Early-sixteenth-century account books from Langenburg district mention spelt, rye, and oats as the most common forms of payment for rents and dues in kind. These hardy cereals, especially spelt, remained the most important strains of cereals in early modern Hohenlohe – indeed throughout Southwest Germany – until more productive strains of wheat replaced them in the early twentieth century. The widespread use of spelt in Southwest Germany dated from the time of the Alemanni of the early Middle Ages, who developed this cereal strain to grow on the poor soils where they settled. Spelt resisted frost and withstood excessive rainfall much better than wheat. Its hard outer husk protected the kernels from disease and mold and thus made it a grain that farmers could store easily for a long time. Rye also grew well in this climate. Strong stalks allowed rye crops to withstand excessive rainfall or sudden rainstorms or hail. Farmers valued its strength in harsh weather so much that they often mixed rye with spelt or other crops to give the fields more resilience during heavy rainfalls. Rye did not yield as much grain as spelt or wheat in a good year, but farmers apparently preferred a reliable low-yield crop. Oats, the third most common crop, served two purposes. In good years it served as cattle feed. In lean years the oats could be mixed with other grains to bake a "mixed bread." These crops may not have produced high yields every year, but they minimized the risk of catastrophic losses in any one year. See Hans Jänichen, *Beiträge zur Wirtschaftsgeschichte des schwäbischen Dorfes*, Veröffentlichungen der Kommission für geschichtliche Landeskunde in Baden-Württemberg, ser. B, vol. 60 (Stuttgart: W. Kohlhammer, 1970), 86–100.

25

cultural productivity for the marginal producers provided a household with only the barest minimum for survival.[10]

On the eve of the Peasants' War the number of peasants tilling marginal lands was on the rise. By about 1500 population growth had already made it increasingly difficult for marginal peasants in Upper Swabia, the Neckar valley, and Franconia to bear easily their burdens of seigneurial rents and dues. This boom had only just begun in Hohenlohe. In Langenburg district the rent rolls and imperial tax registers indicate that few new households were added to the old ones between 1456 and 1470; and just as few came between 1470 and 1528.[11] The steward of Langenburg did note that "newly cleared lands" had been entered into the account books each year between 1514 and 1521.[12] But this would be only the first stirrings of a land hunger that would become much stronger after 1530.

The boom had no doubt started earlier in the rural hinterland of Öhringen and in the Kocher valley. The Kocher valley not only had the advantage of easy access to the market at Öhringen, and hence to markets in Heilbronn, Wimpfen, and Schwäbisch Hall as well, but this valley and the area immediately around Öhringen also offered more land to settlers than the narrow Jagst valley and a climate better suited to viticulture. The records allow only a shadowy glimpse of the agrarian expansion in this area. The best evidence of the demand for land and the economic opportunities this offered farmers and winegrowers comes from a careful study of the career of Wendel Hipler, Hohenlohe's ambitious secretary to the counts of Hohenlohe and later leader of the peasant armies in the Peasants' War.

In many respects this university-educated official was nothing more than a landholder who wheeled and dealed in an active land market around Öhringen. Hipler was already a wealthy man in 1498 when one finds evidence of him renting Michel Lenz four *Tagwerk* of newly cleared land. Near Finsterrot, not far from Öhringen, he continued to clear land, built new buildings, acquired a mill, and consolidated the properties into two estates he called Platzhof and Stolzeneck.[13] Like other propertyholders in this age of agrarian expansion, Hipler also provoked bitter conflicts with his neighbors, nearby villages, and even the church over rights to property. He acquired new lands, cleared them, and

[10] Jan De Vries's example of a family of five members farming eight hectares of land is instructive in this regard. He calculates that a seed–yield ratio of 1:4 allows the peasant household to feed itself and 1.4 other persons. But when it falls to 1:3 – and Atzenrod had only 1:3.4 – then he figures that any surplus vanishes and a shortfall occurs. See *The Economy of Europe in an Age of Crisis, 1600–1750* (Cambridge: Cambridge University Press, 1976), 34–5.
[11] L/L "Reichssteuer- und Schatzungsbuch Amt Langenburg 1525–1568."
[12] ALARL 1514–21.
[13] Gerd Wunder, "Wendel Hipler: Hohenlohischer Kanzler, Bauernführer um 1465–1526," *Schwäbische Lebensbilder* 6 (1957), 66–7. A *Tagwerk* is the amount of land that can be worked in one day.

improved them so aggressively that he became embroiled in protracted legal fights with townsmen and peasants near Öhringen in 1514.[14] The agrarian boom had begun to usher in a new period of land hunger. And with it came heightened conflict over land in Hohenlohe's villages.

The growing numbers of tillers of marginal soils had a solution to their problems with low agricultural productivity: Plant vineyards. The great demand for wine in fifteenth-century Germany no doubt made this shift to viticulture an attractive alternative to cereal production. Wine production flourished all along the Upper Rhine, the Neckar, the Main, and the Mosel rivers. And it was important to winegrowers in the Kocher and Tauber valleys of Hohenlohe as well.

By the early sixteenth century, however, wine production had passed its peak, leaving winegrowers still more exposed to the risks inherent in the trade. Viticulture had always involved risks. From the time that a winegrower cleared a rocky hillside for a vineyard he encountered uncertainties that made production a tricky affair, prone to setbacks that could ruin his household economy if he were not careful. In Hohenlohe there were the added risks of a climate where frosts tended to come earlier than in the warmer valleys of the Neckar and Upper Rhine.[15] Every winegrower therefore had to select the site of a vineyard carefully. He had, moreover, to calculate outlays of labor and capital with great care because he gambled in taking a grain field out of production for several years before it could produce the grapes that would bring a new cash income. These uncertainties no doubt lay behind the special pleas of winegrowers who joined in the Peasants' War in 1525 to free them from labor services during the harvests and to abolish tithes on the vineyards.[16] Both levies aggravated the uncertainties inherent in this trade.

Even more ominous for winegrowers and for merchants dependent upon the trade, the demand for wine had passed its peak by 1500. Hohenlohe, lying far from the major cities of South Germany on poorly maintained roads, was a distant rural hinterland even for the towns that would have been the natural consumers of its agricultural products: Schwäbisch Hall, Crailsheim, Ansbach, Rothenburg o.d.T., and Heilbronn. Because prices had to be high enough to bear the high costs of overland transportation, it seems likely that the Hohenlohe markets felt the weakening of demand for wine before other wine-producing regions. Townsmen from Öhringen, the center of the wine trade in Hohenlohe, complained as early as 1490 that commerce had fallen off and that fields near the town lay abandoned.[17] In fact wine prices throughout Germany had entered a period of sharp fluctuation and decline by the early sixteenth century. This

[14] Ibid. 70–1.   [15] Nestle, "Witterung und Klima," 41–123.
[16] Ferdinand Oechsle, *Beiträge zur Geschichte des Bauernkrieges in den schwäbisch-fränkischen Grenzländern* (Heilbronn: Carl Drechsler, 1838), 258–9.
[17] Ibid. 60–9.

economic uncertainty may not have provided the immediate spark for rebellion in 1525. But it helps explain the fact that the rebels came first from the winegrowing area around Öhringen and then drew strength from among the winegrowers of the Kocher and Tauber valleys.

Patrimonial domination and the House of Hohenlohe

Patterns of lordship or domination deeply influenced the way agrarian expansion transformed Germany's peasant societies in the sixteenth century. It is easy, however, to exaggerate the effective power of lords to direct the expansion or to mold peasant society to their own purposes at the beginning of the century. It is true that in the German Southwest in the late fifteenth century many lords, those of the House of Hohenlohe among them, scrambled to consolidate their lands and improve their revenues, employed serfdom to control the movements of peasants, and used their judicial powers to round off their dominion over land and people.[18] No lord, however, not even the relatively powerful princes of the House of Hohenlohe, could refashion agrarian society at will. Lords could encourage agrarian expansion, foster trade, and perhaps extract peasant surpluses more effectively than ever before. But they still had only limited power to impose order and stability in their domains as village society entered a period of stressful change.

Since authority of a princely house over its subjects depended partly upon its standing in the Holy Roman Empire, it is important first to place the House of Hohenlohe within the still fluid hierarchy of the empire in 1500. In the context of imperial politics, the House of Hohenlohe ranked as a princely house of some regional standing behind the largest secular and ecclesiastical states of South Germany. The princes of Hohenlohe, along with the other counts of Franconia, had largely freed themselves of the direct authority of the dominant power in Franconia, the prince-bishops of Würzburg. By 1500 this accomplishment was largely complete and had been reached by direct challenges to Würzburg, by the manipulation of old connections with the emperors, and by the successful bid for the imperial rank of count.[19] Their princely status was

---

[18] For a discussion of these seigneurial initiatives in the fifteenth century see Peter Blickle, *The Revolution of 1525: The German Peasants' War from a New Perspective*, trans. Thomas A. Brady, Jr., and H. C. Erik Midelfort (Baltimore: Johns Hopkins University Press, 1981), 35–57.

[19] The documentation for the late medieval period, critical in understanding the rise of the House of Hohenlohe into the ranks of imperial princes, is fragmentary and not yet thoroughly understood. There is no single study of the rise of the house in the late Middle Ages. Karl Weller, who wrote the best scholarly treatment of the family's history, leaves off his study too early. See Weller, *Geschichte des Hauses Hohenlohe*, 2 vols. (Stuttgart: W. Kohlhammer, 1902–8). Adolf Fischer's comprehensive history of the family into the nineteenth century discusses the late Middle Ages, but several of his facts are incorrect and he often approaches his material too uncritically. See his *Geschichte des Hauses Hohenlohe*, 2 vols. (Stuttgart: W. Kohlhammer, 1866–71). The best recent treatment of the fifteenth century, one that shows just how much more

confirmed when, in the great imperial reform of Maximilian I in 1495, the House of Hohenlohe received additional authority to administer justice, to keep the peace, and to raise taxes in the name of the Holy Roman Empire.[20] Its princes had, in short, successfully entered the ranks of Germany's rulers behind the greater princes of the realm.

The standing of any princely house depended primarily upon its control over land, and, as imperial authority waned in the fifteenth century, most powerful lords tried to consolidate their lands and various authorities over peasants as much as possible. In this process the House of Hohenlohe went much farther than most of the lesser lords and princes in the German Southwest.[21] This is best grasped by looking at the house's lands in a regional context. The lands were centered on the Kocher and Jagst valleys with properties stretching north from Langenburg to Weikersheim. A few scattered possessions, Schillingsfürst, for example, lay farther to the east. To the north of these domains lay the territories of the prince-bishops of Würzburg, still the largest landholders in Franconia in 1500. Along this northern border too were other, much smaller lands: the domains of the Teutonic Knights at Mergentheim, a few patches of territory claimed by the cathedral chapter at Mainz, the tiny estates of some imperial knights, and, in the valley of the Kocher not far from Öhringen, the monastic lands of Schöntal. To the east the prince's lands bordered Ansbach and the imperial city of Rothenburg o.d.T. And, running from east to west on the southern borders, lay the imperial city of Schwäbisch Hall, the small lands of the counts of Löwenstein, and, finally, the land of the largest state in the German Southwest, the Duchy of Württemberg. Between Würzburg and Württemberg, then, the House of Hohenlohe had carved out the largest set of lands of any noble in western Franconia.

revision is needed of this family's history, is Gerhard Thaddey, "Macht und Recht im späten Mittelalter: Die Auseinandersetzungen zwischen Hohenlohe und Hessen um die Grafschaften Ziegenhain und Nidda," *Württembergisch Franken* 61 (1977), 79–110.

[20] See Thaddey, "Macht und Recht," 104–7, for a discussion of the particular significance of the Diet at Worms in 1495 for the House of Hohenlohe. For a brief discussion of the significance of the imperial reform movement for the constitutional development of the territorial states and the Holy Roman Empire see Gerhard Oestreich, "Verfassungsgeschichte vom Ende des Mittelalters bis zum Ende des alten Reiches," in Herbert Grundmann, ed., *Handbuch der deutschen Geschichte*, 9th ed. (Stuttgart: Union, 1970), vol. 2, 366–8. For older, but still very useful, studies of the imperial reform itself see Fritz Hartung, "Imperial Reform, 1485–1495: Its Course and Its Character," in Gerald Strauss, ed., *Pre-Reformation Germany* (New York: Harper & Row, 1972), 73–135; and Karl Siegfried Bader, "Approaches to Imperial Reform at the End of the Fifteenth Century," in Strauss, ed., *Pre-Reformation Germany*, 136–61. For an introduction to more recent approaches to the reform see Heinz Angermeier, "Reichsreform und Reformation," *Historische Zeitschrift* 235 (1982), 529–604.

[21] See the sketch of the broader patterns of political development in Karl S. Bader, *Der deutsche Südwesten in seiner territorialstaatlichen Entwicklung* (Stuttgart: Koehler, 1950). For the specific patterns in Franconia see Hans Hubert Hofmann, "Bauer und Herrschaft in Franken," in Günter Franz, ed., *Deutsches Bauerntum im Mittelalter*, Wege der Forschung, vol. 16 (Darmstadt: Wissenschaftliche Buchgesellschaft, 1976), 443–6.

The patterns of dominance in a territory flowed from the fact that princes treated their lands not as the nucleus of a state, but as a family patrimony to be used for the personal maintenance of the house, its sons, and its dependents. In the case of the House of Hohenlohe one senior prince of the house, attended perhaps by his sons, close male relatives, and personal servants, theoretically held the reins of power over the household, its lands, and its peasants. In practice authority over the territory was often decentralized, since many princes did not hestitate to endow lesser sons with portions of the territory. Around each heir a small court and a separate administrative hierarchy formed to administer the castles, the estates, and the districts under its control. The House of Hohenlohe had repeatedly decentralized authority in such ways in the fourteenth and fifteenth centuries. By the time of Albrecht II (d. 1490) the alienated lands, and the power that flowed directly from control over these lands, had all come back under the control of the senior prince of the house.

After the death of Count Kraft VI in 1503 authority became decentralized once again and would remain so until the dissolution of the principality in 1806. His successors, Counts Albrecht III and Georg I, divided the administration of the territory between their respective courts, one at Neuenstein and the other at Waldenburg, keeping only a bare minimum of administration in common. They pledged in 1511 to keep common foreign and domestic policies, not to sell off patrimonial lands or castles outside the family, and to administer the archive, the town of Öhringen, and the right of common coinage in common.[22] The split they initiated, however, became permanent in 1556 when the two lines separated into two branches of the the House of Hohenlohe: Hohenlohe-Neuenstein and Hohenlohe-Waldenburg. After that date administrative authority devolved repeatedly to other courts created to maintain lesser sons of these two branches of the family (see Figure 1.1). These separate courts, scattered at Neuenstein, Weikersheim, Langenburg, Waldenburg, Pfedelbach, and Schillingsfürst, became the centers of Hohenlohe's small patrimonial states in the late sixteenth century.

The maintenance of the House of Hohenlohe depended in the end upon its successful dominance of its peasants. The authority of these lords, however, should not be confused with the coercive power of a modern bureaucratic state or even with the authority of the larger territorial states in Germany.[23] *Herrschaft* had less to do with government in the modern sense of the word than it did

---

[22] Wunder, "Wendel Hipler," 67–8. See also Fritz Ulshofer, "Die Hohenlohischen Hausverträge und Erbteilungen: Grundlinien einer Verfassungsgeschichte der Grafschaft Hohenlohe seit dem Spätmittelalter" (diss., Eberhard-Karls University, Tübingen, 1960), 91.

[23] For the small patrimonial state versus a bureaucratic state see Hans Hubert Hofmann, *Adelige Herrschaft und souveräner Staat: Studien über Staat und Gesellschaft in Franken und Bayern im 18. und 19. Jahrhundert*, Studien zur bayerischen Verfassungs- und Sozialgeschichte, vol. 2 (Munich: Kommission für bayerische Landesgeschichte, 1962).

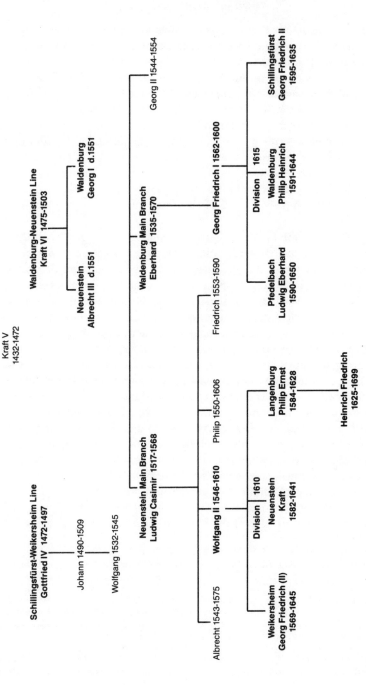

THE HOUSE OF HOHENLOHE

Kraft V
1432-1472

Schillingsfürst-Weikersheim Line
Gottfried IV 1472-1497

Waldenburg-Neuenstein Line
Kraft VI 1475-1503

Johann 1490-1509

Neuenstein
Albrecht III d.1551

Waldenburg
Georg I d.1551

Wolfgang 1532-1545

Georg II 1544-1554

Albrecht 1543-1575

Neuenstein Main Branch
Ludwig Casimir 1517-1568

Waldenburg Main Branch
Eberhard 1535-1570

Philip 1550-1606

Friedrich 1553-1590

Georg Friedrich I 1562-1600

Wolfgang II 1546-1610

Division | 1610

Weikersheim
Georg Friedrich (II)
1569-1645

Neuenstein
Kraft
1582-1641

Langenburg
Philip Ernst
1584-1628

Pfedelbach
Ludwig Eberhard
1590-1650

Division | 1615

Waldenburg
Philip Heinrich
1591-1644

Schillingsfürst
Georg Friedrich II
1595-1635

Heinrich Friedrich
1625-1699

Fig. 1.1. The House of Hohenlohe. The dates refer to births and deaths. Names appearing in bold type denote rulers of significant portions of the county and main branches of the house.

with a lord's personal or patrimonial domination of his dependents and peasants.[24] In the German Southwest this dominance flowed principally from control over the land. It might be broadened, as it was in Hohenlohe, by the lord's authority over serfs or by his authority to dispense justice. The legitimate exercise of these various authorities was sanctioned not by consciously created systems of rational laws, but by the sacredness of custom and religious principle. This is not to say that a lord had absolute power to bend his subjects to do his will. In practice a lord's power to impose order depended far less upon his claims to abstract legal rights over his subjects than it did upon the exercise of authority in concrete situations. And in practice the dominance any individaual prince exercised over peasants was tempered both by a weak administrative hierarchy and by the observance of customary restraints on the legitimate use of authority.

The princes of the House of Hohenlohe did not usually exercise their local dominance in person. Administration took place through a weak three-tiered hierarchy. At the top of the hierarchy the counts recruited officials to serve at the court as their personal servants, scribes, and advisers. Like household servants at other small courts, these officials did not specialize in the performance of any single administrative task. They acted as personal servants assigned sometimes to diplomatic missions, other times to domestic financial affairs, and still other times to ecclesiastical problems. As individuals they may have brought a great deal of personal skill and experience in administrative matters to their jobs, but they also managed the territory with very few written records. Inevitably, too, these servants pursued their own interests, sometimes at the expense of the counts. Wendel Hipler, the famous personal secretary of Count Kraft VI and later Counts Albrecht III and Georg I, served the counts well as their secretary but also built up a sizable set of lands near Öhringen and set himself up as an individual of some considerable power at the court. By 1514 he was threatening enough to Count Albrecht that this count took the extraordinary step of forcing him to sell back his lands, for which he never received compensation. Hipler, however, worked ceaselessly to get even for the insult, first taking his case to the imperial court and later using his old con-

---

[24] I am indebted to David Sabean for this appraoch to *Herrschaft* in the German Southwest. See his stimulating discussion of the problem in *Power in the Blood: Popular Culture and Village Discourse in Early Modern Germany* (Cambridge: Cambridge University Press, 1984), 20–7. For a discussion of the sociological concept of "patrimonial domination" see Max Weber, *Wirtschaft und Gesellschaft: Grundriss der verstehenden Soziologie*, 5th ed., ed. Johannes Winckelmann (Tübingen: J. C. B. Mohr, 1985), 122–76, especially 133–40. The work of Otto Brunner, though problematic in some respects, still has some very important insights into the nature of *Herrschaft*. See his *Land und Herrschaft: Grundfragen der territorialen Verfassungsgeschichte Österreichs im Mittelalter*, 5th ed. (Vienna: Rudolf M. Rohrer, 1956). See also Volker Press, "Herrschaft, Landschaft und 'Gemeiner Mann' in Oberdeutschland vom 15. bis zum frühen 19. Jahrhundert," *Zeitschrift für die Geschichte des Oberrheins* 123 (1975), 169–214.

nections to lead Hohenlohers in rebellion against their lords in 1525.[25] The conflicting loyalties that officials inevitably felt could therefore pose serious problems for the princes' exercise of power in the territory.

The exercise of dominance usually occurred as personal interactions between a few scattered officials and the villagers under their immediate authority. At these lower levels of the hierarchy, however, there were additional limits to the counts' exercise of authority. For a territory as large as Hohenlohe there were surprisingly few officials at the district and village level to carry out the will of the lords. The most important of these officials, the district steward, or *Vogt*, held the responsibility for administering the counts' authority at the district level. His primary responsibility was the supervision of collecting rents and dues, their transport and storage, and imposing fines and penalties on peasants. At the village level, the *Schultheissen*, who represented the steward within the village, aided the stewards in the performance of their duties. It must have been difficult for the counts to make these lower officials accountable for their duties. They operated far from the seats of princely power in Öhringen, Neuenstein, and Waldenburg. Very few of these officials could write in the early sixteenth century, and the records that were kept were often not very accurate. These officials also had limits to their power in face-to-face interactions with peasants. They could not call immediately upon soldiers to overcome peasants' resistance to the collection of rents or dues; the territory had no standing army. And, especially among the peasants who served as *Schultheissen*, they might feel their loyalties to their lord compromised or weakened by conflicting loyalties to commune, family, and personal ambition.[26]

At the lowest level of the administrative hierarchy, officials' authority was attenuated by the need to work through well-organized village communes with considerable authority to govern their own affairs. The *Schultheiss*, for all of his authority and direct ties with the stewards, did not represent the village or direct its main representative body, the communal assembly. By the late fifteenth century the village commune had assumed considerable autonomy and independence in the German Southwest.[27] Late medieval villages formed their own communal assemblies and elected a *Bürgermeister* and other officials to police

---

[25] See Wunder, "Wendel Hipler."

[26] See the discussion of the principality's administrative structures for the eighteenth century in Wolfram Fischer, *Das Fürstentum Hohenlohe im Zeitalter der Aufklärung*, Tübinger Studien zur Geschichte und Politik, no. 10 (Tübingen: J. C. B. Mohr, 1958), 38–82. Most studies of the small territorial states and *Herrschaften* of the German Southwest do not take into consideration the complex tensions in the administrative hierarchy of the early sixteenth century. For a short discussion of the problem see Sabean, *Power in the Blood*, 12–20.

[27] The literature on the medieval German village is vast. For a recent summary of its importance in the political life of late medieval Germany see Peter Blickle, *Deutsche Untertanen: Ein Widerspruch* (Munich: C. H. Beck, 1981), 23–60; and Heide Wunder, *Die bäuerliche Gemeinde in Deutschland* (Göttingen: Vandenhoeck & Ruprecht, 1986). For the region of which Hohenlohe was a part see the comments of Hans Hubert Hofmann in "Bauer und Herrschaft in Franken."

the village's jurisdictions. These assemblies carried sufficient authority to resolve disputes over common fields, pastures, and forests, to hold their own
courts, and to enforce customs later written down as local laws.[28] Some villages
even joined together to form district courts (*Centgerichte*) that resolved disputes
between villages. Confronted with such formidable village institutions, it was
always best to secure the cooperation of the local authorities in their own
subordination.

There is no small irony in the fact that authority depended as much upon
peasants participating in their own domination as it did upon officials exercising
coercive power in the village. Peasants accepted authority only if they shared
in some of the benefits of feudal dominance. The internal security of a territory
like Hohenlohe very much depended upon it. One should not therefore view
lord–peasant relationships as exclusively exploitive or confrontational, although
these relationships were structured primarily to extract surpluses from peasants
through various means. Patrimonial dominance worked in far more subtle and
effective ways than that in maintaining a lord's authority. And the key to peasant
loyalty and obedience was reciprocity. A lord could legitimately press his authority only by providing his peasants with "protection" or, as it was termed,
Schutz und Schirm. This obligation involved a whole range of important services
essential to the stability of any peasant society: military protection, justice, order,
and security.[29] Peasant loyalty was therefore a quality that no lord ever took
for granted. Loyalty was evoked with a customary oath of loyalty, but then it
had to be renewed repeatedly in peasants through concrete actions.

Count Kraft VI (d. 1503), for example, took pains continuously to evoke
loyalty in his peasants. He improved the collection of revenues from his lands
by surveying the territory and carefully recording tenants' obligations in a new
rent book. These included the customary feudal levies of any lord: rents or
quitrents, death duties, entry fines, and tithes. And he frequently commanded
his peasants to perform labor services for a few days every year on his estates,
often to help bring in the harvest of grapes from his vineyards in the Kocher
valley.[30] But he also evoked loyalty from his subjects by protecting them. In
1486 he and Count Gottfried came to the aid of their subjects from Öhringen
and Ingelfingen by distributing supplies of grain and wine, apparently to relieve
them from a famine.[31] In 1490 he protected his peasants again, this time by
suddenly announcing a reduction in the year's carting services to and from his

---

[28] See Gustav Adolf Thumm, "Die bäuerlichen und dörflichen Rechtsverhältnisse des Fürstentums
Hohenlohe im 17. und 18. Jahrhundert" (diss., University of Hohenheim, 1970).
[29] See Brunner, *Land und Herrschaft*, 240–356.
[30] For a discussion of the seigneurial burdens on the land in Hohenlohe see Eckart Schremmer,
Die Bauernbefreiung in Hohenlohe, Quellen und Forschungen zur Agrargeschichte, vol. 9 (Stuttgart: Gustav Fischer, 1963), 41–68.
[31] Oechsle, *Beiträge zur Geschichte des Bauernkrieges*, 60–1.

vineyards in the Kocher valley. He justified his action simply by saying "that the poor people would bitterly complain of [more carting] services" if they had been pressed.[32] In each of these situations Kraft not only legitimized his authority, but his peasants also renewed their promises of obedience. His authority therefore rested as much on displays of grace as it did upon the extraction of rents and dues.

Only through the duration of serfdom did the counts of Hohenlohe have broad powers to govern the everyday lives of their villagers. Serfdom bound a peasant to lifetime servitude to his lord, restricted his mobility, and gave his lord the right to control his marriage choices and the disposition of his property. This odious form of personal bondage had lost significance in the fourteenth century as peasants successfully pressed for more freedoms, but many lords in the German Southwest revived and extended its use in the fifteenth century. Serfdom served both economic and political purposes at this time. Lords could keep their serfs on the land and so halt, and even reverse, the tendency toward declining seigneurial revenues after the Black Death. But the political purposes of serfdom in the German Southwest should not be overlooked either. The claims and counterclaims of German princes, abbots, and petty nobles had created an impenetrable forest of overlapping and conflicting feudal rights in this corner of the Holy Roman Empire. By tightening their hold on their serfs, securing their legal rights over them, lords could extend or round off their control of their territories. For in this region serfdom became a tool of political power at the local level, a building block of what were becoming small territorial states.[33]

The counts of the House of Hohenlohe, for example, used serfdom to build up their power within the relative compact set of lands that became their own political domain. They still relied extensively upon serfdom to control the townsmen of Öhringen and the peasants in its vicinity in 1500. But by this time the counts were also willing to relax their hold over their serfs. To foster agrarian expansion and trade, however, Count Kraft VI moderated the burdens on many serfs who wished to settle in the territory, clear new land, and expand agricultural production.[34] To defuse resistance to his authority in the town of Öhringen, he reduced the burden of taxes on his serfs in Öhringen and gave them broader freedom to move property and engage in trade as a way of encouraging commercial expansion and movement to and from the market.[35]

---

[32] Ibid. 68–71.

[33] See especially Claudia Ulbrich, *Leibherrschaft am Oberrhein im Spätmittelalter*, Veröffentlichungen des Max-Planck-Instituts für Geschichte, vol. 58 (Göttingen: Vandenhoeck & Ruprecht, 1979). See also Saarbrücker Arbeitsgruppe, "Die spätmittelalterliche Leibeigenschaft im Oberrhein," *Zeitschrift für Agrargeschichte und Agrarsoziologie* 22 (1974), 9–33, and Blickle, *The Revolution of 1525*, 29–35.

[34] Oechsle, *Beiträge zur Geschichte des Bauernkrieges*, 70–3.   [35] Ibid. 61–9 *passim*.

In the sixteenth century the princes relied less and less on income from their serfs.[36]

The House of Hohenlohe may therefore have secured its authority over this region, but its dominance rested on only a limited ability to impose order and stability. Some very important powers in fact were either underutilized or still eluded the princes' grasp at the beginning of the sixteenth century. The counts, for example, seem not to have made frequent use of the right to impose imperial taxes. As a result they did not have detailed cadastres listing properties and their assessments. And their peasants were not disciplined to accept a regular burden of taxation.

The princes' judicial authority was also not fully exploited as a tool of domination over the peasant family. In 1418 the princes had acquired the right to hold court in their lands, and this authority seems to have played a significant role in establishing the House of Hohenlohe as princes with a legitimate claim to imperial status.[37] This authority meant that their subjects could no longer appeal directly to the imperial court at Rotweil to adjudicate legal disputes. They came instead to their lords as judges in secular matters. This authority, however, remained circumscribed in the late fifteenth century. For one thing, the bishop of Würzburg still held rights of legal jurisdiction in Hohenlohe and sent courts to make the rounds.[38] And, for another, disputes over peasant marriages, inheritances, and property – critical in intervening in peasant family affairs and in influencing the distribution of property in the village – seem not to have come to the counts' courts in large numbers. Not until after the Protestant reformation in 1556 would the princes of the House of Hohenlohe consolidate all of the judicial powers in the territory in their own hands.

Decay of the church

In late medieval social theory the clergy was imagined as one of three distinct orders, its function to provide spiritual leadership and unity for those who fought and tilled the soil. In practice, of course, the church not only fulfilled a spiritual mission for society but also served as a bastion of the feudal hierarchy, sharing interests with the territorial princes and with the aristocracy. In the Holy Roman Empire the church had a particularly prominent role in upholding

---

[36] Income in Langenburg district declined from forty or fifty *gulden* per year in 1500 to thirty *gulden* or so by the 1620s. By the 1630s and 1640s serfdom had all but disappeared in this part of Hohenlohe. ALARL 1504–1681. See also Schremmer, *Die Bauernbefreiung in Hohenlohe*, 15–22.
[37] Oechsle, *Beiträge zur Geschichte des Bauernkrieges*, 69.
[38] Gunther Franz, "Reformation und landesherrliches Kirchenregiment in Hohenlohe," *Württembergisch Franken* 58 (1974), 120.

the feudal hierarchy.[39] In the parts of Germany near Hohenlohe, in fact, church authorities had a visible role in the hierarchy as feudal lords with vast land-holdings. Most of Franconia to the north and east of Hohenlohe was dominated by the powerful prince-bishops of Würzburg and Bamberg; and not too far to the south a cluster of important abbeys and monasteries held sway over large parts of Upper Swabia. The striking feature of the church in Hohenlohe, however, was its unusual weakness as an independent institution. It still played a part in the feudal hierarchy, but it was destined to do so under the influence of the House of Hohenlohe.

The church's weakness came largely as a result of its lack of significant landed properties in Hohenlohe. No monasteries or other major ecclesiastical institutions held land in this territory. The Öhringen *Spital*, the center of church authority in the region, controlled some properties in and near the town, but these properties did not constitute a significant concentration of land. In the rural parishes there may have been a very few insignificant properties, but they would have been used for the immediate support of a parish priest and nothing more. Without land the church could not command the authority over peasants that came from *Grundherrschaft* or from any of the other forms of lordship. Instead the church exercised its authority through the operation of the *Spital*, itinerant courts, and parish priests. And in each case the princes challenged church authority and weakened its independent influence over Hohenlohe's small townsmen and peasants.

The erosion of church authority was most apparent at its center in Öhringen. Here too the influence of the House of Hohenlohe over the church was strongest and clearly evident for all to see. In theory the prince-bishops of Würzburg controlled the *Spital*, made appointments to its offices, and exercised its various ecclesiastical responsibilities in the town. In this part of Franconia, however, by the late fifteenth century the prince-bishops found it difficult to administer their offices very efficiently and responsibly. For the counts had acquired the patronage rights over the church and many parishes, and used these powers to control appointments to clerical posts. Count Kraft VI showed up his own power – and the church's lack of it – over the *Spital* in the 1490s. In response to the popular view of the clergy in the town as corrupt and immoral he acted decisively to punish their moral offenses and began to reform the administration of the church.[40] He did not achieve the same control over the church that other

---

[39] The literature on the church on the eve of the Reformation is enormous. For an introduction to the conditions in Germany see Bernd Moeller, *Deutschland im Zeitalter der Reformation*, Deutsche Geschichte, vol. 4, 2d ed. (Göttingen: Vandenhoeck & Ruprecht, 1977), 36–46.
[40] Gunther Franz, "Reformation und landesherrliches Kirchenregiment in Hohenlohe," 123–5; Johann Christian Wibel, *Hohenlohische Kyrchen- und Reformations- Historie, aus bewahrten Urkunden und Schriften und nebst einem Vorbericht von der Grafschaft Hohenlohe ueberhaupt* (Onolzbach: Jacob Christoph Poschens, 1752), vol. 1, 192–201, 262–3, 276–9.

territorial princes and imperial cities already had over ecclesiastical affairs in their communities. He deepened the association of the church with the House of Hohenlohe, however, and laid the foundations for the future incorporation of the church into the patrimonial state during the Reformation.

This erosion of church autonomy left the exercise of religious authority in a confused state on the eve of the Reformation. The princes eagerly intervened in ecclesiastical affairs in order to weaken the authority of the bishop of Würzburg, but they were in no legal or practical position to assume full responsibility for the church in the territory. This pattern was particularly evident in the countryside. The bishop had exercised his authority over rural Hohenlohe parishes through an itinerant court, the *Sendgericht*, in the late Middle Ages. The court convened, in theory, every year in the territory to test local religious beliefs, supervise the performance of religious services, and adjudicate legal disputes, especially in marital affairs. Kraft VI ordered parish priests, however, not to send their legal disputes to Würzburg any longer; they were to send their cases to his court.[41] During his rule Kraft obviously tried some cases involving adultery in Öhringen, but he seems not to have tried very many.[42] It may have been that parish priests and Hohenlohers hesitated to take their cases to him because of his questionable legal claim to authority in this matter. Whatever the reasons, Kraft's actions tended to contribute to the decay of the bishop's power in the territory but without establishing in its place a strong religious authority. That would come only after the reformation in the 1550s and 1560s.

Some reformers had a more clearly conceived vision of how to reform the church in the late Middle Ages. In the minds of some of the most radical of them, reform of the church was bound up with a complete restructuring of the feudal hierarchy in the empire, beginning with the office of the Holy Roman Emperor and extending down to the parish priest. The composer of the famous "Reformatio Sigismundi" in 1439 lamented the failure of church councils to rid Christendom of a corrupt papacy and church hierarchy, declaring:

> Obedience is dead.
> Justice is grievously abused.
> Nothing stands in its proper order.[43]

This intellectual looked back to the past for his guide to the present and found it in the model Christian society under the ancient emperor Constantine. A pious leader would appear like a knight, he thought, and he would reform the

---

[41] Franz, "Reformation und landesherrliches Kirchenregiment," 127–8.
[42] Ibid. 128; see also the cases cited in Wibel, *Hohenlohische Kyrchen- und Reformations- Historie*, vol. 1, 270; vol. 3, 201–2, 205–6.
[43] This passage comes from the English translation of the "Reformatio Sigismundi" in Gerald Strauss, ed., *Manifestations of Discontent in Germany on the Eve of the Reformation* (Bloomington: Indiana University Press, 1971), 4.

entire Holy Roman Empire by confiscating ecclesiastical property, abolishing serfdom, and establishing justice at every level.[44]

The call for a radical restructuring of church and society was heard at every level of German society, even in the small towns and villages of rural Hohenlohe. Here the most dramatic call for reform heard in the late fifteenth century came from a propertyless youth, Hans Böhm, the Drummer of Niklaushausen. This lad from the Tauber valley claimed to have received a special mission from the Virgin Mary to preach to the common man. In 1476 he launched himself into a series of sermons sharply attacking the papacy and the clergy for their moral laxity, their worldliness, and their accumulation of property.[45] His denunciations of the abuse of wealth and power soon included secular princes as well. But he did not always dwell on the wealthy and the privileged; he also called for a positive reform of the church and feudal society. His was a more egalitarian vision than that held out in the "Reformatio Sigismundi." Böhm foresaw a society soon to come in which all would live as brothers and sisters, where no one would claim special privileges or collect rents and dues: "Princes, ecclesiastical and secular alike, and counts and knights should only possess ᴽs much as common folk, then everyone would have enough. The time will come when princes and lords will work for their daily bread."[46] Perhaps ten to a hundred thousand pilgrims from the region, including Hohenlohe, flocked to Niklaushausen to hear Hans Böhm deliver sermons and to watch him perform miracles. The bishop of Würzburg, with the support of other secular and ecclesiastical lords, eventually had the youth imprisoned, tortured, and burned at the stake for heresy and sorcery.

This episode brought into relief many of the fractures and strains in the agrarian order in this part of Germany. This was a peasant society entering a prolonged period of stressful social change. The sources of the social tensions and changes lay partly in the inherent uncertainties of the peasant economy, partly in the emergence of a more complex village society based on the control of land, movable wealth, occupation, and place in the market economy. Lords added new tensions, however, and aggravated the stresses within the village by encouraging agrarian expansion and by improving their ability to dominate villagers. The places of different groups within the agrarian hierarchy itself,

---

[44] See Richard van Dülmen, *Reformation als Revolution: Soziale Bewegung und religiöser Radikalismus in der deutschen Reformation* (Munich: Deutscher Taschenbuch, 1977), 16–17. The so-called Revolutionary of the Upper Rhine made a similar, but even more radical, appeal for restructuring the feudal hierarchy in Germany.

[45] For the most recent discussion of the Drummer of Niklaushausen see Klaus Arnold, *Niklaushausen 1476: Quellen und Untersuchungen zur sozial-religiösen Bewegung des Hans Behem und zur Agrarstruktur eines spätmittelalterlichen Dorfes*, Saecula spiritalia, vol. 3 (Baden-Baden: Valentin Koerner, 1980).

[46] Norman Cohn, *The Pursuit of the Millennium*, rev. ed. (London: Oxford University Press, 1970), 228.

however, remained fluid and unstable, for lords did not yet have the ability to redirect peasant loyalties away from the family and the village. Lords could use their dominance to bring overwhelming power to bear against individuals, much as the bishop of Würzburg did against Hans Böhm, and so maintain the feudal order in the countryside. But that power remained limited. When whole villages refused to cooperate, when villagers hesitated to pay their rents and dues, then that power could be called into question. In a moment like that, the lords' power to dominate the village might vanish suddenly, with all the liberating and intoxicating effects of a magical spell being broken.

2

Peasants' War and reformation

No set of events illustrates more clearly the tenuousness of order and the weakness of princely domination of the countryside than do the risings of 1525. During the Peasants' War villagers not only challenged the authority of their lords and called into question the fundamental order of feudal society, they also began to fashion a radical new world to replace it. In some ways, the dynamics of the revolt were determined by the social, political, and economic strains common to many rural societies in Europe at the beginning of this long period of agrarian expansion in the sixteenth century. But the revolt also had its roots in the electrifying religious and political climate of South and Central Germany in the early 1520s. For the leaders of the German peasants, as they drew up grievance lists and hammered out political programs for the new order, built upon the bundle of complex ideas associated with the early evangelical movements.

One must be careful not to read into these plans the ideas of Luther, Zwingli, or any other great reformer, although these reformers certainly influenced the shaping of some of them. These political plans, like the revolt itself, must be understood in the context of the complex inner dynamics of the peasant movements, the shifting, often contradictory, goals of the groups that made up the armies. Still, what was at stake in 1525 was the future shape of the agrarian order itself, who would have the power to shape it, and, above all, how religion would be domesticated to fit the changing social and political relationships in the countryside.[1]

Some of the peasant armies developed unmistakable social-revolutionary tendencies, a religious and political radicalism that, had it ever been realized, would have swept away the feudal order as contemporaries understood it. But, while noting these tendencies, one must exercise caution, for the movements never achieved the cohesiveness, the unity, the clear revolutionary direction that some scholars see in the peasant movements of 1525. The confusing nature

[1] For a discussion of the literature on the Peasants' War see the Bibliographical Essay.

of the events of the revolt resulted partly from the fact that not all villagers, not all armies, broke completely or easily with traditional notions of authority. Peasants and their leaders continued to defer to old forms of authority, as contradictory as this seemed at times, and hesitated, or found it impossible, to break openly with forms of domination in which they still shared some of the fruits. Far from Upper Swabia, far from the radical heartland of the Twelve Articles, in the villages and small towns of Franconia, the Neckar valley, the Odenwald, and Hohenlohe, this pattern was particularly evident. Here some social-revolutionary tendencies clearly developed. But no "early bourgeois rev- olution," no "revolution of the common man" ever took place.[2] The fractures in the movements proved too great to be overcome, the political plans incomplete and contradictory, the peasants' armies too weak before the princes' armies to win the day in battle. The time was too short for peasant leaders to hammer out of the diverse, fractured movements a cohesive new order.

Origins

Every peasant movement bears the marks of the society and the circumstances of its origins, and the peasant armies of 1525 proved no exception to this rule. The risings had their origins in a bundle of tensions – economic, social, political, and religious – common to many small towns and villages of South and Central Germany in the early 1520s. Some involved conflicts woven into the everyday practices of domination common since the fifteenth century. Others stemmed from the unusual rural and urban unrest of the early 1520s. Some scholars see in these tensions a "crisis of feudalism," a crisis of the whole late medieval agrarian order.[3] But no wrenching, thorough crisis of the whole feudal order lay behind the risings that would take place in Franconia and Hohenlohe in 1525. The agrarian conflict of the spring of 1525 seems to have come instead against the backdrop of a cyclical and *short-term* crisis in the agricultural econ- omy. This crisis did not strike every village or social group equally, nor did it come everywhere at the same time. The conflicts piled up in only *certain* rural areas: districts and villages where viticulture and rural industry predominated. Herein lies the most important clue to the origins of the risings, and to the dynamics of peasant movements themselves in 1525.

Subsistence crises struck agricultural communities with predictable, almost

---

[2] The position I take accords more with the view of Richard van Dülmen than it does with Adolf Laube, Max Steinmetz, and Günter Vogler or with Peter Blickle. See van Dülmen, *Reformation als Revolution: Soziale Bewegung und religiöser Radikalismus in der deutschen Reformation* (Munich: Deutscher Taschenbuch, 1977), 41–59.

[3] See, for example, Peter Blickle, *The Revolution of 1525: The German Peasants' War from a New Perspective*, trans. Thomas A. Brady, Jr., and H. C. Erik Midelfort (Baltimore: Johns Hopkins University Press, 1981), 68–86.

disturbing, regularity in the late Middle Ages, and had little to do with a deep structural crisis of the whole agricultural economy. Some of the structural features of premodern agriculture made the subsistence crisis an everyday part of village life: low agricultural productivity, the absence of secure storage facilities for grain, high transportation costs, and inefficient systems of food distribution. But the growth of population in the countryside, the development of a substantial class of cottagers and wage laborers, made some areas like Upper Swabia more prone to crises toward 1500.[4] Even in a land not yet heavily burdened with a large population of cottagers and day laborers, subsistence crises were also the order of the day. But they tended to be less severe. In rural Hohenlohe, for example, villagers seem to have met the local needs for grain. But when crops failed for two, three, or more years and local supplies of grain became depleted, famine would have come to this land. During such a crisis a familiar cycle ran its course: Villagers hoarded grain supplies and could no longer pay taxes, rents, and dues, and, as the famine spread, panic and fear set in.[5] In the fifteenth century, subsistence crises occurred in South Germany every eleven years or so.[6] The towns contributed to the panic, for they hoarded their own supplies of grain or tried to secure sources of grain at the expense of the village.

The crop failures of the early 1520s bred precisely this kind of climate of fear of shortages and suspicion of authority. Harvest failures struck Franconia in 1502–3 and again in 1515, but then became chronic, striking the region almost every single year between 1517 and 1524.[7] The unrest, however, spread somewhat unevenly through the countryside: The harvest failures seem to have struck some villages harder than others, and some not at all. In the parts of Franconia where population growth was already well under way, where villages were dominated by sizable communities of smallholders and landless laborers, the effects of the crop failures were devastating. Even in the best of years these householders, as we noted in the last chapter, lived on the margin of subsistence. "For every one [peasant] that comes out all right," the margrave of Ansbach and Bayreuth wrote early in the sixteenth century, "there are about fifty poor country folk who have hardly any bread and are daily in need of supplies for their households."[8] The unrest that had spread throughout the region by the

---

[4] See David Sabean, *Landbesitz und Gesellschaft am Vorabend des Bauernkrieges: Eine Studie der sozialen Verhältnisse im südlichen Oberschwaben in den Jahren vor 1525* (Stuttgart: Gustav Fischer, 1972).

[5] For a general survey of this problem see Wilhelm Abel, *Massenarmut und Hungerkrisen im vorindustriellen Europa: Versuch einer Synopsis* (Hamburg: Paul Parey, 1974).

[6] Wilhelm Abel, *Strukturen und Krisen der spätmittelalterlichen Wirtschaft*, Quellen und Forschungen zur Agrargeschichte, vol. 32 (Stuttgart: Gustav Fischer, 1980), 63–8.

[7] Rudolf Endres, "Probleme des Bauernkrieges in Franken," in Rainer Wohlfeil, ed. *Der Bauernkrieg 1524–26: Bauernkrieg und Reformation: Neun Beiträge* (Munich: Nymphenburger, 1975), 94–5.

[8] Cited in Rudolf Endres, "Zur sozialökonomischen Lage und sozialpsychischen Einstellung des

end of 1523 seems to have concentrated in the lands of the prince-bishops of Würzburg and Bamberg, the lands in which such groups could compose up to 50 percent of the population.[9] For Hohenlohe, however, a land with a smaller population of smallholders and comparatively few landless laborers, one finds no evidence at all of crop failures or rural unrest before 1525.

In villages where cereal cultivation had given way to viticulture, to specialized cash crops, the crisis spread quickly and deeply. For winegrowers and laborers quickly exhausted whatever stores of grain they held in reserve and had to pay high prices for grain and bread as supplies became scarce. These communities suffered not simply because the crops failed, but because the wine trade itself had entered a period of erratic decline and adjustment. The incomes of winegrowers seem to have fluctuated sharply in the decades around 1500.[10] The swings in prices and demand for wine tended to accentuate the tensions between merchants and the small producers of wine, between the rich and the poor, the privileged and the unprivileged. The patrician families of the imperial city of Rothenburg o.d.T., for example, weathered the crisis by virtue of the monopoly they held on local commerce and the fortunes they had accumulated. But their privileges and wealth aroused discontent among the region's winegrowers, who still had to pay their customary exactions despite losses in income. Other types of tensions surfaced in a town like Öhringen where the crisis revived the bitter resentments against the privileges of the clergy and the restrictions placed on commerce by the counts of Hohenlohe. A number of small merchants, their positions unprotected by trade monopolies, lost their fortunes in the wine trade in the years before the rebellion. Many, as a result, harbored enmity toward those who held the reins of power: the clergy, the magistrates of the town council, and the counts of Hohenlohe.[11]

The crisis of the early 1520s therefore struck the communities of the Kocher valley, Öhringen, and the town's rural hinterland in much the same way that an earlier crisis had in 1490. At that time, the counts had defused unrest by relaxing labor services and other burdens. In 1525 the counts would face alliances of these same communities demanding relief from harsh exactions, though this time on a much larger scale.

'Gemeinen Mannes': Der Kloster- und Burgensturm in Franken in 1525," in Hans-Ulrich Wehler, ed., *Der deutsche Bauernkrieg 1524–1526*, Geschichte und Gesellschaft, Special Issue no. 1 (Göttingen: Vandenhoeck & Ruprecht, 1975), 70.
[9] See ibid.
[10] For this point I am indebted to Franz Irsigler, "The Economic Causes of the German Peasants' War, 1525," unpublished paper presented to the Sixteenth Century Studies Conference, St. Louis, Missouri, October 28–30, 1982. See also Ernst Kelter, "Die wirtschaftlichen Ursachen des Bauernkrieges," *Schmollers Jahrbuch für Gesetzgebung, Verwaltung und Volkswirtschaft im Deutschen Reiche* 65 (1941), 1–42.
[11] Ferdinand Oechsle, *Beiträge zur Geschichte des Bauernkrieges in den schwäbisch-fränkischen Grenzlandern* (Heilbronn: Carl Drechsler, 1838), 82–3.

But there were important differences after 1520. More than the crises of the late fifteenth century, the crisis of the early 1520s was a crisis of rural industry as well. Since cycles in rural industry often followed the ups and downs of the agricultural economy, tensions in many small towns inevitably became heightened in the wake of a drawn-out subsistence crisis. Many craftsmen were, after all, no more than part-time farmers, winegrowers, and gardeners who supplemented their income with work in their small shops and so inevitably felt the pinch when crops failed. But the protracted subsistence crisis had additional consequences for artisans and laborers. In the wake of a subsistence crisis, demand for industrial products – cheap textiles and metal goods, leather goods, pots, wooden tools, for example – fell off sharply as consumers were forced to pay out larger shares of their income for bread and supplies of grain.[12] In and around Rothenburg o.d.T. and Mergentheim (the two centers of the Tauber valley rising), Ansbach, and a whole cluster of other small Franconian towns, the crisis affected small peasant producers, craftsmen, and merchants linked up to the small-craft industries.[13] To make matters worse, an ill-timed currency reform in 1524 made economic adjustments following the crisis particularly difficult. As in 1482, 1491–3, and 1512 when the authorities devalued the coinage, wages were cut, in one swift stroke, for all artisans and laborers. Waves of unrest rolled through a number of German cities as a result.[14]

None of these economic tensions made a rebellion unavoidable. What was critical was how lords and princes responded to the crisis, whether they relaxed seigneurial burdens and taxes or pressed ruthlessly ahead with little regard for local circumstances. For during a short-term economic crisis local attention focused on the particular practices of domination lords used to extract resources from peasants, craftsmen, and laborers, and whether lords extended or withheld their protection in a time of hardship. If some lords showed restraint in extracting rents and dues in these years, if they drove in the customary rents and dues with less harshness than in good years, it would not have been unusual. Rather than arouse deep unrest, as we noted in the case of Hohenlohe in the late fifteenth century, many lords were apt to back off from their customary exactions.

A number of lords, however, sharpened the effects of the crisis by responding with indifference to villagers' pleas to reduce the burden of taxes, tithes, rents, and dues in these years. Some lords intensified the crisis by driving in even the most ordinary of rents and dues. Others over the years had contributed pressures of a different sort by gradually reducing sources of income for vil-

---

[12] Ernst Labrousse, *Esquisse du mouvement des prix et des revenus en France au XVIIIe siècle* (Paris: Librairie Dalloz, 1933).

[13] For a discussion of society and economy in Rothenburg see Paul Eilentrop, *Verfassung, Recht und Wirtschaft in Rothenburg o/T. z. Z. des Bauernkrieges* (Marburg: Spannagel & Caesar, 1909).

[14] Irsigler, "The Economic Causes of the German Peasants' War, 1525."

lagers. Restrictions on access to village common fields, forests, and fisheries, limits on sheep raising, the demands for labor services: All of these burdens had gradually become more onerous over the years.[15] Still others added new burdens on top of the old ones. In Franconia these tended to be the ecclesiastical lords. The church dominated the land in Franconia, after all. Laymen in this region often protested against the rigorous administration of ecclesiastical properties to maximize returns, the levying of a heavy burden of taxes in ecclesiastical lands and the economic advantages secured by abbeys, monasteries, and cathedral chapters as a result of their privileges and exemptions from taxes.[16] But a few bishops and abbots added to the unrest by imposing new and heavy burdens of taxes in the early 1520s. In the bishopric of Bamberg, on top of the usual burden of seigneurial rents and dues, the tax on wine, and a regular tax, came three new taxes: a war levy in 1519, a consecration tax in 1522, and another war levy in 1524. The consecration tax alone was a 10 percent levy on every household's assessed taxable wealth.[17]

The timing of these new levies could not have been worse. For they came precisely at the time when the harvest failures spread through Franconia and aggravated tensions in the countryside. At the territorial assembly in the bishopric of Würzburg in 1523, for example, a number of representatives warned Prince-Bishop Conrad von Thüngen prophetically:

> The prince well knows that the largest portion of the chapter's subjects are winegrowers, peasants, and laboring people, that they provide for themselves by hard work, and are so loaded up with rents, quitrents, taxes, tithes, and other burdens, that a man worth 1,000 fl. can hardly feed himself, his wife, and children; a new levy, and another crop failure following it, could be the cause for a revolt.[18]

But these pleas went unheard. In 1523 and 1524, as the crops failed again in many villages, refusals to tithe swept through the region. The foundations for an early modern tax revolt were clearly laid.

The revolt, once it began, took a far more radical course than other tax revolts, and part of the reason for this lay in the spread of evangelical ideas in the 1520s. For the itinerant preachers of the early Reformation focused popular criticism on the clergy and gave religious legitimacy to the mounting resistance against tithes and the power of the church. The evangelical movements of the early 1520s presented a number of faces to townsmen and villagers, and so they cannot be summed up with simple reference to Luther's ideas. The tracts

---

[15] Rudolf Endres, "Der Bauernkrieg in Franken," *Blätter für deutsche Landesgeschichte* 109 (1973), 38–9.

[16] See Henry J. Cohn, "Anticlericalism in the German Peasants' War 1525," *Past and Present* no. 83 (1979), 3–31.

[17] Endres, "Probleme des Bauernkrieges in Franken," 94–5.

[18] Cited in Endres, "Zur sozialökonomischen Lage und sozialpsychischen Einstellung des 'Gemeinen Mannes,'" 70.

of Thomas Müntzer, Johann Hergot, and others found a readership in Franconia, for example, although one does not yet know the distribution or influence of such tracts with any certainty.[19] Nor is it clear how villagers, who still lived in an oral culture, understood these pamphlets, the popular sermons preached from the rural churches, and the rumors that ran through the taverns and marketplaces.[20] But this much is clear: Popular enthusiasm for Gospel mixed freely with anticlericalism and popular notions of social justice. In 1519 the firebrand popular preacher of Rothenburg, Dr. Teuschlein, not only condemned the Jews, but he denounced the payment of interest, tithes, and other burdens as unchristian as well.[21] In the tense and charged atmosphere in Bamberg after the prince-bishop levied the consecration tax in 1522, the preacher Johann Schwannhausen freely linked the Word of God with a call for social justice. He called for the distribution of church property to the needy, and sided with those who refused to pay clerical taxes. He was careful, however, not to condemn authority itself.[22]

With hindsight we can point to a number of incidents and some near-revolts in 1523 and 1524 that hinted that after several years of harvest failures popular expectations were running high for lords to extend protection from customary or extraordinary burdens. In Franconia these incidents had three factors in common: They took place primarily in the winegrowing districts and in the ecclesiastical territories; they focused on very specific practices of domination, taxes, or dues (tithes, for example); and they began to base local appeals on the Gospel. In May, for example, townsmen from Forchheim, a small town under the authority of the bishop of Bamberg, seized control of the town and forced the town council to swear loyalty to the commune. On the following morning, five hundred peasants from the surrounding countryside marched into the town to join them, and together they presented their grievances to the bishop as five articles. The townsmen and villagers wanted relief from specific burdens – restriction on the freedom to fish and hunt, certain tithes, and the consecration tax – and an end to the clergy's exemptions from local taxes.[23] Jörg Kreutzer, a preacher called to preach the Gospel in the town, rallied support for the grievances from among the town's sizable population of im-

---

[19] Endres, "Probleme des Bauernkrieges in Franken," 96–7.

[20] See Robert Scribner, "Oral Culture and the Diffusion of Reformation Ideas," *History of European Ideas* 5 (1984), 237–56, and *For the Sake of Simple Folk: Popular Propaganda for the German Reformation* (Cambridge: Cambridge University Press, 1981). See especially the path-breaking study of Franziska Conrad, *Reformation in der bäuerlichen Gesellschaft: Zur Rezeption reformatorischer Theologie im Elsass*, Veröffentlichungen des Instituts für europäische Geschichte Mainz, Abteilung für abendländische Religionsgeschichte, vol. 116 (Stuttgart: Franz Steiner, 1984).

[21] Günther Franz, *Der deutsche Bauernkrieg*, 11th ed. (Darmstadt: Wissenschaftliche Buchgesellschaft, 1977), 179.

[22] Rudolf Endres, "Probleme des Bauernkriegs in Hochstift Bamberg," *Jahrbuch für fränkische Landesforschung* 31 (1971), 107–8.

[23] Franz, *Der deutsche Bauernkrieg*, 95–6.

poverished smallholders and artisans.[24] The movement, however, was quickly suppressed.

The risings of 1525 therefore took place at the end of a string of harvest failures and took root in areas particularly vulnerable to short-term economic crises. The regions most vulnerable to the short-term crisis of the early 1520s all became centers of the rebellion: the Tauber valley around Rothenburg, the valley of the Neckar River and the Odenwald, the Upper Main valley near Bamberg, the middle Main valley north of Würzburg, and the valley of the Ries around Schwäbisch Gmünd. The *overall burden* of rents, dues, and taxes was therefore not as important as the *timing* of the taxes, the *harshness* with which ecclesiastical lords drove them in, and the sudden sharpening of criticism of the clergy as a result of the spread of the evangelical movements. The small but localized revolt in Forchheim by itself did not signal the coming of a large-scale rebellion. Such resistance to specific taxes and practices of domination was common enough in times of economic crisis. What was ominous, however, was the scale of resistance to tithes, rents, and ecclesiastical taxes in 1523–4, for tithe and rent strikes had spread throughout Franconia, preparing the way for the sudden and dramatic broadening of resistance in the spring of 1525.

Dynamics of revolt

Given the origins of the risings in the economic crisis of the early 1520s, the inner dynamics of the peasant movements in 1525 inevitably revolved around demands for relief from specific economic burdens and practices of domination. These demands for relief, however, did not spring full-blown from the harsh economic conditions of the early 1520s alone. They evolved out of the expectations of reciprocity at the center of lord–peasant relationships. Traditional practices of domination, as pointed out in the last chapter, rested not on crass coercion or outright exploitation. No lord, not even the powerful prince-bishops, commanded the administrative technology and personnel to exploit peasants so one-sidedly in 1525. A lord's dominion over his lands still depended on peasants actively sharing in the process of their own domination. The line between pressing lords for relief or resisting authority by engaging in rent or tithe strikes and outright rebellion was therefore a confusing one. What constituted revolt or rebellion was not even clearly defined in imperial and local law.[25] Everyday resistance to seigneurial and state exactions in times of crisis

---

[24] Endres, "Probleme des Bauernkriegs im Hochstift Bamberg," 106.
[25] See Winfried Schulze, *Bäuerlicher Widerstand und feudale Herrschaft in der frühen Neuzeit*, Neuzeit im Aufbau, vol. 6 (Stuttgart–Bad Cannstatt: Frommann Holzboog, 1980), 73. Schulze has also shown how lords and princes first began to channel conflict into legal institutions after the frightening experience of 1525. See his "Die veränderte Bedeutung sozialer Konflikte im 16. und 17. Jahrhundert," in Wehler, ed., *Der deutsche Bauernkrieg, 1524–1526*, 277–302.

could pass over easily, almost imperceptibly, into revolt. The dynamics of revolt in 1525 grew out of these everyday relationships of authority and resistance.[26]

Other conditions made it difficult for Germany's princes and lords to suppress a major rising once it began. The fractured and decentralized nature of lordship made lords vulnerable before massed assemblies of villagers. Few lords so dominated their lands that a local rebellion, once it began, could be broken up easily. Vast stretches of the countryside in Franconia – the Tauber valley, the Neckar valley and the Odenwald, the Franconia–Swabia borderlands, and the Ries valley – still lay divided among small, weak lords with scattered lands and overlapping jurisdictions. The Tauber Valley and the Neckar Valley–Odenwald armies, the two largest peasant armies of Franconia, gathered momentum precisely in rural areas such as these. They quickly drew in villagers from weak and scattered lordships, forced a few isolated lords to sign treaties, and then boldly began to demand a restructuring of the political, religious, and social order in the region. The movement in the Swabia–Franconia borderlands and in the Ries valley took advantage of similar weaknesses in the feudal order in those regions. Even the most powerful lords, the prince-bishops of Würzburg and Bamberg, could not contain the revolts that gathered momentum in their outlying districts and jurisdictions. The Tauber Valley, Neckar Valley–Odenwald, and Bildhausen armies all mobilized villages in areas far from the centers of the bishops' power and eventually seized the city of Würzburg itself.[27]

The slowness with which military forces could be mobilized also helps account for the initial helplessness of lords before the peasant armies. Scholars have often commented on the military weakness of Germany's princes and lords in 1525. The most vulnerable of all may have been the lords of Franconia, for none of the region's petty princes, prince-bishops, and lords could call up troops quickly in times of crisis. When townsmen and peasants gathered in Bamberg and Würzburg and presented their grievances, the prince-bishops had no soldiers at their command to disperse the assemblies. To organize

---

[26] Günther Franz and Peter Blickle argue that peasants could only mobilize such massive risings by grounding their actions in divine law. So long as villagers appealed to the "old law," grievances remained focused on local concerns, making it impossible for villages to unite across territorial borders to challenge seigneurial authority. The argument, as others have pointed out, overlooks the fact that lords and peasants often made no distinction between the "old law" or custom and divine law. The argument also does not take into account the extent to which peasants were empowered by custom to demand that lords protect them, that lords meet their reciprocal obligations to provide relief and security. See Franz, *Der deutsche Bauernkrieg*, 1–3, 80–91, 119–27; Blickle, *The Revolution of 1525*, 87–93. See also the insightful analyses of Heide Wunder, " 'Altes Recht' und 'göttliches Recht' im Deutschen Bauernkrieg," *Zeitschrift für Agrargeschichte und Agrarsoziologie* 24 (1976), 54–66, and the discussion by Peter Bierbauer, "Das göttliche Recht und die naturrechtliche Tradition," in Peter Blickle, ed., *Bauer, Reich und Reformation: Festschrift für Günther Franz zum 80. Geburtstag am 23. Mai 1982* (Stuttgart: Eugen Ulmer, 1982), 210–34.

[27] For the literature on the revolts in Franconia see the Bibliographical Essay.

military aid from the Swabian League in late April, Prince-Bishop Thüngen of Würzburg fled the city, an act which enabled the radicals to topple the town council, seize control of the city, and open the gates to the peasant armies then converging on it from three directions. The prince-bishop of Bamberg, in a similar way, provoked his own subjects into rebellion when he called out the nobles to come to the aid of the Swabian League in suppressing the risings. From the middle of March to the end of May the peasant armies would confront no troops of their rulers. In that time, the rebels turned their disorganized bands into disciplined peasant armies, captured the fortress at Weinsberg that protected the Neckar valley, and laid siege to the Marienberg overlooking Würzburg. Only the arrival of troops from the Swabian League in early June brought the risings to an end.

Rulers would have had no need for military forces if everyday practices of domination could have defused unrest quickly and surely. Most such practices at the local level were well suited to defuse unrest on a small scale, to punish individuals or small groups. But few lords could yet channel protests into established institutions where the momentum of a movement could be contained, weakened, and gradually broken up by drawn-out negotiations and piecemeal concessions. Where this was indeed possible, a lord sometimes broke the momentum of the local revolt before villagers became well organized. Faced with the first wave of violent unrest in Bamberg, the prince-bishop of Bamberg hurriedly formed a commission to handle the grievances of his subjects. For three weeks the townsmen and villagers of Bamberg focused their attention on the legal process of submitting lists of demands and then allowed the commission to formulate its recommendations. This legal procedure no doubt slowed the momentum of the rebellion and eventually helped to pacify the townsmen. Still, the commission could not contain a second wave of anticlerical and antinoble violence that swept the countryside in early May, a wave of violence that led to the smashing of Bamberg's monasteries and castles.[28] The efforts to channel the protests in Würzburg into the territorial assembly also failed.[29] Only a few crafty and powerful lords – the patricians of the imperial cities of Nuremberg and Windesheim, for example – completely defused local unrest with timely reductions in rents, tithes, and taxes.[30]

[28] See Endres, "Probleme des Bauernkriegs im Hochstift Bamberg."
[29] Hans-Christoph Rublack offers a useful theoretical understanding of the Würzburg rising as taking place in a series of stages. The moderate, constitutional stage of the revolt failed to contain the revolution, and radical leaders then allied themselves with the peasant armies. See Jürgen Bücking and Hans-Christoph Rublack, "Der Bauernkrieg in den vorder- und oberösterreichischen Ländern und in der Stadt Würzburg: Ansätze zu einer Theorie des Bauernkrieges," in Bernd Moeller, ed., *Bauernkriegs-Studien*, Schriften des Vereins für Reformationsgeschichte, no. 189 (Gütersloh: Gerd Mohn, 1975), 58–68.
[30] Endres, "Probleme des Bauernkrieges in Franken," 105–6. See also Lawrence P. Buck, "Civil Insurrection in a Reformation City: The *Versicherungsbrief* of Windesheim, March 1525," *Archiv*

A number of lords, however, at least slowed the spread of unrest by making timely concessions. Villagers pressed their lords to protect them from taxes, rents, and dues on a number of occasions, after all, and seasoned lords well understood how to coax recalcitrant townsmen and villagers into obedience by relaxing the burdens temporarily. Such tactics could break or split a movement. The patricians of Rothenburg, skillful and practiced masters of political domination of the town and its rural environs, deflected the Tauber valley revolt from the city with this classic tactic.[31] After the city's artisans and peasants had mobilized and presented grievances to the town council, the patricians deftly split the movement in two with concessions to the urban faction alone. To the city's artisans and the "town peasants" they granted tax relief, reductions in various seigneurial burdens, and representation on the city council. Rothenburg's peasants and their Tauber valley allies went away empty-handed.[32] "As all the rich gathered together alone in the chamber, I and the other poor went away with bitterness," one Rothenburger later remembered of the negotiations.[33] In May, however, the city was forced to open its gates to the Tauber Valley Army. The politics of everyday domination, even when carried out in a skillful and cunning way, could not in the end turn back a disciplined peasant army.

Franconia's small lords, however, often had no choice but to capitulate to massed assemblies of peasants and townsmen. Many of these lords, as the Knights' Revolt of 1523 had shown, had entered a period of decline as authority and power shifted to the advantage of the princes. They also administered their small domains themselves or, like the counts of Hohenlohe, dominated their peasants through weak, thinly manned administrative hierarchies. Their stewards and village *Schultheissen* had little power with which to face down even a small force of organized peasants. Rothenburg's peasant bands, for example, abandoned by their allies in the town, turned on the weak and small lords of the central Tauber valley. These weak lords capitulated quickly and signed treaties. Their submission gave the peasants, at first weak and disorganized, a string of easy victories. The Tauber valley rebels then joined forces with peasants from the lands of the Teutonic Knights, whose lord also was powerless to bring them to heel. At Mergentheim, far from the reach of the agents of the prince-bishop of Würzburg, peasant leaders started to organize the Tauber

für Reformationsgeschichte 67 (1976), 100–17, and "The Containment of Civil Insurrection: Nürnberg and the Peasants' Revolt, 1524–1525" (Ph.D. diss., Ohio State University, 1971).
[31] See Eilentrop, *Verfassung, Recht und Wirtschaft in Rothenburg.* For a detailed study of lordship and rural society in the Tauber valley see Heinrich Heerwagen, *Die Lage der Bauern zur Zeit des Bauernkrieges in den Taubergegenden* (Nuremberg: J. L. Stich, 1899).
[32] For a concise summary of the complex events in Rothenburg see Eilentrop, *Verfassung, Recht und Wirtschaft in Rothenburg,* 7–11.
[33] Cited in Franz, *Der deutsche Bauernkrieg,* 179.

51

Valley Army itself.[34] The Neckar Valley–Odenwald Army would also form up in a comparable region of weak lordships.

From the vantage point of peasants, what was new about the protests in 1525 was the calculated politics of turning out massed, well-organized assemblies before the seats of princely and lordly power. Before such gatherings a lord's power could be held in suspense or visibly weakened by forced oaths of loyalty to the assembly or by acts of violence. Leaders of the peasants from the Tauber valley, the Neckar valley, the Odenwald, and Hohenlohe seem to have understood the force that a noble's capitulation would have in loosening the bonds of authority in the region. The rump of the Tauber valley movement, once rebuffed before the gates of Rothenburg, quickly moved down the Tauber valley, mobilizing peasants as it went, plundering castles and monasteries and forcing a series of weak and small lords to sign treaties with the group.[35] In the Neckar valley and the Odenwald, the movement first gained momentum by sacking the monastery at Schöntal and then forcing, in a massed assembly, the submission of the counts of Hohenlohe. The sacking of the fortress at Weinsberg and further plundering of other castles set off a whole new wave of antinoble and anticlerical violence throughout Franconia. In Bamberg the acts of violence were carefully carried out by disciplined bands of peasants and directed strictly against the symbols of nobles' power: the castles.[36] Such tactics naturally did not always work. In the Franconia–Swabia borderlands, several assemblies of peasants presented their grievances or requested mediation of their disputes and then peacefully melted away.[37]

The alliances that held these movements together were thus fragile and broke apart easily. Leaders seem to have drawn bands of peasants and urban craftsmen together through a variety of practical political ties – communal bonds, common local goals, alliances of convenience, coercion, or deference to a common authority or lord – and such alliances fractured all too easily. Rothenburg's patricians easily exploited what was a loose and uneasy alliance of three social groups: the city's artisans, its own town peasants, and the peasants from the city's villages. Each group pressed its own separate lists of demands on the council. The two factions of peasants shared common goals – relief from taxes, death duties, tolls, tithes, serfdom, rents, restrictions on common fields, and other seigneurial burdens – but the town peasants still abandoned their rural allies as soon as their own demands were met.[38] The artisans also left the

---

[34] Ibid. 181–2.   [35] Ibid.

[36] See Endres, "Zur sozialökonomischen Lage und sozialpsychischen Einstellung des 'Gemeinen Mannes,'" 76–7.

[37] Franz, *Der deutsche Bauernkrieg*, 213–14.

[38] F. L. Baumann, ed., *Quellen zur Geschichte des Bauernkriegs aus Rotenburg ob der Tauber* (Tübingen: Litterarischer Verein in Stuttgart, 1878), 76–8, 132–5. For a discussion of the complexities of these alliances see Thomas Robisheaux, "*Ackerbürger* and Town Revolts During the Peasants' War," unpublished paper, University of Virginia, December 1976.

alliance, for, though they too pressed for relief from the city's oppressive taxes, the craftsmen were easily won over to deference when the patricians conceded them new positions in the city government and in the guilds.[39] The townsmen of Bamberg never joined the peasants in the second wave of risings in the middle of May; their goals had already been secured at the end of the first wave of unrest in the territory. Peasants from the Franconia–Swabia borderlands failed repeatedly to draw urban craftsmen into voluntary alliances at all and gained town support only through forced alliances.[40]

The making of a well-organized and disciplined peasant army carried the assault on authority one step further. The three transregional peasant armies of Franconia – the Tauber Valley, Neckar Valley–Odenwald, and Bildhausen – could obviously mass their might against local lords and force them into submission. The Tauber Valley Army, as it mobilized near Mergentheim, began to weld together into a single unit local movements drawn from a hodgepodge of territories: small lordships along the Tauber River, the domains of the Teutonic Knights, the southern lands of the bishop of Würzburg, eastern Hohenlohe, the town of Mergentheim, and, eventually, the city of Würzburg itself. The army took over local political functions and demanded of its recruits that they observe all the principles of Christian brotherly love.[41] The army itself, its rigorous organization laid out in the Ochsenfurt Field Ordinance of April 27, was advised by a peasants' council.[42] The army's discipline and practical loyalties to the village commune kept the movement together despite its weak leadership. The balance began to shift, slowly to be sure, away from the localism that weakened looser associations of peasants and townsmen. A new political culture of the common man was being fashioned for Franconia.

The Neckar Valley–Odenwald Army and Hohenlohe

The risings therefore tended to unfold in three stages. Villagers first presented lists of local grievances, a customary step, one very much a part of the give-and-take of lord–peasant relationships in this period. When lords refused to make concessions or made an effort to suppress the assemblies, villagers expanded the scale of resistance by taking a second step: They forced lords to sign a treaty or began to destroy castles and monasteries, the symbols of noble and clerical power. A number of the peasant movements in 1525 never moved very far beyond this scale of mobilization. But some certainly carried the assault on authority to a third and more radical stage: the making of a disciplined transregional peasant army committed to the making of a new rural order. But

---

[39] Baumann, ed., *Quellen zur Geschichte des Bauernkriegs aus Rotenburg*, 119–39 passim.
[40] See Franz, *Der deutsche Bauernkrieg*, 212–16 passim.
[41] Oechsle, *Beiträge zur Geschichte des Bauernkrieges*, 143–4.
[42] See Blickle, *The Revolution of 1525*, 131.

regardless of the stage of mobilization, the scale of the risings, and the organization of the rebels, what was important was the way in which a space was opened up wherein customary authority became suspended. How this was done, and the consequences of this process, are best understood if we examine one such case in detail: the revolt in Hohenlohe and the making of the Neckar Valley–Odenwald Army.

The revolt did not get under way in this region until late March, two months after the risings had begun along the Upper Rhine and in Upper Swabia. But the rising spread quickly, the authority of the lords eroding away with breathtaking speed. Here the first two stages of the revolt tended to run together. Once peasant bands from Oberschüpf and Unterschüpf, two villages deep in the Odenwald, marched out of their villages on March 26, they rallied peasants around a banner emblazoned with the symbol of rebellion from the Bundschuh risings: the heavy black peasant boot. The peasants of the Odenwald "swarmed out like bees," as one observer remembered it, and began assembling in the Jagst valley, far from the centers of princely power in the region. Many villages never even took the time to compile local lists of grievances.

The structure of lordship itself in the region allowed the bands to assemble quickly against little effective opposition. For few lords of this region held uncontested dominion over their villages; most held lands or exercised powers attenuated by the conflicting claims of other lords. The region lay at the periphery of power for the two most powerful lords of this region, the archbishop of Mainz and the duke of Württemberg. The imperial cities of Heilbronn and Wimpfen, two urban powers on the western edge of the region, also held lands along the Neckar River and could have played a part in suppressing the rebels at the start of the rising. But the bands that mobilized in their lands gathered up sympathizers swiftly and then moved out of these territories to meet up with the Odenwalders assembling in the Jagst valley. Here, at the center of the region, one found a maze of lands held by small and weak lords, imperial knights, a few monasteries, the Teutonic Knights at Mergentheim, and the counts of Hohenlohe, soon preoccupied with the rising in their own lands. The peasants flocked to an isolated corner of the Jagst River valley, far from the centers of lordly power: the Cistercian monastery of Schöntal.

Why these bands moved so quickly to force demands on the lords of the region is difficult to say. The bands displayed a marked anticlericalism right from the start, and this may have helped undermine the obedience and the deference owed the ecclesiastical lords of this region. The refusal of ecclesiastical lords to relax taxes, rents, and dues in 1523–4 may have so eroded respect for the clergy that the next step in resisting these burdens, repudiating the clergy's claims to legitimate power as lords, came quickly once the rising had begun. Certainly the leaders of the two bands of villagers focused the discontent of their followers on the local clergy, their lands, wealth, power, and privileges. Within days after the villagers began pouring into the Jagst valley, in fact, the sacking of the Schöntal began. The anticlerical violence, however, was rarely wanton, senseless, and arbitrary. The destruction of the monastery and the instruments of the monks' seigneurial rule – rent books and account ledgers in particular – amounted to a stripping of the clergy of the right to rule as legitimate lords. This act was obviously a wildly popular one. Once rumors of the sacking spread through the region, peasants from nearby lands began to flock to Schöntal.

In some ways this assembly of peasants could be compared to the massive crowds which had assembled at Niklaushausen fifty years earlier. Both assemblies formed up quickly, spontaneously, and drew together peasants from all over western Franconia. Both also drew upon the anticlericalism that was never far beneath the surface of events in this region. The Drummer of Niklaushausen had preached against the worldliness and corruption of the clergy, promising his listeners divine vengeance and justice for the poor. Jörg Metzler, Jäcklein Rohrbach, and the other peasant leaders at Schöntal also railed against the clergy and denounced the riches and power of the church. But this time, instead of listening to sermons and waiting for miracles or divine intervention, the peasants swiftly took action against the clergy and destroyed Schöntal. The time of waiting for divine intervention was past.

Customary tactics of political domination failed to break up these bands. This process is best illustrated with the case of Hohenlohe, where the counts lost control of Öhringen with stunning speed and then were forced to sign a treaty with the peasant army. On the night of April 2, as peasants were still flocking to Schöntal, a band of conspirators seized the keys to the town gate and spread the alarm to other townsmen. Early the next morning, they opened the gates to peasants from the surrounding countryside, who began streaming into the town and onto the marketplace of the town at the foot of the cathedral. There the townsmen and peasants formed "the assembly at Öhringen" and faced a pitifully small set of representatives of the counts' government: a single steward and two servants. In a single stroke, the assembly had made itself master of the most important town in the land.[43]

The urban and rural components of this movement aimed at rather different goals. The townsmen, for their part, wanted to expand the autonomy of the commune. The tensions that gave rise to the grievances they presented the steward were nothing new. In a small territorial town such as Öhringen, the power of the territorial prince and the clergy still set strict limits to the political

[43] The best narrative account of the events of the Peasants' War in Hohenlohe, accompanied by documents, is Oechsle, *Beiträge zur Geschichte des Bauernkrieges*, 57–244.

autonomy of the urban commune. Townsmen seized the opportunity of the rural unrest to press their own grievances, most of them moderate.[44] They asked for the right to confirm appointments to the town council; to examine, but not actually control, the town's account books; and to make sure that Öhringen's market was held in an orderly fashion.[45]

These townsmen, however, aimed at more than the old goal of expanding communal autonomy. They called for a "reformation," the first mention of such a reform in the Neckar valley–Odenwald movement. What kind of new order townsmen and peasants actually intended to create with this rallying cry depended very much on the local context. The reformation of a territorial town often meant something quite a bit less sweeping than the vision of a new order hinted at when, later, the peasant army took up this idea. In this case, the townsmen wanted to make it clear that they intended it as no rebellion. The preacher at Öhringen, they said, "preached that God's Word was unsuited for a riot." They did make it clear, however, that they saw a local reformation as part of the evangelical movement sweeping through many lands of the empire:

The commune holds out to you [the counts of Hohenlohe] that, wherever a common reformation is ordered, or made by worldly or spiritual authority, that it conform justly and uniformly to Gospel law and the law. And, as it is carried out in other principalities, counties, and lordships, so we want to assure you that we will be helpful and useful to you, our lord, in such matters.[46]

Though they never spelled out precisely what they meant by a reformation and deferred to the will of the counts in this matter, they clearly sought to break the power of the clergy in the town. They urged the counts to strip the clergy of their privileges, making them ordinary townsmen, to put the church's property to work for the common good, and to call a pastor to preach the uncorrupted Word of God.[47]

In any revolt individuals participate for a bundle of reasons, and one often cannot easily distinguish religious or political ideals from personal ambition and the pursuit of local power. Certainly many of the leaders at Öhringen seem to have been guided, at least in part, by the loss of family fortunes and by personal feuds. Some of them had suffered heavy losses in the wine trade in recent years, and the demands to make the clergy pay the consumer tax on wine and to use the *Spital*'s properties for the common good suggest that they blamed the clergy for the economic problems of the town. Conrad Henn, a petty merchant "who bought wine," as the steward noted in the inventory of his properties, felt the pinch of a trade in decline and plagued by sharp swings in the market. The prominent leaders of the movement – Bastian Daub, Hans

[44] See Blickle, *The Revolution of 1525*, 116–20.
[45] Oechsle, *Beiträge zur Geschichte des Bauernkrieges*, 255–8.
[46] Ibid. 262.   [47] Ibid. 258.

Weiss, Stoffel Schmid, Michel Treffz, and Helias Faust – judging from the number of vineyards and the "impressive stocks of winemaking equipment in their houses and cellars, all depended heavily on the wine trade as well.[48] Claus Salb too had lost a fortune in the past few years.[49] A number of these men also harbored grudges against members of the town council or the counts. The feud of Wendel Hipler, the former chancellor who lost a sizable personal fortune to the chicanery of the counts, was well known. He was not actually present at Öhringen in these days, but he later became a prominent leader of the Neckar Valley–Odenwald Army.[50] A movement led by these men would almost inevitably be attracted to the vehement anticlericalism of the revolt and the demands of the peasants gathering at Schöntal.[51]

The peasants shared some grievances with the townsmen. But they tended to focus their attention on pressing for relief from exactions that did not appear in the townsmen's protests. These villagers also came from the region most vulnerable to the decline of the wine trade or to harvest failures. The peasants who sacked Schöntal came from the winegrowing communities of the Neckar, Kocher, and Jagst river valleys, all of these valleys linked up, like arteries to the heart, to the trading centers at Heilbronn and Wimpfen. The peasants at Öhringen came from villages near the town that were also a part of this market network: Michelbach, Pfedelbach, Zweiflingen, Verrenberg, Weinsbach, Kappel, and Sölbach. Their articles reflected their dependence on the wine trade, and they asked for relief from specific burdens that hindered viticulture: tolls, the tax on wine, tithes, and labor services at harvest time. They also sought to keep as many sheep as they wanted, to have free access to the forests for firewood, and to have entry fines, death duties, and serfdom abolished.[52] The Twelve Articles of the Peasants, that radical and popular program of the Upper Swabian rebels, did not strike deep sympathy here at first. A copy of the articles came into the hands of the Hohenlohe peasants as they crowded into the town marketplace and, though they urged the program on the steward, they did not fully understand what the document meant. The counts, as they wrote in their grievances, were "to take them to someone with the wit to explain many of these murky articles to us."[53]

Confusion tended to reign during the first days in which such a popular assembly gathered and presented its grievances. Were the villagers and towns-

---

[48] This evidence comes from the inventories of property of peasant leaders after the revolt had been defeated. See Karl Schum, "Sühneforderungen und die Aufrührer im Bauernkrieg: Ein Beitrag zu seiner Geschichte," *Württembergisch Franken* 54 (1970), 42–55.
[49] Oechsle, *Beiträge zur Geschichte des Bauernkrieges*, 82–3.
[50] See Gerd Wunder, "Wendel Hipler: Hohenlohischer Kanzler, Bauernführer um 1465–1526," *Schwäbische Lebensbilder* 6 (1957), 61–85.
[51] See Oechsle, *Beiträge zur Geschichte des Bauernkrieges*, 82–4.
[52] Ibid. 258–9.   [53] Ibid. 258.

men rebels or not? The actors themselves often could not decide. Villagers often requested lords to relax seigneurial burdens, to provide protection. For this reason one can overestimate the importance of the actual content of the grievance lists. To the actors caught up in the petitioning process, the public gestures and acts that surrounded the presentation of grievances often carried greater weight. The counts of Hohenlohe, for example, when they heard of the assembly gathering at Öhringen, showed no alarm about the content of the grievance lists presented to them. What alarmed them were three public acts that suggested disobedience, a lack of deference to authority: the seizure of the key to the city's gates, the harsh reception accorded the steward, and the forcing of other villagers into the town against their will.[54] For the counts these acts suggested that villagers were stirring up a revolt. The leaders of the assembly, for their part, contested this view. They saw their assembly as a legitimate gathering of petitioners:

It's an evil opinion that we don't regard you as lords, or don't want to hold you as such. It is rather out of pressing, obvious causes, only the smallest part of which he [the steward] understood and took away, that we hope for God's and your grace as poor aggrieved people, and by that to get relief.[55]

As notes flew back and forth, the debate centered not on the grievances but on the interpretation of the public acts that may or may not have signaled disobedience. Each side tried to press on the other its own interpretation of the events. Whether the assembly actually constituted a "rebellious revolt" at this stage, as the counts insisted at one point, is therefore open to doubt.[56]

What is clear is that the counts tried to keep the dispute within the bounds of the lawful process of petitioning and arbitration. Rigidity and harshness – outright exploitation, in fact – may have set in in the everyday practice of domination in some lands in the early 1520s. But this certainly had not occurred everywhere. In the early days of the rising, a number of lords seem to have been groping toward a settlement with the peasants, even outright acceptance of some of the peasant demands, if this could be accomplished without shaking authority to its foundations. The counts of Hohenlohe assured the assembly at Öhringen on April 7 that they looked on their grievances "with sympathy," that, though they found no evidence that the Twelve Articles were founded on the Gospel, they would accept whatever settlement to the dispute the empire imposed. So Counts Albrecht and Georg proposed the setting up of an imperial commission of arbitration or a committee "of twenty impartial judges, ten from us and ten from you, with a headman," to hear out the complaints. The com-

---

[54] Ibid. 260–1.   [55] Ibid. 261.   [56] Ibid. 260.

mission would resolve the conflict.[57] The plan came to grief, however, not for lack of precedent – lords and peasants sometimes appealed to arbiters to help resolve their disputes – but because the assembly melted away to join up with the massed peasantry at Schöntal.

The negotiations in 1525 between a local lord and his subjects often broke down once rebels from other lands joined hands with local villagers. Such an expansion in scale of the movement made an arbitrated settlement to a local dispute impossible. In this particular case we can only speculate about the reasons why Hohenlohers suddenly broke up their assembly at Öhringen and began to flock to Schöntal after April 6. The presence of a sizable army only a few hours from Öhringen, one might argue, was bound to radicalize the movement sooner or later. The pull of anticlericalism, the desire to force on the clergy a reformation, acted as a powerful magnet drawing in the peasants from the whole region. Other villagers, it is important to point out, would have found recruitment into the assembly impossible to avoid. Already there were reports of peasants forcing reluctant villagers into the fold.[58] Finally, though no written evidence supports this view, some of the leaders of the Öhringen assembly may have already hatched a plot to bring the full mass of the assembled peasantry into Hohenlohe itself, seize Öhringen and Neuenstein, and force the counts into submission. For a few days later, on April 10, the "Bright Army," as its leaders styled the assembly at Schöntal, now several thousand strong and flush with new recruits from all over Hohenlohe, moved suddenly on Neuenstein and seized the town.

The forced submission of a lord to a treaty, the next step in the erosion of princely power, was a calculated and carefully staged spectacle. The effects of such a public display were electrifying for those who took part, for here the peasants inverted the relationship of lord to peasant symbolized in the ritual swearing of public oaths of obedience to a lord. Where whole communes or district assemblies were turned out to swear new oaths of loyalty and obedience to a lord, now a lord would be forced to submit to a treaty with the peasantry, if not before a massed assembly then before chosen peasant leaders.

The submission of the counts of Hohenlohe to a treaty took place on April 11, at Grünbühl, not far from Neuenstein. Counts Albrecht and Georg were allowed to turn out in the company of ten of their own men on horseback, a significant gesture that acknowledged their status as counts. The peasants, however, provided the military escorts for the occasion, a gesture peasant leaders calculated to mean "that we [the peasants] are powerful."[59] At the meeting on the green, the counts tried, one last time, to admonish their subjects to obedience, a harangue that failed to impress the peasant leaders. Humiliated when

---

[57] Ibid. 262–4. [58] Ibid. 265, 278. [59] Ibid. 266–7.

the leaders refused to defer to their authority, the two counts signed a treaty binding them and their descendants "to abide by a reformation established, ordered, and decided upon by the whole bright army" and grant the articles presented by the Öhringen assembly.[60] The wording of the treaty was significant, for it suggests that no longer would the peasantry await a reformation introduced by the counts, the princes of Franconia, or the empire. "You are no longer lords," one peasant was heard to say, "but peasants and we are the lords of Hohenlohe."[61] The power to determine the course of the reformation now lay with the peasant army itself.

The submission of the counts marked a turning point in the making of the Neckar valley–Odenwald movement, for the peasants had effectively suspended the everyday authority of the clergy and the princes in the territory. The treaty, it should be remembered, did not actually release peasants from their subordination to the counts. But it did not bind them to customary obedience either. The treaty committed both sides to submit their disputes to a nonpartisan committee of twenty-four judges, headed by an impartial overseer – a panel like the one the counts originally proposed.[62] But the document neither specified who these judges were to be nor set a date for the committee to convene. Since the framers of the treaty nowhere spelled out the actual content of the expected reformation, the precise terms of domination were therefore left up in the air, suspended, creating a state of affairs not unlike carnival when authority was, in a more lighthearted way, held in suspense until normalcy returned. But in this case the suspension of authority in 1525 left those who held power in a far more dangerous position than did carnival, for it left unclear to what order one would, in the end, return.

Feudal authority in the Neckar valley and the Odenwald collapsed rapidly after this point. One lord after another capitulated to the peasants and signed a treaty similar to the one signed at Grünbühl. The most important victories over lords came under the wing of the army that split off and marched off toward the Neckar River. Some Hohenlohers left to join the Tauber Valley Army at Mergentheim. The majority, however, remained at Neuenstein, then formed up into bands and marched westwards, forcing the counts of Löwenstein to sign a treaty, and then moved off in the direction of the imperial city of Heilbronn. The most electrifying triumph of the peasants came soon after this. On Easter Sunday, in a surprise attack, the peasants stormed Weinsberg, the duke of Württemberg's formidable defensive redoubt overlooking the Neckar valley. Heilbronn then surrendered immediately and allied itself with the peasants. In rapid succession other nobles and small towns in the Odenwald and Neckar valley surrendered to the peasants and signed treaties. Even the dom-

[60] Ibid. 267.   [61] Ibid. 100.   [62] Ibid. 268–9.

inant lord of the region, the archbishop of Mainz (who, as chancellor, also headed the government of the Holy Roman Empire), was forced to sign a treaty submitting to terms imposed by the Neckar Valley–Odenwald Army.[63]

These new triumphs, the most stunning victories of the peasants in 1525, came about as the peasant bands became better organized. Before the peasants had moved on from Heilbronn and Weinsberg, their leaders reorganized them into an army, giving them a stricter organization and imposing rigorous military discipline. In command of the army stood Götz von Berlichingen. This experienced mercenary captain, a noble who held lands in the Jagst River valley, had joined the movement after the fall of Weinsberg. A peasant council similar to the one that governed the Tauber Valley Army advised the military commanders and made political decisions. To impose discipline on the troops the council imposed the death penalty for desertion, admonished the peasants to continue to abide by local laws, and promised swift, effective punishment for anyone who proved disobedient.[64]

By early May all of western Franconia lay at the feet of the peasant army. Formal authority was suspended; the power to order a reformation had fallen to the peasants.

Peasant reformation?

In the midst of this confusing world of suspended feudal relationships, peasant leaders drew up plans for a radically new order: a peasant reformation. For this reason the events of 1525 should be seen as an extension of the evangelical movement as a whole. That many leaders meant to break the power of the clergy – even strip them of their property in some places – and foresaw a nobility shorn of many rights, privileges, and incomes there can be no doubt. Such reforms, had they ever been carried out, would have swept away the pillars of authority in a region like Franconia where the clergy and small nobles still dominated the land. And yet the plans of the peasant armies remained ambiguous, incomplete, even contradictory, for authority, however weakened or hollowed out it was, was still understood in traditional terms.

Up to this point I have placed little emphasis on the role of evangelical ideas in shaping the goals of the peasant movements. But certainly many of the peasant leaders, and probably the foot soldiers of the armies as well, came to see themselves as agitators for a reformation. Whether peasants and townsmen

---

[63] Franz, *Der deutsche Bauernkrieg*, 191–5.
[64] Günther Franz, *Quellen zur Geschichte des Bauernkrieges* (Munich: Oldenbourg, 1963), no. 107, 342–5.

based their actions on the Gospel right from the start, as they seem to have done in some parts of southern Germany and Alsace, remains unclear.[65] Pressing demands against the lords, even entering into alliances with other communes to force terms on a lord, did not require, as we noted above, a radically new understanding of political legitimacy rooted in divine law or the Gospel. Still, right from the start of the risings in Franconia, townsmen from a number of small towns – Rothenburg, Bamberg, Mergentheim, and Öhringen, to name only a few – demanded that pastors be summoned to preach the pure, uncorrupted Word of God in their churches. Farther out from the towns, in the rural areas where the first assemblies of peasants began to come together, evangelical ideas do not seem to have come sharply to the fore until after local grievances were presented. Once the transregional peasant bands began to suspend customary authority in a region, however, local demands receded into the background and villagers pressed for a reformation.

In the most radical of the Franconian peasant armies, the Tauber Valley Army, peasant leaders foresaw an agrarian order governed by principles of divine law and social justice and a partial leveling of the social hierarchy. That they linked the idea of a reformation to a complete restructuring of lord–peasant relationships suggests that reform would include not simply the clergy, but the nobility as well. Addressing the soldiers of the army assembled in camp on April 27, the army leaders first hinted that the whole range of rents and dues would be reordered in a future reformation.[66] Later, after the army had marched back to Rothenburg and assembled outside its walls, Florian Geyer, the commander, made it clear to the notables of the town that such a restructuring of lord–peasant relationships would also have to conform to divine law:

And what the Holy Gospel establishes, so should it be established; what is there laid down, so must it be laid down now and remain. In the meantime, one should give to the lords neither interest, tithes, rents, death duties, nor anything like them, until, through the reformation established by ones learned in the holy, divine, and true scriptures, it is established whether or not one is obliged to pay the worldly and spiritual authorities.[67]

In addition, the army wanted to strip the nobles of their privileges, to make them equal before the law with the common man and to have the castles – those symbols of noble privilege, luxury, and power – torn down, broken to

---

[65] See Blickle, *The Revolution of 1525*, 87–93, 155–61. See also his *Gemeindereformation: Die Menschen des 16. Jahrhunderts auf dem Weg zum Heil* (Munich: Oldenbourg, 1985); and Conrad, *Reformation in der bäuerlichen Gesellschaft*.

[66] Horst Buszello, *Der deutsche Bauernkrieg von 1525 als politische Bewegung mit besonderer Berücksichtigung der anonymen flugschrift an die Versamlung gemayner Pawerschaft*, Studien zur europäischer Geschichte, vol. 8 (Berlin: Otto Hess, 1969), 35.

[67] Cited in ibid. 35–6.

pieces. They would then be free to join the "Christian Brotherhood" of the Tauber valley.[68]

Yet the assault on authority remained incomplete. On the essential issues of power and authority the peasant leaders, as far as the evidence goes, remained surprisingly silent. Nowhere did they discuss overturning completely the hierarchy of authority. Nor did they offer up plans for a new government based on the communal or federal principle, as the rebel leaders clearly did in Upper Swabia and Tyrol.[69] Whether the leaders of the army intended to restructure authority completely or whether they actually continued to defer to traditional forms of princely authority remains unclear. What is clear, however, is that the Tauber Valley Army, at least in the principles laid out to the magistrates of Rothenburg, deferred to learned reformers for guidance in establishing a reformation. And, as contradictory as this may seem, the army was willing to let the nobles continue to hold their personal properties and to keep their horses and other symbols of noble status.[70] The framers of the new order therefore envisioned a world ruled by the principle of social justice. But the agrarian order would not be turned completely upside down.

The Neckar Valley–Odenwald Army, in contrast, never fully agreed on the shape the agrarian order and a future reformation would eventually take. Here too the written plans called for a reformation and for a just social and political order. The wording of the plans, however, suggests a bitter political struggle behind the scenes, one that seems to have pitted the army's moderate leaders – Wendel Hipler, Götz von Berlichingen, Count Georg von Wertheim, and Friedrich Weigandt – against others who wanted to carry out a more radical assault on the structure of authority in the region.

In the Amorbach Declaration, a reform proposal drawn up on May 4, the moderate leaders tried to tone down the revolutionary implications of the Twelve Articles, already embraced by the army as part of its program. Expressing concern about the "errors, dissension, and misunderstandings that have grown up among the common folk and the freedom that the [Twelve] Articles would be able to give," the leaders reinterpreted the articles in ways that guaranteed less freedom to peasants than the framers of the articles intended. They agreed with the proposal to give communes the right to call their own pastors and agreed with the articles that called for the abolition of the small tithes and serfdom; none of these articles would seriously harm the power of the secular lords of the region. But they called for the mere suspension of labor services, death duties, and some other dues until a reformation was ordered. They never supported the permanent abolition of these seigneurial rights. These leaders

---

[68] For a discussion of the Tauber valley goals see Blickle, *The Revolution of 1525*, 130–1.
[69] See ibid. 97–104, 125–54; and Buszello, *Der deutsche Bauernkrieg von 1525 als politische Bewegung.*
[70] Buszello, *Der deutsche Bauernkrieg von 1525 als politische Bewegung,* 39.

also insisted that villages pay for the right to fish in common waters or for the use of common pastures and that they abide by the orders of the local authorities in matters concerning the forests.[71] And, in specific orders addressing the problem of discipline in the army, the leaders admonished the peasants to continue to defer to the established authorities: "In all towns, villages, and hamlets all subjects should remain obedient to their established authorities, and should not refuse punishment or obligations."[72] The army council, in fact, saw itself as a guarantor of order and peace in the territory and promised to investigate any reported disobedience or crime. Not surprisingly, the army refused its full support of this plan.[73]

The movement seems never to have overcome this split fully, and as a result plans for the future political and social order remained incomplete. The Heilbronn Peasants' Parliament, which was to have assembled representatives from Franconia, Swabia, and the Upper Rhine, might have helped leaders to reconcile the conflicting interpretations of the Twelve Articles and perhaps clarified the course that a reformation was to take. The meeting, however, broke up prematurely after the forces of the Swabian League won their victory at Böblingen on May 12 and began their march on Heilbronn.

What little we can glean of the debates in the army about the future order comes from the detailed advisory plan drawn up by Wendel Hipler, that old veteran of princely and peasant politics from Hohenlohe. What is striking about this document is Hipler's vagueness on the critical issue of a future reformation. What kind of society and political order would it bring about? Who would introduce it? How would one reconcile the conflicting goals and plans of the armies? All of these questions Hipler never clearly addressed. The current structure of the empire, the essential relationships of property, domination, and hierarchy in the agrarian order, never came into question in Hipler's mind. He showed no interest in a radical restructuring of lord–peasant relationships. He did hint that the church would be stripped of its properties and that the common man could count on reductions in tithes, consumer taxes, and death duties. But he saw this taking place through legal arbitration, where everyone, "the rich and poor," also the princes and the nobles, would be treated with equal fairness.[74] If Hipler had had his way, the armies would have concentrated their efforts on the practical task of consolidating their hold on parts of South Germany. He suggested that they consider coordinating their efforts against certain princes, possibly seek aid from the powerful elector of Saxony, and perhaps carry the war against the two electors of Cologne and Trier. On the whole, the plan therefore suggested a far less ambitious reform than the framers

[71] Franz, *Quellen*, no. 107, 342–4.   [72] Ibid. 345.
[73] Blickle, *The Revolution of 1525*, 132.
[74] Franz, *Quellen*, no. 122, 370–1. For discussions of Hipler's plans see Blickle, *The Revolution of 1525*, 132–3, and Buszello, *Der deutsche Bauernkrieg von 1525 als politische Bewegung*, 43–46.

of the Twelve Articles and the earlier peasant leaders of the Bright Army itself ever intended.

Defeat and aftermath

The inability of these two armies to frame a clear conception of a new order, let alone to carry it out, serves as a reminder of the difficulty the movements encountered in sustaining a radical assault on authority in 1525. The split between leaders and the rank and file, dissension over the goals of the armies, and continued weaknesses in the organization and discipline of the troops weakened the peasant armies as the confrontation with the military forces of the princes approached.

These weaknesses and fractures surfaced in the final weeks of the rebellion. At Würzburg, where the three Franconian armies had joined forces, the moderates and the radicals failed to reach agreement on the terms they wished to impose on the bishop's troops that continued to hold out in the fortress at Marienberg. Some, the circle of moderate Odenwalders around Götz, proposed simply that they accept the Twelve Articles. Others, the radical Taubertalers, insisted on the surrender of the fortress and all other castles in the bishopric and the payment of 100,000 fl. indemnity. When the garrison refused these harsh terms, the armies had little choice but to begin a hopeless siege. As the troops of the Swabian League approached Würzburg, panic began to set in. The rebels from Würzburg proposed one desperate, final plan that would call for submitting all of the disputes to a territorial assembly. But this last bid to stave off a military defeat fell through. The ten-thousand-man army of the Swabian League recaptured Heilbronn and Weinsberg and then cut to pieces the remnants of the Tauber Valley and Neckar Valley–Odenwald armies at Königshofen in a bloodbath on June 2. Two days later the Bildhausen Army surrendered to the forces of Prince John of Saxony. The fates of the last rebels were therefore sealed, and soon thereafter Würzburg and Bamberg fell. The revolts were at an end.[75]

Some princes and lords introduced harsh reprisals against the peasants. Several leaders of the rebellion were executed and their properties confiscated or given over to others. Most lords systematically made the rounds in their territories, moving from community to community, receiving new oaths of loyalty and obedience and meting out punishments where they thought appropriate. The counts of Hohenlohe, for example, confiscated the property of some of the leaders of the revolt and executed some of them. Öhringen, that forcing house of the rebellion, was made to hand over any leaders it found and lost all of its privileges as a town. All Hohenlohers swore new oaths of loyalty and

---

[75] Franz discusses these events, and the causes of the peasants' defeat, in some detail; see *Der deutsche Bauernkrieg*, 203–8, 279–94.

promised never to give aid to rebels again.[76] The humiliating treaty of April 11 was retrieved and the seal affixed to it ripped off. The counts' subjects, like others in the region of the rebellion, had to bear the costs of a heavy indemnity levied by the Swabian League.[77]

Still, no prince had the state apparatus, the sure, unchecked power, that would later come from improved practices of domination. Many petty princes could not, as a result, impose order in the countryside on whatever terms they wished. Rather than run the risk of sparking off another peasants' war or discouraging immigration into rural areas depopulated by the revolt, many lords soon relaxed their efforts to drive in burdensome exactions. Some even extended new political rights to peasants.[78] A number of prominent princes and lords from Upper Swabia, lords who had tended to refuse to extend protection to their peasants during the crisis of the early 1520s, eased off on serfdom, granted more secure terms of land tenure, and sealed the concessions with treaties.[79] In Hohenlohe, the counts obviously wished to encourage immigration into their lands and, though they no doubt feared further unrest, they returned to well-tested practices that eased unrest over heavy dues or assessments. They reluctantly carried out the collection of the indemnity, assessing each peasant household to pay the tax. But by 1531 they were again easing off on the collection of taxes, tolls, and other dues.[80] They showed no signs of pressing a seigneurial offensive at the expense of their subjects. The counts remained uncontested lords over Hohenlohe, but order remained tenuous and uncertain.

What was certain in the aftermath of the revolt was this: The peasant reformation had been crushed. For this reason the Peasants' War marked the most important turning point in the early development of the evangelical movements. That the idea of a reformation could inspire such sweeping and breathtaking visions of a new, more egalitarian agrarian order serves as a reminder that the precise course of the reformation remained very uncertain before 1525. Before the defeat of the peasants the movement seems to have enjoyed a great deal of popular support, support that waned rapidly as the power to order a reformation fell to the princes and the magistrates of the imperial cities.[81]

---

[76] Oechsle, *Beiträge zur Geschichte des Bauernkrieges*, 203–5; Schum, "Sühneforderungen und die Aufrührer in Bauernkrieg."

[77] See Thomas Sea, "The Economic Impact of the German Peasants' War: The Question of Reparations," *Sixteenth Century Journal* 8 (1977), 75–97.

[78] See Thomas S. Sea, "Schwäbischer Bund und Bauernkrieg: Bestraffung und Pazifikation," in Wehler, ed., *Der deutsche Bauernkrieg 1524–1526*, 129–67. For a more extensive discussion of the consequences of the revolt see Thomas Klein, "Die Folgen des Bauernkrieges von 1525: Thesen und Antithesen zu einem vernachlässigten Thema," *Hessisches Jahrbuch für Landesgeschichte* 25 (1975), 65–116.

[79] Blickle, *The Revolution of 1525*, 165–82.

[80] Oechsle, *Beiträge zur Geschichte des Bauernkrieges*, 206–7.

[81] See Blickle, *The Revolution of 1525*, 183–5; van Dülmen, *Reformation als Revolution*, 59–62; and especially Conrad, *Reformation in der bäuerlichen Gesellschaft*, 156–75.

Religion would be domesticated in the course of the sixteenth century, of course, the clergy stripped of its control of the church and ecclesiastical properties. Religious discipline would slowly be made to conform more closely to the needs of the social order. That would eventually mean that religion would fit more closely the needs of princes and lords to improve the practice of domination in the countryside, although not without ambiguous and unintended results. That would be a long and difficult process, however, one that would stretch into the early decades of the seventeenth century. But before that could happen the solidarity of the peasant commune would have to erode in other more insidious ways: from within village society itself.

3

~~~~~~

Rich and poor

Some events alter a society, dramatically setting it on a new path for decades or generations to come. But many do not. They pass away quickly, their effects merging almost imperceptibly into the stream of other events altering day-to-day social relationships at a slower but steadier pace. This latter pattern was often the case in the wake of the great peasant uprisings of early modern Europe. For in the countryside the pace of social change was often slow, the structures of everyday life resilient and difficult to change at one blow.

The Peasants' War was one such event in the sixteenth century. The revolt, despite the hopes it aroused among the peasantry and the fears it spread among the nobility, marked less of a turning point than is commonly understood. In most lands of South and Central Germany one can detect few sharp breaks with the past in the decades immediately after 1525. For the revolt came and went quickly and left few lasting structural changes in the day-to-day practice of domination and in the social relationships at the heart of the village community. The hurried deliberations in 1526 at the Diet at Speyer on the rebellion and the peasants' grievances, the small treaties concluded in some territories in the late 1520s, the criminalization of resistance to authority clearly spelled out in the imperial law code in 1532, the slow funneling of disputes into the courts, and the heated discussions concerning authority and obedience: All showed the heightened concern among elites about order and domestic security in the years following the revolt.[1] But none of these measures altered the everyday practice of domination at the village level quickly. For the exercise of power continued to rest on the give-and-take between lord and peasant, the

---

[1] For a stimulating look at the legal methods of controlling conflict after 1525 see Winfried Schulze, "Die veränderte Bedeutung sozialer Konflikte im 16. und 17. Jahrhundert," in Hans-Ulrich Wehler, ed., *Der deutsche Bauernkrieg, 1524–26*, Geschichte und Gesellschaft, Special Issue no. 1 (Göttingen: Vandenhoeck & Ruprecht, 1975), 277–302; and Helmut Gabel and Winfried Schulze, "Folgen und Wirkungen," in Horst Buszello, Peter Blickle, and Rudolf Endres, eds., *Der deutsche Bauernkrieg* (Paderborn: Ferdinand Schöningh, 1984), 322–49.

need to legitimize authority and to secure cooperation, to display restraint and offer protection, to know when and how to apply force at the local level.

Permanent shifts in the exercise of power came about only slowly in the sixteenth century. And they would be accompanied by repeated and frustrating setbacks, by periods of extreme fluidity and uncertainty. To see one event as the turning point in this process is therefore to miss the significance of the deeper and more subtle changes taking place in sixteenth-century society.

Land of paupers

The evidence points instead to the tenuousness and the uncertainty of social order in the decades after 1525, the difficulty in countering forces that would continue to undermine the stability of rural communities well into the early seventeenth century. The structure of authority had rested on two pillars in 1500: the practices of domination by lords and princes and the power of the village commune. The revolt clearly revealed the weaknesses of feudal authority in the countryside in 1525, the difficulty of lords when faced with well-organized and disciplined peasant armies. But in the decades after the revolt that other pillar of the social order, the village commune, was also undermined and weakened. For the demographic and social changes that had fed the conflict in 1525 – the growth in population, the competition for land and other resources, the stratification within the village, and the increasingly complex economic ties with the broader world – continued to polarize village society and further undermined the late medieval institutions of order and stability. As the gulf between wealthy tenant farmers and the village poor widened in the decades after the revolt, the social foundations of the commune therefore eroded away. The village commune, that source of stability in the South German countryside, the focal point of peasant political allegiances, progressively lost its cohesion after 1525.

One development aroused fears of disorder and the decay of communal values perhaps more than any other change in the sixteenth century: the spread of poverty. The idea that pauperism bred sedition was, of course, an old notion, one easily revived in a time of rural and urban unrest. The idea was in conflict with Christian notions of compassion toward and understanding of the poor, of course, but it also tended to complement the new reflections on pauperism, charity, and social order among German humanists and religious reformers in the middle decades of the sixteenth century. The leaders of towns and religious reformers almost everywhere in Germany began to reorganize poor relief in these years, and as they did so they slowly undermined the notion of charity as an expression of the reciprocal and personal ties between individuals. The reforms tended to institutionalize and bureaucratize poor relief, to sharpen the social gulf between the poor and everyone else, and to direct relief at improving the moral life of the poor. The organizers of charity tended to look upon foreign beggars and the landless poor, groups that grew rapidly in the middle of the century, as dangerous and undisciplined elements, as carriers of sedition, disease, and immorality. "Many in a country, and no food or livelihood for them, is more harmful than useful," wrote Johann Becher. "It makes loafers, thieves, murderers, rebels, beggars – better that a country have no communities than one such wretched community."[2]

These new social attitudes probably reinforced the perception of disorder and decay in the social order more than the objective dimensions of poverty itself. For few riots and rebellions were actually organized and led by the truly hungry and impoverished in the sixteenth century. Still, pauperism, by almost every objective measure, was growing at an alarming pace by the middle of the sixteenth century.[3] (Pauperism had come earlier in some regions. The South German cities, Nuremberg, Augsburg, and Ulm, for example, and the areas of rural industry already supported sizable populations of propertyless and landless residents by the early sixteenth century.)[4] The reform of poor relief came later in the rural areas of Germany. But the fear of social disorders spread here as poverty grew. Even lands like Hohenlohe, thinly populated stretches of countryside in the late Middle Ages, were fast becoming lands much more densely populated. They were becoming lands of paupers.

In the County of Hohenlohe the first signs of massive rural poverty appeared in the last third of the sixteenth century. Here population trends still lagged a few decades behind the more densely populated areas of South Germany. Population growth took place in two stages. In the first stage, a period extending from about 1500 to 1560 or 1570, the population grew steadily, especially after the Peasants' War. When the steward completed his survey of taxable households in Langenburg district in 1528, about 150 households stood on the tax rolls; one generation later, in 1553, the number had increased to 224 (see Graph 3.1). But the growth continued uninterrupted. In 1573 the number stood at 332 households, a total population of perhaps 1,500 to 1,600 villagers, twice the number in 1528.[5] The growth slacked off, population even contracting in

[2] Cited in Oskar Jolles, "Die Ansichten der deutschen nationalökonomischen Schriftsteller des sechszehnten und siebzehnten Jahrhunderts über Bevölkerungswesen," *Jahrbücher für Nationalökonomie und Statistik* N.S. 13 (1886), 214.

[3] For the general problem of pauperism in Germany in this period see Wilhelm Abel, *Massenarmut und Hungerkrisen im vorindustriellen Europa* (Hamburg: Paul Parey, 1974), and Willi A. Boelcke, "Wandlungen der dörflichen Sozialstruktur während Mittelalter und Neuzeit," in Heinz Haushofer and Willi A. Boelcke, eds., *Wege und Forschungen der Agrargeschichte*, Festschrift für Günter Franz (Frankfurt a.M.: DLG, 1967), 80–103.

[4] See Erich Keyser, *Bevölkerungsgeschichte Deutschlands*, 2d ed. (Leipzig: S. Hirzel, 1941), 365–83.

[5] The precise number of residents per household in Hohenlohe is not precisely known. The estimate of 1,500 to 1,600 villagers in 1573 rests on the assumption that the average size of rural households lay between 4.7 and 5.7 individuals. These figures come from studies of population

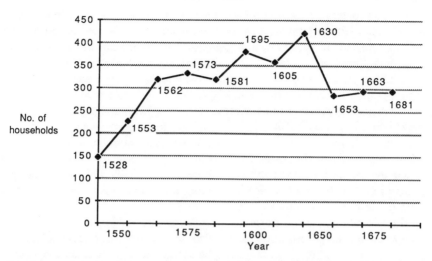

Graph 3.1. Number of taxed heads of households in Langenburg district, 1528–1681 (1). *Sources:* Graphs 3.2a, b; L/L "Schatzungsanlage Amt Langenburg 1663."

the 1570s, but then continued to grow well into the early seventeenth century. Population grew at a slower pace in this stage, and setbacks and periods of stagnation came repeatedly. Population density reached its peak in the early modern period in 1630: 421 households, a total population of perhaps 2,000 invididuals.

By the 1560s this rural society was poised on the brink of a wrenching subsistence crisis. For by that time the rural economy had become more prone to such crises; the larger population of the late sixteenth century did not have the land or the material resources to survive very easily in the new age of dearth that was beginning (see Table 6.2). The famine of 1570–6 marked the beginning of a long series of famines and unfolded in classic fashion. The first unfavorable signs came in the cold and harsh winters of 1568–9 and 1569–70, two years in which unusually low temperatures, ice, and snow heavily damaged the winter spelt and rye crops. These two crop failures were no local affairs, for they obviously affected large parts of Central Europe, triggering a general subsistence crisis. The cities and towns of South Germany and northern Italy, their granaries depleted, therefore began buying up supplies of grain throughout the South German countryside. By the spring of 1570 supplies were scarce, prices outrageously high. The hunger grew worse, however, as one bitterly cold winter followed another right through 1574. In the early 1570s Franconian town

in Schleusingen district in the County of Henneberg and the village of Dachau in Bavaria. See Keyser, *Bevölkerungsgeschichte Deutschlands*, 370–1.

magistrates, petty princes, and nobles, the counts of Hohenlohe included, expressed fear that the famine would cause unrest among the rural poor if relief did not come soon.[6] But the famine continued; in Hohenlohe the winter grain crops failed again in 1575–6.[7] Not until 1576 did the crisis ease.

The connection between poverty and rebellion, as we have noted, was rarely a direct one in early modern Germany. Hunger alone almost never triggered the small peasant rebellions that became increasingly common after 1560. This proved true in Franconia in the 1570s as well, for no rebellion ever came at this time. But this period did mark a small turning point of another type: The population boom of the sixteenth century suffered its first serious reversal. When the steward surveyed the households of Langenburg district again in 1581, the population had declined: Fourteen households on the rolls in 1573 were no longer to be counted.

The famines indicated a growing concern about the problems associated with the spread of rural poverty in Germany. From this time petty princes and nobles struggled to master the instability and the social dislocations created by pauperism. In some areas the growth of the urban and rural poor so utterly transformed community life by the late sixteenth century that few officials could enter a new place and leave unaffected by the wretchedness they saw around them. Lutheran visitors in the parishes of Hohenlohe in 1556, despite the fact that they had explicit instructions to inquire into religious beliefs and practices, instead often noted the shocking living conditions of the village poor. In Unterregenbach, the visitors reported when they returned to Öhringen, the majority of villagers "went begging because of poverty."[8] In report after report to the counts of Hohenlohe in the 1580s, stewards and officials "worried that the poor people will complain bitterly [about new taxes] because the people live in great poverty and have enough to worry about with rents and other dues at the same time."[9] Pauperism therefore engaged the attention of the counts directly, partly because it made it difficult to collect rents, dues, and taxes, but also because they too feared that poverty bred sedition. "Unfortunately I have seen all too well in a short time," wrote Count Wolfgang in 1587, "that the common man is so poor that many cannot buy a loaf of bread for their own households, let alone pay their taxes."[10]

These worries did not simply reflect social prejudices and fears: Much of South Germany had in fact become a land of paupers. This pattern held even for the County of Hohenlohe, a land often seen as one of wealth and plenty. That image, however, stems from a later date, from the eighteenth century, for

[6] See Rudolf Endres, "Zur wirtschaftlichen und sozialen Lage Franken vor dem Dreissigjährigen Krieg," *Jahrbuch für fränkische Landesforschung* 28 (1968), 5–52.
[7] LAN 42/14/9. [8] PAÖ 93/3/7, 1556.
[9] LAN 42/14/48, October 1, 1580; 42/14/152, April 3, 1587.
[10] LAN 42/14/152, April 3, 1587.

Table 3.1. *Cotters in Langenburg district, 1553 and 1581*

Village	Tenants		Cotters		% cotters	
	1553	1581	1553	1581	1553	1581
Billingsbach	34	51	9	19	26.5	37.3
Oberregenbach	15	20	2	1	13.3	5.0
Unterregenbach	31	30	3	7	9.7	23.3
Raboldshausen	24	26	2	10	8.3	38.5
Nesselbach	24	37	2	2	8.3	5.4
Bächlingen	26	39	2	5	7.6	12.8
Langenburg	29	51	2	5	6.7	9.8
Atzenrod	22	39	1	6	4.5	15.4
Hürden	7	11	0	3	0	27.3
Binselberg	6	6	0	0	0	0
Brüchlingen	4	6	0	0	0	0
Kupferhof	2	2	0	0	0	0
Total	224	318	23	58	10.3	18.2

Sources: L/L 5, 1553; 17, 1581.

here too rural paupers had come to dominate the countryside in the sixteenth century, at least in numbers. The rent rolls from Langenburg district, for example, give no hint of large numbers of landless poor in 1470. Even if villagers divided land unequally at this time, even if only a few families held sizable farms while others farmed only small plots of land, at least every villager could acquire land somewhere, clear and cultivate it, and eke out a living. By 1553, however, a number of villagers could no longer acquire land (see Table 3.1). These landless villagers, the cottagers, were evenly distributed among most of the communities of Langenburg district. Atzenrod, Bächlingen, Langenburg, Nesselbach, Raboldshausen, Oberregenbach, and Unterregenbach, all of these settlements had their share of village poor. They formed nowhere a significant majority at this time. Only in Billingsbach did the village poor stand out in terms of numbers: Nine of the thirty-four households in the village had only a cottage for their families.

By the 1580s, shortly after the first devastating series of famines, most of the villages and small market towns had sizable numbers of households that held no land. The first cluster of these households in an area such as Langenburg district was naturally to be found in and around the small market town at its center (Table 3.1). Ten to 15 percent of the households in the town of Langenburg and in the two neighboring villages (Atzenrod and Bächlingen) held no arable land in 1581. Other villages in the Jagst River valley, Hürden and Unterregenbach, also housed a substantially larger number of cotters, up to 30 percent of the households. But the largest clusters of village poor grew

73

up, in this district at least, in the villages on the Hohenlohe plain, in Billingsbach and Raboldshausen. Nearly 40 percent of the households were mere cotters in 1581. These households had no land at all, no fields to provide for their subsistence needs; often they had no property worth recording in the tax assessments at all. Whatever livelihood they earned came from wage labor. The social conditions in these villages a century before, in the time of an abundance of land, were by contrast an almost idyllic time of plenty, a peasant fantasy of surplus and prosperity, a real-life *Schlaraffenland.*

The boom transformed the physical layout and social life of almost every rural community. Many small market and noble residence towns, once hardly distinguishable from the villages that surrounded them in the late fifteenth century, became burgeoning centers of local population. This was perhaps already the case for the larger towns, the nerve centers of local trade and commerce. Öhringen and Neuenstein probably already had neighborhoods given over to the poor in 1500. But the population growth completely altered that next tier of market towns smaller than these regional centers, towns like Ingelfingen, Kirchberg, Langenburg, and Weikersheim. Settled within the walls of tiny Langenburg in 1470, for example, was a smaller population than that of the nearby village of Bächlingen. By 1553 that was no longer the case (see Graph 3.2b). The town expanded eastward, down the road that led to Atzenrod and Gerabronn. A whole new quarter, a suburb made up of ramshackle houses of the town poor, grew up just beyond the town gates. In 1592 thirty-seven houses clustered within the walls of this market town, most of them along the narrow main street that led up to the castle; an additional eleven houses made up the suburb. Fully one-third of all the new buildings came in the sixteenth century.[11] Rounding out the picture of this larger, slightly more imposing, town was the castle, rebuilt in the fashionable new style of the Renaissance by Count Wolfgang in the 1580s and 1590s.[12]

Population never grew evenly in any rural region in the sixteenth century. The growth instead tended to cluster in specific towns and villages: those communities near market or residence towns and along trade routes, or settlements in which one could still acquire land and work. This pattern held for Hohenlohe as well, even, on a smaller scale, for the district of Langenburg, a district no longer as remote and isolated as it was in the fifteenth century. The town of Langenburg naturally housed one important cluster of the region's rural poor. In the villages near the town one would also find the densest concentrations of the new poor: Atzenrod, Bächlingen, Nesselbach, and Ob-

---

[11] Gustav Bossert, "Recht und Brauch in Langenburg im sechszehnten und siebzehnten Jahrhundert," *Württembergische Jahrbücher für Statistik und Landeskunde* (1910), 81.

[12] On the rebuilding of the castle and its transformation into a small palace see Gerhard Thaddey, "Neue Forschungen zur Baugeschichte von Schloss Langenburg," *Württembergisch Franken* 63 (1979), 13–46.

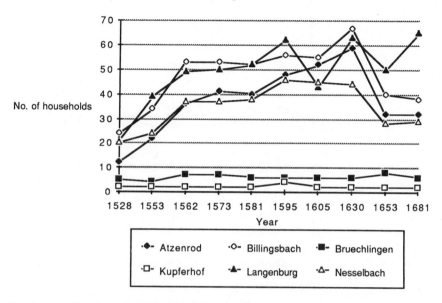

Graph 3.2a. Number of taxed heads of households in Langenburg district, 1528–1681 (2). *Sources:* L/L "Reichssteuer- und Schatzungsbuch 1528–1568"; 1528; 5, 1553; 4, 1562; 7, 1573; 17, 1581; 24, 1595; 27, 1606; 28, 1606; "Schatzungsanlage Amt Langenburg," 1630, 1653, 1663, 1681.

erregenbach. Here villagers could clear new arable lands from the slopes of the Jagst valley or plant vineyards (see Graphs 3.2a and b). To the north and east of the town villagers and townsmen could also clear land from forests, bring new fields under the plough, or clear pastures for their cattle. Billingsbach and Raboldshausen became large, compact villages in this way. Peasants in these two villages had the added lure of easy access to the markets along the Emperor's Highway, the main trade route not far to the east.[13] Rothenburg o.d.T., Gerabronn, Rot am See, Crailsheim: All of these towns became centers of trade for the eastern and northern districts of the County of Hohenlohe (see Chapter 6).

Land and surpluses from the land were the most sought-after resources in the late sixteenth century. By the 1580s and 1590s land could not be easily acquired in the densely populated areas of South Germany – the valleys of the Rhine, Neckar, and Main rivers – but it could still be had in some parts of Hohenlohe. Few of the village poor, however, could acquire plots of the best land in the territory, those lands that stretched along the floors of the Kocher and Jagst valleys or the best lands on the plain. By the late sixteenth century

[13] ALKI 351/1, 1589; 351/2, March 22, 1589; 351/3, March 22, 1589.

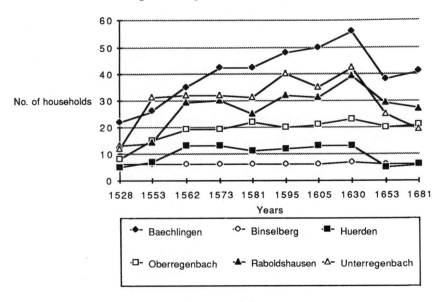

Graph 3.2b. Number of taxed heads of households in Langenburg district, 1528–1681 (3). *Sources:* See Graph 3.2a.

these lands were largely locked up in the compact farms held by the tenant-farmer elite. The poor had to settle instead for the marginal lands of Hohenlohe, those on the slopes and rim of the river valleys, lands cleared from forests or former wastes. Many of them took up the difficult tasks of land clearing eagerly, however, since any amount or quality of land was better than none at all. "I shall be completely destitute," explained Hans Hanselman d. J., a cotter with only a house and a few tiny plots of land near Unterregenbach, "unless I get several fields which, along with my day labor, might help me to feed my small children."[14] Smallholders from Atzenrod, Bächlingen, and Langenburg completely cleared the Mühlberg, the slope of the valley below the town; it became a patchwork of vineyards and tiny fields. The forests north and east of the town also fell victim to the new cultivators. If they had had their way almost no forest at all would have been left standing.

The passion for felling trees and clearing new fields so endangered the forested lands of the district that the stewards stopped the clearing in order to protect sources of firewood.[15] "Generally, everywhere in the district," the stew-

---

[14] ALAL 1080, [1590?].
[15] See Walther Hubner, "Die geschichtliche Entwicklung der Forstgesetzgebung in Hohenlohe bis zum Jahre 1650" (diss., Freiburg im Breisgau, 1968), and Gustav Adolf Thumm, "Die bäuerlichen und dörflichen Rechtsverhältnisse des Fürstentums Hohenlohe" (diss., University

ard noted in the rentbook of 1562, "the waste on the slope and other abandoned lands that once provided communal cattle walks and pastures have been steadily eaten away by the land clearing."[16]

Land was not the only magnet that drew the poor into a new community. The promise of work, even at low wages, held out its attractions as well. This was particularly true in the small towns, where the princes undertook a great deal of construction work on their castles, where old medieval fortresses became fashionable Renaissance palaces, and where the building boom in general created new opportunities for work. But this was not the only work to be done. The counts still employed the largest number of agricultural laborers in the territory. Their compact estates had long since been broken up and leased out to tenants, but the counts still kept a few estates, some in the Kocher valley, others in the Tauber valley near Weikersheim, and one small farm at Lindenbronn not far from Atzenrod. All of these estates employed seasonal laborers. A laborer could also find work in the counts' vineyards or in the vineyards of other villagers, for maintaining the vines was a labor-intensive activity. And, as we shall see in Chapter 6, smallholders and laborers could take up a craft, setting up shop in their houses and employing their children to help out. Shoes, wooden utensils and tools, rope, pots, and cloth were in demand on what was rapidly becoming a large regional system of markets in Franconia.

Finding out the social origins of the village poor is a difficult task, for the records are silent about many of the details of their everyday lives. What little one can piece together suggests that they came from many sources, that the paths that led individuals and families into poverty were many and complex. Some certainly originated as branches of older families from the region, the families that already held compact farms or smallholdings. In the 1530s, 1540s, and 1550s it was likely that many children who could not inherit the farms set off on their own, cleared new land, often in the same or in a nearby village, and established a household independent of their parents. Low mortality rates – at least lower compared to the high mortality rates of the century following the Black Death – perhaps enabled families to reproduce themselves and add a small surplus to the local population. But since parish records do not begin until 1587, long after the population boom got under way, this idea remains only a hypothesis. If it were true, however, it would account for the recurrence of several key names in the rent books – the Hanselmanns, Weissmüllers, Schmidts, and Bauers, for example – who turn up not just as tenant farmers but also as smallholders and laborers by the late sixteenth century. Such a

---

of Hohenheim, 1970). For a discussion of the clearing of forests in the sixteenth century see Wilhelm Abel, *Geschichte der deutschen Landwirtschaft vom frühen Mittelalter bis zum 19. Jahrhundert*, Deutsche Agrargeschichte, vol. 2 (Stuttgart: Eugen Ulmer, 1962), 140–2.
[16] L/L 4 (1562).

pattern would also be in keeping with the Europe-wide pattern of slightly lower mortality rates in the sixteenth century.[17]

Many also came as immigrants. No precise statistical data on this problem are available, but petition protocols from the 1590s suggest that immigration played an important role in expanding the ranks of the village poor into the very late sixteenth century. Between 1594 and 1602 fifty-six petitioners requested permission to take up permanent residence in Langenburg district alone. Fifty of them, the vast majority, were accepted.[18] Most of them clearly became smallholders, day laborers, and artisans, but a few came to Hohenlohe as brides and grooms marrying into the old tenant-farmer families. The counts required that every immigrant show his ability to support himself and his family, that he have a craft, some wealth, or at least the promise of marriage into an established household. Hans Beiser, a smith, for example, received permission to set up shop in Unterregenbach in 1592, but only on the condition that he bring with him into the village his inheritance of fifty *gulden*.[19] These requirements for settlement seem not to have been a hard-and-fast policy, however. Endris Schoppert, a teamster from Unterregenbach, became a resident with the lame excuse that he "would marry shortly and that he needed lodging."[20] The absence of stiff requirements for residence might help explain why poor immigrants still came to Hohenlohe in the 1590s. Many of the towns of the region – Schwäbisch Hall, Rothenburg o.d.T., Nördlingen, for example – had already raised the requirements for citizenship to discourage a flood of paupers from taking up residence in their communities.[21]

The numbers of poor households continued to grow into the early seventeenth century, although at a slower rate, and reached its peak in 1630. This year marked a watershed in the demographic history of early modern Hohenlohe. After that year the overall population fell steeply: Between 1630 and 1653 Langenburg district as a whole lost roughly one-third of its population. In the survey of 1630 the district boasted 421 households, in 1653 only 283 (see Graphs 3.2a and b). The losses fell unevenly across the district. The heaviest losses came in Billingsbach, Oberregenbach, and Atzenrod. Each of these villages lost at least 40 percent of its population in this period. Langenburg, Raboldshausen, Bächlingen, and Nesselbach suffered severe losses as well, between 20 and 36 percent. Only Unterregenbach and the tiny hamlets of Kupferhof, Brüchlingen, and Binselberg came away from the terrible losses of

[17] For a review of the problem of mortality rates in the European demographic system see Michael W. Flinn, *The European Demographic System, 1500–1820* (Baltimore: Johns Hopkins University Press, 1981), 47–64.
[18] ALSPL 1592–1602.   [19] ALSPL, November 4, 1592.
[20] ALAL 1080, December 5, 1625.
[21] The town of Nördlingen, for example, raised the requirements for citizenship from 50 to 100 fl. in 1585, and then to 200 fl. in 1607. See Christopher Friedrichs, *Urban Society in an Age of War: Nördlingen, 1580–1720* (Princeton, N.J.: Princeton University Press, 1979), 55–7.

population with modest or no losses. But all of these losses paled in comparison with the comparative devastation in Hürden; only five of the village's thirteen houses were occupied in 1653.

These losses were common in Germany during the decades of the Thirty Years' War. Günther Franz has calculated that Germany lost roughly one-third of its population during this crisis.[22] So Hohenlohe suffered no more than most areas, and certainly less than parts of North and Central Germany turned into wastelands by the Catholic and Protestant armies in the 1630s and 1640s. Some of these losses certainly resulted from military actions against the civilian population. But plague and famine took far more lives than the war itself. Many impoverished villagers died in the terrible famines between 1630 and 1635, the worst of the early modern period. Many more died in the epidemics of plague, first in 1626, then on a much larger scale in 1634–5. Many villagers who survived these horrors then died from malnourishment or disease after 1635, or, since the land was laid waste by the two armies, they left the area and joined the masses of refugees who crowded Germany's highways in search of food and safety. The decline continued into the 1640s. One final, devastating famine of the war years took the last toll of victims between 1648 and 1650 (see Chapter 8).

The calm came after 1650. The numbers of households stabilized quickly in the late seventeenth century at about 283 or 293 households in Langenburg district, roughly two-thirds of the prewar population level. Only the town of Langenburg recovered its losses quickly and reached once again its earlier size of sixty to sixty-five households. But the overall population did not grow again until the early eighteenth century. The long cycle in population had finally run its course.

Old families and the market in land

A few communities, scattered across the rural landscape like a great archipelago, remained outwardly untouched by the population boom. These villages deserve special attention, for they point to a pattern hidden in the aggregate population statistics of the sixteenth century: remarkable stability and continuity in the midst of the population boom. They also provide one of the first sets of clues for understanding how the control of land and property could create, maintain, and reproduce social order and hierarchy by the late sixteenth century.

The village poor made no inroads in these communities, or they made very few. For all of the land in these villages remained locked up in a few compact

---

[22] Günther Franz, *Der dreissigjährige Krieg und das deutsche Volk: Untersuchungen zur Bevölkerungs- und Agrargeschichte*, Quellen und Forschungen zur Agrargeschichte, vol. 7, 3d ed. (Stuttgart: Gustav Fischer, 1962), 5–52 passim.

farms. The hamlets of Kupferhof, Brüchlingen, Binselberg, and, to a lesser extent, Hürden, typified this type of settlement in Hohenlohe. In each of these hamlets a handful of old tenant-farmer families held tight to all of the village land: Never was it carved up into smaller plots, divided permanently into smaller and smaller farms. Some of the oldest, and soon to be some of the wealthiest, peasant families of the area held farms in these hamlets: the Englarts and Krantzes in Kupferhof; the Schneiders, Wagners, Breiders, and Englarts of Brüchlingen; and the Reuses, Schmidts, Schumms, Hanselmanns, and Schuelers of Binselberg. Day laborers came and went from nearby villages, as did the children and servants. But these hamlets maintained an amazingly stable demographic regime in the unstable and uncertain world of the sixteenth and seventeenth centuries (see Graphs 3.2a and b).[23] As the numbers of village poor grew, as village society became more complex and stratified, prone to severe subsistence crises, these tenant-farmer families enjoyed a stability and continuity that hearkened back to the last decades of the fifteenth century.

Common wisdom in the sixteenth century looked to the propertied classes as the bulwark of order, the foundation of stable authority and hierarchy. But the stability these households achieved came at a high price for the society as a whole, for their domination of the village lands contributed to the impoverishment that took place around them. In almost every community of Hohenlohe transformed by the population boom, crowded with the village poor, old tenant-farmer families continued to hold the lion's share of the village's lands. A careful scrutiny of any of the rent books often turns up the same family names as holders of the most coveted of these properties in this period, the *Höfe*. In Langenburg district these families, to name only a few, included the Prenners and Krauses of Atzenrod, the Hanselmanns and Wierts of Oberregenbach, and the Franck and Weissmüller families of Unterregenbach. They formed the core of what was becoming a village elite.

The origins of this stable elite lay partly in developments in the late Middle Ages. One of the expressions of the rough-and-tumble peasant egalitarianism of the late Middle Ages was the power of the village to develop customs and practices of inheritance that shaped the availability of land. The origins of local customs remain obscure, of course, and one cannot determine in most cases when a particular set of inheritance customs became common in any single area. In a land like Hohenlohe one will never know precisely at what point in the fourteenth and fifteenth centuries the custom of impartible inheritance took hold. Surely this was an idiosyncratic local development, for impartible inher-

---

[23] Arthur Imhof has analyzed, in fascinating detail, the demographic regime of one such hamlet in Hesse. The patterns he found for Laimbach, especially the way in which these propertyholders placed the stability of the household and property above all else, are not unlike similar such households in Hohenlohe. See *Die verlorenen Welten: Alltagsbewältigung durch unsere Vorfahren – und weshald wir uns heute so schwer damit tun* (Munich: C. H. Beck, 1984).

itance did not take root in the German Southwest as a whole. The Upper Rhine, Kraichgau, the Neckar valley, the Hegau, and Swabian Alb: All became lands of partible inheritance. Only for a few areas – the Black Forest, Klettgau, Upper Swabia, the Hohenlohe plain, and some few other isolated areas – can one follow, in the rent books and district account books, how specific farms remained intact, passed on to a single heir.[24] A few scattered records suggest that this was the practice in late-fifteenth-century Hohenlohe. But none indicate that the practice was imposed by the counts. In 1498 Count Kraft issued a decree defending the rights of children to family property, but the document makes no mention of impartible inheritance.[25]

Few princes long remained unconcerned about the interconnections among population, inheritance, and a stable property order. For unchecked population growth only exacerbated the problems associated with rural poverty, and, in areas where partible inheritance prevailed, weakened the fiscal foundations of the state. Those rulers who had the power and the authority to intervene in local inheritance practices therefore usually favored the maintenance of large compact farms. These farms could bear the burden of taxes and rents more easily than smallholdings that were barely able to keep a family alive.

One cannot determine with certainty when the counts of Hohenlohe decided that impartible inheritance would be essential for the maintenance of the integrity of village property and the social order. But this much is certain: The first written records of their support date from the middle of the sixteenth century, the decades when population pressure on the land became particularly acute. In 1562 Count Ludwig Casimir decreed that "no subject may divide or split up his holdings" without his permission.[26] After this date his stewards made a concerted effort to make sure that impartibility was upheld, at least with regard to the territory's compact farms. In the survey of assessed wealth in 1581 they classified all the properties of the districts according to three types: compact farms, smallholdings, and houses.[27] The massive survey of village property in 1605–6 culminated this trend. The rent book of Langenburg district bearing this date became the official record of all properties in the district, each propertyholder and heir and each transfer of a plot of land carefully recorded.[28] In 1634 Chancellor Assum, after carefully looking over the rent books and other records from the archives of Hohenlohe–Langenburg, noted that rarely had a tenant farmer been allowed to divide a farm.[29] When Count Heinrich Friedrich confirmed the rule of impartible inheritance in 1655, he

---

[24] See the discussion of inheritance customs in Southwest Germany in Helmut Röhm, *Die Vererbung des landwirtschaftlichen Grundeigentums in Baden-Württemberg*, Forschungen zur deutschen Landeskunde, vol. 102 (Remagen: Bundesanstalt für Landeskunde, 1957).
[25] ALKI 6/4, 1498; 234/78, 1503.   [26] ALGAL 175, February 26, 1562.
[27] L/L "Schatzungsanlage Amt Langenburg, 1581."
[28] L/L 27 (1606); 28 (1606).   [29] ALKI 233/19, June 12, 1634.

therefore did nothing but reaffirm what had been policy for a hundred years and custom for even longer.[30]

Theory and practice, law and everyday social reality often diverged in the sixteenth century. The custom of impartible inheritance therefore introduced stability in the village property order only in the measure in which it was actually practiced. The temptation to sell property to newcomers or to merchants with the capital to buy up peasant land, the pressure to divide up the family patrimony among contending heirs could break up the old compact farms within a few short generations. But that clearly did not happen in Hohenlohe. Tenant-farmer families made certain that their farms rarely came up for sale to "outsiders," to those buyers who were not kinsmen. Indeed the tendency for farms to pass from father to son or from father to daughter's husband meant that these properties rarely passed into hands of new settlers or immigrants. A sample of 332 land transfers from Langenburg district between 1552 and 1600 illustrates just how effectively these old families managed to control access to these properties. Seventy-five percent of the sales of farms involved the passing on of the property to sons, daughters' husbands, or other kinsmen. And when a farm did pass out of the family's hands, it did so because of the absence of a suitable heir or because of a bankruptcy in the family. Endris Kutroff's children, for example, inherited their father's substantial farm worth 720 fl. in Billingsbach. But they sold it to Hans Schuman in 1591 because the "six small children had their father's and mother's burdens and among those were enormous debts."[31]

Rural property seems to have circulated in two separate spheres of exchange: a sphere ruled by the politics of kinship, and a second sphere where the raw force of supply and demand governed the exchange of property. The circulation of the compact farms must be understood in the context of this structure of the market in land and property. These properties never passed freely from hand to hand as if there were a free and open market in land. These coveted lands circulated as if they were a part of a sphere of economic exchange separate and apart from the circulation of other properties. Few families had access to this exclusive economic sphere. Normally an outsider had no chance to bid for one of these properties at all, since the negotiations for a farm's sale took place only within the family. Parents, the heir, siblings, the spouse and her family: All negotiated the sale of the farm. The "buyers" did not pay what one could construe as a market price for the farm. They paid instead what Hohenlohers called a "child's price" for the property. This sum included a bundle of payments, all of them bound up with inheritance and kinship obligations: payments

[30] Eckart Schremmer, *Die Bauernbefreiung in Hohenlohe*, Quellen und Forschungen zur Agrargeschichte, vol. 9 (Stuttgart: Gustav Fischer, 1963), 30–4.
[31] ALARL 1552–3 to 1555–6; 1557–8; 1572–3; 1577–8; 1583–4; 1590–1; 1591–2; 1594–5; 1597–8; 1599–1600.

to the retiring couple if they were retiring once they passed on the farm; deductions for the heir's portion of the patrimony and his wife's dowry; debts to siblings who did not inherit the farm; and other debts.[32] The whole transaction, in short, was inseparable in the eyes of tenant-farmer families from inheritance and the rituals of courtship, engagement, and marriage (see Chapter 4).

The other sphere of exchange contrasted sharply with this exclusive circle of property transactions. Here small properties, fields, vineyards, pastures, and houses changed hands briskly, and kinship ties and inheritance customs played a much weaker role in determining the circulation of property. Almost any villager or immigrant could acquire these properties so long as a buyer could put up the cash or arrange the credit to do so. Only 45 percent of the small-holdings and a mere 20 percent of the houses passed from kinsman to kinsman. This market in smallholdings and cottages, more open than that for the compact farms, suggests that ties of kinship were weaker among the smallholders who engaged in these transactions. These properties also turned over rapidly, especially in years of crisis, as in the 1570s and 1590s, for few individuals held these properties long enough to pass them on to an heir. Hohenlohers called these plots the *wälzende Stücke*, the "plots that turn over," and the name seems appropriate for the way in which these pieces of land changed hands quickly in the late sixteenth century. Many villagers, now living on the margin of subsistence, certainly had difficulty keeping plots of land at times; they would be sold off in times of crisis. Still, this hurly-burly of a land market made it possible for some smallholders to stitch together plots into a fairly sizable set of lands. An immigrant could therefore easily find a niche, even if that niche was only an insecure or temporary one.

Every elite naturally seeks to restrict access to certain properties, to coveted goods, to sought-after symbols of status, and to its women. And when some families successfully exclude outsiders or individuals of lower rank from the most coveted goods in a society they create a powerful foundation for dominating any society.[33] In a peasant society these coveted goods are land and women, of course, and with the strict adherence to impartible inheritance Hohenlohers had at least taken the most valuable properties, the *Höfe*, out of general circulation. The village elite would make sure that women too did not circulate freely. But that change came slightly later, in the 1570s and 1580s, and as a consequence of the Reformation.

[32] See Schremmer, *Die Bauernbefreiung in Hohenlohe*, 40–1.

[33] Mary Douglas and Baron Isherwood argue that many societies, even complex capitalist societies, create separate economic spheres for certain goods. In each case the social effects are strikingly similar: the reinforcement of social hierarchy. See *The World of Goods* (New York: Basic Books, 1979), 131–46.

Wealthy tenant farmer, poor smallholder

Old categories of social thought often acquired new meaning in the sixteenth century. Forms of address remained traditional, but their content had altered irrevocably. So it comes as no surprise that villagers came to look upon the tenant farmers not simply as one kind of propertyholder, as one group in the village distinguished for its service to the lords with teams of oxen. Often they were looked upon as an elite, even a class at times, whose wealth and status contrasted sharply with the wretchedness of smallholders and paupers. In times of tension, of conflict within the village, a rough subsistence calculus was often employed, one that drew clear lines between those who produced surpluses and those who produced little or none. "As our neighbors they [the tenant farmers] well know how badly we can support ourselves," the angry cotters of Langenburg district complained in 1599. "A number of our tenant farmers have so much more than they actually need for the household's subsistence, but we need every scrap to stock up our barns and to supply our small households."[34] The notion reflected the idea at the heart of the German *Hausvaterliteratur*. Every house should be self-sufficient, production geared toward subsistence needs and not the accumulation of surpluses.[35] But this was not an abstract notion, one borrowed from classical philosophy. The subsistence calculus captured the harsh social reality of the 1580s and 1590s directly, concretely.

All social theory captures only a small part of reality, of course, and the subsistence calculus of the late sixteenth century was no exception. The distribution of wealth within the village was more complex and subtle than this, the distinctions among some groups of households fluid and shifting. Yet the central idea reflected accurately what had occurred during the population boom of the sixteenth century: The village elite had come to hold the lion's share of all village wealth. Two major changes, occurring simultaneously, seem to have taken place in the distribution of wealth in Langenburg district, for example. A few propertyholders – the upper 20 percent of the households – steadily increased their share of the total wealth of this society (see Table 3.2 and Graph 3.3). These households held 44 percent of the assessed taxable wealth in 1528, 49 percent in 1553, and, in 1581, 62 percent. Within this group, the greatest increases came among the households in the upper 10 percent. This small group accounted for only 27 percent of the wealth in 1528, but for 43 percent in 1581. Part of this concentration of wealth can be explained by the fact that the bottom 60 percent of the households simply grew in numbers: There were

---

[34] ALKI 356/4, May 20, 1599.
[35] See Otto Brunner, "Das 'ganze Haus' und die alteuropäische 'Ökonomik,' " in his *Neue Wege der Verfassungs- und Sozialgeschichte*, 2d ed. (Göttingen: Vandenhoeck & Ruprecht, 1968), 103–27.

Table 3.2. *Distribution of wealth in Langenburg district, 1528-81*

Poorest ___% of households	% of wealth		
	1528	1553	1581
10	1.4	0.9	0.5
20	4.3	2.7	1.5
30	8.8	5.8	2.9
40	14.8	10.9	5.3
50	23.2	16.7	9.3
60	33.0	25.0	15.9
70	43.9	36.4	25.2
80	56.5	51.2	37.9
90	73.5	69.4	57.3
100	100.0	100.0	100.0

Sources: See Appendix Tables A.1, A.2, and A.3.

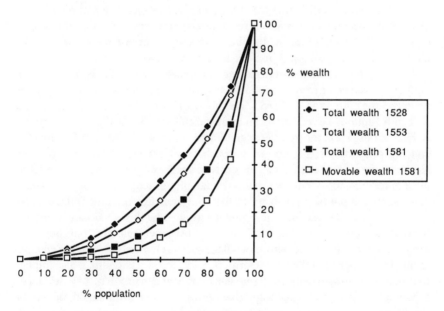

Graph 3.3. Distribution of wealth in Langenburg district, 1528–81 (Lorenz curve).
Sources: Tables 3.6, A.1, A.2, A.3.

many more paupers in 1581 than in 1528. But these villagers also amassed new wealth, wealth accumulated at the expense of their village poor through trade.

In many peasant societies villagers look upon the accumulation of wealth as a zero-sum game: One household cannot amass wealth without others losing it. One individual's gain is almost certainly another's loss. The circulation and distribution of material goods naturally takes place in more complicated ways than this, but in a society with fixed resources this notion was not an inaccurate one. In this case, what the village elite gained, the smallholders and paupers lost. The gulf that was certainly beginning to open between the groups in 1500 became unbridgeable by 1580. In 1528 the poorest 60 percent of the households from the district held 33 percent of the wealth. By 1553 their share had slipped to 25 percent, by 1581 to a mere 16 percent. That this group of householders suffered the most in this development comes more sharply into focus when one compares their fortunes with those from the middling ranks. These middling households – those in the sixtieth and seventieth percentiles – managed to hold a relatively fixed share of the wealth: 24 percent in 1528, 26 percent in 1553, and 22 percent in 1581. The Gini Index, a measure of relative equality in a statistical sample, shows just how unequally wealth was divided by 1581. The index stood at .3812 in 1528. By no means was this an equal distribution of wealth; that only occurs when the index approaches zero. But this was as equal as wealth would ever be distributed in early modern Hohenlohe. In 1553 the index stood at .462, and in 1581 it reached .5884.

The fluid and shifting circumstances as population grew, the high social mobility, the absence of firm institutional structures, and the web of kinship often hindered the formation of hard social boundaries between groups in the late sixteenth century. Yet one finds an unmistakable trend in a village society such as Hohenlohe. Here the gulf between wealthy and poor, between the propertied and the propertyless, became so great that nascent class relationships were clearly taking root. Wealth alone, of course, provides only the crudest foundation of class relationships: The fact that a few families monopolized the total wealth in a society did not necessarily mean that they constituted an identifiable class. Yet if one looks deeper into the problems implied by this unequal distribution of wealth, if one follows the logic of the subsistence calculus, one begins to discover other clues to the nature of village social relationships. For the calculus implied not simply that the tenant farmers held substantial wealth, it also implied that they held properties of a particular quality and type, that they developed a particular place in the economy that set them apart from smallholders and the village poor. To what extent was this true?

Certainly when one examines village property relationships closely the social distinctions appear even sharper, the gulf that separated the elite from the village poor more concrete and easy to grasp. For the overall distribution of wealth closely mirrored the distribution of certain types of properties, and movable or commercial wealth as well, within the village. The village elite, for example, that upper caste of 20 percent of the households identified earlier, held properties of a very similar type. Thirty-nine of the fifty-eight households

86

Rich and poor

Table 3.3. *Propertyholders in Langenburg district, 1581*

Decile (wealth)	Cotters	Smallholders	Tenant farmers	Millers	Tavernkeepers
1	27	1	0	0	0
2	29	0	0	0	0
3	22	7	0	0	0
4	13	16	0	0	0
5	3	26	0	0	0
6	1	28	0	0	0
7	1	28	0	0	0
8	0	18	11	0	0
9	0	7	22	0	0
10	0	6	17	4	2
Total	96	137	50	4	2

Source: LAN 42/16/10, 1581.

in this group held compact farms in 1581 (see Table 3.3). Six additional householders held mills, inns, and the sizable farms attached to them. Only a fragment of this group, thirteen households, came from the ranks of the smallholders (*Köbler*), that is, propertyholders of a second order of smaller farms. That a small group of properties belonged to this elite, and that a group of tenant farmers actually ranked in the third decile of wealth, should serve as a reminder that the categories overlapped somewhat, that the hierarchy was never completely rigid. Still, the farther down the scale one descends the more pronounced the shift in types of properties: In the bottom six deciles one finds only smallholders and cotters.

The holders of the compact farms completely dominated the total landholdings of the village. One did not need a trained eye to enter a village in Hohenlohe and quickly spot the six or eight sizable farmsteads that stood out in the community. One steward knew immediately when he entered a village where the tenant farmers were: They had by far the largest houses, several barns, and obviously the most fields and pastures in the village. If one were in doubt, the coming and going of villagers to the fields would give you a clue: The tenant farmer was the one accompanied by his laborers and servants, his plough pulled by a sturdy team of oxen.[36] Some precise statistics give more precise meaning to these impressions. In Atzenrod seven tenant farmers – only 14 percent of the propertyholders in 1605 – held 64 percent of the farmland, a total of 279 *morgen* (see Table 3.4). In nearby Bächlingen a village elite of six households – all of which had individual holdings in excess of 20 *morgen* –

[36] ALKI 356/12, [1600?].

Table 3.4. *Land distribution in Atzenrod, 1606*

Size of landholding	Tenants		Land in *morgen*	
(*morgen*)	No.	%	Total	%
0	14	27.4	0	0
0.1-4.9	18	35.3	34.7	8.0
5.0-9.9	6	11.8	41.0	9.4
10.0-19.9	6	11.8	78.4	18.0
20.0-29.9	1	1.9	23.6	5.4
30.0-39.9	3	5.9	103.9	23.8
40.0 +	3	5.9	151.5	34.8
Other	-	-	2.5	0.6
Total	51	100.0	435.6	100.0

Sources: L/L 27, 1606; 28, 1606.

Table 3.5. *Land distribution in Bächlingen, 1606*

Size of landholding	Tenants		Land in *morgen*	
(*morgen*)	No.	%	Total	%
0	7	14.0	0	0
0.1-4.9	23	46.0	47.5	11.5
5.0-9.9	8	16.0	54.1	13.2
10.0-19.9	6	12.0	87.6	21.3
20.0-29.9	2	4.0	47.0	11.4
30.0-39.9	1	2.0	35.5	8.6
40.0 +	3	6.0	139.6	34.0
Total	50	100.0	411.3	100.0

Sources: L/L 27, 1606; 28, 1606.

controlled 54 percent of the land (222 *morgen*) (see Table 3.5). The remainder of the village land was carved up into a maze of tiny plots held by the smallholders and the village poor.

The distribution of movable wealth mirrored this unequal access to land, only more intensely. The tax survey of 1581 was the first systematic survey of movable wealth in sixteenth-century Hohenlohe. Here, in the records describing the methods used to carry out the survey, the notion of "surplus," a flexible and abstract concept when it was used in other contexts, was given concrete expression, a precise legal definition. What one considered as "surplus" was fixed by imperial law at this time; it included all movable goods beyond "essential needs" of the household. This legal concept was an imprecise one, however,

Table 3.6. *Distribution of movable wealth in Langenburg district, 1581*

Decile	Wealth (fl.)	Cumulative wealth	%	%/100
1	23	23	0.1	.0001
2	42	65	0.3	.0003
3	92	157	0.8	.0008
4	196	353	1.7	.0017
5	607	960	4.6	.0046
6	917	1,877	9.1	.0091
7	1,160	3,037	14.7	.0147
8	2,083	5,120	24.7	.0247
9	3,633	8,753	42.2	.0422
10	11,975	20,728	100.0	.1000
Total				.1982

Source: LAN 42/16/10, 1581.

Note: Hence G = 1 - 2(.1982) + .1 = .7036. (See Graph 3.3.)

one that aroused heated debates for everyone engaged in the tedious business of assessing taxable wealth and collecting revenues: learned jurists, treasury officials, stewards, and even villagers.[37] Still, despite these difficulties, the steward listed all of the "movable wealth" beside every entry. What this included, in practice, were all of the material goods that a household produced for sale on the market or that were acquired through commercial activity: surpluses of grain, all cattle and other livestock, wine, loans to debtors, hoards of cash, and silver plate. An analysis of the results shows an enormous inequality in the distribution of this type of wealth: The top fifty-eight households held 75 percent of all of movable wealth in Langenburg district (see Table 3.6 and Graph 3.3). This distribution suggests the strikingly different places the tenant farmers, the smallholders, and the village poor held in the market economy.

A look at the top fifteen householders in this group shows why: These individuals dominated the production and distribution of food. Jörg Kraus, Hans Schneider d.A., Thoma Kellerman, Hans Hanselman, Jörg Prenner, and Michel Scheurman: These men held the largest and the most valuable farms in Langenburg district. Four individuals – Burck Plomenstock of Bächlingen, Wolff Heuser's widow from Oberregenbach, Veit Albrecht of Hürden, and Simon Weissmüller of Unterregenbach – were millers and so stood at the center of the distribution and sale of grain in the district. They not only controlled the properties attached to the mills, they also held considerable stores of grain that they sold on local markets. The two innkeepers, both of them exceptionally

[37] LAN 42/13/1, 1577; 42/14/58, November 16, 1580.

wealthy, occupied a similar position in the economy. Lienhart Preunger and Enndris Franck of Nesselbach not only tended their inns but also engaged heavily in the alimentary trade; both had amassed considerable stores of wine, grain, and livestock. Even Wendel Scheurman, Bartel Erman, and Hanns Eberhardt – all of them listed as smallholders in the survey – were actually petty merchants from Langenburg who controlled an important part of the grain trade by the early 1570s.[38] Together these fifteen householders held stocks of grain, cattle, wine, silver, and other goods worth 9,405 fl., or 45 percent of all of the movable wealth in the district. The steward assessed their total wealth at 28,410 fl., 30 percent of the total wealth of the district. By the measure of any subsistence calculus these propertyholders had little in common with smallholders and the village poor.

The vast majority of the remaining householders in the district, by contrast, disposed of little not needed for the immediate needs of their families. Their entries in the survey were short, the list of movable goods they might sell on the market in no way comparable to the village elite. No one would have confused a tenant-farmer household with the sparsely furnished households of these smallholders and cotters. Not all of them were without stocks of grain, wine, and cattle. The middling sorts of households – those in the seventh and eighth deciles – held most of the remaining movable wealth in the district. But those households below them, the lower 60 percent of the households, disposed of very little movable wealth at all, a mere 9 percent of the total in the district. Here one found bare, sparsely furnished cottages or a set of rooms in a house shared between two or more families. Each of these families had only the barest furnishings: a bed, table, and chair, a few pots or pans for the hearth. The steward might find a goat or two or a sheep sharing the house with them, but only rarely did one find a calf or cow in these households. Most telling of all, none of these households disposed of that which they needed most of all in this age of dearth: supplies of grain. For most village households in the late sixteenth century the ideal of the self-sufficient household remained precisely that: an ideal, a metaphor perhaps loaded with rhetorical power, but one that could only draw attention to the wealth of the few and the wrenching poverty of the many.

This process of social stratification carried implications for political, religious, and social order at every level of society, from the smallest hamlet in South Germany to the court of the emperor in far-off Vienna or Prague. For the struggle to create social order in the midst of disorder, the attempt to impose social discipline and hierarchy, would inevitably become bound up with the search for political and religious order in the empire as a whole. The power of Germany's petty princes in the empire, the shape of state and feudal authority

[38] ALKI 10/1, 1572; 10/2, 1572.

at the local level, the ability of the state to extract taxes, the shape of religious reform: Each of these problems led back, in one way or other, to the village, the cornerstone of feudal authority. Here the search for order in the sixteenth century was played out in all of its complexity. And it was a process bound to involve not simply the elites of this rural-based society, but villagers as well.

Part Two

Search for order

4

~~~~~~

Reformation, patriarchy, and marital discipline

It is not easy to scan the broad spectrum of popular and learned responses to social conditions in Reformation Germany in the middle of the sixteenth century. Yet, if the pamphlet literature from this period can serve as a guide, one theme often stood out above all others: the fear of social, political, and religious disorder, the perception that the underpinnings of the whole social order were dangerously unstable, uncertain, continually in flux.[1] That many pamphleteers still held up for their readers the social values of a society of orders – hierarchy, social harmony, religious unity, corporate solidarity, the common good, deference, obedience – could only have intensified the feeling for many that society had become unstable. For those ideals bore even less resemblance to social reality in 1550 than they had fifty years before. Out in the countryside, in a rural society like Hohenlohe, specific events and social conditions – the Peasants' War, the fear of rural unrest, the continued decay of the church, the uncertain power of the counts in the empire, the spread of poverty and population growth, the erosion of communal solidarity – lay behind the views voiced by contemporary observers of society. Protestant reformers called to Öhringen in the 1540s and 1550s, for example, were all deeply distressed by the social disorder and decay they saw around them. For devout reformers like Johann Hartmann, steeped in an apocalyptic vision of the world, the disorder and conflict they saw in society were signs of the last days pressing hard upon humanity. From their vantage point this was a society fast losing its moorings.

Over the next several decades German princes, Lutheran pastors, and villagers struggled, each in their own way, to bring order and stability to this society. The agrarian class structure that began to take shape between 1560 and 1620 – the peak of the expansionist phase of the agrarian cycle – was the result of all of their separate efforts to fashion order out of the world. That a

---

[1] For a masterful treatment of the social-psychological culture of fear in the sixteenth and seventeenth centuries see Jean Delumeau, *Le péché et la peur: la culpabilisation en Occident (XIIIe–XVIIIe siècles)* (Paris: Arthème Fayard, 1983).

clearer sense of hierarchy, discipline, and social order would appear, that social boundaries between the groups arranged in the feudal hierarchy would finally begin to harden by 1600 or 1620, was not at all clear in the middle of the century. This search, this struggle, for social order embraced almost every aspect of everyday life, but it was most evident on three primary levels: the family and household, the marketplace, and the state. The reforms that centered on these aspects of rural life never entirely replaced the old bonds of community or the patterns of domination rooted in the princes' exercise of *Herrschaft*: They complemented these older relationships and built up broader horizontal ties based on class and obedience to the territorial state. Many of these changes involved the careful control of property and access to surpluses from the land in an age of land scarcity. But they also involved the control or disciplining of people as well, women, youth, and the village poor in particular.

Reformation and patriarchy

The fluidity of social relationships in the village, the mobility and continuous changes brought on by population growth, opened up a number of avenues for infusing rural social relationships with the values of hierarchy, discipline, and social order once again. Yet no path proved more important in this process than the effort to reform the family, to bolster patriarchal authority, to introduce a strict marital discipline. For all of the social groups in a rural society – princes, pastors, and many villagers themselves – tended to see disorder as the consequence of the decay of the family. Once the Reformation came to Hohenlohe, for example, once the counts had the legal authority and political power to carry out a thorough reform of the moral and religious life in their lands, reformers worked zealously to bolster the values of the patriarchal family. In the eyes of the Lutheran reformers, the family and marital discipline would become the cornerstones of a godly and orderly rural society.

The intellectual roots of this moral crusade to reform the family lay in humanism and the Protestant Reformation. If one were to believe Protestants and humanists, even reform-minded Catholics like Erasmus, marital discipline and family values had fallen into ill repute. The family was in crisis. Luther was by no means the first to complain of the decay of marriage and the family, but he lent force to the notion that the church had devalued the estate of marriage, that moral decay and social turmoil had, as a consequence, increased.[2] In his widely read sermon "On the Estate of Marriage" (1522) he complained that "marriage has universally fallen into awful disrepute" and that booksellers everywhere peddled "page books which treat of nothing but the depravity of

[2] See Steven Ozment, *When Fathers Ruled: Family Life in Reformation Europe* (Cambridge, Mass.: Harvard University Press, 1983), 3–9.

womankind and the unhappiness of the estate of marriage."[3] These views echoed popular opinions evident in many areas on the eve of the Reformation. As early as 1490 Count Kraft VI of Hohenlohe blamed the priests and the local church for the appalling decay of public morality he saw in his own lands. As patron lord of Öhringen's ecclesiastical foundation, he ordered his officials to "drive out and refuse residence to all those who do not live in marriage but who live together [out of wedlock]."[4] Before his own courts, set up in defiance of the bishop of Würzburg, he punished adulterers, gamblers, and others who lived disreputable lives.[5] But these efforts, like the reach of his power, remained limited; they seem to have touched only the townsmen and priests of Öhringen. Only later, in the 1550s, could the campaign be renewed and extended to Hohenlohe's other small towns and villages as well.

Protestant reformers, by contrast, took up the call for the reform of marriage and the family with a vehemence, a sense of urgency and purpose, that was lacking before the Reformation. The difference lay partly in Protestant theology and social theory: The family, in the eyes of reformers, would take the place of the church in indoctrinating Christians with right doctrine and belief. For Luther the family assumed a primary significance in spreading the message of the Gospel. In the family were linked two primary functions: the begetting of children and the raising of them, educating them as Christians. But to meet these taxing responsibilities the father of the family, the patriarch, would have to have secure and unchallenged authority over the members of his family, especially his children, and the dependents of his household. He should rule his household with paternalistic wisdom and compassion, of course, much the same way that God the Father ruled the universe. Lutheran moralists, with the clarity of ideologues, never saw patriarchal authority as oppressive or enslaving. From their vantage point the patriarchal family would liberate men, women, and children from the oppressive rule of monks and priests. But obedience and submission from the children was still essential.[6] The family was to become a godly institution, as God had intended it to be, a cornerstone of worldly stability and harmony.[7] The patriarchal family would therefore help secure the triumph of Protestantism.

This view of the family carried with it a sweeping condemnation of the laws governing marriage. From Luther's point of view the problem was twofold. The medieval church, for one, had elevated celibacy and life in the cloister as

---

[3] Cited in ibid. 3.

[4] Johann Christian Wibel, *Hohenlohische Kyrchen- und Reformations- Historie*, 4 vols. (Onolzbach: Jacob Christoph Poschens, 1752–5), vol. 2, 383–7; Gunther Franz, "Reformation und landes-herrliches Kirchenregiment in Hohenlohe," *Württembergisch Franken* 58 (1974), 123–8.

[5] Wibel, *Hohenlohische Kyrchen- und Reformations- Historie*, vol. 1, 270.

[6] See Gerald Strauss, *Luther's House of Learning: Indoctrination of the Young in the German Reformation* (Baltimore: Johns Hopkins University Press, 1978), 108–31.

[7] See Ozment, *When Fathers Ruled*, 9–25.

the way of life most favored by God. Canonists since the time of Gratian and Peter Lombard had therefore considered marriage to be acceptable, but less than desirable, a means of curbing man's carnal lust. This normative bias created enough confusion for the laity, in Luther's opinion, but further chaos arose from the application of canon law to disputes over marriage in the ecclesiastical courts. According to canon law, marriage was nothing more than a spiritual union of two individuals. Two individuals could become legally married if they showed "marital affection" for one another, exchanged vows, and then engaged in sexual intercourse.[8] The individuals who exchanged the vows did not have to seek a priest to perform this sacrament, nor did they need the consent of their parents. Marriage was a private contract and a sacrament, not a public institution. This legal view often came into conflict with secular ideas about marriage. Lawyers and judges who considered disputes in the ecclesiastical courts often considered marriages to be relationships that, in the eyes of the community, were mere instances of concubinage. Even worse, these liaisons became "secret marriages," marriages contracted without the consent of the family and parents.[9] The result, Luther concluded, was the weakening of the institution of marriage and the inevitable corruption of the family.[10]

Luther therefore argued for the secularization of marriage, for the return of authority over this institution to the community and the state. He also revised the meaning of marriage itself in two important ways. He rejected, on the one hand, the church's subtle distinction between engagement and marriage, and argued instead that marriage itself began with the engagement. Even more important, he insisted, on the other, that a match became binding only when the parents gave their consent.[11] Luther drew upon a variety of sources – scripture, canon law, imperial law, Germanic custom – in making this argument. He touched upon a particularly important point for village society when he argued that the family's wealth and prestige depended upon the wise and judicious choice of marriage partners for children:

---

[8] For an introduction to the articles on marriage in canon law see especially Gabriel Le Bras, "La doctrine du mariage chez les théologiens et les canonistes depuis l'an mille," in *Dictionnaire de théologie catholique* (Paris: Libraire Letouzey et Ane, 1927), cols. 2123–317, and Beatrice Gottlieb, "The Meaning of Clandestine Marriage," in Robert Wheaton and Tamara K. Hareven, eds., *Family and Sexuality in French History* (Philadelphia: University of Pennsylvania Press, 1980), 49–83.

[9] See especially R. H. Helmholz, *Marriage Litigation in Medieval England* (Cambridge: Cambridge University Press, 1974), 25–73; Gottlieb, "The Meaning of Clandestine Marriage"; and James A. Brundage, "Concubinage and Marriage in Medieval Canon Law," *Journal of Medieval History* 1 (1975), 1–17.

[10] Hartwig Dietrich, *Das protestantische Eherecht in Deutschland bis zur Mitte des 17. Jahrhunderts*, Jus ecclesiasticum, vol. 10 (Munich: Claudius, 1970), 53–5.

[11] Ibid. 56; Klaus Suppan, *Die Ehelehre Martin Luthers: Theologische und rechtshistorische Aspekte des reformatorischen Eheverständnisse* (Salzburg: Universitätsverlag Anton Pustet, 1971), 69–70.

If I raised a daughter with so much expense and effort, care and trouble, diligence and work and had bet all my life, body, and property on her for so many years, should she not be better protected than a cow who had wandered into the forest that any wolf could devour? Should my child be so available that any boy, perhaps a stranger or an enemy to me, would have power and free access to steal her secretly from me and take her home without my knowledge and consent? Does anyone want to leave his money and property lying about so openly that the first one who comes by can take it? Every reasonable person must concede, I say, that this is violence and injustice that could be easily avoided if one prohibited secret engagements.... No boy would be able to win a child from a pious man or presume to become an heir of property that he had not acquired if he knew that it were useless even if he made a thousand secret engagements.[12]

Every pastor should therefore announce engagements before the congregation. Then a public, and not a private, wedding should be held. Luther argued, of course, that no parent should force his child into a prearranged match.[13] But his work still amounted to a passionate and popular appeal for parental and community control over marriage.

Social reform with a goal as sweeping, as fundamental, as this was accomplished neither as swiftly nor as thoroughly as reformers envisioned. The reform of marriage practices, once begun, took decades to accomplish in Protestant Germany. In the cities patriarchal values and marital discipline could be enforced more easily than in the countryside. Already in the 1520s, urban magistrates of Strasbourg, Nuremberg, and Zürich had rejected the judicial authority of the church, disbanded local ecclesiastical courts, and established consistories. The magistrates also drew up new marriage codes, often as part of church and police ordinances, and these laws denied the binding authority of marriage vows made in secret and required a public wedding. One cannot say much as yet about the activities of the Protestant consistories over long periods of time, but, if the example of the Zürich marriage courts is typical, the new judges spent a considerable amount of time trying cases of contested engagements and making sure that couples made their marriages public.[14] Protestant states followed the cities' lead in the 1530s, 1540s, and 1550s. In 1539 the elector of Saxony formed a consistory at Wittenberg to oversee marriage practices in accordance with the new Saxon marriage code.[15] Once new marriage laws were established, once consistories or courts could administer the laws, the reform of popular marriage practices could begin in earnest.

The Reformation and the moral crusade to reform the family and marriage

---

[12] Martin Luther, "Von Ehesachen," in *D. Martin Luthers Werke: Kritische Gesamtausgabe* (Weimar: Herman Böhlaus Nachfolger, 1910), vol. 30, pt. 3, 208–9.
[13] Ozment stresses this point about Luther's message; see *When Fathers Ruled*, 39–41.
[14] Ibid. 32–7.
[15] Dietrich, *Das protestantische Eherecht*, 87–9.

came somewhat later still in Germany's small Protestant states. Obstacles stood in the way of reform in these states even for princes eager to introduce the Reformation as early as the 1530s and 1540s. The major obstacle was the opposition of Emperor Charles V to the Reformation. Powerful princes of the empire – Elector Fredrick the Wise of Saxony, Landgrave Philip of Hesse, Duke Ulrich of Württemberg – could perhaps defy the emperor and the Concordat of Worms and push ahead with Protestant reforms. But the petty princes, still fearful of the emperor's power, hesitated to flout his authority so boldly and openly. Besides, religious reform still rested on no secure foundation in imperial law. For petty princes, whose legal rights within the empire still remained unclear, the weakness of imperial law remained a barrier to reform. The legal foundation for religious reform would not be reasonably secure until the Peace of Augsburg.[16] In addition, Protestantism was still associated with the taint of religious radicalism, revolt, and disorder, a legacy of the stormy 1520s and the spread of Anabaptism in the 1530s and 1540s.

So many small princes, when they introduced the Reformation, did so comparatively late. The Reformation in Hohenlohe was typical in this regard. Counts Albrecht III and Georg I undertook no bold reform of the church in the wake of the Peasants' War. They encouraged moderate reforms in Öhringen and sympathized with those who complained about the decay of the church in the 1530s.[17] But they did not edge into the Protestant camp until the mid-1540s, and then only with reluctance. A number of conditions in the empire and their small principality had changed by this time. The Schmalkaldic League, the defender of the Protestant cause, remained outwardly powerful at this time, undefeated until 1547. The Reformation had also made deep inroads in the most important lands around Hohenlohe. The Duchy of Württemberg, the margraviate of Ansbach, the imperial cities of Heilbronn, Rothenburg o.d.T., and Schwäbisch Hall: All of these neighbors pushed ahead with their own reformations. The isolation, the decay of the church and clergy, the changed political circumstances within the empire perhaps made the counts more inclined to call Caspar Huberinus, a noted Lutheran preacher from Ulm, to Öhringen to introduce a reform in the church services in 1544. But they moved cautiously and set limits on the reform: Huberinus was not to abolish the mass and had to respect the priests of the ecclesiastical foundation. Between 1544 and 1551 the modest foundations for a later reformation were laid.[18]

[16] Gunther Franz, *Die Kirchenleitung in Hohenlohe in den Jahrzehnten nach der Reformation: Visitation, Konsistorium, Kirchenzucht und die Festigung des landesherrlichen Kirchenregiments 1556–1586*, Quellen and Forschungen zur württembergischen Kirchengeschichte, vol. 3 (Stuttgart: Calwer, 1971), 13–15.
[17] See Franz, "Reformation und landesherrliches Kirchenregiment," and Wibel, *Hohenlohische Kyrchen- und Reformations- Historie*, vol. 1, 192–201.
[18] Franz, *Die Kirchenleitung in Hohenlohe*, 13–15.

Reformation, patriarchy, and marital discipline

Certain reformers left a decisive imprint on the course of a local reformation, and Hohenlohe proved no exception. During his tenure as preacher in Öhringen, Huberinus may have had to move cautiously, the practical effects of his reforms remaining limited, but he set the direction of the Reformation once it was fully introduced beginning in 1556.[19] He also brought vigor to the campaign to reform the family and marriage. His sermons, delivered at Öhringen and Ulm and later published as a popular devotional work, emphasized the importance of the patriarchal family for a godly society. He called upon secular and spiritual authorities to cooperate in grounding the church, Christianity, and the state in a strong, stable patriarchal family. Only in this way could one be certain that parents could teach their children and servants sound Christian belief and doctrine.[20] He also warned that this task would be a difficult one, that Satan could employ a bundle of tricks to undermine marriage and the family, that vigilance would be needed. Only in this way would the patriarchal family become the foundation of peace, harmony, and stability in the worldly order:

The evil enemy often stirs up those harsh words with which married couples curse each other so that many times great misfortune, misery, and despair come of it. Wherever he finds a small entry he will dig and bore until he has slipped in with his whole body. So young married couples should truly be warned that they should not turn a receptive ear to the deceitful enemy and that they should not let themselves become bitter with each other. For if he comes into your house he will be a good-for-nothing, a harmful and seditious guest.[21]

His popular catechism, one of the most widely read devotional tracts of the Lutheran reformation, drove home the same arguments in shortened form.[22] Here he made it clear that the success of the reformation depended upon the

[19] For a full treatment of the Reformation in Hohenlohe see ibid. and Thomas Robisheaux, "Peasants and Pastors: Rural Youth Control and the Reformation in Hohenlohe, 1540–1680," *Social History* 6 (1981), 281–300.
[20] Strauss, *Luther's House of Learning*, 125. Huberinus became one of the most important writers of Protestant devotional literature in the sixteenth century, influencing Protestant pastors throughout Europe. See Gunther Franz, *Huberinus–Rhegius–Holbein: Bibliographische und druckgeschichtliche Untersuchung der verbreitesten Trost- und Erbauungsschriften des 16. Jahrhunderts*, Bibliotheca humanistica et reformation, vol. 7 (Nieuwkoop: B. de Graaf, 1973). See also Huberinus's popular devotional handbook for the heads of households, *Spiegel der geistlichen Hauszucht, Jesus Sirach genannt* (Nuremberg: Ulrich Newber and Johann von Berg's heirs, 1556), and his sermon collection, *Mancherley Form zu predigen von den fürnembsten Stücken so inn der Christlichen Kirche teglich gelert und getriben sollen werden* (Nuremberg: Ulrich Newber and Johann von Berg's heirs, 1565).
[21] Caspar Huberinus, "Die achte Predig Vom heyligen Ehestand: Vber den Text Matthei am 19," in *Mancherley Form zu predigen*, 72b–74.
[22] Caspar Huberinus, "Ein Predig darinnen die summa des ganzen Catechismi begriffen ist," in *Viertzig kurtze Predig vber den ganzen Catechismum: Für die Hausvaeter ir Gesinde zu lehren* (Nuremberg: Johan von Berg and Ulrich Newber, 1561), B–C.

patriarch taking over the task of doctrinal instruction in his family.[23] The catechism was therefore explicitly designed to guide him in that pious undertaking.

But the reform needed more than sermons and catechisms if it were to take hold. For marital discipline would not only have to be taught and inculcated, it would also have to be rooted in law and imposed on the everyday practice of courtship and marriage, even if that meant using the full force of the state. Here Huberinus also showed the way, although he merely continued a trend well established by the 1540s. The old itinerant courts of the bishop of Würzburg had, by this time, long been withdrawn from the territory. Huberinus encouraged Count Albrecht to step into the vacuum left by the absence of these courts, to hold his own marriage courts more frequently, to use his judicial power to punish immorality more sternly. And he advised the count on the cases that came before the marriage court held at Öhringen in 1546.[24]

One cannot determine very much about his work with this court. But his ideas about the significance of marriage and the patriarchal family for the whole social order were well known. In his catechism, Huberinus made it clear that marriage was no ordinary social institution: God had created it to maintain order and stability in society:

He then decreed that marriage also [was] good and placed parents and magistrates in His place and commanded [them that they] should give witness, rule over, and protect this institution as the highest authorities on earth in the secular order. They should also guide, lead, and initiate the people into [marriage] so that men should conform and hold to these two governments. God the Father therefore appointed fathers and mothers and the authorities to rule in His place and confirmed this through the fourth holy commandment: Thou shalt obey thy father and mother.[25]

These ideas help explain the extraordinary place that marital discipline and patriarchal authority would come to have in Protestant Hohenlohe.

The church ordinance of 1553 marked the next step in giving marriage a new social meaning in this rural society. Huberinus probably helped to write this law, and it followed closely the trends in other Protestant states. The code, like other Lutheran church and marriage laws, denounced all "secret marriages." Young people were now required to marry only with the permission of their parents. The church's supervision of marriage was also tightened: Pastors were to question a couple thoroughly before the wedding and to announce their engagement three times from the pulpit. The law also required a public church ceremony, a sharp break with practice before this time. "The

---

[23] Caspar Huberinus, "Vorrede," in *Viertzig kurtze Predig.*
[24] Franz, "Reformation und landesherrliches Kirchenregiment," 135.
[25] Caspar Huberinus, "Ein Predig darinnen die summa des ganzen Catechismi begriffen ist," B–C.

married couple should be blessed in the church before the altar as in other reformed churches," the law read, "namely, that they, their kinsmen, and neighbors should come into the church, hear God's word, receive God's blessing, and have a Christian prayer from God's words."[26] With this church ordinance, the direction of family reform in Hohenlohe was clearly laid.

The work of the reformers who came after Huberinus was to deepen and broaden the reformation, to extend the campaign for family and marriage reform into every village of the territory. This became legally possible once Count Ludwig Casimir introduced a full reformation in 1556. This pious ruler repeated the bans on "secret coupling" in the church ordinances of 1556 and 1559.[27] But he went much further in 1572 and laid down a comprehensive new Marriage Law. The code itself contained nothing unusual for a Protestant territory; its drafters borrowed heavily from the marriage code of the Duchy of Württemberg. The Marriage Law declared all "secret marriages" to be illegal, without any binding legal force, and made it clear that parental permission was essential for making a match a permanent one: "No one, man or woman, still under the authority of his or her parents shall secretly promise marriage; rather every child, girl or boy, should marry honorably with the advice, previous knowledge, and consent of the parents or, in their absence, the next of kin and guardian."[28] The law went on to require local pastors and state officials to report any secret engagements to the court; an inquiry would be held and the offenders duly punished. And, to make sure that every villager understood the law, pastors were directed to read a shortened version of the ordinance to their congregations at least four times every year.[29]

All of these measures must be seen against the backdrop of the Lutherans' goal: the creation of a godly society, a society that required individuals to conform outwardly and inwardly to God's will. In the case of marriage and family reform that meant, of course, conforming to the will, the power, of the ruler. The administrative structures of a small state, however, were poorly suited to achieve these ends. To police the church laws effectively, to impose marital discipline in practice, required an unprecedented expansion of the apparatus of the state. A petty ruler could perhaps justify this new authority with an appeal to custom; a lord, after all, carried moral and spiritual responsibility for the salvation of his subjects. But these measures, because they aimed at such a total reform of the moral lives of villagers, were often justified by other arguments as well. For Count Ludwig Casimir's new religious adviser, Johann Hartmann, the justification was a religious one: These final days before the

---

[26] Gunther Franz, ed., *Grafschaft Hohenlohe*, pt. 1 of *Württemberg*, vol. 15 of *Die evangelischen Kirchenordnungen des XVI. Jahrhunderts* (Tübingen: J. C. B. Mohr, 1977), 78.
[27] Franz, ed., *Grafschaft Hohenlohe*, 82–7.
[28] Ibid. 176.   [29] Ibid. 172.

Apocalypse demanded an extraordinary effort to combat Satan and establish a godly society.[30]

The first visitations in Hohenlohe in 1556 and 1559 were therefore carried out by the state and church in the heat of apocalyptic expectation. The results of these systematic inquiries into the conditions in the parishes clearly disappointed the visitors.[31] Everywhere they found disturbing evidence of pastors poorly prepared to carry out their duties, of popular immorality and disorder, "disobedient children who do not treat their parents with the usual honor, but who treat them rather disgracefully and unscrupulously."[32] Many of these conditions persisted, largely unchanged, into the 1570s. In the visitation of 1571 visitors discovered that young people still contracted secret marriages in defiance of their parents.[33]

Church visitations alone, however, could never reform the family and bring about marital discipline. A large territorial state like the Duchy of Württemberg, a state with a rapidly developing centralized bureaucracy, could perhaps make the visitation into an effective tool of state and church domination at the local level. But a small state could only carry out visitations infrequently, and with less centralized control, for they required time, personnel, bureaucratic organization, and money. The state and church lacked all of these resources in Hohenlohe. The state never developed a centralized church administration, one that could exercise the same degree of control over villagers as that achieved in Württemberg. But the reformers and the counts could improve and expand the marriage courts in the principality. This continued the trend of the fifteenth century. The courts came under the authority of the counts, of course, and formed part of the small state's direct administration of the church after the reformation.[34] The reach of the courts was limited at first: Cases from the 1550s and 1560s still came primarily from the towns of Öhringen, Neuenstein, and Waldenburg. The extension of the courts' power into the northern parts of the territory, into the countryside around Ingelfingen, Weikersheim, and Langenburg, took several decades and reflected the loose control over the church in these areas.[35] Only in the 1580s and 1590s did counts of Hohenlohe-Langenburg and Hohenlohe-Weikersheim establish marriage courts in these areas. But by 1600 the new Protestant marriage court system was firmly in place.

---

[30] Franz, *Die Kirchenleitung in Hohenlohe*, 40–1.
[31] For a more general discussion of the visitations and their results see ibid.; Robisheaux, "Peasants and Pastors"; and Gustav Bossert, "Beiträge zur Geschichte der Reformation in Franken," *Theologische Studien aus Württemberg* 1 (1880), 173–212, 253–80, and "Die kirchlichen Zustände der Grafschaft Hohenlohe-Neuenstein im Jahr 1571," *Blätter für württembergische Kirchengeschichte* N.S. 30 (1926), 2–42.
[32] PAÖ 93/3/7, 1556.   [33] ALGAL 553/2, 1571.
[34] Franz, *Die Kirchenleitung in Hohenlohe*, 147–50.   [35] Ibid. 61–2.

The courts in this land, even when the reformation was largely completed in the 1580s, still lacked the autonomy and the power of consistories in many Protestant lands and cities. In the Protestant imperial cities, in Württemberg and Saxony, the consistories and special tribunals became permanent institutions with the sole purpose of policing the moral life of the state's subjects. But the magistrates of Hohenlohe's courts never became specialists in the business of marital discipline and moral improvement. The count of this land called his courts on an informal and ad hoc basis, and drew the judges and advisers from among his court officials and advisers and the territory's pastors; all of the magistrates, in other words, had other primary posts and sat in judgment of cases only when called to do so.[36] The courts, as a result, only occasionally launched examinations on their own initiative. They depended instead upon parish pastors, village officials, and villagers themselves to bring cases to their attention. The weaknesses of this administrative system obviously slowed the campaign to reform the family and made moral reform difficult to achieve in the 1550s and 1560s. But once the church had established a well-trained and dedicated Lutheran clergy in the parishes and the pastors began to work closely with the courts in the 1570s and 1580s, a more rigorous policing of marriage practices in the countryside got under way.[37]

Marital discipline in the village

The history of religious and moral reform in the Reformation was a complex one, however, far more complex than the look at the elites of this society has so far shown. One should therefore not look at the campaign for marital discipline in village society as one orchestrated simply from above, as a relentless campaign to suppress popular culture. The laws and the rhetoric of the reformers perhaps suggest that this was a dogmatic and harsh crusade carried out by elites against village culture. But the dynamics of social change were more complicated than this in the sixteenth century, the power of elites to refashion village culture more limited and tenuous than the sermons and church ordinances would lead one to believe. One should rather look at the progress of this moral campaign as a shift in the way in which a complex discourse about marriage and the family within the village was carried out.[38] For villagers played an important role in the process of creating marital discipline in this village

---

[36] Ibid. 30–7, 137–40.
[37] Ibid. 48–62.
[38] I have borrowed this idea from David Sabean. See his *Power in the Blood: Popular Culture and Village Discourse in Early Modern Germany* (Cambridge: Cambridge University Press, 1984).

society. Without the cooperation of certain groups in the village the reform would never have been carried very far.

This does not mean that villagers accepted marital discipline without question, that the Lutheran law appealed uniformly to all groups. Nor does it mean that all of the bearers of local culture resisted the reforms. The campaign instead played upon generational conflicts, social tensions, and rivalries already present in the village, and, because it favored some groups of villagers – the propertied elite, fathers, mothers, certain factions of kinsmen, the guardians of minor children – found a receptive foundation for reform. The campaign became, in short, inextricably intertwined with the bundle of conflicts related to the struggle for land and power within the village and the peasant family in the late sixteenth century.

The reform of marriage and the family can therefore only be understood in the context of the social conditions in the village at this time. The rise in population, the scarcity of land, the rapid spread of rural poverty, and, after 1570, the ever present threat of famine: All of these conditions meant that families survived only through carefully protecting their land and resources. The access to land and wealth, in addition, was inseparably bound up with courtship and marriage, as we have seen, and the intensified effort to reform the family only made this connection more important. The appeal of marital discipline and stronger patriarchal authority cut through all ranks in the village: It worked to the advantage of any propertyholder seeking more effective control over family land and wealth. But the appeal seems to have been particularly strong for the village elite: Family elders could arrange their children's marriage alliances more easily, terminate any unwanted secret marriages, and thereby tighten the controls on access to family property. Patriarchy, Protestantism, and the control of wealth and property were all inseparable from one another in a land like Hohenlohe.

The records of the marriage court therefore cast light on a timeless social problem: the tensions between family elders and village youths, parents and children, the propertied and the propertyless. These tensions ran deep in the late sixteenth century, for elders and youths were often at odds over courtship, marriage, and inheritance. Peasant elders apparently shared with Lutheran pastors the belief that young people required careful supervision and social controls. Whenever the watch was slackened, so ran the lament of a number of parents before the marriage court, youths would take advantage of the opportunity to find secret lovers or spouses. Young men and women from all social strata worked together as servants or laborers in the households of tenant farmers, after all, and they mingled freely. The head of a household was supposed to supervise his young workers and servants carefully, "to protect them and shelter them," as one village father put it, but the close living quarters still afforded numerous chances for young people to engage in illicit sex and courtship.[39] Lienhard Dietz's daughter, for example, served as a maid in the prosperous household of a Künzelsau miller in the 1550s. When the miller's son clandestinely asked for her hand in marriage, she slept with him, assuming that they were now married, and then bore him a child out of wedlock.[40] A pastor told this story about a young woman to the court:

She went to serve at a tenant farmer's household and not long after that a number of soldiers found shelter there. With these men she drank the entire day and night and went by night to Regensbach. On the third day, a soldier came by and asked for this whore's brother and kinsmen and what they then talked about no one in the village knows, because no farmers were home except for her relative, Simon. He would have nothing to do with them. And with that the maid packed together her clothes and ran off with the soldier.[41]

Masterless children and women: These were the threats to a patriarchal family order.

The social contacts between the sexes, which seemed so uncontrolled, undisciplined, and threatening to some villagers, were an integral part of the youth culture of this period. The documents do not reveal much about these relationships, and so one can only speculate about their meaning in the context of youth culture as a whole in the sixteenth century. Yet clearly village youths sought opportunities to escape the immediate authority of their elders and to strike up love affairs and courtships on their own. Wedding celebrations, dances, festivals, and markets: All of these were occasions for courtship and love. One official reported that Hans Streckfus's courtship of Ursula Schneider of Ingelfingen began in 1579 when he asked her to dance with him at a festival. She understood the risks she ran if she allowed him to propose secretly to her, however, so she put him off with the argument that "I could not take any man without my mother's knowledge and consent or I would bring a curse down on her house."[42] Hans Götz of Unterregenbach, on the other hand, struck up an illicit courtship with Appolonia Köhler at a wedding.[43] The occasion of a wedding drew youths from the surrounding area to a village, and they filled the streets and taverns, drinking, shouting, playing games, and singing bawdy songs. Then, "at night," as one pastor observed, "young servants get together in barns and other places without regard for male or female sex."[44] Try as one might, no amount of state supervision and control, no amount of church oversight and discipline, could ever suppress this youth culture.

But the state and church could discipline individuals by helping to break up

[39] ALGAL 649/55, [1615].   [40] ALGAL 617/2, November 27, 1560.
[41] ALGAL 630/12, December 1583.   [42] ALGAL 626/2, 1579.
[43] ALGAL 637/58, September 4, 1596.   [44] ALKI 56/6, December 27, 1680.

Table 4.1. *Marriage court cases in Hohenlohe-Langenburg, 1550-1680*

Offense	No. of cases	%
Engagement	110	44.7
Sexual offense	56	22.8
Divorce	30	12.2
Miscellaneous disputes	20	8.1
Adultery	17	6.9
Marriage within third degree of kinship	13	5.3
Total	246	100.0

Sources: ALGAL 616, 1550, to 712, 1680.

illicit and, from the standpoint of parents, unwanted alliances. For the marriage courts, once in place, worked tirelessly in terminating the illicit engagements brought to their attention. An analysis of 246 cases from the court of Hohenlohe-Langenburg between 1550 and 1680 illustrates just how consistently the courts supported parents who wished to control the courtship and engagement of their children (see Table 4.1). The magistrates of this court concentrated their attention on punishing youths for contracting secret engagements or for engaging in illicit sexual relationships. In this sample of cases, the judges examined 110 cases of contested engagements – 45 percent of the total – and they terminated all of those relationships in which youths did not have the explicit permission of their parents to marry. The cases involving premarital sex should also be reckoned as part of this campaign. In 56 of these cases (23 percent of the total) magistrates punished youths for engaging in premarital sex: The offending youths were sent off to prison for a week or two before being returned to the authority of their parents. The courts considered other types of disputes that involved violations of the Marriage Law of 1572: divorce, adultery, marriages within the third degree of kinship, and other miscellaneous marital conflicts. From a statistical point of view, however, these offenses were never as important as the cases involving the marital discipline of youths.

The heads of village families and guardians played the most prominent and aggressive role in bringing these contested engagements to the attention of the magistrates. In 80 of the 110 cases of contested engagements one can determine who initiated the investigation by the magistrates. In 39 cases (49 percent) parents or guardians were the ones who pressed the court to investigate an illicit engagement (see Table 4.2). The goals of these inquiries, whatever the details of the story the complainants told the magistrates, were all closely

Table 4.2. *Groups initiating marriage court cases in Hohenlohe-Langenburg, 1550-1679*

Initiated by	No. of cases	%
Village parents	39	48.7
Youths	23	28.8
Pastors and officials	18	22.5
Total	80	100.0

Sources: ALGAL 616, 1550, to 712, 1679.

interrelated: the breaking up of an illicit relationship, the enforcement of the authority of the parents over the family's marriage alliances. Every child, one father told the court, "must seek the parent's consent beforehand because, if one or another of his own children contract a marriage on his own, he would give them neither a *heller* nor a penny for their dowries for the rest of this life."[45] Others expressed similar sentiments.

Old notions died slowly in the sixteenth century, however, and one finds evidence in these records of some youths fighting to maintain an older, or at least different, idea of marriage and engagement. Many youths continued to believe that an oral promise, sometimes given without their parents' consent or simply implying their consent, constituted a binding engagement. Their parents may not have liked the match, they may even have opposed it, but the words spoken in private, the words that promised a future marriage, still carried a binding force for these young people. All of the sermons and the visitations of the Reformation, the dire threats read from the pulpits, and the renewals of police laws from the chancellery never seem to have made much of an impact on the young people who put forward such ideas before the court. Almost all of the twenty-three youths who brought their own cases before the new Lutheran marriage courts, in fact, tried to have vows spoken in private recognized as a binding marriage. Young women in particular often put forward this argument in their own defense. The conflict between the two notions of marriage was an unequal one, however, even though the old conception lingered well into the seventeenth century. For all a parent had to do was testify that he or she opposed the match and the magistrates declared the bond illicit, the liaison terminated.

Parish pastors also began to keep a watchful eye on young people and the relationships they struck up with each other. The church ordinances and the Marriage Law of 1572 admonished pastors to carry out this oversight. So pastors

---

[45] ALGAL 659/32, March 8, 1636.

carried out their own investigations, asking questions around the parish, requesting the parents of a couple who were to wed to stop by the parsonage for
a quiet talk. The web of gossip reached everywhere in the village; it was thick
and rich, and a good pastor knew how to tap into it. They also denounced
individuals to the court who seemed, in their view, to act suspiciously. Lutheran
pastors and village officials brought eighteen such cases to the attention of the
magistrates in the sample from Hohenlohe-Langenburg. Wolfgang Schott, a
vigilant pastor from Unterregenbach, reported in 1583 that Hans Hershl and
Anna Legir had appeared before him to announce their engagement. Suspicious
of their intentions, Schott explained to the court that he

questioned Anna as to why her father had not come along and whether he too consented.
She replied that her father did not help her and that he therefore did not question
anything she did. I was not satisfied with such an answer, but demanded her father's
consent.[46]

Hans and Anna, their plans shattered, left the pastor's house and never returned.
How often pastors put an end to such relationships informally, invoking the
authority of the Marriage Law, one cannot know. But power did not have to
be exercised repeatedly to be effective. The quiet threat of an inquiry certainly
chilled more than a few courtships.

The campaign to introduce a stricter marital discipline took time to achieve
results. In the cities, magistrates perhaps achieved results comparatively quickly
and effectively; they had, after all, highly developed institutions of government
and social control at their disposal. But in a small state like the County of
Hohenlohe marital discipline took much longer to establish. The crusade began
to reach its peak of activity only in the 1580s and 1590s. A comparatively weak
church administration, delays in introducing a trained parish clergy, and the
resistance of villagers to the early reformation perhaps account for the relatively
few cases that came to the attention of the judges from Hohenlohe-Langenburg
in the 1550s and 1560s (see Graph 4.1). But these problems were overcome
by the 1580s and 1590s, and the zealous Protestant ruler, Count Wolfgang,
pushed ahead with the campaign for moral discipline more effectively than any
of his predecessors. The religious zeal of this ruler, however, cannot alone
explain the steady increase in the number of cases that came before the marriage
courts. For reform still depended upon the efforts of villagers. Population
pressure, the threat of famine, and severe shortages of land appear to have led
many village elders to intensify their efforts to manage their children's marriages
with caution. The courts kept up a relatively high level of activity through the
1620s. Only then, as the apparatus of the state began to collapse during the
Thirty Years' War, did the campaign slacken.

[46] ALGAL 630/4, 1583.

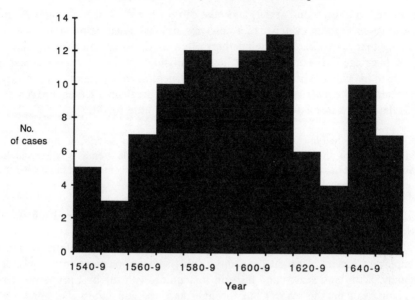

Graph 4.1. Contested engagements before the marriage court, Hohenlohe-Langenburg, 1550–1659. *Source:* ALGAL 616–712.

The campaign to break up secret engagements carried important social consequences for a society increasingly divided between wealthy and poor, the propertied and the propertyless. Parents from all social strata improved their control over the marriages of their children, but wealthy tenant farmers benefited most of all from the power and authority to control children's marriages. They could now arrange marriage alliances with more care, certainty, and control, and with much less worry about entanglements that damaged the family's status and honor or that brought unwanted claims to the patrimony.

Alliances with the tenant-farmer families were the most desirable in rural Hohenlohe, and villagers often tried to secure a match with a tenant farmer, a miller, or a wealthy widow. Some of these courtships seem to have been hopeless gambles, others desperate and bold ventures, still others carefully thought-through plots. But they all had one aim: to secure claim to a farm or a handsome set of properties. A marriage to old Jopp Breuninger of Kupferhof, one tenant farmer well known for his wealth, was to have been the prize in one such affair in 1615. Caspar Schumann's daughter apparently worked for him as one of his servants, and, when she and her father tried to ensnarl him in an unwanted marriage alliance, Breuninger presented his case to the marriage court. Schumann, for his part, demanded that Breuninger "marry my daughter, lead her to church and street, and take care of her."[47] But the judges of the court discovered no evidence of a valid vow and dismissed Schumann's claims, noting that poor girls and their fathers often tried to trap "wealthy peasants" into marriage.[48] Breuninger went home, still single and free to seek a match more to his liking. Michel Schneider from Brüchlingen, another tenant farmer, appealed to the marriage court in a similar way to break up a secret engagement his daughter had made with a man who had too little wealth:

I knew that he had lousy prospects.... Consider that he had no craft or other work to look forward to, that he could support neither a wife nor children as a father should, but rather that he would soon no longer be able to make ends meet and must need the help of other people.[49]

The court terminated the liaison. Each such broken tie hardened the social barriers between the tenant farmers and the village poor.

The courts, in short, offered the chance to control more carefully the most important means of upward mobility in this society: marriage into a wealthy family. With land scarce and difficult to acquire, with the best properties circulating not on the market but through marriage and inheritance, only one possible path for upward mobility lay open for many young people: making a favorable match. But now the marriage courts blocked that path, not always, of course, but enough to emphasize the social distance that separated families in the village. When Leonhard Scheuermann, a day laborer, tried to snare his employer, the wealthy widow, Ottila Keeser, his effort failed miserably. Scheuermann approached the widow Keeser with all the guile ascribed to suitors of widows in the sixteenth century. One evening, while they were drinking at a tavern and complaining to each other about their family problems, Scheuermann made his move. "[He] gave me his hand," she later said before the marriage court, "and now wants to force me to marry him, putting on as if I accepted him." She made it clear to the magistrates, however, that she "never, at no time, thought of marriage, and her or anyone else would not be able to say so in truth."[50] The court, as a result, ruled the liaison illegal and not binding.

One can see in these cases how wealthy tenant farmers defended their social position and property and kept their hands free to seek out alliances that fit into their families' strategies better. The young suitor Michael Würzberger, a man of modest means but immodest ambitions, hoped that he could bluff his way into a favorable match. But he approached his quarry in a more direct way than Scheuermann did, honoring the formalities of an openly negotiated marriage. The details of his courtship of Wendelbar Bauer, the daughter of the

[47] ALGAL 649/55, [1615].   [48] ALGAL 649/61, [1615].
[49] ALGAL 652/61, December 10, 1626.   [50] ALGAL 650/57, April 2, 1619.

tenant farmer Peter Bauer, have not been preserved. But he seems to have made such a good impression that he was able to begin marriage negotiations with her father one evening in a tavern in Langenburg. The bargaining collapsed, much to the embarrassment of the old man, when he finally discovered that Würzberger "could not support her with either money or property."[51] The angry father, the honor of his daughter and family at stake, swiftly brought a complaint against the young man so that the liaison between him and his daughter could be officially annulled. When asked why he had tried to bargain for Wendelbar Bauer's hand in marriage, the young man lamely replied that he had had too much to drink that night, that he could not freely contract a marriage without his parents' permission. "They sent me out to learn a trade," he said, "and if I let myself get married without their permission they would renounce me as their child, not to mention the fact that they would not help me out or advise me."[52]

The history of these failed courtships and broken social ties points to the way in which marital discipline became a mechanism for maintaining the social hierarchy, for defending property and family honor. The cases discussed above show villagers keenly aware of the hierarchy of wealth in the village and their place in it. But some who came before the court never brought up worries about property when discussing their cases. The dispute involved other, intangible qualities: honor and shame. After Bartel Schmied of Unterregenbach became engaged to Ursula Ehrmann, for example, he felt publicly disgraced when she ran away to Waldenburg with another man. With his father at his side, the young man requested the magistrates to terminate his engagement because "she deceived me and ran away with a wicked boy without my knowledge or my father's."[53] Ursula Ehrmann also brought shame on her own family, and her stepfather appeared before the court to condemn her and her behavior. "My daughter let herself be misled by her bad, ill-tempered spirit," he said, "moved away and wanted to place herself in service elsewhere."[54] The judges not only sent her to prison, ordering her to be fed a wretched diet of bread and water, they also banished her from the territory.[55]

Honor resided in the individual in this village society. But that fund of honor could change, darken, and turn to shame. When that happened, the disgraced individual pulled his whole family – in some extreme cases, his whole community – after him into ill repute. Women in particular carried the honor of the family in their person, and an obedient, pious, and morally pure woman – the ideal in this patriarchal society – became a symbol of family honor in the village. A woman who became disobedient and undisciplined could therefore threaten the honor of the family and the community. Village women sometimes

[51] ALGAL 652/33, August 5, 1622.   [52] ALGAL 652/35, August 28, 1622.
[53] ALGAL 630/23, [1586?].   [54] ALGAL 630/24, [1586?].   [55] ALGAL 630/25, February 23, 1588.

turned out in groups in Hohenlohe to abuse and taunt a woman suspected of dishonorable behavior with men. They worked much like a female charivari: They reinforced patriarchal values and marital discipline.[56] Once they became outraged by some disreputable act, they took their case to the streets and publicly humiliated the woman for all to see. Poor Ursula Schreiner, one such woman accused of moral indiscretions in Ingelfingen in 1629, found herself besieged by the women of the town, "who did all kinds of bad things, shouted almost the entire day at her, and made her to suffer." The crowd suspected that she had slept not just with one man but with others, and they wanted to know how far the dishonor had spread in the community. And, when they received no answer from her, they went to the pastor to badger him for answers to their questions.[57] Such a crowd not only shamed a woman, it pointed up the disgraceful behavior of men as well.

The protection of family honor during courtship could become a worrisome business for many families, even very respectable families, once the standards of Protestant marital discipline took hold. For tensions remained between the demands of the law and the quietly sanctioned practices of local custom. The authorities required that couples carry out their courtship and engagement publicly, not secretly, and that they should abstain rigorously from sexual intercourse until they were properly married. But this latter requirement of the new marital discipline, the repression of sexuality, could never be fully enforced. Local custom, in fact, continued to sanction sex before the public wedding.[58] This practice was known as *Fenstern* in Franconia: the right of the young man to slip into the window of his betrothed under cover of darkness and there spend the night. In the intervening time, however, before the couple publicly solemnized their vows, their parents could still deny them permission to marry. Parents could take the couple to court and state that they disapproved of the match, and the union would be terminated. When this happened, the young woman often bore the brunt of this scandal, for by that time she might very well have become pregnant.

[56] For a discussion of charivari see Natalie Zemon Davis, "The Reasons of Misrule," in her *Society and Culture in Early Modern France* (Stanford: Stanford University Press, 1965), 97–123; E. P. Thompson, " 'Rough Music': Le charivari anglais," *Annales E.S.C.* 27 (1972), 285–312; Roland Bonnain-Moerdyk and Donald Moerdyk, "A propos du charivari: discours bourgeois et coutumes populaires," *Annales E.S.C.* 32 (1977), 381–98; André Burguiere, "The Charivari and Religious Expression in France during the Ancien Régime," in Robert Wheaton and Tamara K. Hareven, eds., *The Family and Sexuality in French History* (Philadelphia: University of Pennsylvania Press, 1980), 84–100; and Martin Ingram, "Ridings, Rough Music and the 'Reform of Popular Culture' in Early Modern England," *Past and Present* no. 105 (1984), 79–113.
[57] ALGAL 652/39, January 10, 1629.
[58] See Karl-Sigismund Kramer, *Volksleben im Fürstentum Ansbach und seinen Nachbargebieten (1500–1800): Eine Volkskunde auf Grund archivalischer Quellen*, Veröffentlichungen der Gesellschaft für fränkische Geschichte, ser. 9, vol. 15 (Würzburg: Kommissionsverlag Ferdinand Schöningh, 1961), 221–3.

How often young women fell into shame and disgrace in this manner one cannot determine. The numbers were perhaps less important than the way in which these scandals were used to teach the lessons of marital discipline. For Lutheran pastors and village gossips held up these cases as warnings for the whole community; scandalous stories drove home to young people the importance of obedience, honor, and piety. The courtship of poor Margarethe Volker became the stuff of one such scandal in Hohenlohe. When her suitor, the son of a local tenant farmer, began to make nightly visits to her room, she feared for her honor. She knew that she could never marry him. She told him "to leave her in peace," she later told the court, "because I am poor, have no bed or anything else to offer, and that, even if he wanted to marry me, his parents and brothers and sisters would never consent to it." But he charmed her anyway, she explained, saying "that he wished the devil would take him if he slept with a girl and did not honor her with marriage." He told her that she "was rich and beautiful enough for him and he, not his parents, would have to live with me." She eventually consented and slept with him. Whether his flattery had weakened her or whether he actually raped her one will never know. When she became pregnant, she tried to make him marry her, and she pleaded her cause desperately before the court. But the court rebuffed her pleas and broke the bond.[59] She and her family were disgraced.

The tight controls on courtship and marriage contributed to a slow rise in the average age at first marriage. Before 1560 and 1570, young men and women may have been able to defy their parents' wishes, marry, clear some new land on the edge of the village, and begin a new household. At that time the courts functioned imperfectly, the laws being difficult to enforce. By the seventeenth century an early escape from the patriarchal authority of the family was much harder. Young men, as a result, often postponed marriage until they were older and more established and could count on the support of their families. Men from Langenburg parish first married at a median age of 24.0 years between 1610 and 1619, but between 1680 and 1689 they married at 26.2 years. Women, however, continued to marry at about the same age, 24, throughout the seventeenth century.[60] The increase in the median age at first marriage for men conformed to the general trend toward later marriages throughout western Europe. In seventeenth-century France peasant men married at 27 and women at 25, an increase from the average age of 21 to 22 in the late sixteenth century.[61] In England, the median age at first marriage for men rose from 25.8 between 1560 and 1646 to 26.4 between 1647 and 1719. The median age for women

[59] ALGAL 638/30, December 30, 1608.   [60] Robisheaux, "Peasants and Pastors," 297.

[61] André Burguiere, "De Malthus à Marx: le mariage tardif et l'esprit d'entreprise," *Annales E.S.C.* 27 (1972), 1133; Jean-Louis Flandrin, "Mariage tardif et vie sexuelle: discussions et hypothèses de recherches," *Annales E.S.C.* 27 (1972), 1351–78.

increased from 25.9 to 27.5 in this same period.[62] The new patriarchy, in short, was fully established.

Rites of passage

These social changes can be more clearly grasped by examining the new significance attached to the rituals of betrothal and marriage in the sixteenth century. Once a private family affair, betrothal and marriage became a public ritual, carefully watched and supervised by the state and the church. Like any rite of passage, the rituals, in their mature form, performed a distinctive social function for the whole community: They separated a couple from their siblings and peers; prepared them, their kinsmen, and the whole community for an improvement in their status; and then incorporated them into the new web of kinship and property relationships that came with marriage.[63] In the context of the social changes of the sixteenth century the meaning of these rituals was unmistakable: This became the public rite of passage into the ranks of propertyholding villagers.

Before the sixteenth century one cannot speak of marriage as a public ritual. In late medieval society a betrothal and the blessing of the marriage never were clearly linked up in one ritual process. The church did not everywhere require that couples appear before a priest to receive a blessing. So villagers always attached more significance to the betrothal. In this ritual, the parents and other family members negotiated the property arrangements for the marriage and then sealed the agreement as an alliance of two families.[64] The custom continued, with many regional variations, into the sixteenth century. The promise of marriage itself reflected the importance of the betrothal as an affair of the whole family. As Luther noted, villagers recognized vows as binding only when spoken with the consent of the parents or guardians. "I want to have you if you bring a dowry of a hundred *gulden*," a lad might have said. Or he could have made this promise: "I want you if your parents and mine want it." Villagers paid careful attention to the precise words spoken, as the cases from Hohenlohe suggest, and became suspicious of ambiguous promises, such as "I want you" or "I want to take you."[65] The negotiations at the time of the betrothal itself

[62] E. A. Wrigley, "Family Limitation in Pre-Industrial England," *Economic History Review* 2d ser. 19 (1966), 86.
[63] See Arnold van Gennep, *The Rites of Passage*, trans. Monika V. Vizedom and Gabrielle L. Caffee (Chicago: University of Chicago Press, 1960).
[64] Emile Friedburg, *Das Recht der Eheschliessung in seiner geschichtlichen Entwicklung* (Leipzig: Bernhard Tauchnitz, 1865), 21–5, 79, 93; Ingeborg Schwartz, *Die Bedeutung der Sippe für die Öffentlichkeit der Eheschliessung im 15. und 16. Jahrhundert*, Schriften zur Kirchen- und Rechtsgeschichte, vol. 13 (Tübingen: Ekkehart Fabian, 1959).
[65] Luther, "Von Ehesachen," 211–12.

invoked frank talk about wealth, money, debts, financial obligations, the precise property arrangements of the marriage. One tenant farmer, explaining his daughter's betrothal, summarized these negotiations in this way: "I asked whether he [the groom] could match the dowry and he replied, yes, he would gladly do so . . . and we gave each other our hands on the marriage."[66]

Visible symbols and ritualized gestures sealed the new alliance. The practices in Hohenlohe involved two separate symbolic exchanges, a private one between the bride and groom and a public one involving the families. When a young man had spoken the proper words of betrothal and they were accepted, he then offered his bride a penny or other coin. This practice continued an old custom from the Middle Ages, and some argue that it once symbolized the purchase of the bride. But in this sixteenth-century context, the meaning was more simple and direct: The coin symbolized the existence of a personal union and the property commitments that underlay the match. Later, the male relatives of the bride and groom gathered for a festive evening or day in the village tavern. Here they celebrated the match, and cemented the family alliance, with the drinking of wine, a rite called the *Weinkauf* in this part of Franconia. From this moment on, the match was a licit marriage. The parish pastor still had to read the banns three weeks in a row, but the bond could now be broken only by recourse to the marriage court.

Before the Reformation the celebration would have ended at this point, the marriage now complete. But the Lutheran church required a public wedding to complete the marriage, and so the ritual process was extended, made public and subject to the controls of the state-run church. By no means did this mean the suppression of popular customs in this part of the ritual process. Peasant custom mixed freely at this stage with Lutheran ceremoniousness, license with religious discipline, gaiety and frivolity with stern piety. The pastors and state authorities rarely approved of the way in which the typical three-day marriage ritual unfolded in rural Hohenlohe. But they could not always give the cele-brations the godly seriousness and restraint called for in the Marriage Law and the police ordinances. The families of the bride and groom, for example, felt the need to cement the property ties and kinship bonds with lavish gift giving and feasts. They gathered on the first day, usually a Saturday, sharing meals and exchanging gifts to symbolize their commitment to the couple and to each other. The Marriage Law required that the feasts and gift giving be kept within bounds. A couple with a joint conjugal fund of 100 fl. were allowed only two tables for their feasts, couples with 100–200 fl., four tables, and those with more than 200 fl., six tables.[67] But villagers rarely held to these limits. A wedding was,

[66] ALGAL 652/33, August 5, 1622.   [67] Franz, ed., *Grafschaft Hohenlohe*, 290–1.

after all, a demonstration of social status and wealth, and many celebrated these occasions with what the authorities considered excessive spending for food, drink, and entertainment.

The church dominated the festivities of the second day, however, for on this day the couple and the wedding party solemnized their union with the wedding ceremony. The law required that the ceremony occur punctually at ten o'clock in the morning. But the celebrants were not always on time, and some arrived at the church boisterous and disorderly from the "morning soup."[68] But once the ceremony came to an end, the families again took control of the occasion: They held a feast that began at noon and lasted well into the evening. While the couple then disappeared to consummate the marriage, the wedding dance took place. Pastors disapproved of these long festivities on Sunday afternoons and evenings, the expense, and the disorderliness, but all they could do was to encourage the secular authorities to police them and discipline the "excesses."[69] Still, by the seventeenth century no pastors reported that marriages took place without a wedding ceremony in the church. What was once a separate rite, infrequently performed, had become part of one ritual process.

The festivities, however, had not yet come to a close. One day remained, and the celebrations on this day revealed another dimension of the ritual process: social criticism, mockery, and play. A ritual as involved and lengthy as this involved a clear rhythm: Periods of extreme control and discipline gave way at certain times to license, play, and frivolity. The feasts and dancing that followed the church ceremony already point to this pattern. These activities perhaps involved jokes and lighthearted criticism, but, up to the third day, one finds little evidence of any explosive release of youthful mischief or open mockery of the social values and the religious discipline implicit in the ritual process from the first day.[70] That took place on the third day in a Hohenlohe wedding celebration. On this day the controls and the discipline fell away. On this day room was made for all of the stressful and ambiguous attitudes, all of the sharp and bitter-edged emotions, that a marriage could call forth in this rural society.

Youths, those most affected by the new marital discipline, dominated the scene. They filled the streets and the taverns. One cannot reconstruct all of the activities that took place on this day, but they seem to have been of three types. Some youths pulled pranks on the members of the wedding party and poked fun at the institution of marriage itself. "All kinds of deviltry and frivolity are practiced by young people on the wedding guests in which the wedding

[68] ALKI 56/8, December 20, 1680.
[69] ALKI 56/6.5, December 17, 1680; 56/9, December 19, 1680.
[70] For one anthropologist's analysis of the implicit structure of the ritual process see Victor Turner, *The Ritual Process: Structure and Anti-Structure* (Chicago: Aldine Press, 1969), and "Passages, Margins, and Poverty: Religious Symbols of Communitas," in his *Dramas, Fields, and Metaphors: Symbolic Action in Human Society* (Ithaca, N.Y.: Cornell University Press, 1974), 231–74.

day and holy matrimony are not honored, but scorned and desecrated," one pastor observed.[71] Others made fun of the church and the wedding ceremony itself. They ridiculed the Lutheran wedding ceremony by "singing holy songs and, because these people were already drunk, either made the songs crazy or derided them."[72] In mockery of the disciplined and restrained ritual behavior demanded by the church, village youths took to the streets, drinking, dancing, and "making all kinds of wickedness," as another pastor described the occasion in his village. Finally, in flagrant violation of the church's admonishments, "young people, both men and women, get together in a barn or somewhere else" to play games, sing bawdy songs, and "hold secret dances."[73] One Lutheran pastor thought these youthful activities fully as raucous and sacrilegious as a Catholic carnival.[74] For many youths these activities amounted to no more than a day of fun and relief from the seriousness of the occasion. But the activities gave vent to social criticism as well, and youths openly ridiculed the values of marital discipline, hierarchy, and social control on this day.

Over the course of many years these rites probably reinforced these very values. For the rites gave village youths a chance to learn the meaning of these values even if it was only to poke fun at them, ridicule them, and turn them upside down by singing a bawdy song or by playing a prank. But if this were the case, the point was lost on the local authorities. The counts of Hohenlohe and their pastors continued to regard dances and unsupervised festivals as a disruption of the everyday order and godliness they wished to preserve. Count Philip Ernst repeatedly banned *all* dances, first in 1586, then again in 1588 and 1592. He did this for a simple reason: to suppress "all disorder, unseemly leaping, turning, throwing around, shouting, and other lewdness, to defend good moral order."[75] In 1592 he expressed his goal more directly: These measures were to make "youths into honorable family members."[76] The pastors of Öhringen also linked the suppression of dances with "the preservation of marital piety."[77] As one pastor complained, echoing the complaints of the first visitors to Hohenlohe's parishes, youths had too many opportunities to fall into "unseemly love." He wanted all dances to end at six o'clock in the evening "so that girls and boys end at the right time of the day and go home again to their masters, lords, and mistresses."[78]

Despite admonitions, the everyday stuff of government decrees in this period, the transformation of the rituals of betrothal and marriage was complete by the early seventeenth century. The two rituals had become part of a single ritual

[71] ALKI 56/12, January 5, 1681.
[72] ALKI 56/6.5, December 17, 1680.
[73] ALKI 56/6, December 27, 1680.   [74] ALKI 56/6.5, December 17, 1680.
[75] Franz, ed., *Grafschaft Hohenlohe*, 521–2, 578–88.   [76] ALGAL 1/20, 1592.
[77] ALGAL 578/5, [1624].   [78] ALGAL 578/1, [1624].

process, a public rite of passage, charged with intense religious, social, and emotional meaning in this rural society. The whole celebration, from beginning to end, was no quaint holdover from the medieval past. Whatever fragments the rituals incorporated from the village culture of the late Middle Ages were now transformed, set into a new social context, given a meaning and purpose they never had before. The early modern rituals of marriage were very much a product of the search for order in the sixteenth century. They were meant to *create* order, to *impose* social discipline in a world many saw as unstable and in flux. That they also lifted a couple out of their familiar milieu as youthful dependents and settled them, with lavish displays of good will and wealth, into a world of propertyholders was also no accident. For only a minority of youths in a land like Hohenlohe ever made that transition. For all of these reasons the rituals became the most visible expression of the everyday social order in the village, and of many of its cracks, fissures, and tensions as well.

5

~~~~~~

Defending the patrimony

If we look back over the campaign to reform the family in the sixteenth century, this basic process was at work: The religious and moral ideals of the family were slowly made to fit the social conditions in the countryside. In the late Middle Ages, many laymen considered the church's ideals of marriage and the family to be a threat to social order, corrosive of marital discipline and morals in the society as a whole. With the Reformation, that began to change. The order that came to family life by the early seventeenth century – the firm rule of peasant elders over village youths – came about once the church and state embraced the ideal of the patriarchal family and then imposed, with the cooperation and help of village elders, as strict a marital discipline as the society would bear. Without this alliance, without solid social support for the patriarchal family in the countryside, any new marital discipline would have been difficult to establish.

A similar pattern is evident when we turn to a second, but equally important, aspect of family reform: the effort to grasp the patriarchal family as a set of property relationships. For the state this effort marked a departure from past practice. It grew out of the state's new pastoral mission and its rapidly rising fiscal needs in the middle of the sixteenth century. By the early seventeenth century, when new cadastres were complete, no longer was the village as a corporate unit quite so central to property relationships as it once had been. The peasant household, its property carefully surveyed and inventoried, had begun to replace it. Within the village this emphasis on the family and the household as the center of all property relationships was not entirely new. For villagers understood property as so bound up with family relationships, so inseparable from blood and affinal ties, that they readily used terms about property as metaphors for social relations. "As the old saying goes," one experienced district official said, commenting on popular marriage practices in Hohenlohe, "when two single youths marry each other, they put property and blood together."[1] When villagers fell into disputes over family rela-

---

[1] A district official from Kirchberg recorded this saying in 1707, but it had no doubt been in popular use for a long time before the eighteenth century. ALKI 33/22, May 16, 1707.

tionships, they were not simply arguing about the proper place of youths in the village. They were also mapping out property relationships and struggling for power over family patrimonies. Any movement supporting marital discipline would therefore inevitably spill over into efforts to control peasant property and inheritance as well.

The state's effort to grasp the peasant family as a set of property relationships established a solid community of interest between the princes and village propertyholders. Both princes and peasants sought to preserve peasant property in the sixteenth century, the one in order to establish the fiscal foundations for the state, the other in order to conserve family wealth and property as land became scarce. The relationship, however, was never free of conflict. And the degree of state management of peasant property and inheritance varied from land to land. But everywhere the social effects tended to be the same: The boundaries between the propertied and the propertyless, between the wealthy peasant elite and the village poor, tended to harden. What became the foundations of the agrarian order – what confirmed the domination of the prince over the village and helped reproduce the social hierarchy within it – was therefore this: broader social control over women, youths, and property.

Nowhere was this trend more evident than in Hohenlohe. The drive to bolster the patriarchal family in this land came to hinge not simply on marital discipline, but on the practice of impartible inheritance. We have already noted the consequences for village society as a whole by 1580: Tenant farmers, millers, tavernkeepers, and a handful of petty merchants and wealthy artisans became the masters of village property and society. But the practice had similar social effects within the family as well. Whenever a propertyholder – a male head of the household, a widow, a young heir – triumphed in a dispute over the patrimony, he played out, on a small scale, the social drama taking place in the society as a whole in the sixteenth century. For only a fortunate few, the victors in the desperate struggle for property, were allowed to enter the ranks of the village elite, with all the land, movable wealth, favorable marriage prospects, and control over the patrimony that came with it. Those youths and women who lost these contests paid dear. Unless they could recoup their fortunes with a favorable marriage alliance, unless they could establish themselves in a new household or trade with a portion of the patrimony, they faced bleak prospects as smallholders, artisans, and laborers.

The state and peasant property

Only gradually did German princes acquire the power to police the complicated transactions by which peasants passed on property from one generation to the next. And by no means did this transition come about easily or smoothly. If we look at the problem over two centuries, between 1500 and 1700, we can discern at least three waves of reform, three periods in which the state struggled to extend its power to regulate the property relationships at the center of the peasant family: the first efforts around 1500, often weak and ineffective; a second wave of reform beginning in the second or third quarter of the century; and, finally, a renewal or, in some small states, a final bureaucratization of family property relationships beginning around 1640 or 1650.[2] Each of these waves of reform was accompanied by setbacks, the state's power over peasant property relationships not becoming fully secure until the middle of the seventeenth century. In the large territorial states, in Austria, Bavaria, Saxony, and Württemberg, state intervention to shape village property relationships went farther and rested on secure foundations earlier than was possible in the small German patrimonial states. In Hohenlohe, for example, the reform of the late sixteenth century met with only partial success. More lasting and thorough state controls would come about only in the wake of the Thirty Years' War.

One of the striking features of the agrarian order in 1500, as we have already noted, was the extensive control villagers had over the disposition of land and property. Almost everywhere in the German West heritable land tenure had become firmly, irrevocably established as the cornerstone of lord–peasant relationships. Here and there a few princes sought to bring order to the local customs governing inheritance. Some introduced written law codes; others attempted to intervene more systematically in local disputes. But two obstacles stood in the way. The princes, for one, had only a limited ability to dominate the internal affairs of the village. Few of them could impose a uniform code of laws and set aside well-established customs of inheritance or even challenge the authority of village and local courts to rule on property disputes.[3] Church authorities, for another, also stood in the way. The ecclesiastical courts still exercised authority over marriage and family conflicts. Both of these checks on state power were at work in Hohenlohe in the late fifteenth century. In 1498 Count Kraft VI condemned the local practice of cheating children out of their share of the family patrimony. But there his intervention seemed to stop. In the decree he showed no understanding of local customs – the one-third–two-thirds rule, the key to this land's inheritance practices, was not even mentioned – and he proposed no method to intervene rigorously in disputes on a

---

[2] In Upper Austria the state seems to have acquired considerable authority over property relationships by the end of the sixteenth century. Elsewhere, in the smaller states of the empire, the final consolidation of the state's power over property tended to come later, often not until the end of the Thirty Years' War. See Hermann Rebel, *Peasant Classes: The Bureaucratization of Property and Family Relations Under Early Habsburg Absolutism, 1511–1636* (Princeton, N.J.: Princeton University Press, 1983).

[3] Rolf-Dieter Hess, *Familien- und Erbrecht im württembergischen Landrecht von 1555 unter besonderer Berücksichtigung des älteren württembergischen Rechts*, Veröffentlichungen der Kommission für geschichtliche Landeskunde in Baden-Württemberg, ser. B, vol. 44 (Stuttgart: W. Kohlhammer, 1968), 4–14.

regular basis.[4] And the count could also enforce the decree in only a few towns, Öhringen, Neuenstein, and Ingelfingen, all of them centers of princely power.

The state's drive to make the devolution of property an orderly, more publicly scrutinized, process therefore tended to come later in the sixteenth century. The more settled political and religious climate in the empire after 1552 seems to have been an essential precondition for this development. Protestant princes, their authority over family and marriage law finally secured by the Peace of Augsburg, could then reform marriage laws and the closely related laws governing inheritance and family property as well.[5] Another major obstacle – the ecclesiastical courts – also fell once the Protestant reformation was introduced in a territory. Once ecclesiastical authorities no longer obstructed state power at the local level, state courts could begin to expand their jurisdiction over property disputes. The fiscal demands of the empire and the territorial state also began to increase in the middle of the century, and drove state officials to draw up detailed cadastres of village and household property in the 1560s, 1570s, and 1580s. These initiatives on the part of the state also came as population growth in the countryside reached new peaks, as famines began to occur with disturbing frequency, and as conflict over scarce land intensified. For all these reasons any dispute over a family's patrimony was now much more likely to become a vital matter of state, village, and family concern.

Hohenlohe is instructive in this regard, for it shows how the drive for marital discipline soon spilled over into efforts to police the family's property relationships. The interest of Protestant reformers in village property relationships did not come from any deep or profound understanding of local inheritance customs. Ignorance and misunderstandings about local customs, in fact, were more the rule in the early years of reform. The reformers showed little grasp of the role of property disputes in family discord in the early years of reform. The language of their sermons, the church ordinances of 1553 and 1558, and the parish visitations bear testimony to this view; nowhere do they attribute strife to local inheritance customs, to disputed marriage contracts, or to the pressure to defend the patrimony from land-hungry children and relatives. When the parish visitors found conflict during their rounds in 1556 they simply ascribed it to the moral and doctrinal shortcomings of the local priests and the laity. The ignorance of the visitors is understandable. The first generation of reformers in this small Protestant land were all trained to see family strife in moral and religious terms. And they tended to come from outside the territory: Caspar Huberinus from Augsburg; Matthäus Lilienfein, Gallus and Johann

[4] ALKI 6/4, 1498; ALGAL 33/1, 1503.
[5] For the broad outline of this development see Hartwig Dietrich, *Das protestantische Eherecht in Deutschland bis zur Mitte des 17. Jahrhunderts*, Jus ecclesiasticum, vol. 10 (Munich: Claudius, 1970).

Hartmann, and others from Württemberg.[6] They had, as a result, no knowledge of local inheritance customs.

The 1560s and early 1570s marked a turning point. Why the reformers began to take an interest in inheritance practices is not entirely clear. Some of them may have learned about local customs during the visitations carried out in 1556, 1558, and 1571. But if they did, this knowledge was not reflected in the visitation reports. Visitors were carefully instructed to inquire into church ceremonies, the catechism, attendance at church, baptism, and popular morality. Nowhere was there a mention of inheritance customs.[7] A more likely position to learn about property disputes, however, was as a magistrate on a marriage court. Practical experience from the early courts was probably reflected in the territory's marriage ordinance of 1561, for this ordinance almost certainly established the first laws concerning marriage contracts.[8] But, wherever the reformers gained their knowledge and experience, by the early 1570s they clearly considered orderly and publicly scrutinized property settlements as an essential part of the marital discipline they wished to impose in the territory. In the Marriage Law of 1572, Count Ludwig Casimir decreed that a couple must settle all of the property arrangements of the marriage, the inheritances of any existing children included, in the presence of their parents, the next of kin or guardians, and one of the count's local officials.[9] With this step the state began to make the passing on of property a more public process.

The means to enforce these laws, however, were not firmly in place until the early seventeenth century. All of the obstacles that slowed marital reform – slow and cumbersome communications, the weak administrative control of rural districts far from Neuenstein, resistance to state authority – also slowed the effort to police peasant property relationships as well. But there were other, more serious obstacles to state controls. The small towns and villages of the territory still tried local cases of disputed inheritances before their own courts. And, even if these courts started to pass on more of these cases to the chancellery for a ruling, the magistrates who looked into the disputes had no uniform law code by which to try them. On occasion, these state officials acquired written copies of a community's customs, the earliest surviving example of which came

---

[6] Gunther Franz, *Die Kirchenleitung in Hohenlohe in den Jahrzehnten nach der Reformation: Visitation, Konsistorium, Kirchenzucht und die Festigung des landesherrlichen Kirchenregiments 1556–1586*, Quellen und Forschungen zur württembergischen Kirchengeschichte, vol. 3 (Stuttgart: Calwer, 1971), 29–30.

[7] See, for example, the detailed instructions to visitors in 1558 and 1571. Gunther Franz, ed., *Grafschaft Hohenlohe*, pt. 1 of *Württemberg*, vol. 15 of *Die evangelischen Kirchenordnung des XVI. Jahrhunderts* (Tübingen: J.C.B. Mohr, 1977), 120–33, 161–70.

[8] Copies of this ordinance have not survived, but Gunther Franz argues that later references to it indicated that it contained regulations of property settlements. See ibid. 171–3.

[9] Ibid. 187–90.

from Ingelfingen in 1549.[10] But not every community compiled local laws. Most villages preserved the customs as oral traditions, and so villagers often changed and manipulated them according to circumstances. In 1578 the princes attempted to draw up a general law code for the territory, to write down all of the customs and systematize them. But the effort failed. Not until 1738 did the territory have a uniform law code.[11]

Any rigorous intervention in property disputes would also require local officials to have a detailed knowledge of local property, fixed and movable alike. But this knowledge too local officials did not have in the 1570s. Officials would complain that no one could uncover all of the properties of a family, that loans, debts, even the holding of parcels of land, could not be easily sorted out, and that villagers themselves were reluctant to provide them with such detailed information.[12] State officials would not carry out a detailed survey of the taxable wealth of peasant households until 1581, and even then the survey was of limited value in grasping the whole complex of properties, movable wealth, debts, and loans that constituted a family patrimony. In this survey, the stewards listed the propertyholder by name, then assessed the taxable value of his or her farm or set of landholdings, and wrote out a brief inventory of the household's movable wealth. They did not survey the properties attached to the farm – the sizes and precise locations of fields, forests, vineyards, and pastures were not recorded.[13] Officials would acquire such a detailed knowledge of peasant property in Langenburg district only in 1605–6, the year the massive new cadastre of peasant properties in the district was finished.[14]

All of these instruments of domination – new laws, courts, better administrative control over local officials, surveys of wealth and property, the power to carry out inventories of property – were essential for the state to regulate peasant property and inheritance effectively. Without them the maze of property relationships that ran through the peasant family and household was impossible to grasp. There is evidence that in a highly centralized state like Austria the state had already made significant inroads in controlling property, inheritance, and land tenure by the 1590s.[15] But the smaller patrimonial states never acquired such centralized control over property and the family, at least not until the seventeenth century. Until that time enforcement was not uniform, but spotty and even arbitrary.

---

[10] ALGAL 618/1, 1549.
[11] ALKI 6/3, 1578.
[12] Officials gave up on the attempt to survey peasant property in the late 1570s for these reasons. For a fuller account of resistance against the surveys see Chapter 7.
[13] LAN 42/16/10, 1581.
[14] L/L 27 (1606); 28 (1606).
[15] See Rebel, *Peasant Classes*, 21–32, 120–69 passim.

Power, property, and inheritance

One might expect that this extension of state authority would have reduced family and village strife, that the campaign, however slow it was to become effective, would at least have made the devolution of property a more orderly and publicly scrutinized process. But this was only partially true. For the practice of inheritance, carried out in the context of the byzantine world of family and village politics, did not lend itself easily to state controls and oversight.

Inheritance customs themselves were not easily codified and enforced. They were preserved as oral traditions, not as laws in a lawbook, and so were still subject to continual change in the middle of the sixteenth century. Taken out of their social context, written down and codified, these customs may have given state officials the illusion of a coherent set of laws at work, a structure of property relationships that molded family relationships from one generation to the next. But the opposite was true. The customs only came to life in the hands of the villagers themselves, not as rational laws separate and apart from social action, but as rules that had meaning only in the actual practice of passing on and defending the patrimony. Villagers continually argued over the key principles in the customs, the justice of them, and the practical ways in which the principles were to be carried out.[16] What we can piece together about inheritance practices in Hohenlohe between 1550 and 1630 is instructive in this regard. Here we can discern what the principles of inheritance in the village were, at least as far as the inquiries into customs and the court cases of disputed inheritance illuminate them.[17] But it is clear that agreement on the principles did not stop villagers from arguing over how these were best carried out. For peasants treated these customs only as rough rules, rules easily manipulated to fit the relationships of power in the family.

The principles themselves were simple and, for the most part, common to all lands in which impartible inheritance held sway. But they also set up deep and unresolvable tensions within the peasant family. For custom called for the

---

[16] The key conceptual idea of this chapter – that inheritance customs must be placed in their social context, that they were malleable – builds on Jack Goody's theoretical studies on the devolution of property. See *Production and Reproduction: A Comparative Study of the Domestic Domain*, Cambridge Studies in Social Anthropology, no. 17 (Cambridge: Cambridge University Press, 1976), and "Inheritance, Property and Women: Some Comparative Considerations," in Jack Goody, Joan Thirsk, and E. P. Thompson, eds., *Family and Inheritance: Rural Society in Western Europe, 1200–1800* (Cambridge: Cambridge University Press, 1976), 10–36.

[17] The second written record of the customs comes from Langenburg district in 1578. Officials made note of these same principles in Ingelfingen district in 1632, in several investigations later in the seventeenth century, and in the extensive reports on inheritance customs in the early eighteenth century in preparation for the law code issued in 1738. ALGAL 618/1, 1549; 18/39, n.d.; ALKI 18/45, n.d.; 6/3, 1578; 33/5, October 8, 1632; 33/21, February 24, 1657; 33/7, 1663; 33/11, April 16, 1707; 33/22, May 19, 1707; 33/14, December 29, 1709.

Search for order

propertyholder to keep the family farm together, to pass it on undivided, but at the same time to provide equally for all of the natural children and heirs out of the patrimony. In practical terms, this meant that the compact farm – the house and barns, the attached fields, pastures, vineyards, and forests – was to be passed on intact to only one heir. The other heirs, the natural and adopted children of the couple, were not disinherited, at least not in theory. They were to receive cash settlements based on the value of the entire patrimony. Not all villages in Hohenlohe embraced these principles; a few communities from the river valleys treated all the family property, the land included, as partible.[18] But the princes, their officials, and the tenant farmers, most of whom lived in villages and hamlets on the rolling Hohenlohe plain, treated the compact farms as impartible property, while the wealth of the family, the patrimony as a whole, remained partible. The customs therefore favored not strict impartibility, a rarity in any case, but tended toward preferential partibility, that broad gray area where the two were mixed up.[19]

This custom alone was enough to create tensions in the village family. But two additional principles made the devolution of property a particularly contentious affair, laden with perhaps more potential for conflict than customs in other lands. One was a rule unique to Hohenlohe, a rule roundly condemned by village women, children, state officials, and, on occasion, even by men. At the moment the executors divided a family's patrimony, they applied a principle that worked insidiously and cruelly against the interests of women, their kinsmen, and their heirs. When a spouse died, a woman was left with only one-third of the patrimony (the *dritteil*); a man, two-thirds (the *zweyteil*). The rest, divided in equal parts, went to the children. Even a woman's dowry, property usually kept separate and distinct from the marital fund elsewhere, was absorbed into the whole and divided up among the heirs. Asked about this shocking custom in 1632, three old men from Crispach, a village near Ingelfingen, explained:

[18] See Wolfgang Saenger, *Die bäuerliche Kulturlandschaft der Hohenlohe Ebene und ihre Entwicklung seit dem 16. Jahrhundert*, Forschungen zur deutschen Landeskunde, vol. 101 (Remagen: Bundesanstalt für Landeskunde, 1957), 41–2. For a discussion of the practices in the eighteenth century see Eckart Schremmer, *Die Bauernbefreiung in Hohenlohe*, Quellen und Forschungen zur Agrargeschichte, vol. 9 (Stuttgart: Gustav Fischer, 1963), 30–40.
[19] For a general introduction to inheritance practices in early modern Europe see Goody, Thirsk, and Thompson, eds., *Family and Inheritance*; for early modern Germany see Helmut Röhm, *Die Vererbung des landwirtschaftlichen Grundeigentums in Baden-Württemberg*, Forschungen zur deutschen Landeskunde, vol. 102 (Remagen: Bundesanstalt für Landeskunde, 1957); Hess, *Familien- und Erbrecht im württembergischen Landrecht;* Lutz K. Berkner, "Inheritance, Land Tenure and Peasant Family Structure: A German Regional Comparison," in Goody, Thirsk, and Thompson, eds., *Inheritance and Family*, 71–95; and "The Stem Family and the Developmental Cycle of the Peasant Household: An Eighteenth-Century Austrian Example," *American Historical Review* 77 (1972), 398–418.

The custom of this village makes it extremely difficult for the parents, but even more so for the widowed mother left behind. She not only loses her husband, the one who feeds her and takes care of her, but also is left with [only] the third of the whole property by her own children, and is then allowed to be driven into beggary – all of which goes against natural and Christian love.[20]

Some villagers complained that women from nearby lands married into Hohenlohe families with reluctance, that the one-third–two-thirds rule discouraged prospective marriage partners from moving to the territory. Women and their families from outside Hohenlohe feared that their dowries would be irretrievably lost or, at the best, sharply reduced when they married into a Hohenlohe family. Nonetheless the rule was accepted as custom.

This was not all. Each time a propertyholder passed on the family patrimony, a crisis loomed, for the customs provided no rules for the succession to the farm itself. In some lands, villagers provided for an orderly succession to the farm by prescribing a certain son – some designated the oldest, others the youngest – as the heir destined to take over the farm on the father's death. But officials reported no comparable custom for Hohenlohe. The succession was left open, each family working out the issue on its own. And in practice families showed no clear preference for one son over another. Propertyholders often set up a daughter and a son-in-law as heirs to the farm, even when sons could have taken over the property. These rules, or the lack of them, made the succession a struggle for power in the family, a struggle sometimes carried out subtly but at times brutally and violently, and almost always with lasting bitterness and enmity. Succession was often a time of conflict and crisis.

On the whole, propertyholders tried to conserve wealth as the succession was arranged, to defend the patrimony from the burdensome claims of many heirs. Two strategies stand out as particularly important in this process. The most common strategy was for propertyholders to prolong the devolution of the property as long as possible, acknowledging the legitimacy of kinsmen's claims, while dribbling out payments for years or even decades. A parent, for example, commonly refused to divide up the patrimony when a spouse died, even though he or she was clearly required to do so. Custom was remarkably malleable when it came to defending this practice. As some villagers from Langenburg district explained to an official in 1578, custom made an exception when it came to widows and widowers: "So long as a living spouse continues to sit in the widowed state, then he owes the children not a thing." Only when he or she remarried was the property actually to be passed on.[21] In hard economic times – the 1570s, the 1590s, and the 1620s and 1630s in particular – parents often died before paying off the inheritances, marriage properties, or

[20] ALKI 33/5, October 8, 1632.   [21] ALGAL 18/43, 1578.

129

dowries of their children, passing on the unfulfilled claims as debts to their heirs. For children to acquire inheritances – the marriage properties and dowries that were deducted from the inheritance – might very well take a lifetime.

Such a practice might have conserved wealth, but, in an age of land scarcity, rapidly eroding wages, and increasingly bleak prospects for smallholders, rural artisans, and laborers, the postponement of an inheritance was a decision charged with the fear of ruin, poverty, and loss of honor among the heirs. Such practices inevitably weakened the prospects of youths and siblings eager to set up their own households. When Anna Seybold of Langenburg "hardened in the widow's state," as the expression went, her sons battled her relentlessly, but in vain, to have her split up the 300 fl. she owed them. Jorg, the most eager of the sons to get his share, complained to the court that she had promised him the bathhouse and that he desperately needed it so he could set up a household with his soon-to-be wife from Strasbourg. Besides, he protested, his mother seemed eager to marry again, this time to a worthless and poor man of eighteen who could bring little to "her enormous household."[22] Anna, for her part, did not dispute the claim, but she argued that she was not yet obligated to hand over the children's share of the patrimony, that to do so now, in 1624, would mean her complete ruin.[23] Her husband had left her a pile of debts when he died, a legacy not uncommon as the economic crisis of the 1620s set in. Still, her sons could not establish themselves until she paid them off.[24]

The other strategy for defending the patrimony involved parents disinheriting their children outright. Villagers went about this practice not crassly, but shrewdly, and often not with the intent of harming the interests of their children. They did so by remarrying and then merging the patrimony, and their children's future legacies along with it, with the property of the new spouse. Such an arrangement usually meant dispossessing the children of the first marriage of at least part of their inheritances. For widows and widowers often promised a new spouse a share in the patrimony, a "child's part" of the inheritance. Even more threatening for the children, the new spouse also acquired the use rights to his or her stepchildren's property, lawfully guaranteed until the children came of age and claimed it. These stepchildren could press no claims to their stepparents' property, however, or to the marital fund created at the time of the new marriage. On the whole, then, remarriage worked against the interests of the children of the first marriage and any other heirs. As Chancellor Assum

---

[22] ALKI 227/1, February 11, 1624.   [23] ALKI 227/8, November 20, 1624.

[24] In this case, and in many others, the enormous debts piled up by villagers in the early 1620s made the devolution of property an extremely difficult problem for youths and propertyholders alike. Anna Seybold had a handsome legacy in the Langenburg bathhouse; assorted properties – 5 1/2 *morgen* of fields and 2 1/2 of pastures – 265 fl. in cash; a number of pigs, sheep, and cattle; and a store of grain. But she had also inherited 1,100 fl. in debt, a massive sum for this period, a sum she probably would never be able to pay off.

observed in 1616, perhaps with only slight exaggeration, these practices led to "great disorder, and poor orphans have suffered severe reductions [in their inheritances]"; parents often "absorb virtually the entire inheritance and leave only a small amount for the heirs."[25] But the practices remained common ones, for the relatively high death rates of the early modern period virtually guaranteed that most men and women would marry not once, but two times or more.

The state might have tried to systematize inheritance customs, even to impose new laws and intervene in disputes on a more regular basis. But state officials could never root out the persistent conflict, the lasting enmity between kinsmen, and the endless intrigue over property in the peasant family. All the state could do was to make the devolution of property, an inherently conflict-laden and unequal process, a bit more orderly and public. In the Marriage Law of 1572, Count Ludwig Casimir required that spouses adopt the children of a first marriage, that they make the children "legal and natural children" (*rechte und naturliche Kinder*) and not stepchildren. To do so, the surviving parent and the new spouse drew up an *Einkindschaft*, a contract obligating the couple to treat all of the children in the marriage as if they were of the same blood. In legal terms, this meant that all children, those of the first and second marriage alike, would "take equal shares in the inheritance in all ways as if all the children were born of their own blood; property would come equally from both [parents]."[26] The couple were to announce the *Einkindschaft* at the time of their marriage and settle all the outstanding inheritance claims on the patrimony. Some kinsmen and guardians insisted upon this arrangement as protection for the children. But villagers often made such agreements orally, leaving open the possibility for disputes later over the status of kinsmen. These conflicts would be tempered only slowly in the seventeenth century as villagers were forced to draw up written marriage contracts and children's property settlements before local officials.

There is no small irony in the fact that state practice aimed at conserving peasant property, keeping the compact farms in particular intact, while at the same time trying to protect youths and women from losing their shares of the patrimony. The princes and state officials of Hohenlohe never seem to have been aware of the contradictions implicit in their policies. Counts Wolfgang II and Philip Ernst, and the latter's trusted chancellor Assum, became shrill when condemning the injustice of local inheritance practices, lambasting villagers for "driving legal heirs into poverty," as one decree from 1592 had it.[27] Yet they seem never to have understood that such practices were inevitable in a society in which most of the land remained locked up in large compact farms that were to pass, undivided, to one propertyholder at a time.

To understand more clearly how villagers conserved property in practice,

[25] ALKI 33/3, 1616.   [26] ALGAL 33/14, December 28, 1709.   [27] ALKI 1/20, 1592.

and how these practices reproduced and reinforced the social order of the village, it is useful to analyze a series of important inheritance disputes. In a social order as staunchly patriarchal, as biased toward men and male property rights as this, one would perhaps expect to find family patriarchs, the old men in the village, and their sons at the center of these conflicts. But that is only partially true, for many disputes, perhaps the most bitterly contested ones, tended to revolve around two other powerful figures in the peasant family: the widow and the son-in-law. At least a close look at property and kin relations in Hohenlohe suggests as much. Among the known cases of property transfers between kinsmen in Langenburg district between 1552 and 1600, a total of eighty-one cases, only slightly more than half (51.4%), involved the passing on of property directly to a son. In the remainder of the cases, propertyholders passed the property on to other kinsmen: their widows (23.5%) and sons-in-law (13.6%), but also brothers (4.9%), stepchildren (3.7%), and even a daughter's son or a sister's husband (2.4%).[28] This sample does not seem out of the ordinary for the region. In a larger sample for this same district from the late seventeenth century, similar patterns prevailed. Women and young men were therefore able to acquire much more power over property and kinsmen in the patriarchal family than is commonly assumed.[29]

In the following three cases we shall look more closely at the roles of three family members – the widow, the son, and the son-in-law – in defending the patrimony. It is best to see each of these heirs as the new center, the hub, of a web of shifting kin relations. Once control over the property and the patrimony fell to an heir, all of the kin relations around him or her were altered. Other members of the family, blood relatives and affines alike, were suddenly placed in positions of dependence as weaker claimants to the patrimony. The heir's blood relatives depended upon this control over the patrimony in order to acquire their own inheritances and dowries. To a great degree, the futures of an heir's unmarried siblings and children hinged on his or her power and good will. Relations with the affines – the stepchildren, a stepmother, and a father-in-law and brother-in-law in these three cases – changed as well. When an heir came under pressure to conserve family wealth, the affines were likely to be the first to suffer. For in the calculus of kin relations, blood relatives almost always counted first and affines second.

General social conditions in the village and the power of the state played important roles in each of these cases. For this reason one should bear in mind that these conflicts took place at three different stages in the agrarian cycle: the first in the 1550s, as the agricultural economy continued to expand rapidly; the

---

[28] I have gleaned the following records for this sample: ALARL 1552–3 to 1555–6; 1557–8; 1572–3; 1577–8; 1583–4; 1590–1; 1591–2; 1594–5; 1597–8; 1599–1600.

[29] See Jack Goody, *Production and Reproduction*, 86–98; "Strategies of Hiership," *Comparative Studies in Society and History* 15 (1973), 3–20, and "Inheritance, Property and Women."

second in the 1590s, a decade of contraction and famine; and the third in the 1620s and early 1630s, the years of the agrarian crisis. They also involved families rather wealthy by contemporary village standards; two ranked among the wealthiest village families in the whole land, and one was a smallholder family of slightly better than average means. This too is important, for, though they do not give us a glimpse of the more desperate struggle for survival being waged below them among the village poor, they do show us how disputes over property and kin reproduced and reinforced the social order at the top of the village hierarchy.

The widow

It would be tempting to look at women in this patriarchal society as exploited wives, widows, and servants, as pawns whose primary role it was to labor in the household and cement family alliances. This view contains a kernel of truth, as we pointed out in the last chapter. But women, widows in particular, played a far more aggressive role in defending the patrimony, in protecting their own and the family's wealth, than is commonly assumed. Once we break through the rhetoric of the Lutheran pastors, once we look beyond the letter of the laws to the actual practice of inheritance, peasant women appear in a rather different light. Here, within the network of kinship ties created by blood relations and marriage, women often carved out places of power essential if property and wealth were to be conserved.

The case of Barbara Wittig, a shrewd miller's wife, illustrates what an essential role widows played in defending the family patrimony. The power she acquired seems to have rested on three foundations: the family's wealth, her manipulation of inheritance customs, and help from her kin. In 1535 she married the miller of Ingelfingen, Michel Wittig, and settled into life at the mill, right on the Kocher River. Miller families, more than other village families, prospered during the agrarian boom of the sixteenth century. The Wittigs held considerable properties – the mill itself, the attached lands, and several houses in the town, all assessed at 450 fl. – and stood to accumulate more wealth as the town, and the surrounding countryside, grew in population. The Kocher River valley broadens out just above Ingelfingen, the river itself running almost due west for several more miles before it empties into the Neckar. Because of the width of the valley, the gentle angle of the slopes, the long stretch of slopes facing the south and sheltered from the wind and warmed by the sun, and the town's place along the main road between Neuenstein and Bad Mergentheim, the town and the area around it had become a thriving center of viticulture and local commerce. In addition, the counts had made the town the administrative center of the Kocher valley. For all these reasons the small town's population grew rapidly in the sixteenth century, and the Wittigs, as millers, were well placed to prosper from this expansion.

Barbara's marriage, however, seems to have aroused fear, and possibly dissension, in the Wittig family. For with this marriage came an element of uncertainty about the future of the substantial family wealth and landholdings in and around Ingelfingen. The fact that Michel Wittig drew up a property settlement before the marriage suggests as much, since most villagers relied only upon oral agreements at this early date; written contracts would not become the norm for another fifty or seventy-five years. And in that document we can see the source of the concern: the future of the ten Wittig children.[30] For Michel Wittig the marriage was his second, his first, to Barbara Kress, having come to an end only recently with her death. Ten children survived this marriage, and each of them had a legitimate claim on the patrimony.

The agreement was intended to protect the children's claims to the patrimony, to make for an orderly and certain disposition of the family's wealth. The death of the children's mother meant that Michel was now obligated to pass on to them the one-third, the maternal inheritance, or at least inventory the family's assets and formally divide them. This he did. He promised the children 150 fl., each to receive 15 fl. But the children's patrons – Melchior Kress, their maternal uncle, and Wendel Contz – obviously wanted more than this. Michel assured them and his children that any new wife – the new Barbara was probably in mind – would become a "legal mother" to them, not a stepmother, and that the new couple would set up an *Einkindschaft*. This clause protected them "as equal heirs" in the family if children were to issue from the second marriage. That the kinsmen went on to insist, in the last part of the settlement, that Michel and his next wife treat them "as a father and a mother" suggests how anxious they must have been about the future of the children and the family property. For they may have feared that the new wife would act like a stepmother toward them and cheat them out of their inheritance. "It is extremely dangerous when children come under stepmothers and stepfathers," one Hohenlohe jurist later noted, "because such stepparents show no natural affection or good will toward their stepchildren."[31] Behind this legal arrangement one can sense, from the start of this marriage, fear of the woman's power, fear of a stepmother.

Such fears of the woman's power were often well founded. For when the family came to the next critical moment in the devolution of the property, the death of the patriarch, a wife could quickly assume considerable power. This Barbara Wittig did when her husband died, sometime in the early 1550s. Precisely why she emerged as the defender of the Wittig patrimony is unclear; the foundations of her power within the family were no doubt laid long before Michel actually died. What is clear is that she moved swiftly and decisively to

[30] ALGAL 618/3, 1535.   [31] ALGAL 33/14, December 28, 1709.

protect the family's handsome set of properties from being broken up or run into debt through satisfying the claims of the Wittig children. She did not accomplish this all at once. She first "hardened in the widow's state," checking carefully with Ingelfingen's officials to make sure that she could do this legally. She refused to divide up the estate, moved into one of the Wittig houses in the town, and began to manage all of the properties – including the mill with its lucrative income – on her own. As she explained before the town's magistrates, "I was not obligated to divide" the estate at that time.[32] She was right, and she cited the town's law in her defense.

But this really marked only the beginning, for Barbara soon showed a tenacious will to keep her hold on the property and not let the claims of the other heirs burden it. In reading the court records and the testimonies about the dispute that swirled up around her we see a shrewd and calculating propertyholder at work, one certain of the justice and the legality of her acts. Once she had occupied the mill and the properties, she purchased them and claimed the properties for her own. But this was not all. She secured her hold on the properties, delivering a crushing final blow to the hopes of the fourteen children from her first marriage, with one final act: She remarried. With this she merged the Wittig wealth with that of her new husband. She reminded her fourteen children, who took her to court to contest these actions, that widows had extraordinary powers to protect themselves, their children, and the family legacy when they were threatened with poverty. And then she appealed to the authorities for protection from Michel Wittig's fourteen children. "Town law should not break my case," she argued before the magistrates, "but should support me."[33] The Wittig properties were to remain together, the claims of the children handled as best they could be. But control over the mill, the houses, and the attached properties was to pass to the widow Wittig and her new husband.

Every such effort to conserve family property placed children and heirs at a disadvantage. For those who lost a dispute over the patrimony or whose claims were put off faced diminished prospects or even a slide into poverty. At least the fourteen Wittig children – ten of them from Michel's first marriage, four from his second to Barbara – saw the dispute with their mother in these terms. For them the suspicions that surrounded a stepmother were all confirmed; in their eyes she was a common thief. "She has everything from our [father] and mother," the children pleaded before the magistrates, "and she is stealing all of this against all justice." They argued that she owed them 300 fl., the two-thirds of the patrimony, that "it was our beloved father's last decree that the children should be settled with the two-thirds before a [new] marriage." And, arriving at the crux of the matter, they charged her with planning to take a new

---

[32] ALGAL 618/6 [1550s?].   [33] Ibid.

husband without their knowledge: "Why in God's name did she set up this man [her new husband] in our two-thirds, in our paternal inheritance and this property?"[34] Should the mill, the lands, and the houses not be returned to them, it would "ruin all of us children [and force us] into begging."[35] We do not know the outcome of this dispute before the Ingelfingen court. In all probability the widow and her new husband held onto the mill and the other properties but were obligated to settle the inheritances of the Wittig children. Whether the children would actually have received their share of the patrimony is a separate matter.

Regardless of the outcome, the case points to the widow as a figure of power in the peasant family, very often the pivotal figure who held the patrimony together through a time of crisis. In a land like Hohenlohe her power seems to have been essential if the compact farms and large blocks of landed property were to pass undivided from one propertyholder to the next. For though women never outnumbered men as propertyholders at any given time – only 5 percent of households in 1581 were headed by widows – every family passed through a phase in its developmental cycle in which a widow was likely to acquire some control over the farm and the patrimony. In those times, the pressures from children to split up the patrimony, to dissipate the wealth accumulated over the course of a generation, would be enormous. If the widow gave in, if two-thirds of the family's wealth were actually distributed among the children, the farm would be overburdened with claims and debts that it was unlikely to meet. But when the widow did not, when she hardened in the widow's state and put off the claims, the properties remained intact and the patrimony was defended and passed on as if its life, and not those separate lives of the children, mattered most of all.

The son

Control over the patrimony did not always pass to the widow. In the majority of cases, as we have seen, the farm, the attached lands, and the power to manage the patrimony fell to a son. Often the property no doubt devolved in an orderly fashion, the claims of all the heirs being settled satisfactorily and conflict kept to a minimum. But sometimes it did not. Because custom did not prescribe a clear line of succession, and because the heir to the farm acquired a great deal of power over property and kin, the succession could split the family into feuding factions. Among Hohenlohers the unstated rule, the fundamental pattern of kin and property disputes, seems to have been a clear one: Blood relatives almost always lined up against affines. What was often unclear, however, what

---

[34] ALGAL 618/4 [1550s?].   [35] ALGAL 618/5 [1550s?].

created endless uncertainty, doubt, and suspicion among family members, was who would acquire final power over the patrimony. Sometimes the affines, as in the last case, triumphed in such a dispute, and control over the property was wrenched away from the sons and their blood relatives. But more often than not, as in the dispute over the Weissmüller legacy in 1591, the blood relatives won out and set up a son in control of the farm and the patrimony.

For the villagers engaged in this dispute the stakes were substantial. Indeed the outcome would have consequences for the social and economic order of the whole middle Jagst valley. Whoever entered into old Simon Weissmüller's legacy would become one of the wealthiest and most powerful propertyholders in the entire region. In the cases of most regions' wealthy propertyholders, those who dominated the village landholdings and who held the lion's share of movable and commercial wealth, we can see only the shadowy outlines of their ties in the village and in the region. In this case, however, we can see in some detail how, by the 1590s, a village family had built up a substantial fortune and established ties that ran from village to village throughout the region.

From his mill at Unterregenbach Simon had built up a small village empire, one held together by kinship, property, alliances with other families, and ties of indebtedness that stretched up and down the valley and into the villages on the plain above it. A marriage alliance had been essential to the building up of this Weissmüller empire; only with the help of Kunigunde Seyfrid, her dowry, and her family was Simon able to purchase the mill in 1561.[36] By 1581 he had become a dominant figure in the village and in the regional economy. In the tax survey from that year he ranked as the third wealthiest householder in all of Langenburg district. The mill, the attached arable land and pastures – among the most desirable lands in the village, since they were spread out along the valley floor – the house, and his enormous stores of grain were valued at 2,619 fl. Even more significant, as a pivotal figure in the local grain trade he had amassed a fortune of 439 fl. in movable wealth.[37] By 1591, the year he died, over 200 fl. of his wealth was invested in loans to villagers from Billingsbach, Raboldshausen, Brüchlingen, Unterregenbach, Oberregenbach, and other villages.[38] In a region in which the majority of propertyholders had become smallholders, cottagers, small craftsmen, and laborers, old Simon Weissmüller therefore stood out as an extremely rich man, a dominant figure in the commercial economy, a creditor of some importance.

The passing on of this considerable legacy, and the power over other villagers that came with it, created a small crisis in the valley. The origins of the bitter dispute that broke into the open in 1591 lay in the jockeying for power within the Weissmüller family itself. Before 1587 the blood relatives of Simon the

---

[36] ALKI 215/8, October 29, 1591.
[37] L/L "Schatzungsanlage Amt Langenburg 1581."   [38] ALKI 215/4 [1592?].

elder seem not to have feared for the future of the patrimony. The property appeared secure, though to whom the mill and all the properties at Unterregenbach would actually pass was an issue that did not yet seem settled. There was an obvious favorite, though. Old Simon and his wife had had seven children, three boys and four girls, and the second son, Hans, would have been a natural choice as heir to the mill. The miller's trade would have come naturally for Hans, or to any of the other children, for that matter, for they had all worked at the mill. The couple had "raised them up at the mill (as a father would)," one official reported, "so he did not let them sit around, but would have had them work and help out."[39] The old miller had, in fact, helped establish his oldest son, Simon the younger, as the miller in nearby Eberbach, only a mile or two down the Jagst River from the Weissmüller mill at Unterregenbach. The two oldest daughters had made favorable matches, Ursula with Stoffel Wagner in Mittelbach, Anna with Hans Holch in Bächlingen. The other children, Els, Appel, and young Hans, were younger than Hans. If all had gone well, when old Simon died Hans, the second son and still a minor at sixteen, would have been the obvious choice as heir to the mill.[40]

But all did not go well. By the time Simon the elder died in 1591, other relatives of the Weissmüllers stood ready to press home their own claims to the properties. As was so often the case in property disputes, a woman, a widow, stood at the center of the controversy. We do not know the full story behind old Simon's marriage to Margarethe Hanselmann, his second wife, in 1587. From the vantage point of the Weissmüller children, the match was unwanted, done "against the will of the kinsmen," as they later explained to state officials.[41] But from her own, and her family's, point of view, a finer match could not have been conceived, or more carefully timed, for if she could establish herself at the mill and raise up some of her own children, she might very well be able to lay claim to the properties as a widow. Had Margarethe Weissmüller pulled off this coup, the Hanselmanns, already well-to-do tenant farmers, would have become one of the wealthiest clans in the district. Margarethe's father, Hans Hanselmann, held a compact farm in Oberregenbach, the companion village of Unterregenbach a short walk upstream, assessed at 1,100 fl. in 1581. Like his new son-in-law, Hans Hanselmann had also prospered on the grain trade – he had a substantial store of grain worth 460 fl. Other Hanselmanns held farms of similar size and worth: Simon, a farmstead in Oberregenbach, and Bastian, an estate in the hamlet of Binselberg.[42] With these kinsmen, her own blood relatives, at her side, Margarethe prepared to press home her claims to the Weissmüller properties.

[39] ALKI 215/8, October 29, 1591.   [40] ALKI 215/12 [1591?].   [41] Ibid.
[42] LAN 42/16/10, 1581.

Who would lay claim to the patrimony, who would actually control the properties when a propertyholder died, was an issue that could be left unsettled for years. Certainly some power to settle the issue lay with the patriarch. But power also lay with his wife, especially if she expected to be a widow soon, and with the favored heir. Who actually held the power in the Weissmüller family between 1587 and 1591 is difficult to say. The issue seems clouded, unclear, beset with claims and counterclaims. The power of old Simon to dispose of his property, to line up an heir, does not seem to have been unconditional. Simon probably favored Hans as heir to the mill; at least his claim seemed secure enough for Margarethe to agree initially to pass on the mill to him in 1591. But the widow soon showed her own power when she repudiated the agreement and prepared to seize the properties for herself and her own son.[43] But her position in the Weissmüller family was by no means secure. She had never overcome the taint of being an outsider in the family. She had become a stepmother, not a "legal and natural mother," to the children, and the family had never received her full dowry.[44] In addition, a powerful faction rallied around Hans and the other young Weissmüller children: the elder brother, Simon; their older sisters' husbands, Stoffel Wagner and Hans Holch; and the wealthy tavernkeeper of Nesselbach, Adam Franckh. Still, the Weissmüllers did not hold all the power, or the dispute that broke out upon Simon's death would never have gone to court.

State officials did not intervene in every such dispute, but when they did their power, and not that of the factions, decided the issue. In one regard the decision should have been a simple one: The patrimony would be inventoried and then divided, one-third passing to the widow and two-thirds to the children. Neither the Weissmüllers nor the Hanselmanns contested this. But who would acquire the mill and its properties? Here custom provided no rule, no sure guide as to the final disposition of the property, though custom did allow the widow "to harden in the widow's state," to postpone the division of the property until later. So it seems odd, if not arbitrary and unjust, that the magistrates awarded control over the properties to Hans on December 8, 1591.[45] Why they did so is not clear. It may have been that her father's failure to deliver the dowry compromised her claims to the property. Or the magistrates may have been suspicious about her decision to repudiate an earlier settlement with the children. They may also have doubted her ability to carry on with the work of the mill. She did not have a new husband, nor was her own son old enough to work at the mill. Or it may simply have been that the magistrates wanted the mill, a key piece of property in the district, to pass quickly to a young man able and eager to take up the work. Simon left behind over 1,000 fl. in debts,

[43] ALKI 215/12 [1591?].   [44] Ibid.
[45] ALKI 215/9, December 8, 1591.

after all, and paying them in the 1590s was a difficult task.[46] Whatever the reasons, the mill and its properties passed to Hans, and Margarethe and her son left.

In theory, who acquired control over the property should not have mattered, for the whole patrimony was to be divided up. In practice, however, it always mattered a great deal, for with control over the property came the power over the patrimony, the power to pay off, or withhold, the other heirs' claims. For young Hans Weissmüller this power now became the means by which he conserved the Weissmüller wealth and patrimony. He occupied the mill and agreed, along with assuming responsibility for all the debts, to pay off Margarethe, his stepmother, her share of the estate, a sum put at 1,400 fl. The payments were fixed at 70 fl. a year.[47] But he never paid off this debt. In 1611 Margarethe, now living in Künzelsau, took him to court, charging that he still owed her and her son over 600 fl.[48] The court was not able to help her very much. Hans admitted to state officials that he owed her the money. But he refused to pay her, arguing that he needed the returns from the mill to pay off debts to his own blood relatives and to provide dowries and inheritances for his own children.[49] The court found that Hans Weissmüller owed Margarethe the money, but that she too was still in debt: She should pay the Weissmüllers the remaining 100 fl. of her dowry.[50] For practical purposes, the widow's claims were being put off, set aside, while the young miller channeled the family wealth to his siblings and children.

The power to control the patrimony was therefore power to conserve wealth, to pass it on to only a few kinsmen while putting off the claims of others. In the last case we saw how a widow could accomplish this by "hardening in the widow's state." But in this case the tables were turned on the widow when the young heir disbursed funds from the patrimonial lands to only one set of heirs: his own blood relatives, his siblings and children. From the vantage point of these blood relatives – Hans Weissmüller's unmarried sisters, his younger brother, and the children in particular – the heir's control over the patrimony was essential, for they would need funds from that patrimony, their own inheritances, to purchase a farm or another property or make a favorable marriage alliance.

The same practices that secured these villagers' futures, however, put others – the widow and her child, the stepbrother of the Weissmüller children – at risk. The widow lost not only part of her dowry but also some of the money settled on her for the mill. The family property remained intact, the heirs settled

---

[46] ALKI 215/14, 1592.   [47] ALKI 215/10, December 8, 1591.
[48] ALKI 215/16, June 15, 1611; 215/21, August 15, 1611.   [49] ALKI 215/20, June 15, 1611.
[50] ALKI 215/28, February 29, 1612.

with their shares of the patrimony, but little wealth was set aside to cushion the widow's slide into the ranks of smallholders or the village poor.

The daughter's husband

Despite all of the complex differences between families, all of the subtle variations in strategies to conserve family wealth and property, one theme emerges in each of the disputes that came before the courts: a search for order and stability within the family, for power and control over property and kin. What is ironic about this sometimes desperate search for order and stability is that it bred as much fear, instability, and factionalism in the family as it did harmony and unity. In times of a succession crisis or hard economic times the unity of a family and its broad network of kin could give way quickly to a protracted and bitter conflict, to confusion over property and kin relations until the dispute was resolved.

This image sums up the conditions I have described for the late sixteenth century. But it is even more apt for the second quarter of the seventeenth century, the decades of the Thirty Years' War. For in the 1620s all of the social and economic conditions that made succession to the peasant farm a contentious and difficult issue – the scarcity of land, the fear of famine, peasant indebtedness, the erosion of living conditions for laborers and artisans – became suddenly much worse (see Chapter 8). One cannot say with certainty that the incidence of family strife increased after 1620, that the numbers of disputed inheritances making their way into the courts of Hohenlohe increased. But what is certain is this: The records of disputes become more complete and more voluminous, the tone set by the participants in the conflicts more bitter and desperate than ever before. In this regard, the battle waged for control of Kilian Schnerer's property between 1625 and 1635 was typical. But this case had a slightly unusual outcome: Control over the property passed to a son-in-law, the propertyholder's daughter's husband, as contemporaries preferred to call him. The dispute pitted blood relatives against affines, a father and his son against a son-in-law, a pattern common enough in any family dispute. This time, however, the son was destined to lose his father's land and position.

Why control over a family's property and patrimony passed to a son-in-law is a question not easy to answer. A propertyholder, on occasion, had no choice but to devolve property in this manner. Failure to produce a male heir made it likely that a daughter and her husband would inherit the family farm or lands. But villagers in Hohenlohe did not always pass on property to a daughter's husband as a last resort. Here propertyholders could choose to pass on farms to a number of kinsmen, to widows, brothers, stepchildren, and sons-in-law, as well as to sons. In this particular case, for example, the beginnings of the dispute lay in the agreement Kilian Schnerer drew up to make his son-in-law, and not one of his sons, the preferred heir to his small farm in Langenburg. What seems to have driven Schnerer, an old man nearing retirement, to set up his son-in-law as his heir was security, the desire to be provided for in his old age. At least Schnerer explained his drawing up of the contract in these terms. "I gave half of my house, and all that went with it, to my youngest daughter," he explained in 1627, "in the hope that we [he and his wife], in our [old] age, would have someone in whom we might trust."[51] Why his son Hans could not provide for his security he did not explain. Instead, in 1625, he signed over half of his land, and with it half of his house, to Anthoni Glockh, his daughter's husband. The remainder would pass to him at Schnerer's death. In return, Glockh promised to support Schnerer and his wife in their old age.[52]

When the agreement was made no family crisis seemed imminent. Indeed the records of the Schnerer inheritance dispute suggest that old Kilian managed the passing on of the patrimony in a remarkably orderly and thorough way. He seems to have taken pains to avoid conflict in the family, to treat every heir, whether a son or a son-in-law, fairly and equitably. Every one of them – he had two sons and four sons-in-law – received a fair portion of the patrimony from Schnerer. When state officials inventoried his property in 1631 (probably after the death of his wife) and asked the family to account for every child's portion of the patrimony, they found that Schnerer had already given each one a roughly equal share, whether in money or property: his sons, Hans and Georg, 266 fl. and 253 fl. and nine *batzen*, respectively; and his sons-in-law, Jeremias Reisinger, Johann Schmidt, Jacob Obermüller, and Anthoni Glockh, 137 fl. and four and one-half *batzen*, 304 fl., 384 fl. and six *batzen*, and 300 fl., respectively.[53] But these sums tell only part of the story, for, like all reckonings in an inventory, they were only rough money equivalents of material goods and gifts – beds, linens, land, medicine, candles, wood, furniture, wine, pigs, cows, and cash – that Kilian had given his sons and sons-in-law over the years.[54] Each of these items, each small gift, symbolized the ties of dependence and kinship that knitted this family together.

Schnerer's strategy for passing on the patrimony began to come apart in a frightful way in 1627. And as it did, the family itself fell into a bitter and protracted dispute. The rapid deterioration of economic and social conditions in the region in 1626 and 1627 certainly played a part in heightening the domestic tensions. In those years the crop failures, chronic in this region since the early 1620s, were particularly severe, the shortages of grain and bread

[51] ALKI 233/3, April 27, 1627.
[52] ALAL 370, January 24, 1625.
[53] ALKI 239/14, September 4, 1631.
[54] ALKI 239/1, April 2, 1611; ALAL 370 [1631?]; 370 [1631?]; 370, July 5, 1631; 370, September 11, 1631; 370, June 27, 1631.

increasingly acute. In addition, the state levied a new burden of war taxes in 1627 that fell on village households with unusual harshness (see Chapter 8). The Schnerer household itself would have been able to survive any normal crop failures without much difficulty. Schnerer and Glockh together held not only the small farm, but also six or eight additional parcels of arable land, some vineyards, and several pastures. Even in the terrible year 1631, when most households were being crushed into poverty by the war taxes, this household still had some oxen and cattle, and reserves of grain and wine.[55] Still, even this wealthy household would not have been able to survive the extraordinary exactions without cutting back on food or selling off some reserves for the cash the state demanded in taxes.

What was more threatening in 1627, what split this family into warring factions, however, was a bitter struggle for power and property within the Schnerer family itself. The dispute unfolded in two stages: the first an open and public attempt to strip Glockh of his property and position; and, when the first failed, a second plot against Glockh, this one to deny him the property promised him in the future. Old Kilian Schnerer lay behind both of these plots to disinherit his son-in-law. Why their relationship soured so quickly after 1625 is difficult to say. Schnerer, when he petitioned the court to annul his agreement with Glockh, argued that his son-in-law no longer provided for him, that Glockh, who was supposed to be as obedient and loyal as a child, had turned into a tyrant:

Against all hope he has shown himself to be a lion in sheep's clothing, and with all the means in his hands, hostile, vile, disgraceful, his spirit like a monster and a lion; he has made it known, with words and open deeds, that he wants not only to be the master and lord of the house, but that I am to be obedient and subordinate to him.[56]

Glockh, who knew his rights before the law, was much more circumspect in his testimony. All he would say was that the contract protected him, set him up as the lawful heir, and so it should remain in force.[57] The magistrates agreed with him. The first round of the dispute therefore came to an end on April 20, 1627, when the court ruled that Schnerer must honor the contract, that Glockh remained the legal heir to the property.[58]

In the next phase of the dispute, Schnerer created a legal crisis not simply for the family but for the state as well. For he called into question a cornerstone of state policy, the impartibility of land, and with it, implicitly at least, the foundations of the entire property order. Had Schnerer triumphed in this dispute, had he actually disinherited Glockh and the principle of partibility been established in this land, the legal underpinnings of the agrarian order

---

[55] ALAL 370, June 6, 1631.   [56] ALAL 370, February 3, 1627.
[57] ALAL 370, April 3, 1627.   [58] ALAL 370, April 20, 1627.

could have been undermined. His plan was a simple one. Schnerer no longer challenged Glockh's claim to his half of the property; instead he tried to cut him off from inheriting the other half. In 1630 Schnerer drew up a contract with his son Hans in which he sold the son his half of the property for 325 fl. – the half promised to Glockh when Schnerer died – and promises of support for him and his wife for the rest of their lives.[59] The scheme was a clever one. For Glockh would have been left with only half of the smallholding, and this portion of the farm, especially in the economic crisis of the early 1630s, was inadequate to support a family. The settlement would have improved the position of young Hans, however, since he already held other lands in nearby Atzenrod, and could, with some effort, combine them to support his family. In effect, Schnerer tried to divide his farm, to break it up permanently, even if the two parts as separate farms would not have been able to support a family comfortably.

The case tested the new power of the state to order family property settlements, to prop up the social order and to keep family farms from breaking up. But for five more years, before the state and Glockh prevailed over Schnerer, the issue remained unresolved as officials inventoried the estate's assets, jurists offered up legal opinions, and everyone awaited old Kilian's death. Chancellery officials seemed worried about the legal implications for the whole territory raised by this case. Soon after Schnerer drew up his new contract, Chancellor Assum passed on the documents to jurists in Tübingen for their opinion. Their opinion, while it supported Glockh's claim to remain heir to the property, did not entirely please Assum. The jurists ruled that the terms of a marriage contract had to be fulfilled, that Schnerer had no right to repudiate an agreement so essential to a family's property arrangements.[60] Assum, however, was more concerned about the principle of impartibility and the possible effects of partible inheritance on the whole territory. "No peasant is allowed to divide his farm among his children, to sell to two of them a half part without the permission of the state or the lord," he wrote in 1634. If this were allowed, he argued, then children would break up a property within twenty years, splintering the farm into parcels so small that no family could be supported.[61] When Schnerer died and Assum made his final ruling on the case in 1635, he therefore awarded the whole property, undivided and complete, to Glockh. Hans Schnerer would have to leave.[62]

The pivotal issue in this dispute, as in the other disputes over property, was this: How would property be held together, the family's lands and wealth protected from burdensome claims and not scattered among contending heirs? In its final ruling the state made it clear that the integrity of property, the rule

[59] ALAL 370, 1630.   [60] ALKI 233/8, December 10, 1612.   [61] ALKI 233/19, June 12, 1634.
[62] ALKI 233/24 [1634?]; 233/32–3, March 23, 1635.

of impartibility, must come first, the separate interests of the kin second. But this rule was only a public articulation of a policy in which most propertyholders themselves shared. Even old Kilian Schnerer shared in this view until he felt driven, as a last resort, to try to split his farm between his son and son-in-law. The custom of impartibility, the rule that Kilian Schnerer counted on in 1625 to protect his own and his wife's livelihood, was also a rule that the state would uphold at all costs, even if it meant overturning Schnerer's last will and handing the farm to his daughter's husband.

Inheritance, kin, and the social order

The process of devolution was therefore a complicated and troublesome process, one far more complex than inheritance customs alone would lead one to believe. For within each family and household the practice of inheritance involved two tendencies, two simultaneous processes that together worked to reproduce the social order.

The first part of that process, the acquisition, accumulation, and setting aside of property and wealth, acted as a powerful buttress for the position of the tenant farmers, the millers, the tavernkeepers, and some smallholders in the village. This part of the process made it possible for the bulk of the landed property in the countryside – the compact farms, the mills, the taverns, the smallholdings, and often the lands attached to them – to remain intact, protected, as much as was possible, from the burdensome claims of kin. How certain sons, widows, and sons-in-law acquired these coveted lands and how the remainder of the patrimony was actually divided up and passed on to other kinsmen was a process influenced by a number of conditions, all of them subject to change: the shrewdness with which family members manipulated custom; the balance of power between blood relatives and affines; the ages of the heirs; the alliances of family members with powerful persons in the village or with local authorities; the availability of land; the marriage market; the family's movable wealth and debts; the strength of individual personalities; luck and circumstance; and, by the early seventeenth century, the power of the state.

This concentration of wealth and power in the hands of only a few propertyholders was complemented, even somewhat undermined, by a second tendency: the continual redistribution of accumulated wealth, the splitting up of the patrimony and its dispersal among kinsmen. The practices of inheritance in Hohenlohe may have favored the continuity and integrity of property over the pressing and immediate demands of youths, women, and siblings in the sixteenth century. But the passing on of the patrimony never took place as a single act, as one event in the life cycle of the family. It acted on the family wealth and property of this rural society like the ebb and flow of the tides on a great string of barrier reefs. Property was built up and concentrated here and there in large masses, but it was also broken up on occasion, creating new and unexpected flows and concentrations of wealth. Positions of power and wealth in the family were never assumed to be permanent in this society. They could change hands suddenly and dramatically, opening up, and closing off, opportunities for family members through birth, death, and marriage. And an individual's fortunes could also change through the actions, both well-intentioned and wicked, of kinsmen with power over the patrimony.

Every family and household of tenant farmers and millers formed a small social world of its own in the late sixteenth century, a small hierarchy of wealth and power within the village society. The patriarchal family, the household, the extended networks of kinship and property ties, inheritance practices: These were the foundations of power, the instruments of domination of the village elite. That society included a circle of individuals, some related by blood, others by marriage, that often cut across all strata within the village. It often included smallholders, craftsmen, laborers, servants, even those threatened with destitution and utter dependence. All of them had claims on the family patrimony. All of them watched and waited for opportunities to secure those claims, to improve their social status and standing within the network of kin. At a time when population growth, social stratification, and, as we shall see in the next chapter, the expanding market economy all pulled the social order apart, these ties of property and kin formed the primary bonds of social cohesion, the foundations for stability and hierarchy in the agrarian order.

6

~~~~~~

The unchristian economy

Whatever stability the strict control of landed property introduced in family and village social relationships was inadequate to contain the threat to agrarian order that came from another quarter in the sixteenth century: market relationships and new sources of commercial wealth. By the end of the sixteenth century lords and peasants in Hohenlohe no longer looked upon market activities as peripheral or supplementary to the local economy. Whether for good or ill the place of villagers in the agrarian order depended as much on securing cash incomes to maintain their social standing as it did on securing access to landed property. Established tenant farmers needed movable wealth, not land, to endow sons and daughters in their marriages. Young heirs also needed cash incomes to meet the heavy burdens of family inheritance claims. The village poor, even if they did not have to meet as burdensome a demand in inheritance obligations as did tenant farmers, certainly needed cash incomes to buy grain, bread, and other food supplies to survive. As the century wore on, in fact the pressure to secure cash incomes in the market economy would increase steadily as the princes levied a more regular burden of taxes. These burdens were to be paid, if at all possible, in cash.

Market relationships proved far more difficult to order than did family and property relationships. With family and property relationships the authorities and villagers could appeal to old ideals of Christian patriarchy, to respect for local custom, and to new courts to manage conflict over property and status in the family. But market relationships never succumbed easily to idealistic appeals to conscience or to order imposed by community and state controls. Especially when market relationships assumed such importance in village life after 1560 did they prove difficult to order. This is not at all to suggest that market relationships supplanted family ties, village loyalties, or relationships with lords in Hohenlohe's agrarian society. The relationships villagers forged in the marketplaces complicated family bonds, introduced new sources of conflict between old village factions, and added an additional layer of social distinctions based on the acquisition of commercial wealth to older identities based on property.

At the beginning of the new period of market expansion in Hohenlohe one event seemed to foreshadow the way in which the conflict inherent in these new relationships would eventually be structured, but never completely tamed. In 1572 Hohenlohers denounced three wealthy tenant farmers and petty merchants to the court for engaging in a host of marketing practices disturbing to the community. Bartel Ehrman, Martin Heinrich, and Wendel Scheuermann, all of them from Langenburg, had apparently bought up grain in the surrounding villages, exported it to markets and towns outside of the territory, and then used their ill-gotten profits to make usurious loans to impoverished neighbors who could not afford to buy bread.[1] All this they had done during the terrible famine of the early 1570s. The records do not mention how the dispute was resolved, but the fact that the count and his officials took such a deep interest in the case was in itself important. Just as the princes had begun to order the family and inheritance in the early Reformation, so too they were now drawn into the marketplace to impose order between a wealthy peasant elite and the village poor.

Market expansion

The integration of Germany's rural areas into broader market economies took place in roughly two stages in the sixteenth century. The stages, corresponding roughly with the two phases of the agrarian expansion of the sixteenth century, were quite different in character: an initial period of steady expansion from 1450 to 1560 and a second phase of much more rapid growth from 1560 to 1640 or 1650. In the initial stage of expansion the inflation of grain prices played the most important role in drawing peasant economies into broader market economies. In Würzburg, not far from Hohenlohe, this initial period of inflation was clearly evident in the prices of rye. Prices doubled between 1511–20 and 1531–40 and then leveled off, even declining slightly at times, to 1551–60.[2] During this period of inflation, cities drew tight into their orbits rural areas in their immediate hinterland. Here they found and secured their supplies of grain. On occasion merchants foraged far and wide into the countryside in this period to provision urban markets with grain. After the shortages of grain in northern Italy in 1553–4, for example, merchants bought up supplies of grain deep in the hinterlands of South Germany.[3] But rural areas like Hohenlohe, as we saw in Chapter 1, remained peripheral regions for the cities and were not yet fully integrated into the regional market economies on a permanent basis.

---

[1] ALKI 10/1–2, 1572.

[2] Wilhelm Abel, *Geschichte der deutschen Landwirtschaft vom frühen Mittelalter bis zum 19. Jahrhundert*, Deutsche Agrargeschichte, vol. 2 (Stuttgart: Eugen Ulmer, 1962), 70.

[3] See Wilhelm Abel, *Massenarmut und Hungerkrisen im vorindustriellen Europa: Versuch einer Synopsis* (Hamburg: Paul Parey, 1974), 60, 64–7 passim.

The unchristian economy

The second explosive period of market expansion after 1560 ended the relative isolation of regions once peripheral to the South German market economy. As in the first period, the inflation in grain prices played the most important part in expanding the sphere of market activity. This time, however, in contrast to the earlier period of inflation, grain prices rose at a much faster pace and reached extraordinarily high levels for the early modern period as a whole. Rye prices at Würzburg, for example, rose rapidly after 1560 and by 1580 stood at roughly double those of 1550 and four times those of 1510.[4] The inflation in this period originated, as in the earlier period of expansion, partly in the increased demand for grain and bread from a burgeoning population. But to this demand came two extraordinary factors that pushed prices up at a much more rapid pace than in the early sixteenth century: a prolonged series of harvest failures between 1568 and 1576 and the now regular search of merchants from South German, Italian, and Dutch cities for secure sources of grain deep in the German countryside.[5]

For the rural hinterlands of Germany this second period of spectacular inflation had far-reaching consequences. It meant above all that local prices began to fluctuate in response to the rhythms of trade that animated the broader market economies. No longer would local supply and demand alone determine prices in the small regional markets. After 1560 or 1570 a region such as Hohenlohe experienced the same general price trends, with some regional variations, that sent prices in the cities continually upward into the early seventeenth century. The first evidence of this for Hohenlohe came in the 1570s and 1580s when peasants and local officials complained bitterly about the exceptionally high prices for grain in their communities. These years had become "these dear times" or "these hard times." Spelt prices in Hohenlohe-Langenburg, after perhaps stagnating temporarily around 1600, continued to rise rapidly after 1610 and reached their peak for the period, at almost three times the prices of 1601–10, sometime in the 1620s (see Table 6.1). Then, following the general pattern of prices everywhere in Central Europe, grain prices declined in the 1630s and continued to do so well into the late seventeenth century. By the 1660s prices had fallen back to roughly the levels of 1601–10.

Although prices in Hohenlohe began to fluctuate in unison with those of the South German market economy, this did not mean that local fluctuations in supply and demand had become unimportant for the agrarian economy. A number of unpredictable factors could send grain prices up or down: local harvest failures, inefficiencies in the distribution of grain, extraordinary demands by troops during the Thirty Years' War, currency adjustments, sudden demand for grain from outside the territory. In the district of Langenburg the

---

[4] Abel, *Geschichte der deutschen Landwirtschaft*, 70.
[5] Abel, *Massenarmut und Hungerkrisen im vorindustriellen Europa*, 70–111.

149

Table 6.1. *Median prices of spelt in Langenburg district, 1601-70*

Year	Price (fl. per *malter*)	Index
1601-10	1.5	100
1611-20	3.4	227
1621-30	4.3	287
1631-40	2.7	180
1641-50	2.2	146
1651-60	1.9	126
1661-70	1.4	93

Sources: ALARL 1607; 1608; 1611; 1615-16; 1616-17; 1620-1 to 1622-3; 1624-5 to 1634-5; 1637-8; 1639-40 to 1641-2; 1644-5; 1645-6; 1647-8; 1649-50; 1650-1; 1651-2; 1654-5; 1657-8; 1658-9; 1664-5; and 1666-7.

Note: These prices represent the median yearly prices for spelt paid by villagers at state granaries. They therefore do not necessarily reflect the prices paid for grain on the open market, although their movements tended to follow general price trends for the seventeenth century.

Table 6.2. *Famines in Langenburg district, 1570-1683*

Year	Villages	Reported causes
1570-6	All	Harsh winters
1588-9	Billingsbach, Unterregenbach	Dearth
1600	Langenburg, Bächlingen, Hürden	Harsh winter
1601-2	Langenburg	High prices
1611-12	All	Dearth; high prices
1612-13	Unterregenbach	Bad weather
1620-1	All	Harsh winter; high prices
1623-30	All	Dearth; high prices
1632	All	Dearth; troop quarterings
1634-5	All	Hail; troop quarterings
1648-50	All	Rain; troop quarterings
1660	Eberbach	Hailstorms
1661	Binselberg, Raboldshausen	Rainstorms
1663-4	Binselberg, Raboldshausen, Nesselbach	Hailstorms
1666-7	Binselberg, Nesselbach	Dearth
1677	All	Dearth
1683	All	Dearth

most important reason for these sharp fluctuations seems to have been local harvest failures. These recurred at distressingly regular intervals from the terrible winters and famine of 1568–76 right to the end of the Thirty Years' War in 1648 (see Table 6.2). The worst of these dearths began as simple harvest failures in 1620 and then expanded into a chronic shortage of grain in the 1620s culminating in the catastrophes that came with the troop movements into the region in the early 1630s (see Chapter 8). Not until population had declined and a great deal of the marginal land had gone out of production after the 1640s did the frequency and seriousness of these dearths lessen somewhat. This rural hinterland may have become an integral part of a market economy, but the unpredictable short-term economic cycles still largely followed the ups and downs of local harvests.

The economic integration of remote rural areas into the broader South German market economy was accomplished primarily through the expansion of secondary and tertiary markets in small towns. The primary urban markets, those concentrated in the great imperial cities, had expanded spectacularly during the commercial expansion of the fifteenth and early sixteenth centuries. Even though most of these cities retained their significance as the centers of commerce in South Germany after 1550, however, they no longer grew at the pace of the earlier period. Within their orbits they had stimulated the growth of secondary markets that, in part, served as transshipment centers for moving grain supplies and other agricultural products to the larger urban centers. For western Franconia, the region of which Hohenlohe was a part, four imperial cities stood at the apex of the regional pyramid of markets: Dinkelsbühl, Heilbronn, Rothenburg o.d.T., and Schwäbisch Hall.[6] Wimpfen may still have handled some commerce into and out of Hohenlohe, but it was fast becoming of secondary importance to Heilbronn. All of these cities deepened their market connections with the surrounding countryside after 1570. And they did so through the whole cluster of long-established secondary markets that served them: Öhringen, Mergentheim, Crailsheim, Markbreit, and Ansbach. All of these secondary markets assumed more importance for Hohenlohers as centers of trade in the late sixteenth century.

For most villagers, however, the most important links with the broader market economy occurred through the small periodic markets at the bottom of the regional hierarchy of markets. Among these markets there was spectacular growth in the sixteenth century. Within Hohenlohe itself and near the borders, these markets probably handled the bulk of the trade in agricultural products and small manufactures. The small markets on the Jagst River servicing the rural districts of Langenburg and Kirchberg, for example, provided the primary

---

[6] For short discussions of the significance of these market centers see, for Dinkelsbühl and Rothenburg o.d.T., Erich Keyser and Heinz Stoob, eds., *Deutsches Städtebuch: Handbuch städtischer Geschichte*, vol. 5, pt. 1: *Bayern* (Stuttgart: W. Kohlhammer, 1971), 151–2, 463–4; and, for Heilbronn and Schwäbisch Hall, ibid. vol. 4, pt. 2: *Südwest-Deutschland*, 113, 207. For a discussion of the place of Schwäbisch Hall in the South German market economy see Gerd Wunder, *Die Bürger von Hall: Sozialgeschichte einer Reichsstadt, 1216–1802*, Forschungen aus Württembergisch Franken, vol. 16 (Sigmaringen: Jan Thorbecke, 1980), 88–93.

links between villagers and the broader market economy. The counts of Hohenlohe opened a new market at Kirchberg in 1551, another in Nesselbach in 1569, and still another in the town of Langenburg in 1576. In each case the merchants from the larger market towns of Rothenburg, Schwäbisch Hall, and Dinkelsbühl immediately applied for, and received, permission to visit these markets regularly.[7] This did not mean that villagers from the area sold their agricultural products to merchants only in these markets. Langenburgers themselves frequently drove teams of cattle to Schwäbisch Hall or Rothenburg for sale. And some tenant farmers were known to load their wagons with grain to sell direct to buyers in the markets of the imperial cities.[8] A number of tenant farmers in fact began to engage in the unlawful, but never successfully suppressed, practice of "private marketing." In this case tenant farmers bypassed the official markets entirely by selling direct to merchants who went from house to house or farm to farm buying up surpluses of grain.

The authorities encouraged this expansion of commerce by attempting to fit each market into a niche in the broader market economy. The timing of a market was continually reappraised and adjusted so as to make it as attractive for merchants and peddlers to attend as possible. When the counts of Hohenlohe established the weekly and yearly markets at Langenburg they investigated thoroughly the dates of the other important markets in nearby Ansbach so as to avoid conflicts.[9] Establishing markets specializing in certain commodities also became more common. Ingelfingen, Öhringen, and Weikersheim specialized, for example, in the wine trade in Hohenlohe.[10] Langenburg and Kirchberg held special yearly markets for cattle.[11] To buy and sell small manufactured goods one frequented the markets in Mergentheim, Ingelfingen, Rothenburg, or Ansbach.[12] And at the great yearly fair held at the Mooswiesen near Crailsheim, not far to the east of Hohenlohe, one could buy and sell most anything in a carnival-like atmosphere. None of these small regional markets attracted the attention of the great merchant houses of South Germany. Most of them were known as *Krämermärkte*, or "peddlers' markets," indicating that trade was carried out by small itinerant merchants who bought and sold a wide variety of goods in small quantities.[13] All the same, these markets linked up as a network,

[7] ALGAL 3/1, 1551; 1/1, 1569.
[8] ALGAL 7/3–4, October 5, 1611; 7/6, 1617; 7/7, February 14, 1617; 7/8, December 20, 1601.
[9] ALGAL 7/12, 1576.
[10] Keyser and Stoob, eds., *Deutsches Städtebuch*, vol. 4, pt. 2: *Südwest-Deutschland*, 123–4, 194, 294.
[11] Ibid. 126, 137 (page for Langenburg).
[12] Ibid. 163, 123–4; and vol. 5, pt. 1: *Bayern*, 463–4, 48–9.
[13] For a general discussion of the importance of peddlers in linking rural areas to markets see Fernand Braudel, *Civilization and Capitalism, 15th–18th Century*, vol. 2: *The Wheels of Commerce*, trans. Siân Reynolds (New York: Harper & Row, 1982), 75–80.

their timing and special function creating, together with Heilbronn, Rothenburg, Schwäbisch Hall, and Dinkelsbühl, an integrated market economy.

Peasants and the market economy

These markets drew almost every villager to a greater or lesser extent into the market economy. For tenant farmers and smallholders in Hohenlohe the relatively high prices for agricultural products and the more efficient distribution system made it more attractive to export grain, wine, and cattle out of the territory. The earliest evidence of this activity for Langenburg, of course, comes from the spectacular case of profiteering in 1572. Bartel Ehrman, Martin Heinrich, and Wendel Scheuermann may have aroused a great deal of communal anger with their commercial activities, but they were also quick to take advantage of the opportunities to profit from Hohenlohe's new place in the market economy. Other tenant farmers and smallholders followed them in the 1580s and 1590s, and they too sometimes drew criticism for their heavy participation in the export trade. Others too found their place in the market economy: butchers, bakers, artisans of all types, winegrowers, and laborers. Some went to sell their goods, others went to buy. Whole communities now focused their attention on the place of different villagers in the market, the prices paid for food at the marketplace, the practices of sellers and buyers, and the accumulation of movable wealth won on the marketplace.

From the early 1570s the expansion of trade benefited one group of villagers in particular: tenant farmers and propertyholders with sizable landholdings, millers, and petty merchants. The concentration of movable wealth in the wealthiest 5 to 10 percent of the households was already apparent in the survey of taxable wealth undertaken in 1581 in Langenburg district (see Chapter 3). But by the early seventeenth century tenant farmers, millers, and merchants were suspected of hiding enormous fortunes gained through trade. Old Jop Breunger of Kupferhof, who had been long suspected of hoarding grain and selling it to the poor at usurious prices, was discovered in 1612 to have a hoard of wealth in his household. His land, cash hoard, supplies of cattle, wine, and grain, and outstanding loans totaled approximtely 3,700 fl., twice the amount of his assessed wealth for taxes.[14] Investigators discovered in Jacob Abel's house at Unterregenbach a whopping 4,600 fl. in property, more than three times the still substantial estimate of 1,330 fl. registered in the account books.[15] And, in a case that particularly shocked villagers in the Jagst valley region, officials

---

[14] ALGAL 738/1, September 8, 1612.   [15] ALGAL 738/1, September 8, 1612.

found that the wealthy and powerful tavernkeeper at Nesselbach, Endres Franckh, had amassed a fortune of 8,600 fl.[16]

Only a small elite of peasants could position themselves in the South German market economy to amass commercial wealth on this scale. To do so a villager had to have properties large enough to produce grain supplies sufficient to meet his own household needs plus regular surpluses to sell on the market. Whether a household could produce enough grain to meet its own needs depended upon three main factors: size of landholdings, seed–yield ratios on the farm's lands, and the number of children and dependents in the household. A household in Hohenlohe with exceptionally fertile lands that gave a seed–yield ratio of 1:7 or 1:8 could produce enough to feed its members with as little as 5.25 *morgen* of land. To remain self-sufficient, however, this same household would have had to have only two or three family members and no additional dependents. The head of a large household of eight to ten family members and dependents, on the other hand, would struggle to remain self-sufficient even if he or she had as much as 18 *morgen* of land to farm. In order to be relatively certain of producing sufficient supplies of grain for the household and having surpluses to sell on the market, a household needed 18 *morgen* of land or more to farm.[17]

Tenant farmers with large compact farms and a few smallholders who could assemble a sizable estate from various plots of land were, then, the only groups who entered the market with hopes of selling grain for a profit. One might visualize this group as an elite at the top of a fluid economic hierarchy of three strata in village society. In the early seventeenth century this group, namely those who disposed 18 *morgen* of land or more, composed at the most 22 percent of the households in Langenburg district (see Graph 6.1). Below them came the households whose position in the market might oscillate. In good years, and at times when they had few other demands on the household, they might sell a small surplus on the market; in bad years they had to buy grain to feed their families. Perhaps 21 percent of the households, those holding between 5.25 and 17.9 *morgen* of land, fell into this category. The majority of households in this sample (52 percent) never produced enough grain on their small plots of land to feed themselves; they entered the market on decidedly weak terms as buyers of grain in a time of high prices and dearth. As grain prices continued to rise into the 1620s and market relationships deepened, the number of Hohenlohers who entered the market on disadvantageous terms continued to rise. In 1630 fully two-thirds, and probably more, of the households in Langenburg district could not produce enough grain to meet their own needs.

[16] ALGAL 740/11, December 1619.
[17] I base these statistics on household self-sufficiency on the systematic study of peasant grain production undertaken in the district of Langenburg in 1622. For a detailed discussion of the basis for these measurements see Appendix B.

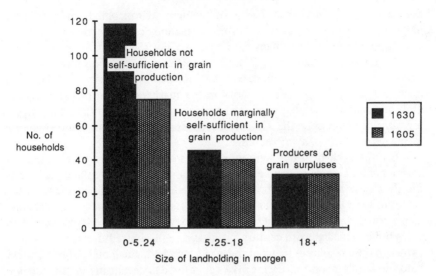

Graph 6.1. Self-sufficiency of peasant households in Langenburg district, 1605–30 (Atzenrod, Bächlingen, Binselberg, and Langenburg only). *Sources:* L/L 27, 1606; 28, 1606; "Schatzungsanlage Amt Langenburg 1630."

For the majority of peasants, participation in the market economy brought only impoverishment, heavy debts, and acute vulnerability to famine. Without sufficient land to feed their families, they had to buy grain or bread on the local markets at high prices. Smallholders and cottagers with no reserves of grain or money faced starvation repeatedly after 1570. And their position became more tenuous with each unpredictable swing in the price and supply of grain. In 1607, for example, the smallholders of Oberregenbach and Unterregenbach found that "after we poor, along with our wives and children, had eaten the grain planted in our small fields we could not even borrow any more in our village."[18] Driven to desperate measures during these famines, smallholders and the village poor went into debt "to buy bread and other food at the baker's" even if that meant compromising their future income and welfare. As one smallholder put it during the famine of 1611–12, to repay his debts for buying food that year he would have to "cut back on my own and my wife's bread."[19]

With each cycle of famine and indebtedness, smallholders, cottagers, and the village poor were driven into greater dependence upon the market economy for their livelihood. They had, of course, to purchase their grain or bread on

[18] ALARL 1607–8/B8, July 12, 1607.   [19] ALARL 1611–12/B6, March 15, 1611.

the market. But to do so they had to supplement their income from inadequate plots of land with cash incomes. For these smallholders, winegrowers, artisans, and day laborers, participation in market activity was no peripheral activity: Their incomes fluctuated sharply with the ups and downs of prices and wages. For the villagers in this position, and this included the majority in Hohenlohe, making a profit on the sale of goods in the market was out of the question. Only one economic strategy made sense in what was for most villagers a struggle for survival: Minimize the chances of economic disaster by supplementing income from a diversity of sources.[20]

Viticulture still held out some hopes for some villagers eager to acquire a cash income. Unable to acquire fertile farmland on the Hohenlohe plain or in the river valleys, many smallholders continued to plant small vineyards on the slopes of the valley walls. Smallholders from Bächlingen, Unterregenbach, and Langenburg, for example, covered the southern slopes of the Jagst valley with vines by the late sixteenth century.[21] Viticulture maximized the use of the only two economic resources many of these villagers had: small plots of poor, rocky land and family labor. Since wine prices continued to decline in the late sixteenth century, only the poorest smallholders desperate for a cash income undertook such projects willingly. In Bächlingen smallholders with 10 *morgen* of land or less devoted approximately 25 percent of their agricultural production to viticulture in 1606, those with 10 to 19 *morgen* slightly less than that. But Bächlingen's tenant farmers planted none of their land in vines; they preferred to keep it in arable and pasture (see Graph 6.2).

Not even the most desperate smallholders depended exclusively on viticulture for a living. The high risks of crop losses in viticulture, the low and declining prices for wine, and the rising prices for grain made it worth while to keep at

---

[20] Economists and economic anthropologists sometimes assume that peasants pursue economic thinking at odds with the "rational" pursuit of economic self-interest. The dichotomy has led to the conclusion among some developmental economists that peasants do not therefore respond rationally to economic opportunities. Leaving aside for a moment the problem of *motives* – these are far too complex and difficult to ascertain in individuals even in situations where profit making seems to prevail – and concentrating simply on the *behavior* of peasants, it is obvious that they appear to have adopted a classic rational approach to their economic conditions: risk-aversive strategies designed to minimize losses in an uncertain economic environment. Even in the most highly industrialized economies of the West, firms pursue risk-aversive strategies in times when profits cannot be easily realized or in times when uncertainty makes it important that losses be minimized. The problem of risk minimization still needs a great deal more consideration in discussions of peasant economies. See, for example, James C. Scott, *The Moral Economy of the Peasant: Rebellion and Subsistence in Southeast Asia* (New Haven, Conn.: Yale University Press, 1976); Samuel L. Popkin, *The Rational Peasant: the Political Economy of Rural Society in Vietnam* (Berkeley and Los Angeles: University of California Press, 1979); and Sutti Reissig Ortiz, *Uncertainties in Peasant Farming: A Colombian Case*, London School of Economics, Monographs on Social Anthropology, no. 46 (London: Athlone, 1973).

[21] Gustav Bossert, "Recht und Brauch in Langenburg im sechzehnten und siebzehnten Jahrhundert," *Württembergische Jahrbücher für Statistik und Landeskunde* (1910), 95–114.

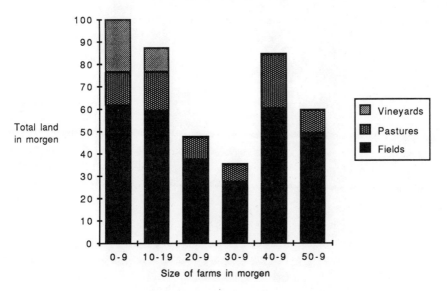

Graph 6.2. Land use in Bächlingen, 1606. *Source:* L/L 27, 1606; 28, 1606.

least some land in grain production even if the yields on these lands were low and unreliable. When Count Wolfgang of Hohenlohe directed peasants to continue planting vineyards on Bächlingen's Mühlberg, the land rising up the slope behind the mill to Langenburg, some villagers simply refused to cooperate. "A number of the day laborers point out that they have no other arable land, but many children to feed," the *Schultheiss* reported in 1597. "If they plant vines on small plots that once gave them a half-year's supply of grain, they fear that they could not feed their children."[22] Winegrowers in Bächlingen who understood the agricultural conditions of the Jagst valley also explained that the vineyards often failed to produce reliable harvests of grapes because of the climate. Besides, these villagers pointed out, the labor costs were often excessively high to maintain the vineyards properly and, above all, winegrowing increased one's dependence on the market for grain and bread.[23] The tendency in the 1610s and 1620s, in fact, was to convert vineyards back to arable. By 1630 smallholders had severely curtailed their production of wine (see Graph 6.3).

Despite the efforts to secure sources of cash income and grain, smallholders still could not avoid going deep into debt by the early seventeenth century. Since the princes prohibited peasants from taking out loans from merchants

[22] ALKI 358/18, January 24, 1597.   [23] ALKI 358/37, December 2, 1598.

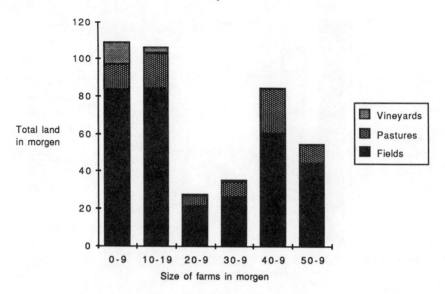

Graph 6.3. Land use in Bächlingen, 1630. *Source:* L/L "Schatzungsanlage Amt Langenburg 1630."

outside of the territory, only two official sources of credit were available to
Hohenlohers: other villagers and small townsmen from Hohenlohe or the
princes themselves. Of the two, the princes and their patrimonial state assumed
the lion's share of smallholder debts. For some smallholders the loans from
the princes went toward conversion of arable land into viticulture. As Count
Wolfgang noted, peasants could not plant vineyards "at their own expense alone,
which would be beyond their means; they should be sustained in their expenses
by their own villages and other communities."[24] And he should have listed
himself as the smallholders' most important creditor. Bächlingen winegrowers
turned to him for credit in 1596 to purchase thirteen thousand seedlings for
their new vineyards.[25] To Atzenrod's smallholders agricultural improvements
were impossible without the princes'credit:

We are clearing a plot of land near the mill and Our Grace [Count Wolfgang] wants
us to make a vineyard out of it and plant vines there. But if our gracious lord does not
want us to miss any of the work to complete this project then we need grain because
grain in the land is now very dear, and not at all available, and we have neither grain
nor money in reserve and are extremely hard pressed.[26]

[24] ALKI 358/38, December 25, 1598.
[25] ALKI 358/15, November 7, 1596; 358/17, December 13, 1596; 358/29, September 27, 1597;
358/30, September 27, 1597; 358/31, September 28, 1597.
[26] ALARL 1611–12/B18, December 26, 1610.

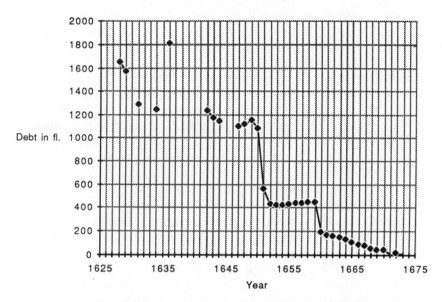

Graph 6.4. Debts of winegrowers from Langenburg district to the state, 1628–73.
Source: ALARL 1628–9 to 1673–4.

Smallholders who depended partly upon viticulture for a cash income in Langenburg district piled up a debt of 1,600 or 1,700 fl. with the government by the late 1620s. Their total indebtedness declined only in the 1640s and 1650s (see Graph 6.4).

Other villagers entered the market as petty craftsmen selling small manufactures to supplement their incomes. Low fixed costs, the ability to mobilize family labor in times of seasonal unemployment, and access to local markets made it relatively easy for almost any smallholder or cottager to make shoes, small leather goods, rope, pots, wooden utensils and furniture, or cloth for sale on the local markets. Production in these craft industries remained very small in scale and never rivaled agricultural production in importance in the regional economy. Smallholders and cottagers who organized their households to produce small crafts also remained independent producers. Merchants from the surrounding cities never organized the widely dispersed craftsmen engaged in such activities into a putting-out system that rivaled the proto-industrial regions of Germany for a share of the export market.[27] Few, if any, products left Hohenlohe destined for the export trade. Craft production in this rural area remained peasant industry, a part-time activity among smallholders and cottagers geared strictly to service local markets.

[27] On the development of rural industry in early modern Germany see the Bibliographical Essay.

Peasant craftsmen therefore took steps to carve out as secure a niche in the local markets as possible. Like craftsmen in other parts of Europe, these peasants protected their markets by organizing small rural guilds. Leather workers, first organized in the Kocher River valley in the early sixteenth century, expanded their guild in 1562 when they acquired the privilege to organize workers in their craft throughout Hohenlohe.[28] The potters followed in 1602, the cobblers in 1603, the tailors in 1614, and the ropemakers in 1617.[29] In each case the craftsmen presented themselves to the princes of Hohenlohe as a corporate group wishing to restrict competition on the local markets to members of their society. In return they promised to make sure that they served consumers by producing goods of quality and by training apprentices carefully in their respective trades. And each of these guilds organized itself on a territorial, not on a village or town, basis. Peasants also worked as barbers, weavers, ironsmiths, wheelwrights, barrelmakers, carpenters, and masons to supplement their agricultural incomes in the sixteenth century, but none of these crafts received privileges to organize guilds until the late seventeenth century.[30]

Despite these efforts, peasant artisans held only a tenuous position in the markets next to competitors from beyond the territory. This weakness is hardly surprising. These Hohenlohers competed with well-established artisans from Ansbach, Mergentheim, Rothenburg o.d.T., and Schwäbisch Hall who specialized in the production of small manufactures. And these urban craftsmen could take advantage of much more sophisticated distribution networks created to service not just the local markets but the entire region. Hohenlohe potters, for example, fought constantly to secure dominance of the local markets and never fully succeeded against their competitors from Ansbach and Hall. In 1603 and again in 1604 the potters protested to the princes of Hohenlohe that foreign potters threatened to ruin their trade and demanded that the interlopers be excluded from the local markets.[31] After years of such complaints the princes finally granted the request in 1619.[32] Even though such bans did not always accomplish their intended goals, it is doubtful that the tiny and weak craft industry of Hohenlohe would have survived without at least some state protection.

As a last resort smallholders and cottagers unable to earn cash incomes in any other way became wage laborers. The major disincentive was the steady erosion of wages in the sixteenth century. This weakening of income for wage

[28] ALKI 98/5, 1562; the privilege was renewed in 1655 (ALKI 98, October 15, 1655).
[29] For cobblers see ALKI 105/1, 1602; and 105/3, [1616 or 1617]; potters, ALKI 108/1, February 28, 1602; tailors, ALKI 107/1, February 5, 1614; and ropemakers, ALKI 110/1, [1617?].
[30] For weavers see ALKI 123/1, December 28, 1668; barbers, ALKI 124, 1670–80; smiths and wheelwrights, ALKI 125/1, May 28, 1677; barrelmakers, ALKI 130/1, June 20, 1677; carpenters and masons, ALKI 133/11, 1683.
[31] ALAL 251, May 1603; 251, December 2, 1604; and 251, May 23, 1612.
[32] ALAL 251, October 25, 1619.

laborers had less to do with nominal wages than with the wage–price scissors brought about by the steady inflation of grain and bread prices.[33] And in the early seventeenth century wages continued to decline, this time at an accelerated pace. By the 1620s day laborers working the vineyards of the counts of Hohenlohe had only 35 percent of the disposable income of workers twenty years earlier.[34] "I went to work in the vineyards," explained Jacob Strauss of Billingsbach during the famine of 1623, "because of pressing need so that I could repay Your Grace [Count Philip Ernst] my past debts."[35] The making of Germany's rural proletariats after 1560 took place in a climate of hunger, fear, and desperation.

Peasants who became part-time laborers also became deeply dependent upon the ups and downs in the seasonal market for rural labor. Work in this labor market meant dependence on two employers: tenant farmers and lords. Tenant farmers, for example, often could not manage their farms simply with family labor. They employed seasonal workers to help out with the planting or harvesting of crops. The lords, however, became employers of much larger numbers of smallholders and cottagers. Day laborers either worked the estates of the lords or helped with the collection, storage, and distribution of rents, dues, and tithes. In the district of Langenburg, for example, day laborers from Bächlingen, Atzenrod, Langenburg, Oberregenbach, and Unterregenbach planted the crops in the spring at Lindenbronn, harvested them in the fall, and mowed hay for winter storage. Others were employed to hoe, prune, fertilize, harvest, cart, and plant new vines in the lord's vineyards near Langenburg.[36] The princes hired a host of other laborers to work as forest workers, fishermen, hare catchers, shepherds, watchmen, and pasture keepers. None of these occupations paid much. But with such employment came the opportunity to petition the princes for gifts of wood, grain, bread, small loans, clothing, or other items necessary to survive harsh economic times.

All of these strategies for survival in the market economy did not protect smallholders, cottagers and laborers from utter destitution. The alarming growth of the urban and village poor in the sixteenth century spurred authorities in almost every community to expand and reform public charity and almsgiving. The motives for doing so always involved a mixture of religious piety, charity, and fear of social unrest. All of these motives guided the reform of public charity in Hohenlohe as well. Upon his death in 1610 Count Wolfgang left a legacy that established a poor-relief fund for Hohenlohe-Langenburg. The decree establishing the fund declared: "God repeatedly commanded us with

---

[33] See Abel, *Geschichte der deutschen Landwirtschaft*, 172–5.
[34] On the counts' estates in Langenburg district, for example, day laborers received a fixed wage of 0.2 fl. per day between 1601 and 1670, but spelt prices in the 1620s stood at almost three times their level in 1601.
[35] ALARL 1623–4/B90, May 12, 1623.   [36] ALAL 640, February 21, 1661.

his holy words that we should take in the poor, the needy, the wretched and help them with our alms." His goal, however, was to help only one group of the village poor: "the house poor or oppressed people who had supported themselves honorably as long as they could, who had behaved piously and honorably."[37] The state established a fund, in other words, for local house-holders, not migrant beggars, who could expect quarterly payments disbursed by local pastors. A few of the village poor might also find shelter at the *Spital* in Döttingen.[38] Most of these "house poor" were indigent widows and orphans who had fallen into destitution upon the death of a male head of the household. As Barbara Ziegler of Bächlingen explained when admitted to the *Spital* in the 1620s, "I stayed with my son for four years, but the food was bad and [he] supported me only with great effort."[39]

Of all the groups in village society, the "house poor" felt the sharp seasonal and yearly swings in a harvest-centered economy most of all. Their fortunes depended also upon cycles in the family, the whims of governments, and the generosity of individuals who took pity on their plight. In the end, however, the numbers of desperately poor villagers fluctuated in unison with agrarian prices and wages. In Langenburg district, for example, the poor-relief fund supported thirty-eight villagers when it was introduced at the beginning of a famine in 1611. As the famine eased, the numbers on the "house poor" list fell, then fluctuated until the beginnings of very hard times for the village poor in 1620. As the prices for grain, peasant indebtedness, and taxes rose to new heights in the 1620s, so the numbers of "house poor" increased once again. By the late 1630s the fund was declining many applicants for relief and pastors were reporting larger numbers than usual of "foreign beggars" found dead from exposure and hunger in Langenburg and the surrounding villages. From a peak of forty "house poor" in 1630 the numbers declined sharply, accelerating when the population of the region suddenly collapsed in 1634–5. It continued to decline until only a dozen or so remained on the list in 1650.[40] By then the economic crisis had passed.

A moral economy?

Against this backdrop of chronic dearth and impoverishment the old debate over the proper place of market activities in a Christian society assumed new relevance. The debate was one-sided, for no one seriously argued that the market should have free rein in ordering social relationships. For scholars in the universities and pamphleteers, especially Lutheran ones who set the tone

---

[37] AL "Almosenrechnung Amt Langenburg," December 5, 1611.
[38] AL "Döttingen Spital Rechnungen," 1621, 1622, 1626, 1636; AK O/26/A1, 1627.
[39] AK O/26/A4/12, January 28, 1653.   [40] ALAlmAL, 1611–54, 1679–84.

The unchristian economy

in the debate, market activity should always be subordinated to the greater good
of the community and the household.[41] Just as François Quesnay and Adam
Smith in the eighteenth century elevated an abstract ideal, the free market, to
a prominent place in their economic theories, so writers like Conrad Heresbach,
Martin Grosser, and Johann Coler championed the ideal of the self-sufficient
household as a cornerstone of a sound Christian economy. They admonished
their readers not to pursue market activities merely to accumulate material
wealth. Market activity was acceptable, but only insofar as it contributed to the
self-sufficiency and social harmony of the household. A good head of the
household whether a lord or a peasant, should order market relationships as
part of the effort to keep the household and the community self-sufficient.[42]
These writers gave voice to the powerful opinion in Germany that had gathered
strength from the early days of the Reformation that markets should be carefully
supervised, that trading activities should be strictly subordinated to the needs
of the community.

But *who* should control the markets and police the commercial transactions
that took place? How should sellers and buyers structure the relationships they
established at the marketplace? In an age of chronic and unpredictable dearth,
command over the production and distribution of food supplies did not appear
to the authorities or to consumers to be a neutral economic activity. Those who
produced surpluses of grain and food and those who controlled their distribution
through the market had the power to dominate individual consumers, families,
and whole communities with no choice but to buy their food on the marketplace.
When shortages came – and come they did with disturbing regularity between
1560 and 1650 – the decision to sell grain to consumers in local markets or
to export it to towns outside the territory determined who would suffer from
hunger and who would not. Dearth then was not simply an economic problem.
It was a social and a political problem at the same time. Whoever dominated
the markets and controlled the distribution of grain and food held power over
a community's lifeblood, especially when so many households could not produce
enough grain to support themselves.

Who would dominate the markets themselves and the relationships established there was a question never fully resolved in the sixteenth century. Pro-

---

[41] For discussions of the ideas contained in the Lutheran *Hausvaterliteratur* see Otto Brunner,
"Das 'ganze Haus' und die alteuropäische 'Ökonomik,' " in his *Neue Wege der Verfassungs- und
Sozialgeschichte*, 2d ed. (Göttingen: Vandenhoeck & Ruprecht, 1968), 103–27, and especially
his *Adeliges Landleben und europäischer Geist: Leben und Werk Wolf Helmhards von Hohberg 1612–
1688* (Salzburg: Otto Muller, 1949), 240–86. Much remains to be done, however, to understand
the intellectual world of these writers.
[42] See, for example, Conrad Heresbach, *Rei rusticae libri quattuor* (Cologne: Johannes Birckmann,
1570); Johann Coler, *Calendarium oeconomicum et perpetuum* (Wittenberg: P. Helwig, 1592); and
Gertrud Schröder-Lembke, ed., *Martin Grosser, Anleitung zu der Landwirtschaft*, Quellen und
Forschungen zur Agrargeschichte, no. 12 (Stuttgart: Gustav Fischer, 1965).

ducers, merchants, consumers, and state authorities all fell into conflict at one
time or another in fitful and haphazard attempts to control market exchanges.
In the 1520s and 1530s the diet of the Holy Roman Empire tried repeatedly
to administer prices, control coinages, and curb the abusive practices of Germany's powerful urban merchant houses. The diet, however, failed in the end
to acquire meaningful power over Germany's rapidly expanding market economy.[43] Then in the middle of the century the territorial princes took the initiative
to control market activities. The princes often saw themselves as *Hausväter*, or
"fathers of families," responsible for making certain that the markets provided
the territory's towns and villages with secure supplies of grain and food at
affordable prices.[44] The extension of state controls over markets occurred in
fits and starts after 1560 and proceeded not so much as a carefully thought-
through policy as it did as a series of expedient measures taken out of desperation
during subsistence crises. Taken as a whole, however, the market ordinances
aimed at creating a moral economy in which market exchanges served the
subsistence needs of consumers, not the desires for profit of the producers and
sellers of grain.[45]

Princes of territories with particularly volatile grain markets battled constantly
after 1560 to establish a moral economy in their marketplaces. In Hohenlohe,
for example, Count Ludwig Casimir first took steps to extend authority over
the local markets in 1561–2, probably in response to sudden surges in grain
prices in those years. He ordered sellers of grain "to undertake to sell grain
not to the detriment of our subjects, but for their use and welfare."[46] Food
prices were to be regulated, and no sellers would be allowed to export food
out of the territory during years of shortages or famine. Later, when a new
market at Langenburg was established, the princes stated clearly the purposes
of the local markets: "to grant and allow each subject to buy what he needs
for himself and his household on the public market at a fitting and proper
price."[47] Tenant farmers, millers, merchants, bakers, and butchers should all
make food available for the common man in the local market and in their shops
before they exported grain out of the territory. And they should also make
certain to use correct weights in their transactions and never charge more than
a just price for food.[48] The constant issuing of market ordinances in these
territories, however, indicated not a state victory over the forces of supply and
demand, but continuous difficulty in administering prices at just levels and

---

[43] Heinrich Bechtel, *Wirtschaftsgeschichte Deutschlands vom Beginn des 16. bis zum Ende des 18. Jahrhunderts* (Munich: Georg D. W. Callwey, 1952), 90–4, 107–11.
[44] Ibid. 73–83, 94–5.
[45] See the seminal article by E. P. Thompson, "The Moral Economy of the English Crowd in the Eighteenth Century," *Past and Present* no. 50 (1971), 76–136.
[46] ALGAL 175, 1561–2.   [47] ALGAL 7/49, July 24, 1602.
[48] ALKI 100/4, [ca. 1590]; 100/6, [ca. 1590].

policing marketing practices effectively.[49] Tenant farmers, millers, and petty merchants eager to profit from the sale of food always managed to escape rigid controls.

Within the village the efforts to create a moral economy masked another kind of struggle: desperate and, in the long run, hopeless attempts to structure market relationships in ways favorable to the village poor. From the early 1570s on, there is evidence that smallholders, artisans, and laborers took the initiative in drawing the state into conflicts at the marketplace with the producers and sellers of grain. These villagers adopted the language of the moral economy as part of their attempt to force tenant farmers, millers, and merchants to sell grain at just, usually meaning low, prices. In petitions delivered to state officials the village poor of Hohenlohe painted a picture of communities now divided into two hostile camps: those who prospered through market relationships and those who were exploited by them. As one group explained in 1601, sellers of grain appeared obsessed with greed and showed an appalling neglect for the welfare of their neighbors. They charged whatever prices they wanted for their grain, engaged in uninhibited exporting of scarce supplies, and, as a result, "pressed the poor man violently and piteously" into poverty.[50] Echoing provisions in the market ordinances, these desperate consumers called upon the authorities to press vigorously all the controls that would hold the bakers, millers, tenant farmers, and merchants in check: just and fair prices, prohibitions on grain exports, and the end of grain hoarding. Buying and selling at the market should be done morally, in a Christian manner, so as to protect the village poor from starvation at the hands of those who controlled the production and distribution of grain.

These conflicts lent a tense and uncertain atmosphere to market days from 1560 on. No one, especially wealthy peasants, admitted to benefiting from market exchanges. Everyone, buyers and sellers alike, instead complained constantly of being cheated. Among the village poor the suspicion easily spread that particular tenant farmers charged unfair prices or hoarded grain in times of famine. Others suspected the bakers and butchers of falsifying their weights or conducting a secret trade with foreign merchants to sell the bread and meat out of the territory. Still others worried that teamsters made the rounds by night to the tenant farmers buying up stores of grain and slipping across the border to other markets by daylight. For tenant farmers and millers there was always the worry that officials would suddenly appear to investigate charges of overpricing or to search their houses and barns for secret supplies of goods. Bakers and butchers complained constantly that the administered prices were

---

[49] ALKI 16/1, December 10, 1601; 103/1, December 29, 1597; 100/8, 1598; 100/10, [ca. 1598]; 100/11, 1599; ALAL 388, November 1, 1610; ALKI 103/2, August 24, 1611; 103/4, August 5, 1617; ALAL 339, 1618.
[50] ALKI 16/1, December 10, 1601.

ruinously low. And state officials, spurred on by angry consumers, conducted regular campaigns to discipline them for breaking the laws, singling them out for fines and admonishments in 1597, 1598, 1599, 1610–11, 1617, and 1618.[51] In the short run the village poor achieved temporary triumphs when the state intervened on their behalf. In the long run the terms of trade continued to favor the region's peasant elite. Until prices and population fell steeply in the 1640s not the moral economy but the unchristian economy reigned at the marketplace.

The failure to establish stable and orderly market relationships in the rural areas set the stage for an expansion in the state's role in provisioning communities with adequate supplies of grain. Princes of the small patrimonial states in Germany sometimes undertook this task not out of eagerness to find new sources of power, but reluctantly and out of fear that they had no alternative if they wanted to preserve their authority in the countryside. Peasants also expected their lords to come to their aid in times of need. Only a few scattered records document the earliest efforts of the House of Hohenlohe to supply impoverished peasants with grain. This is not surprising, since relief efforts evolved naturally out of the long-recognized obligation of a lord to provide protection to his dependents. In 1561 and 1562 some evidence suggests that stewards and district officials carried out relief efforts on their own, without supervision or guidance from the court. Count Ludwig Casimir in fact suspected that his own officials had loaned out grain at usurious rates to villagers in desperate need of it.[52] The turning point may have come during the terrible famine of the 1570s. Lords and princes throughout Franconia feared a general insurrection if they did not provision hungry villagers with grain, and their relief efforts marked the beginning of a period of active state involvement in supplying communities directly with food.[53]

From the 1580s on, the relief efforts intensified, then were systematized. During the famines of the late 1580s Count Wolfgang personally supervised the distribution of large amounts of grain from his own granaries to poor smallholders and cottagers from Billingsbach and Unterregenbach. These efforts obviously taxed his resources at times. In May 1589 he granted villagers still more supplies of grain, this time noting that "it required more than I [Wolfgang] thought and [my granaries] are now exhausted."[54] The protocols of petitions from Ingelfingen and Langenburg districts from the 1590s indicate that villagers pleaded continually for supplies of grain, sometimes in small

[51] ALKI 103/1, December 29, 1597; 100/8, 1598; 100/10, [ca. 1598]; 100/11, 1599; ALAL 388, November 1, 1610; ALKI 103/2, August 24, 1611; 103/4, August 5, 1617; ALAL 339, 1618.
[52] ALGAL 175, 1561–2.
[53] See Rudolf Endres, "Zur wirtschaftlichen und sozialen Lage in Franken vor dem Dreissigjährigen Krieg," *Jahrbuch für fränkische Landesforschung* 28 (1968), 5–52.
[54] ALKI 351/4, May 9, 1589.

amounts for just one family, other times in substantial quantity for an entire village.[55] The effort to coordinate actions and to keep accurate records began in 1602. In July of that year Count Wolfgang prohibited the export of grain from the territory, this time so as to help district officials to buy up surpluses of grain and stockpile them "so that it can be arranged at any time to help out our subjects."[56] Later he directed his *Schultheissen* to record incomes from rents, dues, and tithes more accurately so that a portion of each year's harvest would be available to loan out to the village poor "so that they would not be too hard pressed."[57]

State distribution of grain, even though it developed haphazardly at first, still had its desired effects. After 1602 villages had relatively secure supplies of grain and the state had a way of countering the chaos that reigned in the markets in times of famine. Improvements in record keeping, a temporary stagnation in prices, and perhaps a lessening in the severity of famines until the 1620s allowed lords and peasants to consolidate the relief networks. By this time the state distribution of grain had become essential for the everyday survival of the village poor. "We poor, our wives, and children have already eaten our grain that we planted on our small plots," a group of desperate Oberregenbachers pleaded to Count Wolfgang in 1607, "and there is none left to borrow and everyone has harvested early and sold [their crops] for cash."[58] For groups such as these the princes now commanded the lifeblood of the community. "We praise and thank the Almighty God that He has richly blessed the House of Hohenlohe with grain," another group of villagers put it in 1611.[59]

The new paternalism

Lords, then, did not take advantage of the agrarian expansion simply as calculating landlords bent on extracting an economic rent from scarce land and resources. The exercise of *Grundherrschaft* made it impossible for lords ever to separate material wealth from the social relationships that produced it. For a prince like Count Wolfgang, steeped as he was in the new Lutheran *Hausvaterliteratur*, the term "economy," or *Wirtschaft*, still meant household management and the careful tending of all the social and political, and even religious, relationships that continued the House of Hohenlohe's dominance over its peasants. The efforts to control the marketplace and to distribute grain to the village poor suggest that princes and lords sought social and economic stability even if it cost the state dear, as it did Count Wolfgang in the 1580s. For these

---

[55] ALGAL 178; ALSPL, 1592–1602.   [56] ALGAL 7/49, July 24, 1602.
[57] ALKI 171/3, September 28, 1602.   [58] ALARL 1607–8/B 9, July 12, 1607.
[59] ALARL 1611–12/B19, 1611.

lords, mastering the rural unrest that came with commercial expansion mattered as much as improving seigneurial incomes. In an age of chronic dearth and, as we shall see in the next chapter, persistent and disturbing peasant discontent, cautious lords tended to place a premium on bringing order to an increasingly complex agrarian society.

This does not mean that lords neglected to improve their revenues in the sixteenth century. German lords showed an attentiveness to the management of their lands and revenues in the late sixteenth century that they had not had in the fifteenth century. The surveys of landed wealth and seigneurial income deserve particular attention, since they indicate more careful management of incomes and the material resources at the disposal of lords. Officials were instructed to survey their properties more frequently and to record in greater detail every rent and due from new lands brought into production. Stewards had carried out new cadastral surveys of land and seigneurial sources of income in Langenburg district shortly after the Peasants' War – in 1528, for example – but they showed more diligence in recording properties and incomes from the middle of the sixteenth century on. New surveys were undertaken in 1553, 1562, 1573, 1581, and 1595.[60] And two extraordinary measures capped these efforts: a detailed assessment and description of all peasant property, both movable and fixed, between 1581 and 1587 and a massive and systematic description of every piece of property in the cadastre of 1606.[61] This final survey became the official record for all property for the rest of the seventeenth century. And, to systematize the record keeping in the yearly account books for each district, the stewards began to keep detailed accounts of every single transaction after 1605.[62] Such records enabled lords to manage their incomes and expenditures with a confidence completely unknown in the early sixteenth century.

These records show just how much lords profited from the agrarian and commercial expansion of the sixteenth century. Lords in every corner of Europe prospered as a result of the boom of the sixteenth century, but the greatest increases tended to come after 1550. As peasants cleared new land and began to pay customary rents, revenues soared. In the 1550s the lords collected 204 fl. per year in rents from peasants in Langenburg district. By the 1590s income from rents had risen to 387 fl.; it then began to reach a peak in the 1620s at around 500 fl. per year (see Table 6.3). Incomes from entry fines and death duties also increased. Because properties changed hands so many times in the late sixteenth century, the lords in fact began to regard entry fines as a major source of revenue.[63] In the 1590s income from fines stood at 888 fl., more than

[60] L/L 5, 1553; 4, 1562; 7, 1573; 17, 1581; 24, 1595. [61] L/L 27, 1606; 28, 1606.
[62] ALGAL 179, 1605. [63] ALGAL 738/24, 1612.

168

Table 6.3. *Average yearly income in rents from Langenburg district, 1550-1689*

Year	Income in fl.	Index
1550-9	204	100
1560-9	-	-
1570-9	319	156
1580-9	319	156
1590-9	387	190
1600-9	433	212
1610-19	453	222
1620-9	509	250
1630-9	519	254
1640-9	522	256
1650-9	522	256
1660-9	522	256
1670-9	522	256
1680-9	522	256

Sources: ALARL 1552-3 to 1683-4.

Note: After 1651 the counts of Hohenlohe transferred the administration of the villages of Leofels, Döttingen, and Kirchberg to Langenburg district. For comparative purposes the figures after 1651 in this table have therefore been adjusted downward to reflect the income from the villages that were under district administration between 1550 and 1649.

Table 6.4. *Average yearly income in entry fines from Langenburg district, 1590-1689*

Year	Income in fl.	Index
1590-9	888	100
1600-9	735	83
1610-19	789	89
1620-9	877	99
1630-9	757	85
1640-9	170	19
1650-9	279	31
1660-9	288	32
1670-9	355	40
1680-9	304	34

Sources: ALARL 1590-1 to 1683-4.

twice the income from rents. It remained at relatively high levels right into the 1620s and 1630s (see Table 6.4). Income from death duties followed a more erratic pattern, but peaked around 1640 (see Table 6.5). Other sources of income added substantially to these revenues. The revenues from tithes, grazing fees, and the sale of wood, grain, and wine on the market all increased during

Table 6.5. *Average yearly income from death duties from Langenburg district, 1590-1689*

Year	Income in fl.	Index
1590-9	181	100
1600-9	186	103
1610-19	164	91
1620-9	217	120
1630-9	371	205
1640-9	43	24
1650-9	249	138
1660-9	140	77
1670-9	88	49
1680-9	127	70

Sources: ALARL 1590-1 to 1683-4.

the boom of agricultural prices in the late sixteenth century. The material wealth of Germany's lords had not been so substantial since the fourteenth century.

Wealthy nobles tended to invest much of their wealth in conspicuous consumption, or, if one looks at their investment from another view, in symbols and tools of social dominance. The most visible symbols of this new wealth and power were the elegant Renaissance palaces built in the countryside by Germany's petty princes and nobles. The House of Hohenlohe engaged heavily in lavish spending of this sort. With the help of the noted architect Jakob Stegle, Count Wolfgang began to expand the castle at Weikersheim into a stunning Renaissance palace in 1595.[64] Not far away work got under way in transforming the castles at Langenburg and Kirchberg as well into more elegant seats of princely power.[65] But of equal, if not greater, importance for domestic order was the investment in less visible sources of social power and dominance. The expenses that went into expanding the state apparatus formed only the most obvious expenditure in this regard (see Chapter 7). The House of Hohenlohe also protected its peasants from dearth by redistributing wealth in the form of loans, rent adjustments, and various forms of relief. In an age of conflict and uncertainty created partly by the expansion of the market economy, the princes exchanged food and guarantees of subsistence for peasants' promises of loyalty.

The paternalism of the late sixteenth century was hardly a new development in lord–peasant relationships in Hohenlohe. The practice of dominance had

[64] Werner Fleischhauer, *Renaissance im Herzogtum Württemberg* (Stuttgart: W. Kohlhammer, 1971), 81; and Walter-Gerd Fleck, *Schloss Weikersheim und die hohenlohischen Schlösser der Renaissance*, Tübinger Forschungen zur Kunstgeschichte, no. 8 (Tübingen: Kunsthistorisches Institut der Universität Tübingen, 1954).

[65] See Gerhard Thaddey, "Neue Forschungen zur Baugeschichte von Schloss Langenburg," *Württembergisch Franken* 1979, 13–46.

always rested on the way in which a lord protected his dependents from adversity (see Chapter 1). The paternalism of the late sixteenth and early seventeenth centuries, however, involved more regular commitments to a much larger number of impoverished peasants than had been the case in the time of Kraft VI (d. 1503).

When the new paternalism developed is impossible to know with any certainty. As in the case of grain distribution, the princes appear to have expanded their networks of paternalism in fits and starts in response to famines and other pressing social and economic circumstances sometime after 1560. A watershed may have been passed in the early 1570s when all of the nobles of Franconia, the princes of Hohenlohe among them, felt compelled to relieve famine in the countryside on a massive scale.[66] Another major development came around 1580 when the princes reformed the procedures peasants had to follow to present petitions to the court. From this time forward the stewards helped peasants to present petitions directly to the princes, and then filed separate reports on each request with the steward's recommendation.[67] By the 1590s several stewards had begun to compile massive volumes of petitions and to organize them for systematic presentation to the counts. And in 1605 Count Wolfgang acquired complete personal mastery over the whole system of rural patronage when he required his stewards to document meticulously every transaction with a peasant and to append the records and reports to the account books for the count and his advisers to review personally.[68] Count Wolfgang and his successors now kept track of every single peasant request for help, the individual circumstances surrounding the request, and the execution of commands in response to the petition. A finer tool of paternalist control over peasants could not be imagined.

The depth and range of social and economic interests bound up in these paternalist ties might be glimpsed by studying the petitions submitted to Count Wolfgang from villagers of Langenburg district in a nine-year period between 1594 and 1602 (see Table 6.6). By this time the stewards had systematized the petitioning process considerably by recording every petition submitted, and the action taken in response to it, in a thick volume of protocols for the district.[69]The volume by no means indicates the full scope of the paternalist relationships that bound Wolfgang to his peasants at this time; it records almost exclusively those petitions concerning the burdens of *Grundherrschaft*. Requests concerning the territorial taxes and labor services were handled separately (see Chapter 7). Only in the new-style account books after 1605 does the vast extent of the patronage system become clear.

[66] See Endres, "Zur wirtschaftlichen und sozialen Lage in Franken."
[67] ALKI 6/5, [ca. 1580].   [68] ALGAL 179, 1605.   [69] ALSPL, 1592–1602.

Table 6.6. *Petitions from Langenburg district, 1594-1602*

Category	No.	%
"Economic" petitions		
Wood	354	26.5
Tax remissions	144	10.8
Requests for land	136	10.2
Loans of grain	135	10.1
"Political" petitions		
Miscellaneous favors	320	24.0
Remission of punishment	189	14.2
Residence requests	56	4.2
Total	1,334	100.0

Source: ALSPL 1592-1602.

Table 6.7. *Petitions for economic relief from villagers of Langenburg district, 1594-1602*

Request	Petition granted No.	%	Petition denied No.	%	Response n/a No.	%
Wood	340	96.0	14	4.0	0	0
Tax reductions & postponements	104	72.2	39	27.1	1	0.7
Land	108	79.4	26	19.1	2	1.5
Grain loans & subsidies	129	95.6	6	4.4	0	0

Source: ALSPL 1592-1602.

Even this small sample of petitions indicates that Count Wolfgang established, and renewed repeatedly, deep personal ties of patronage with almost every single peasant household in the territory by the 1590s. The numbers of petitions alone in proportion to the population of the district suggest the importance of the system for lord–peasant relations. In these nine years villagers from about 370 households submitted a total of 1,334 petitions. The majority of the petitions (58 percent) involved individuals, families, and, quite often, entire villages requesting some form of economic help: supplies of wood, relief from rents and dues, parcels of land, and stocks of grain. What is striking as well was the readiness of Count Wolfgang to come to his peasants' aid (see Table 6.7). This benevolent prince approved approximately 96 percent of all the requests for wood and grain in these years. Requests for relief from rents and dues and land were often looked on with favor as well. About 72 percent of these requests

Wolfgang approved, usually after some negotiation. Those who sought parcels of land had favorable responses in almost four out of five cases. In a strictly economic sense, the prince now functioned as the peasants' main creditor and source of capital loans and as a protector against dearth. Through these relationships Count Wolfgang redistributed the economic resources needed to survive the periodic crop failures, high prices for grain, and devastating cycles of famine that had become a part of villagers' everyday experience since 1560.

Every form of paternalism rests on the ability to evoke loyalty, deference, and fear in those who benefit from a patron's benevolence. In this particular case lords could impose their will on individual peasants or entire communities without the direct use of force or violence. With the wealthy tenant farmers this called for exploiting the vulnerability of these peasant households to death duties and entry fines. From these peasants the princes extracted new promises of loyalty and commitments to stagger payments for several years until the debt was paid. For tenants eager to retire, like Johann Huchbar of Rupershausen, this relief made it possible to establish an inexperienced heir, his daughter's husband, as his successor on the farm.[70] The village poor who asked for help showed a fear of authority possible only in individuals faced with a loss of land or immediate starvation. Hans Morwart of Bächlingen, for example, eagerly renewed his pledge of submission in 1592 when he approached the steward for a loan. He had fallen into debt, as had so many smallholders since the 1570s, and admitted that "to pay my debts I desperately need a considerable amount of money and I do not know where else to turn than to ask humbly that Your Grace [Count Wolfgang] loan me twenty-two *gulden* out of mercy."[71] For others, like Georg Graff of Unterregenbach, the lord's aid enabled them to survive, if only barely. This desperate villager pleaded to Wolfgang "to take pity on my wife and small, helpless children until I get some money and not to drive me away, but, out of mercy, to let me stay."[72] These villagers fell into a form of obsequious deference born out of a fear of hunger.

Property and hierarchy

The comparative stability that becomes noticeable in the agrarian economy in the early seventeenth century came at the expense of village autonomy. As Hohenlohers found their places, either on favorable or unfavorable terms, within the South German market economy, the village lost its significance as the major focal point of villagers' loyalty. The commune, after all, had derived its power from the ability to govern access to limited amounts of *fixed* property: land,

[70] Ibid. December 9, 1592.
[71] ALARL 1623–4/B170, May 16, 1624. [72] ALAL 1080, January 9, 1588.

pasture, woodlands, and water. The new market relationships of the sixteenth century demanded that villagers concern themselves not just with landed property, but also with *commercial* wealth, with money and with place or occupation within the market economy. The bitter conflicts to control the marketplace therefore marked the end of communal solidarity as it was known at the time of the Peasants' War.

Over this complex agrarian hierarchy the House of Hohenlohe imposed order with much more effectiveness than had been possible in the early sixteenth century. Once the small patrimonial state had seized the opportunity to order, with varying degrees of success, the market economy and to distribute grain and other scarce resources in the territory, the princes could make villagers more obedient and compliant. The princes of the House of Hohenlohe, in fact, showed an almost obsessive concern with domestic order and social control of peasants in the 1580s and 1590s. And, as we shall soon see, there was good reason to worry.

Threat of revolt

To the modern observer looking back on the decades around 1580, the patterns of lordly and princely dominance, of paternalistic rule and deference, appear much more settled than they in fact were. Only with hindsight can one see in this period the decisive turning point that it most assuredly was: a watershed when South Germany's lords and princes established secure patterns of dominance over their villagers that would last well into the eighteenth century. Determined and zealous princes had clearly seized the initiative to broaden their authority over their domains and subjects, to use new power to impose order where disorder appeared to reign. That these feudal lords, their secretaries, pastors, and stewards sometimes justified these measures with the passionate rhetoric of religious reform or with time-honored appeals to their villagers' devotion to custom or justice did not matter. The effect was the same. The autonomy of the village commune had been broken. Willingly or not, the descendants of villagers who had fought in 1525 for the freedom of their rural communes were forced to weaken their corporate ties and redirect their loyalties to the territorial state.

But for contemporaries, especially those who knew the circumstances of the small German states well, lord–peasant relationships appeared very much unsettled in these years, even more unsettled than in the two or three decades after 1525. For after 1570 South German and Austrian lords began to experience a wave of peasant unrest every bit as threatening and unnerving as the discontent on the eve of the Peasants' War. Not only did peasants rebel against Habsburg authorities in Upper Austria, a rebellion that dragged on for four long years between 1594 and 1597, but elsewhere in South Germany villagers revolted or carried out such bitter disputes with their lords that imperial authorities often intervened to resolve them.[1] If one listens to the voice of Johann Schuwardt, one of the scores of German pamphleteers in the 1580s and 1590s

---

[1] For the literature on the patterns of revolt in Germany after the Peasants' War see the Bibliographical Essay.

who offered up practical advice to princes and lords on how to instill obedience in their peasants, disobedience, recalcitrance, and outright resistance to authority were the rule of the day.[2]

But rural disorders did not always lead to the classic peasant revolt of this period. Nor did the order and stability that came in the wake of suppressing such unrest necessarily strengthen the early modern state. In the fluid and uncertain circumstances that surrounded a revolt, or the threat of a rising as was the case in Hohenlohe, the precise terms on which villagers accepted the expanded authority of their masters mattered a great deal. In the large territorial states, in the lands of the dukes of Württemberg, or in Bavaria, the outcome of these struggles favored the state. But in the small South German states like Hohenlohe the triumph of the prince was often bittersweet or even illusory. For, even though few peasant leaders dreamed of creating a world without lords, persistent and disciplined opposition to taxes and labor services could set strict limits on the prince's ability to exploit villagers' resources. Petty princes may have mastered the unrest, but, as one looks closely at the disorders in Hohenlohe, one can see that mastering peasant unrest and restoring order and stability could very often weaken the small patrimonial states.

The empire, the small state, and taxes

In the early sixteenth century the levying of taxes posed comparatively few problems for rulers and ruled alike in South Germany. The reason for this is simple: Few of the secular lords and small princes imposed a heavy burden of taxes on their villagers. What taxes they did levy stemmed from the irregular burdens placed on them by the empire. Ever since the Middle Ages the princes had had the obligation to assist the emperor with any war effort that involved the empire as a whole, but only in the late fifteenth century did many princes begin to meet this obligation with cash. In theory a prince had to use his own personal resources. Legally the military levies did not fall on the households of their subjects. When the imperial diet finally did establish the principle in 1489 that princes could tax their subjects to pay imperial levies, the precedent was an important one. But even then most princes were slow to tax their subjects directly. In 1495, for example, the diet levied a "common penny" on the territories, a general tax that most princes refused to impose on their subjects. Other taxes in the early sixteenth century met a similar fate.[3] When the empire

---

[2] See Winfried Schulze, *Bäuerlicher Widerstand und feudale Herrschaft in der frühen Neuzeit*, Neuzeit im Aufbau, vol. 6 (Stuttgart–Bad Cannstadt: Frommann-Holzboog, 1980), 176–7.

[3] For a discussion of the imperial war taxes see Winfried Schulze, *Reich und Türkengefahr im späten 16. Jahrhundert: Studien zu den politischen und gesellschaftlichen Auswirkungen einer äusseren Bedrohung* (Munich: C. H. Beck, 1978); or, for a short and concise treatment, his *Bäuerlicher Widerstand*, 66–9.

pressed urgently for the collection of war taxes in times of emergency, as happened more often after 1500 as the Turks advanced on the southeastern frontiers of the empire, reluctant princes were more likely to collect imperial levies in a rigorous manner. But even at that, the burdens fell unevenly on the small states and came at irregular intervals. In Hohenlohe, for example, Count Albrecht levied only a few such imperial war taxes, one in 1528 and three or four in the 1540s.[4]

Only after 1550 did the imperial taxes begin to pose a disruptive threat to the internal order of the empire. The sheer fiscal burden of the levies guaranteed it. The spiraling costs of fielding a mercenary army and keeping it in the field made these burdens far heavier and more regular than in the past. During the reign of Charles V (1519–55) the empire levied only 73.5 *Römermonate* of war taxes. His successors, ever more pressed to defend the empire against the Turks, had to seek the help of the diet and the princes much more frequently. Between 1556 and 1606 the imperial government imposed 409 *Römermonate* of war taxes on the territories.[5] These extraordinary demands pressed upon the resources of almost every state in the empire. In Hohenlohe Count Ludwig Casimir levied five, perhaps more, separate assessments on his villagers' households in the 1550s and 1560s. The levies fell even more frequently once Rudolf II assumed the imperial throne in 1576.[6] After that time the imperial taxes became a yearly levy on the territory and imposed an unprecedented burden of taxes on the resources of Hohenlohers. Like so many other small territories, by the 1580s Hohenlohe could not meet the yearly levies or pay off the debts that accumulated year after year. The House of Hohenlohe piled up debt upon debt to the empire in these years, and only the most indomitable optimist could have hoped that it could ever meet these crushing demands with any degree of regularity.[7]

The threat these levies posed to the domestic order of the small South German states was more subtle than the fiscal pressure. One could argue, and some historians have, that the petty German princes welcomed this chance to collect the imperial taxes as a sure means of extending their control over their

---

[4] LAN 42/5/5, 1528; 42/5/7, 1542; 42/5/10, 1544; 42/5/11, 1545; 42/5/12, 1548; 42/5/13, 1548; L/L "Reichssteuer und Schatzungsbuch Amt Langenburg 1528–1568."

[5] Schulze, *Bäuerlicher Widerstand*, 68. The *Römermonat* was the standard unit of taxation for military expenses adopted by the empire after 1521. Originally one *Römermonat* was 128,000 fl., or the cost of paying an army of 4,000 cavalry and 20,000 infantry for one month. This army served Charles V for the march to Rome in 1521 and then became the standard unit for the imperial army. See Schulze, *Reich und Türkengefahr*, 77, 179–82, 186–90, 272–5.

[6] LAN 42/16/7, 1577; 42/16/8, 1578; 42/16/9, 1580; 42/16/10, 1581; 42/16/11, 1582; 42/16/12, 1583; L/L 20, 1585; 20, 1587; ALKL II/3/37/1–11, 1586–7, 1594–1602.

[7] A thorough study of the debt problems of Germany's small princely houses and states in these years is desperately needed. According to Gustav Fischer, the young Wolfgang II of Hohenlohe-Neuenstein had interest payments on the house's debts totaling 10,000 fl. a year in 1581 but disposed only 16,114 fl. in yearly income.

subjects. Little evidence actually confirms this view. On the contrary, many petty and weak princes undertook the task of raising imperial taxes with reluctance, fearing that the Habsburgs would use the taxes, and the issue of unpaid debts, as a means of opening them up to influence and pressure from Prague or Vienna. The successors of Charles V never accepted the Peace of Augsburg as more than a temporary setback to the ambitions of the Habsburg monarchy and, after a brief period of regrouping, they continued to extend Habsburg influence after 1580 or so, although they did so in clever and more subtle ways than Charles V had.[8] To fall behind in the payment of imperial taxes in these years or to demonstrate an inability to manage conflict in one's domains might very well invite imperial meddling in the domestic affairs of a small and vulnerable principality. And, just as threatening to these princes, the Imperial Aulic Court showed a disturbing tendency to undermine the smaller princes' control over their domains by siding with peasants in legal disputes over taxes. Imperial commissions of arbitration, sent into small territories and lordships to settle local disputes, had the same effect.[9]

Any imperial or Habsburg intervention in Hohenlohe's affairs would have come at a particularly vulnerable moment for the princes. In the early 1580s all of the Protestant princes of Franconia watched with deep concern as the zealous prince-bishop of Würzburg, Julius Echter, renewed Catholic culture and institutions in his lands and reasserted the bishopric's power in the region for the first time since the Reformation.[10] If the House of Hohenlohe were weakened, its political position in Franconia would also suffer, making it difficult for the counts to establish themselves as counterweights to the prince-bishops of Würzburg and the Habsburg emperors.[11] Perhaps most troubling of all, the princes might lose some power to control their own peasants. Already in other lands, especially those near Outer Austria farther to the south, such an erosion of princely autonomy was well under way.

None of these small states developed the centralized machinery of government increasingly necessary to collect the taxes efficiently. Instead many of the smaller territories remained fractured, their lands and administrative structures often split up repeatedly among contending lines of the ruling princely house. This was so because many of the princes continued to treat their lands as a

---

[8] See Martin Heckel, *Deutschland im konfessionellen Zeitalter*, Deutsche Geschichte, vol. 5 (Göttingen: Vandenhoeck & Ruprecht, 1983), 101–5; and R. J. W. Evans, *The Making of the Habsburg Monarchy, 1550–1700: An Interpretation* (Oxford: Oxford University Press, 1979), 3–41 passim.

[9] See Schulze, *Bäuerlicher Widerstand*, 76–85.

[10] For a general discussion of the Catholic Reformation and the confessional conflicts of the late sixteenth century in Germany see Heckel, *Deutschland im konfessionellen Zeitalter*, 67–127.

[11] On the politics of the House of Hohenlohe in Franconia and in the Holy Roman Empire see Ferdinand Magen, *Reichsgräfliche Politik in Franken: Zur Reichspolitik der Grafen von Hohenlohe am Vorabend und zu Beginn des Dreissigjährigen Krieges*, Forschungen aus Württembergisch-Franken, vol. 10 (Schwäbisch Hall: Historischer Verein fur Württembergisch Franken, 1975).

private family patrimony to be divided, if necessary, to support the heirs of the house. In Hohenlohe Counts Albrecht III and Georg I were the last princes to maintain a unified structure of dominance over the family's patrimonial domains. Between 1553 and 1555 their successors, Counts Ludwig Casimir and Eberhard, formally split the house's lands into two parts, Hohenlohe-Neuenstein and Hohenlohe-Waldenburg, and agreed to administer in common only the town of Öhringen and the archives. Although each promised not to alienate lands to others outside the family, from this time forward their successors did not hesitate to parcel out the family's domains even further. After Ludwig Casimir died in 1568 the Neuenstein power devolved to smaller courts centering on his sons: Philip at Neuenstein, Friedrich at Langenburg and Kirchberg, and Wolfgang II at Weikersheim. Even though Wolfgang eventually reunified the Neuenstein lands, his sons split the state once again into three parts upon his death in 1610.[12] In classic fashion these princes continued to split, re-form, and then again parcel out their properties until on the eve of the French Revolution the Hohenlohe supported a half-dozen or more separate courts.[13]

The burden of the levies fell, then, on princes eager to establish their own small patrimonial states but without the resources to create large bureaucratic institutions to do so. Whatever success these princes had in meeting the imperial demands and in disciplining officials and peasants to accept them depended very much on adapting old methods of patrimonial domination to the new circumstances of the late sixteenth century. And this process required that princes engage themselves personally in the day-to-day administration of their domains in ways their predecessors had never imagined. Count Ludwig Casimir of Hohenlohe-Neuenstein certainly broke new ground in this way in the 1550s and 1560s. In the administrative records he left from these years he appears as a zealous reformer, one who saw the advance of the Turks as an alarming threat and so personally prodded his officials repeatedly to collect taxes promptly and efficiently.[14] He left, however, the collection of the levies to his district officials, much as he did all of the usual business of seigneurial rents and dues.

By the 1570s and 1580s the struggle to master the administration of the taxes intensified and drew the princes ever more deeply into frustrating day-to-day administration. Few small princes tackled the problem in ways that made them feel masters of the situation. Indeed the structures of government threatened repeatedly to break down. But, where one sees the gradual emergence of

---

[12] See Fritz Ulshöfer, "Die Hohenlohischen Hausverträge und Erbteilungen: Grundlinien einer Verfassungsgeschichte der Grafschaft Hohenlohe seit dem Spätmittelalter" (diss., Eberhard-Karls-University, Tübingen, 1960).

[13] See Wolfram Fischer, *Das Fürstentum Hohenlohe im Zeitalter der Aufklärung* (Tübingen: J. C. B. Mohr, 1958), 16–37.

[14] LAN 42/14/1, June 10, 1566.

centralized bureaucratic institutions to administer taxes in Germany's larger territorial states in these years, the smaller states continued to make do with older *decentralized* structures of government. In Hohenlohe one can follow this in some detail after 1577. In the administrative records of Hohenlohe-Neuenstein the counts show an attention to the details of tax collection that Ludwig Casimir never did. While they threatened, wheedled, and cajoled their district stewards and village officials to bring in the levies, they added no new institutions of government to make the task any easier.[15] No central treasury took shape and bookkeeping improved only slowly. As late as 1644 one exasperated chancellery official could still complain that the financial records of the principality were such a labyrinth of confused accounting records that no one could easily estimate revenues and expenditures.[16]

The burden of administering the new taxes therefore fell to the district stewards, officials poorly prepared to collect the levies and keep order should villagers refuse to cooperate. As in the past, these officials relied upon voluntary compliance and cooperation to raise these revenues. From their point of view they had little choice. The imperial war taxes of the 1540s had been collected in this way. And past experience with these levies and with the usual seigneurial rents and dues prepared them to treat the taxes as irregular burdens that might, depending on agricultural conditions, take several months or years to collect. Besides, the stewards received no additional support from the counts and the central administration to collect the levies. The stewards could not appeal to the counts for additional teams of officials to help them or to armed force to intimidate reluctant taxpayers – the territory did not, and never would, have an army. To make matters even more difficult, the stewards had no systematic surveys of peasant wealth in the 1570s upon which to base their assessments of the tax burden on each household. The weaknesses in this administrative structure, coupled with the increasing impoverishment of the rural population, no doubt explain why this small state had fallen so far behind in its payments of war levies to the imperial treasury.

Shrewd princes, however, recognized the need to do all they could to strengthen the hand of their stewards in their efforts to extract revenues. This was the approach favored by the princes of Hohenlohe between 1577 and 1581. All of the princes, their court officials, and the stewards agreed that the old method of tax assessment was a serious hindrance to collection of imperial taxes. According to this method, each householder estimated the total value of his own property, excluding articles of clothing, food, tools, and other items "needed for the daily upkeep of the house and for work."[17] He or she then

---

[15] LAN 42/13/1, 1562; 42/13/1, 1577; 42/13/6, [ca. 1580]; 42/14/9, 1576; 42/14/52, October 9, 1580.
[16] ALGAL 189/3, May 16, 1644. [17] LAN 42/5/25, 1557; 42/13/1, 1562.

delivered up a cash sum to the steward based on this assessment. Officials reported, however, that peasants often underestimated their taxes in this way. In 1577 Countess Anna, with the cooperation of all the other princes, tried to push through a new method of assessment that would require that two or three men from each town and village undertake the assessments in their own communities. Each of the assessors was to take an oath to assess each household's wealth accurately, and she threatened dire punishment to anyone who broke that oath.[18] As in the past, the trick was to secure the voluntary help of peasants in their own exploitation.

Since the 1550s the success of each major reform, each intrusion into villagers' everyday lives, had depended not simply on the counts' exercise of power over their subjects but also on the compliance or tacit compliance of significant parts of the village population. In different ways the wealthy village elite, the smallholders, and the village poor had each willingly cooperated in some extension of princely authority. But this time the princes found no support. Right from the start no Hohenloher would come forward to take an oath and assess his neighbors' wealth. When the burden fell to the stewards and *Schultheissen* they sent back reports that a thorough assessment was beyond their abilities. Who could estimate the value of land scattered in so many village fields, one official wrote? What steward had the time and the personnel to unravel all the overlapping and disputed claims to land and property? And how was anyone to discover all the wealth that villagers concealed in cash, in silver, or in loans?[19] The *Schultheiss* from Künzelsau summed up the problem tersely: The systematic survey of property "would simply not be worth the effort and the costs."[20] The princes, thoroughly discouraged that their stewards did not have the manpower or the coercive force to carry out such thorough surveys, allowed the district officials to return in 1580 to the old methods of self-assessment.[21] The new surveys of taxable wealth undertaken according to these methods were completed between 1580 and 1584, and, even though they provided the stewards with their first revised tax registers since the 1560s, officials complained that the surveys were not as accurate as they should have been. No one, however, would undertake a reform of the system again until 1609.

The making of a tax revolt

Disorder and resistance to the taxes spread wide, and deep, in the South German countryside in the 1580s and 1590s, and the petty princes and lords

---

[18] LAN 42/13/1, 1577; 42/14/58, November 16, 1580.
[19] LAN 42/14/56, November 12, 1580; 42/14/58, November 16, 1580; 42/14/71, December 9, 1580.
[20] LAN 42/14/73, December 10, 1580.   [21] LAN 42/14/76, December 13, 1580.

kept order at times only with the greatest difficulty. To make matters worse, events sometimes tumbled completely out of control as unrest spread from a few scattered villages and territories to almost every community and territory. Those princes who showed no regard for the resistance, who overestimated their power to bend whole villages and districts to their will, courted disaster in these years. Aggrieved villagers showed more willingness to rebel than they had shown in years, and when they did not revolt they showed little hesitation in disputing their lords in the imperial courts; the courts became choked with cases of this sort by 1600.[22] In neither case could beleaguered rulers count on a favorable outcome. So it is not surprising that many princes steered more cautious courses in dealing with the protests and learned to bring about order in less coercive ways. In the best of cases, princes averted a revolt and kept their disputes free of the legal entanglements of the courts, but this took, as the widening resistance to taxes in Hohenlohe shows, a great deal of skill, some flexibility, and luck.

To understand how and why resistance to the taxes spread so widely one must keep in mind that many villagers considered the taxes unjust or illegal. Before 1543 resistance to the taxes could easily be justified, since they rested on shaky legal foundations. Indeed, in the eyes of some villagers – and many German jurists agreed – resistance to the taxes was perfectly legitimate. The reason lay in the fact that patrimonial dominance in the sixteenth century rested, as I mentioned in Chapter 1, not simply on the use of force to intimidate peasants into obedience, but on the recognition of reciprocal obligations of lords and peasants to each other. In extreme cases, as in 1525, Franconian and Swabian peasants interpreted this to mean that nobles should pay the imperial taxes from their own funds, that they should never have passed on the burden of the taxes to the peasants in the first place. "We mean by this [grievance] that we do not owe this money," they wrote, "for the reason that we give rents and dues so that our lords should protect us."[23] In the aftermath of the revolt, the imperial authorities and the German princes condemned this type of resistance to the taxes. The imperial diet in fact established the principle in 1543 that no subjects of the empire could avoid paying their share of the imperial war taxes. Later additions to the imperial law codes elaborated on this idea and made it possible to punish anyone who did not meet an imperial obligation.[24]

But changes in the laws did not put an end to the protests, nor did they make it possible for small German princes to press the collection of the levies with impunity. In the scattered cases of resistance to taxes in the 1540s and 1550s, in fact, peasants show no evidence of changing their expectation that lords would show restraint in exploiting village resources, that protection would be extended to those householders who faced ruinous burdens of taxes. This

---

[22] See Schulze, *Bäuerlicher Widerstand*, 95–114.   [23] Ibid. 68.   [24] Ibid. 73–6.

was evident in one case from 1542 when Counts Albrecht and Georg levied another *Türkensteuer* on their population. When word went out to the villages to deliver over to the stewards one-half *gulden* for every 100 fl. of assessed taxable wealth, some peasants called out their communal assemblies and wrote up petitions to the counts asking for temporary relief from paying their assessments. In none of the requests did these petitioners question the legitimacy of the tax itself. The villagers of Steinheim, who sent a petition to Count Albrecht, professed a willingness to contribute their fair portion of the assessments. They expected the count to protect them, to extend to them special consideration, perhaps even a temporary exemption, because local agricultural conditions made it difficult for them to raise the sums necessary to meet the payments.[25]

When the burden of imperial levies became heavier, then villagers did not hesitate to stiffen their resistance to the burdens and organize protests on a larger scale. Up to 1560 or 1570 resistance remained sporadic and confined to only a few areas. But after that time clashes occurred more often and spilled over into resistance on a broader front. No doubt the deterioration of agricultural conditions, especially in the wake of the famine between 1570 and 1576, made resistance to the taxes more likely. In Hohenlohe the resistance spread geographically in much the same way it had in 1525. Protests tended to come first from the river valleys, from those towns and villages most vulnerable to heavy taxes, and then to draw in the small towns and villages of the Hohenlohe plain. In 1567 villagers from Crispenhofen, one of the largest communities in the Kocher valley, failed to hand over to the steward the sums of money demanded of them in the new assessments.[26] In 1577 reports poured into the chancellery at Neuenstein that Öhringen and almost every other town and village put up resistance to the assessments in some way or other.[27] No longer was resistance a problem confined to impoverished communiites of smallholders, winegrowers, craftsmen, and laborers. Millers, wealthy tenant farmers, petty merchants, and others joined in. Not since that first week in April of 1525 had peasants and townsmen showed such corporate solidarity against princely power – this despite the cleavages that had eroded the sense of community among Hohenlohers.

The gravest threat to public order came when whole communities joined forces and put up solid walls of resistance to stewards and officials. When the princes tried to press the collection of the taxes in the late 1570s several stewards and *Schultheissen* complained of the cool defiance and open hostility shown them as they made their rounds from house to house. In Öhringen townsmen came together as a body to complain that the assessments were too high and requested to have their share of the taxes reduced. Other communities, showing their resistance in a more devious way, "hid their property behind doors that were nailed shut and falsely reported their wealth" in the assessments. Still

[25] LAN 42/2/1, July 13, 1542; 42/2/3, 1542.   [26] LAN 42/14/2, 1567.   [27] LAN 42/13/5, 1577.

others adopted complicated ruses to deceive officials by claiming exemptions for properties that they argued did not belong in the assessments.[28] And of course scores of villagers refused to be enlisted in the survey of properties proposed for 1577. In the past lords had defused this sort of resistance to seigneurial rents and dues by showing restraint in the extraction of revenues or by securing peasant cooperation in their own exploitation. But when the princes tried to use force with unaccustomed harshness, when they pushed ahead with the collection of the taxes without securing local cooperation, it was difficult to evoke loyalty and obedience in their subjects.

Behind all of these protests, conspiracies, and schemes a consistent pattern of behavior is evident. In each case villagers attempted to minimize their fiscal obligations to the state, to structure their new relationships to the state in as favorable a way as possible. For many of them, especially those smallholders, artisans, and laborers who lived quite literally on the margin of survival in the 1570s, scraping together the necessary coppers to pay the tax could mean the difference between bare subsistence and hunger. In case after case villagers linked their reluctance to pay the taxes to the subsistence needs of their households, much as they did to protest unfair prices of food on the marketplace. For Georg Renner, the *Schultheiss* of Langenburg, a reduction or exemption from the tax was essential because, as he himself explained, "as a poor old servant I have several poor properties and parcels here and there with which I have, until now, fed and kept me and my poor wife and children, which are not so fine and splendid as one would like, and to that...I am also deep in debt and need to keep servants for my house."[29] The same worries about supporting his family concerned Adolf Zeseman of Kirchensall.[30]

These villagers neither called into question the legitimacy of the imperial taxes nor disputed their obligation to pay their assessments. The issue was a subtle one, one raised at first in a handful of petitions, but one that assumed greater importance with each new petition or confrontation in the 1580s. How was the state to wield its power to tax peasant households? Would the taxes become fixed, inflexible, levied year in and year out to serve strictly the fiscal purposes of the state? Or would the state bend to peasants' interests in making the taxes flexible burdens, adjustable according to economic conditions and the subsistence needs of householders who wanted protection from economic ruin? To follow the former course was to break sharply with the old patterns of patrimonial dominance. To follow the latter was to adapt those old methods of dominance to an expanded patrimonial state, but to accept all that it implied about honoring reciprocal obligations and showing restraint in the exploitation of peasant resources.

---

[28] LAN 42/13/5, 1577; 42/13/6 [ca. 1580].   [29] LAN 42/12/17 [late 1570s?].
[30] LAN 42/12/13, November 1, 1584.

Threat of revolt

In the 1580s the patrimonial state of Hohenlohe tended to follow the second path. The princes and their officials learned to accept limits in their power to extract revenues from their subjects. Discovering those limits, and finding the right ways to use what power they did command, was at first a disappointing and bitter lesson for the ambitious sons of Count Ludwig Casimir to learn. Right into the mid-1580s they continued to exhort their villagers to accept each levy with patience and obedience, even though the burdens contributed to the impoverishment of many households. More often than not the princes commanded their subjects to submit to the taxes without question and without any special reductions or protection from the levies. When district officials requested postponement of the collection of taxes in 1584, the princes, adopting the arguments of their advisers in the chancellery, rejected the request outright and urged officials "to collect both installments with all loyal diligence."[31] But without the means to add force to the extraordinary demands they were making of their subjects, such efforts were doomed to failure. Tax arrears mounted and Hohenlohe fell ever farther behind in its payments to the imperial treasury.

Accommodating peasant resistance to the taxes was not, then, at least not at first, a well-considered policy of benevolent princes who wanted to protect their dependents from exploitation. On the contrary, the princes were trying to discipline their subjects to accept the taxes strictly on the state's own terms. But they overestimated their own power and underestimated the tenacity of the resistance from district officials and villagers. District officials, for one, showed themselves unwilling or unable to carry out the princes' commands. The stewards and *Schultheissen* saw more limits to the state's power to extract revenues and hesitated to press recalcitrant or uncooperative villagers too far. Several officials even refused to carry out commands to collect taxes in bad years. Others, such as this one, thought it folly to try to squeeze blood from stones, and cautioned against innovations:

It is entirely unadvisable to break with the present order and I advise this for these reasons. Not only among the common man [of Hohenlohe], but also among our neighbors there would be extremely disparaging talk (and other dangers) if we were, in these times, to assess and tax separately his pigs, sheep, cows, and calves. . . . He would be happy with the present order and would have cause to be quite grateful to you, for it is certain that the hunger of these times is wringing him. If we were to assess each and every head of livestock we would find that the common man has sunk into great debt because of the wearisome, expensive, and exhausting year.[32]

Villagers, protected from the full force of the princes' commands by hesitant local officials, could therefore continue to resist taxes without fear of harsh recriminations. If villagers were learning to accept a regular burden of taxation,

[31] LAN 42/14/135, November 23, 1584.   [32] LAN 42/14/44, July 17, 1579.

the princes, for their part, were learning where the limits of their power lay. Benevolence would eventually come, but it would be a virtue born out of the frustrations of power.

One series of events in 1587 shows how the counts began to accept this uneasy state of affairs. The winter of 1586–7 must have been a harsh one, for in March officials were already mentioning in their correspondence how bad the spring harvests had been, how rapidly prices were rising, and how many villagers had finished the winter more impoverished than ever before. Through-out Hohenlohe-Neuenstein local officials had postponed collecting taxes.[33] When it came time to levy another tax, however, even the counts started to waver. Count Wolfgang, who earlier had shown little hesitation in pressing the collection of taxes, ordered his officials to show restraint and leniency this time in collecting the levies.[34] Countess Anna, deeply worried about Hohenlohe's obligations to the emperor and the empire, countered these orders, sharply recalled her subjects to obedience, and admonished the district officials to collect the taxes "without arrears, for no one is to be granted a respite."[35] But by August even she had lost her resolve and watched helplessly as the harvest failures made it impossible to collect the taxes.[36] Subsistence concerns had won out over the fiscal demands of the state.

Storm over labor services

Resistance to taxes by itself rarely made for a revolt in this period. Grievances against rising taxes spread far and wide in almost every part of Germany in this period, but did not necessarily spark a rebellion. In most cases unrest took a turn for the worse only when other grievances made the tax burden unbearable, when the village elite became seriously disaffected and took up leadership in resisting authority and when complex ties between villages broadened the basis of opposition to authority. Precisely these circumstances began to complicate the disorders in Hohenlohe in the years after 1590. No sooner had the tensions from the first wave of protests eased than a new and more vexing cycle of rural protests and disputes broke the peace in the countryside. But these disorders, the storm of controversy over labor services, threatened to get out of hand and spill over into revolt.

As in the case of resistance to taxes, the unrest over labor services began when South Germany's feudal masters, in need of additional labor in the 1580s, sometimes began to put their seigneurial powers to use in novel and particularly oppressive ways. The old bundle of powers that came from *Grundherrschaft* had

---

[33] LAN 42/14/149, March 18, 1587. [34] LAN 42/14/152, April 3, 1587.
[35] LAN 42/14/154, May 25, 1587.   [36] LAN 42/14/156, August 1587.

become so interwoven with the other more recently acquired powers and jurisdictions by the late sixteenth century that one often forgets just how important a role these seigneurial rights continued to play in bolstering princely power in small South German states. Some services, the carting of wood and services at the hunts, for example, remained fixed by custom, and stewards could not easily justify to villagers putting the performance of these obligations to new uses.

But the so-called unmeasured services, or *unbemessene Frondienste*, were a wholly different matter. These services caused a great deal of friction in many territories in the German Southwest in the 1580s and 1590s. Petty princes and lords who could call up villagers to provide these services in no way mounted the sort of feudal offensive then under way in many lands east of the Elbe River. There the nobles robbed villagers of their land and freedom, imposed a kind of "second serfdom," and built up the basis for large latifundia.[37] Here the feudal offensive took on more modest dimensions; never did it seriously threaten the comparatively favorable land-tenure rights and peasant freedoms common to the German Southwest. But in some territories still, when ambitious princes wished to rebuild their old castles in the stylish new Renaissance fashion or when they simply needed extra labor at the harvest, stewards formed up teams of laborers from villagers to help out with the work. When Count Wolfgang began to build his magnificent Renaissance palace at Weikersheim in the 1580s, his stewards turned naturally to Hohenlohers to provide much of the labor. From every district of Hohenlohe-Neuenstein the stewards called out villagers to work as manual laborers or to act as teamsters hauling lumber from the forests or stone from quarries to the site at Weikersheim. When the stewards began to call out villagers for labor services during the planting and harvesting seasons, protests arose almost immediately.

In the unrest that followed, men of wealth, power, and some influence in the villages took the lead. And this fact set these protests apart from the other disturbances and made them potentially more menacing to the authorities from the start. As early as 1583 a few tenant farmers registered their complaints over the labor services.[38] These particular seigneurial dues, like the burden of taxes then beginning to cut into peasant resources, affected different groups in the village in different ways. This stemmed partly from the fact that the work days burdened tenant farmers in particularly obnoxious ways compared with smallholders and cottagers. By custom these wealthier villagers had to put teams of draft animals at the disposal of the stewards and even had to provide the fodder for the animals while they worked for the lords. Since Weikersheim was situated in the northernmost corner of the territory, far from the centers of population

---

[37] See the discussion of the literature on agrarian development in the Bibliographical Essay.
[38] PAÖ 167/1/1/1, 1583; 167/1/1/2, 1583; 167/1/1/3, February 24, 1583.

to the south in the Kocher and Jagst valleys, work days could take the tenant farmers away from their farms for two, three, or more days at a time. Other villagers, while they had to work away from home, had only to provide their manual labor on work days.

To thwart the ambitions of the wealthy and the powerful, no matter what their origins, was in the sixteenth century very often the first step in turning simply disgruntled subjects into potential rebels. In the frightening events that began to unfold in Upper Austria in 1594, and in scores of smaller peasant disturbances farther to the south of Hohenlohe, the cadre of leaders came from the ranks of wealthy and well-connected men who felt their ambitions, or their hold on their property and status, frustrated by their masters in some way or other. The demands for labor services threatened to do precisely this to Hohenlohe's village elite in the 1580s and 1590s. The imperial taxes had not been welcome, to be sure, but tenant farmers, petty merchants, and millers, flush with wealth from commercial agriculture, often bore the burden with relative ease. Labor services, on the other hand, began to obstruct the efforts of families to establish or keep themselves in the circle of the village elite. Not only did the services interfere with work on their farms, thereby reducing their cash incomes, but the services tended to reduce the value of the compact farms, making it difficult for householders to secure heirs and marriage partners. "When someone sells or passes his farm on to a child," the tenant farmers of Langenburg complained in 1583, "no one wants to marry or buy into [the family] because we are so heavily burdened with labor services." So they offered to pay a cash tax, a *Dienstgeld*, in lieu of offering their services.[39] The idea quickly caught on. Tenant farmers and the wealthier smallholders from other parts of Hohenlohe soon joined in the protest and repeated the same offers to pay a cash tax in place of their services.[40] These villagers had a scheme for buying a portion of their freedom.

How to suppress this form of protest was a difficult question for the princes and officials of a small patrimonial state. Officials could intimidate individuals here and there into obedience, but the scale of the resistance and the unity shown by the tenant farmers made this approach unworkable. Besides, the tenant farmers approached the princes deferentially, as petitioners seeking protection from a traditional obligation. But if the princes granted their requests and removed the source of their complaints, the state would suffer an irretrievable loss of power and income. When Count Wolfgang investigated the possibility of commuting labor services to a cash tax, his officials warned sternly that the state simply could not afford such a measure. As his advisers saw the problem, the state depended heavily upon labor services for its day-to-day work:

[39] ALGAL 876/2, 1583.
[40] PAÖ 167/1/1/1, 1583; 167/1/1/2, 1583; 167/1/1/3, February 24, 1583.

"The districts need so many services that they could not make ends meet with a *Dienstgeld*." The steward of Langenburg estimated that a tax would bring in about 2,000 fl. each year from the district but that this sum of money would never be adequate to hire an equivalent amount of labor at current wages.[41] In addition, the advisers warned, smallholders and cottagers would undoubtedly resist the introduction of yet another tax, since they already had difficulty paying the imperial levies. For the moment, Count Wolfgang took no action. But he did urge his district officials to watch the villages carefully for signs of trouble and to communicate directly to him just how much his subjects would bear in the way of services.[42]

In situations like this, discontent could spread in surprising and complex ways and turn into disorders exceptionally difficult to control. A critical point was reached in this case in 1595. This time the old pattern that had asserted itself in 1525 and again in the late 1570s and early 1580s – of discontent spreading out from the impoverished winegrowing communities of the river valleys and from Öhringen – did not repeat itself. The pattern tended to run in reverse, spreading instead from the villages dominated by the wealthy tenant farmers to those of the smallholders, winegrowers, and artisans. This time too the village elite displayed organization, discipline, and aggressiveness that took the stewards and princes by surprise. When the tenant farmers of Langenburg district protested over labor services in 1598 and petitioned for a reduction in the carting services to Weikersheim, Count Wolfgang, fearful that resistance might quickly spread to other villagers and districts, granted the request.[43] His hasty concession, however, shifted the burden of services to the smallholders and cottagers, who did not have the resources to take over the work left undone by the tenant farmers. In an angry letter of protest these villagers complained that additional work and expense were unjust, that "such a burden would be much better and easier carried by many than by a few."[44] Wolfgang, careful not to give cause for unrest to spread more widely again, had his stewards issue a call for the tenant farmers to supply teams of draft animals for the construction work at Weikersheim. This time the tenant farmers flatly refused to cooperate.[45]

At this point one should pause to look at the network of ties that linked villages and enabled scattered actions to coalesce into opposition on a broad front. In the rebellions of the late Middle Ages and in 1525 the village commune pulled peasants together and set its unmistakable imprint on the goals and organization of rebels. At every step of the way during the Peasants' War, from the presenting of grievances to the organizing of large assemblies and the calling

---

[41] PAÖ 167/1/1/3, February 24, 1583.   [42] Ibid.
[43] ALKI 356/2, March 4, 1598.   [44] ALKI 356/2, May 20, 1599.
[45] ALKI 356/5, June 6, 1599; 356/8 [1599]; 356/9 [1599]; 356/10 [1599?].

up of peasant armies, Hohenlohers from every social stratum had united behind the leadership of the village commune. By the late sixteenth century the commune, though still important in some ways, played less of a role in agrarian movements than earlier. Class ties began to supplant the sense of village corporateness or, at the very least, attenuated its hold on villagers. Villagers presented themselves in their petitions not as members of communes but as "tenant farmers," as "smallholders," or simply as "the poor" from whole districts. The smallholders themselves explained the dispute over labor services to local officials in precisely these terms:

It has come about that our ... tenant farmers have made it understood that such [labor services] would be much easier borne by many than by a few. If these [our] neighbors consider, as they themselves well know, how poorly we can help ourselves, and how a number of our tenant farmers have so much more than they need to subsist, things which we cannot spare, things we need to provide for us, our storage bins and our small cottages, they would surely then be quiet.[46]

Eventually the stewards too analyzed the disputes over labor services for the princes as conflicts rooted in local economic conditions and in the property differences that now separated the peasant elite from the village poor.[47] The class rivalries that had been in the making since the rapid population growth of the early sixteenth century and that had become sharper since disputes at the marketplace intensified in the early 1570s now put their stamp on protests against the state.

These tense and uncertain circumstances around 1600 came at a particularly disturbing moment. The Upper Austrian revolt had only just come to an end in 1597, and the shock waves had spread fear of another general uprising far and wide among the nobles of South Germany. Besides, unrest from other sources intensified at this same time. Between 1592 and 1602 imperial taxes fell on householders with unprecedented severity. To make matters worse, crop failures and high prices for food heightened tensions at the marketplaces and in the villages of the territory. These tensions, and the complex overlay of family, class, and village loyalties, made the course of any conflict impossible to predict. At times opposition to labor services fractured along class lines, but on one occasion in 1602 those same ties pulled together all peasants, even if only temporarily, to present one angry and bitterly written petition in protest against the state's burdens.[48] Not since the spring of 1525 had the princes of the House of Hohenlohe confronted such an uncertain, and potentially dangerous, situation in their domains.

---

[46] ALKI 356/4, May 5, 1599.
[47] ALKI 356/12 [ca. 1600]; 356, [ca. 1600].   [48] ALKI 356/5, November 20, 1602.

Return of order

In this unsettled situation how a prince wielded his power to keep order made the difference between keeping an uneasy peace and provoking a rebellion. The most serious mistakes in these years were made by overconfident, misinformed, or unseasoned feudal lords and stewards who misjudged the depth of the unrest and their own power to impose order. Count Wolfgang of Hohenlohe, squeezed though he was between the demands of the empire and the resistance of recalcitrant villagers, showed no signs of doing so. He felt his way cautiously, now taking full advantage of what power he and his predecessors had acquired since the middle of the sixteenth century.

If one steps back for a moment and examines what improvements in the practice of domination lay at hand by this time, it is clear that such a prince wielded formidable, although by no means absolute, power to restore order. The changes varied considerably from land to land, as did the skill with which a feudal lord faced disorder and the possible threat of a rising. But among the lesser princes and counts of Swabia and Franconia in this age Prince Wolfgang, now senior count of his family's house, had become one of the practiced masters of the new politics of domination common in the small patrimonial states of the empire. At the local level he could employ his stewards and village officials with far more efficiency and accountability than was possible in the 1570s. At the court he disposed improved tools of central authority – more complete records and a better-informed and better-trained staff – which enabled him to dispense, or withhold, grain, wood, land, loans of various types, aid in a dispute, or other favors as he saw fit. His network of personal ties with his subjects, like the delicate and almost invisible strands of a spider's web, ran in every direction, linking up the dominant House of Hohenlohe with every village and household in the territory. No small German count would ever dominate his villagers with the ruthlessness and bureaucratic efficiency of the greater princes of the empire. But, if Wolfgang were shrewd, as he appeared to be, he had the means to place the relationships of paternalism and deference in his lands on secure footing.

The reassertion of patrimonial domination demanded careful and deliberate action. The clumsy use of force, as pamphleteers warned, could easily lead to a sharpening of tensions, a lawsuit, or a revolt. A sure way to avoid these problems and ease the way for a peaceful settlement was to open negotiations with villagers on a formal compact or treaty, one that would resolve the conflicts over disputed burdens. Independent lords, abbots, and petty princes of the empire used this method often when protests threatened to get out of hand. Such compacts confirmed as burdens obligations thought to be traditional but that had actually departed sharply from customary arrangements in the past.[49]

[49] For references to examples of this tendency see the Bibliographical Essay.

In the plans Count Wolfgang devised in 1608 and 1609 there is little doubt that he too intended to announce such a compact to secure his state's expanded fiscal powers over its villagers. "The subjects should not complain about their duties and abilities [to perform their obligations]," he wrote. "Under our government, as the authority set here by God, they should perform their duties and yet not be hindered in the pursuit of their livelihoods."[50] Such an agreement would carry a legal, even a constitutional, weight that informal agreements would not. Once the chancellery issued the decree and villagers and townsmen swore to it in their communal assemblies, the agreement assumed the full force of law. In the short term the advantages were obvious. The treaty could consolidate the expanded fiscal powers of the state, its fiscal powers in particular, and commit villagers to submit deferentially to the new burdens.

Certain dangers loomed as well. In these troubled circumstances no petty prince, regardless of how shrewd he might be, could reassert his dominance over villagers on whatever terms he wished. Even if the balance in lord–peasant relationships had tipped decisively against villagers, as it obviously had in Hohenlohe since the 1550s, the practice of domination still bound a lord to honor reciprocal obligations to his villagers. With regard to the broader fiscal powers of the counts of Hohenlohe, this would mean accepting some formal limits to the extraction of revenues from peasant households. But where did those limits now lie? What manner and level of taxes would Hohenlohers bear without withdrawing their obedience and loyalty from their masters? And how would the counts extend protection, as they were bound to do, to the households least able to bear the ruinous burden of yearly taxes? The precise terms of the compact would matter, for the agreement would probably structure fiscal obligations for a long time to come in the territory. Just as the compact held out the hope of securing the state's fiscal powers for the future, it could also hold out the danger of limiting state incomes as well. In the long term rigidity and inflexibility in the practice of domination might set in.

But securing a stable peace, order, and a proper sense of hierarchy and deference obviously mattered most of all. This did not mean that Wolfgang intended to make damaging concessions to villagers. Quite the contrary. He and his officials took advantage of all that they knew about the social divisions in the village, the economic weaknesses, and the political vulnerabilities of peasant communities and households to extract the best terms possible from villagers. As the count and his advisers learned in the lively discussions that took place in district assemblies, explicitly called out for this occasion in 1609, the most effective approach was a time-honored one in politics: Divide and conquer. Officials who studied very carefully the reactions of various factions

[50] ALGAL U/15, October 27, 1609.

to the idea of reform advised the count to introduce a *Dienstgeld*, or labor-service tax, a concession to the wealthy, but to do so in a way that would make it palatable to the majority of impoverished villagers. Wealthy tenant farmers and smallholders, district officials reported, would naturally welcome the commutation of labor services for a fixed yearly tax in cash. This group "would by no means reject the proposal, but would rather be inclined to accept it with humble thanks."[51] But, to soften this blow to the village poor, who would surely resist such a reform, they recommended two measures: a tax graduated according to the number of draft animals a tenant owned and a guarantee that anyone could continue to provide labor in lieu of the *Dienstgeld*. Such a plan might strike villagers as fair and just, since it would distribute the burden of taxes according to the ability of each household to pay.[52]

The final accord, when announced in October 1609, represented a triumph of the patrimonial state over resistance to taxes and labor services. The *Assecuration*, as the accord came to be called, placed the expanded fiscal powers of the House of Hohenlohe on a secure legal footing. And it did so with the compliance of the townsmen and villagers of the territory. The terms of the accord called for the immediate introduction of two taxes, each levied on peasant households once a year but collected quarterly. The first, the *Landsteuer*, or territorial tax, replaced the irregular imperial war taxes with a fixed levy of nine *batzen* per 100 fl. of assessed taxable wealth. But the counts, as a concession to villagers, promised to protect them from future imperial levies, except extraordinary ones, and to pay such taxes from their own personal treasury. The second, the *Dienstgeld* so much discussed since the early 1580s, imposed a tax on each household that was graduated according to the number of draft animals the tenant owned. Here too Count Wolfgang made an important concession. From this date forward he freed Hohenlohers from performing labor services, at least the despised "unfixed" kind. The taxes and the protective measures, the paternalistic senior count announced optimistically in his decree, "will help subjects in the future get along better with their livelihoods and wealth and they, in return, will show us complete and humble thanks."[53]

With this measure the princes of Hohenlohe consolidated their fiscal powers over villagers and brought to an end an era of disturbing agrarian unrest. What complaints remained lasted but a few months into the winter of 1609 and the spring of 1610. The petitions from this period illustrate, in fact, how effectively the accord had worked to weaken organized resistance to the state and to impose taxes at a level many Hohenlohers considered exceptionally heavy. Gone were the reports of widespread resistance so common in the years after 1595. In

---

[51] ALGAL 880/2, June 19, 1609.   [52] ALGAL 880/2, June 19, 1609.
[53] ALGAL U/15, October 27, 1609.

their place came petitions, mostly from individuals, seeking to amend or alter the terms of the agreement here and there. The *Dienstgeld*, for example, amounted to ten *gulden* for tenant farmers with two horses, more than some advisers recommended, and certainly more than many tenant farmers considered reasonable when they heard the precise terms imposed on them.[54] Other tenant farmers complained that the *Landsteuer* had been set too high. In several petitions villagers requested the count to moderate the levy from nine to six *batzen* per hundred *gulden*, even though the higher rate represented a reduction from the twelve *batzen* common in the imperial levies of the 1590s.[55] In none of the reports did officials mention intractable resistance. These wealthy tenant farmers essentially accepted the terms of the accord and with it submitted to the count's authority.

Other villagers did the same, but for different reasons. Artisans, laborers, smallholders, and widows flooded the chancellery with petitions in 1610 protesting, like the destitute widow of Lienhard Büschler of Bächlingen, that the new taxes would utterly ruin their households, since they already lived on the margin of survival:

Because I am old and a poor widow and have only a run-down half a house, and nothing more than my utter ruin and a blind daughter, who cannot support herself, I cannot pay the *Dienstgeld*. Our income and livelihood are simply too small and I have nothing more than my hands with which I work for other pious people.[56]

Count Wolfgang reassured these villagers that he planned to moderate the tax for those who were old or who were unable to pay or who "suffered crop damages from bad wealther."[57] With this paternalistic reassurance the complaints ceased. As Hohenlohers took oaths to abide by the terms of the accord, thirty-three years of agrarian unrest over labor services and imperial taxes came to an end.

Terms of domination

In looking at any of the peasant revolts or rural disorders in Germany at this time one should not automatically assume that peace, when it came, favored the early modern state. Settlements that ended a period of unrest could very well establish terms of domination that would weaken a state. The pattern that Yves Bercé sees in early modern peasant revolts in which the forces of the early modern state repeatedly triumphed over village localism may apply to France,

---

[54] ALGAL 877/17–18, January 16, 1610. [55] ALGAL 877/21, February 14, 1610.
[56] ALGAL 877/35, May 21, 1610. [57] PAÖ 167/1/1, August 2, 1610.

Austria, and Bavaria.[58] But in the smaller states of the empire, where the balance between rulers and ruled was more complex and shifting, the settlement of disputes sometimes weakened the state, often in subtle ways that became apparent only after a period of years had passed. This was the case in Hohenlohe in the ten years after the announcement of the accord of 1609. The same treaty that brought to an end the unrest over taxes and labor services soon weakened the fiscal foundations of the state.

This ironic state of affairs resulted from the structure of taxation established in the accord itself. Each of the three important provisions in the accord – the introduction of a *Landsteuer*, abolition of labor services and the payment of a *Dienstgeld*, and promises of protection in times of hardship – created unintended financial problems for the state. The accord set the rates of taxation for the *Landsteuer* at levels below the actual financial needs of the state. As Chancellor Assum reported in a lengthy opinion on the matter in 1612, the state had established the rates based on property assessments carried out in 1580–1, and these assessments could not be raised without violating imperial laws.[59] In addition, the income from the *Dienstgeld* never compensated the state for the loss of labor suffered when Wolfgang abolished labor services in 1609.[60] Finally, the provisions to relax tax collection in years of economic hardship or crop failures led to difficulties in keeping peasant indebtedness within reasonable bounds as agricultural conditions deteriorated further after 1610. District officials, as a result, began to report alarming shortfalls in revenue.[61] In Langenburg district alone the total indebtedness of villagers to the state rose between 1610 and 1616 from 100 fl. to 1,000 fl.[62] But officials dared not put additional pressure on villagers in a way that would renew protests. As Assum warned in 1612, if unrest spread once again and imperial authorities had to intervene this time to resolve a dispute "we should consider very carefully whether, if this were to happen, the entire territorial tax, or even the privileges of the counts of Hohenlohe might be disputed or endangered."[63]

Restraints such as this on a state provide one clue to the continued prosperity of peasant elites in some corners of the German Southwest after 1600. Without the unsettling fear of further demands from the state, tenant farmers, millers, and petty traders could take further advantage of terms of trade that continued to favor producers and sellers of agricultural products on the marketplace. In Hohenlohe, for example, freedom from labor services allowed tenant farmers

---

[58] Yves Bercé, *Croquants et Nu-pieds: les soulèvements paysans en France du XVIe au XIXe* (Paris: Gallimard, 1974).
[59] ALGAL 738/24, 1612.   [60] ALGAL 743/3–4, 1618.
[61] PAÖ 167/1/1, 1617.   [62] ALARL 1610–16.   [63] ALGAL 738/24, 1612.

to concentrate on farming the land and developing their market activities without the interruption of work days or unexpected demands for draft animals from the stewards of the territory. Tenant farmers acted in these years "as if they were freed on account of the labor taxes," one district official grumbled, "and they no longer show respect for the *Herrschaft*."[64] The precise burden of taxes set by the law also made it possible for these villagers to accumulate considerable fortunes, put money into stocks of grain, wine, or cattle, or loan it out to impoverished neighbors in ways that made it impossible for the state to assess and tax.[65] And, because the assessments of taxable wealth remained frozen at levels fixed in 1580 and 1581, tenant farmers, who profited from the inflation in land and agricultural prices, actually paid lower taxes in 1610 and 1620 than they did in 1580. The terms on which these villagers accepted state authority enabled them to continue to dominate the market relationships right into the 1620s.

Among the village poor, whose ranks continued to swell, resistance to the new fiscal burdens of the state gave way to accommodation and muted social protest within the structure of an expanded patrimonial state. Count Wolfgang had cleverly defused the potential for violent rebellion by exploiting the class divisions between wealthy tenant farmers and the village poor, and this pattern continued after 1610. Even more important, these villagers deepened their dependence on the state for grain supplies, tax remissions, and loans, all necessary more than ever as agricultural conditions continued to deteriorate.

Petitions that streamed into the chancellery during the famine of 1611–12 testify to the importance of these bonds of dependence for the survival of the village poor. In one case, the "poor subjects of Oberregenbach," their supplies of food exhausted, begged and pleaded for supplies of grain because, as they put it, "the Almighty God has richly blessed the House of Hohenlohe with grain and we praise and thank Him for it."[66] Others, like Kilian Kress from the same village, abjectly approached his lord requesting that he postpone, once again, payments on his debts owing to the recent bad harvests.[67] In every case, hungry and frightened villagers tried to manipulate the promises laid out in the treaty that the state would show restraint in extracting revenues in times of hardship. The sheer numbers of these requests, and the tone of desperation that comes through in the petitions themselves, made it difficult for the stewards and the princes to refuse the requests. In effect the small state continually adjusted its fiscal burdens to the ups and downs of the peasant economy. Even though this dependence cost the state dear in some ways, the social and eco-

---

[64] ALGAL 880/5, January 5, 1618. [65] ALGAL 738/24, 1612.
[66] ALARL 1611–12/B19–24. [67] ALARL 1612–13/B17.

nomic relationships that now linked the prince to the village poor were so deep that they could be broken only at the risk of spreading a massive famine in the territory. Order had returned, but the terms that secured it came as a mixed blessing for the state

On the eve of the Thirty Years' War

In looking at South Germany on the eve of the Thirty Years' War one can easily overlook the significance of the calm that settled over the hamlets, villages, and small towns of many lordships, small states, and rural communities. Attention focuses all too quickly on the deepening political crisis in the empire, the instability that would soon spill over into a protracted civil war. Yet the easing of social tensions after three decades of agrarian unrest was unmistakable in many territories. The number of peasant revolts do not tell the whole story about this period, of course, but they do point to an important trend. In the wave of small peasant revolts in the Holy Roman Empire that stretched from 1560 to 1660 the number of revolts dropped off suddenly around 1600, rising again only after 1620.[68] Between 1600 and 1620 the spiral of dispute, confrontation, and conflict that often led to revolt seems to have been broken, if only for a short time. After a century of disruptive agrarian change the foundations for a renewed sense of social order, stability, and hierarchy in many parts of the German Southwest had clearly been laid.

Of course the taming of agrarian unrest alone cannot account for the stability and order one begins to see in these agrarian communities at this time. One must look much deeper than this, for the roots of order actually lay in the patterns of domination and deference now underpinning all spheres of life in the countryside. Whether in the family, on the marketplace, or in lord–peasant relationships themselves, all of the efforts to create order out of the chaotic world of the sixteenth century vastly improved the ability of those with power to dominate those who had little. In general this meant that in a society like Hohenlohe the balance tipped decisively in favor of those who controlled the distribution of property and wealth: lords, but also holders of large compact farms, millers, bakers, tavernkeepers, some petty merchants, and property-holders in general. Those who had comparatively little wealth or property or who entertained hopes of acquiring some – and this included not simply the village poor, but also winegrowers, rural artisans, immigrants, peasant youths, and most women – found themselves caught up in relationships of dependence difficult to break. All of these patterns of domination now stood on a firm

[68] Thomas Barnett-Robisheaux, "Peasant Revolts in Germany and Central Europe After the Peasants' War: Comments on the Literature," *Central European History* 17 (1984), 384–403, pp. 386–7.

institutional footing, secured by the power of the expanded territorial state. At the end of a century of agrarian expansion this once remote rural hinterland now had a complex agrarian hierarchy linked in complicated ways to a broader world.

Part Three

Crisis and recovery

8

~~~~~~

Crisis

In the last four chapters we have examined the search for order in the sixteenth century. Now we turn to the crisis of the seventeenth century, when order gave way to confusion.

To understand the crisis in South Germany a number of characteristics of the agrarian order should be kept in mind. Never should one forget the tenuousness and the uncertainty of the social order, the fact that at every turn, when a measure of stability appeared at long last secure, deep and unresolved tensions still lay not far beneath the surface of events. In Hohenlohe the tensions flowed from the new terms of domination that weakened the state after 1610. The *Assecuration* became an embarrassing liability to the House of Hohenlohe, setting limits to state incomes and, from the point of view of Count Philip Ernst, creating a new sort of chaos in the territory:

As we have repeatedly seen, there has been a striking amount of chaos since the establishment of the *Landsteuer*. Many of the rich are not assessed even half of their worth, not of their fixed property or of their movables. And this has led to considerable trouble and to a decline of our laws. And the poor and those with little property, because of this state of affairs, can avoid their responsibilities only with much greater difficulty.[1]

Domestic harmony may have come, but at a crippling financial cost to the state.

Events on the eve of the Thirty Years' War point to a second important feature of the agrarian order: the way that issues of social order were inseparably linked to political and religious questions in the empire. Most modern scholars pass over this point and interpret the war, and its meaning at the local level, simply in political or religious terms. But to shrewd observers at the time the political impasse in the empire aroused fears about the disruption of social order in the territories. For this reason many Protestants saw the resurgence of Habsburg power, embodied in the vigorous rule of Archduke Ferdinand in Austria and Styria, as a threat to the whole imperial order established since

---

[1] ALGAL 743/3, [1618?].

the middle of the sixteenth century.[2] As Chancellor Assum of Hohenlohe, when asked about the wisdom of pressing state claims on peasant resources more vigorously than before, pointed out, many princely powers still rested on uncertain principles of imperial law. The foundations of the state, and the whole order it underpinned, could come into question if the new emperor suddenly challenged specific rights and privileges of the House of Hohenlohe.[3]

The dynamism and the unexpected violence of the crisis would come, then, from the way the whole agrarian order came suddenly apart, setting in motion events no one could properly control. If we keep in mind the argument of the last four chapters, that order now depended upon new social, property, and market relationships, and that all of these hinged on vastly improved practices of domination within the state, then it follows that the political crisis became inseparable from a crisis of the whole of society. What distinguishes this period from the decades that went before was the sudden and dramatic calling into question of patterns of dominance, and the social relationships linked to them, that had come to underpin the everyday order of life.[4] If one listens to the bitter voice of H. J. C. von Grimmelshausen, who wrote about the war from firsthand experience, the violence of this time came not simply from the harsh and inhuman conduct of the soldiers, but from the way all social, political, and religious order vanished and so contributed to the wild disorder and confusion at every level of society, from the most pretentious court down to the humblest peasant household.[5]

The onset of crisis

Right from the beginning, in fact, the complexity of the crisis lay in the way princely dominance, and the relationships supporting it at every level of society, weakened, and then came into question. For this reason one cannot look simply to the war to explain the decay of order after 1620. In this early stage, when the crisis first set in, the widening sphere of the war and the threat of Habsburg absolutism certainly raised difficult questions about the locus of authority in the empire. An agrarian crisis, however, and the sudden resurgence of old social

[2] See Georges Pagès, *The Thirty Years' War, 1618–1648*, trans. David Maland and John Hooper (New York: Harper & Row, 1970, 46–9. On the interrelationship of secular and spiritual affairs in Austria and the empire before the war see Martin Heckel, *Deutschland im konfessionellen Zeitalter*, Deutsche Geschichte, vol. 5 (Göttingen: Vandenhoeck & Ruprecht, 1983), 100–27; and R. J. W. Evans, *The Making of the Habsburg Monarchy, 1550–1700: An Interpretation* (Oxford: Clarendon Press, 1979), 41–62.
[3] ALGAL 743/3–4, 1618.
[4] In this sense I agree with the main point made by J. V. Polišenský, who sees the war as a conflict between individuals and groups who fought to defend and extend whole social systems. See his *The Thirty Years' War*, trans. Robert Evans (Berkeley: University of California Press, 1971).
[5] *The Adventurous Simplicissimus*, trans. A. T. S. Goodrik (Lincoln: University of Nebraska Press, 1962).

conflicts made worse than ever before, complicated the crisis and linked political problems with questions about the social order. All of this no doubt would have made the 1620s a difficult period of adjustment in any case. But what brought all of these problems together, what quickened the pace of events and pushed lords and villagers alike to call into question all social and political relationships, was the crushing burden of war taxes. By 1627 order threatened completely to dissolve.

The sudden spread of the war westwards from Bohemia into the empire in 1620 can be taken as marking the onset of a crisis in South Germany. Right from the moment the reckless young Frederick V of the Palatinate accepted the crown of Bohemia, the potential existed for a broader conflict, one that would spread to most of Central Europe. But no one foresaw the swift and complete triumph of the forces of the emperor at White Mountain in 1620 and their march, virtually unopposed, into Franconia and the Rhineland. What forces remained at the disposal of the Protestants disintegrated or melted away, leaving the way open for Catholic forces to occupy the Palatinate.[6]

During this stage of the war the armies themselves caused only light damage to most of the territories they marched through. The reason for this lay in the way the troops of both sides moved swiftly through South Germany between 1620 and 1623 and then moved on to northern Germany. Some destruction was inevitable, since the armies, organized and commanded by military enterprisers, lived off the land, forcing subject populations to support the troops with food, transport animals, fodder, supplies, and funds to pay the troops.[7] But in the early 1620s the immediate burdens of the war fell largely on territories, towns, and villages near the major highways leading to the Rhineland. Hohenlohe's position is instructive in this respect. Some villages and towns in the northern and eastern parts of the territory, those situated along or near the east–west highway to Wimpfen and the Emperor's Highway, suffered from looting and pillaging as troops from both armies passed through on their way to the Rhineland. First Protestant forces under the command of Mansfeld, in full retreat, marched quickly through the land in 1621. Fast on Mansfeld's heels came the troops of the Catholic League under Tilly, pressing home their advantage before the Protestants reorganized. But, although some areas suffered terribly, Weikersheim and Schrotzberg in particular, most parts of the territory went unscathed.[8]

---

[6] On the course of the war itself see Pagès, *The Thirty Years' War*; Heckel, *Deutschland im konfessionellen Zeitalter*; and Polišenský, *The Thirty Years' War*. Still useful as a narrative account is C. V. Wedgwood, *The Thirty Years' War* (London: Jonathan Cape, 1938).

[7] The best discussion of this problem is Fritz Redlich, *The German Military Enterpriser and his Work Force: A Study in European Economic and Social History*, 2 vols., Vierteljahrschrift für Sozial- und Wirtschaftsgeschichte, Supplements 47–48 (Wiesbaden: Franz Steiner, 1964–5).

[8] Adolf Fischer, *Geschichte des Hauses Hohenlohe* (Stuttgart: Alfred Müller, 1866), vol. 1, 48–52.

The political crisis was a wholly different matter. The forces of the Catholic League may have moved quickly on to northern Germany, but their stunning success left the emperor Ferdinand free to expand the power of the monarchy and push the cause of the Catholic Reformation at the expense of the German princes.[9] In South Germany the smaller princes, counts, and nobles, their security and autonomy dependent upon the fine political and confessional balance in the empire as a whole, now lay virtually helpless before the power of the emperor.

The most the princes could do was play for time, wait for a general settlement of the conflict, and keep the imperial armies at arm's length. This the counts of Hohenlohe did with remarkable skill, even though they felt more vulnerable than many other small rulers in the early 1620s. For even though the counts made known their official neutrality at the start of the war, it was no secret that the princes sided with the Protestant cause. In the 1590s the sons of Count Wolfgang, Georg Friedrich, Kraft, and Philip Ernst, had each served as officers in Protestant armies fighting in the Netherlands and Hungary. Later, when civil war threatened, Count Wolfgang opened negotiations with the Protestant Union, and even though those efforts fell through in 1610 his successors continued to counter imperial and Catholic power in Franconia in other ways. But the most serious affront to Habsburg power occurred during the uprising in Bohemia, when Count Georg Friedrich came under the imperial ban after he recklessly placed himself at the head of the Protestant army.[10] The reprisals threatened by the emperor Ferdinand aroused a great deal of concern in Hohenlohe, for the whole house could lose some privileges and property, notably Georg Friedrich's lands around Weikersheim. Such measures could wreak havoc in the territory.

Shrewd princes, though they could not accomplish what was politically impossible, might still postpone the inevitable reckoning with the Habsburg monarchy by yet a few years. The hope for this lay in accommodating imperial demands as much as possible while exploiting weaknesses in the fragile alliance Fredinand had stitched together. In this very way Counts Philip Ernst and Kraft kept a semblance of order in Hohenlohe until 1628. They worked frantically behind the scenes, first with the Teutonic Knights, then with Duke Maximilian of Bavaria, to secure a pardon for Georg Friedrich and succeeded; in 1623 the ban was lifted.[11] Then they tried to organize a territorial defense for Franconia

[9] For a discussion of Ferdinand II's policies and the close links between Habsburg absolutism and the Catholic Reformation see Evans, *The Making of the Habsburg Monarchy*; and Heckel, *Deutschland im konfessionellen Zeitalter*, 100–27.

[10] For a fine discussion of the House of Hohenlohe in imperial politics at this time see Ferdinand Magen, *Reichsgräfliche Politik in Franken: Zur Reichspolitik der Grafen von Hohenlohe am Vorabend und zu Beginn des Dreissigjährigen Krieges*, Forschungen aus Württembergisch Franken, vol. 10 (Schwäbisch Hall: Historischer Verein für Württembergisch Franken, 1975).

[11] Ibid. 215–304 passim.

in 1621–2, an effort that eventually foundered over the objections of the Catholic bishop of Würzburg.[12] Finally, the brothers opened direct negotiations in July of 1625 with Count Wallenstein, the new imperial military commander, in an effort to minimize the burden of war taxes levied on the territory. At this point the counts' luck began to run out. Wallenstein, now busy raising a massive army for the Habsburg cause, never honored his promise to spare Hohenlohe a heavy burden of war levies and quartered units of the imperial army in the territory late in the summer of 1625.[13] A reckoning with the Habsburg monarchy and the massive army under the command of Wallenstein was fast at hand.

The intensification of the political crisis could not have come at a worse time. For at the same time the princes were losing much of their autonomy and independence and falling under the heel of Wallenstein's imperial army, agricultural conditions took a sudden turn for the worse. The agrarian crisis that set in, unlike the political crisis, had little direct connection with the war. Its roots lay in the long cycle of demographic growth, now reaching its limits, that stretched back to the late fifteenth century. But, coming as it did when the political crisis reached a turning point, the agrarian crisis made a difficult situation into a near-desperate state of affairs for the whole rural population.

This part of the crisis began as yet another famine in the long chain of famines that had come repeatedly, and with increasing severity, since the 1560s. But this one, unlike most of the ones that went before it, soon threatened the livelihood of every villager, from the poorest laborer to the wealthiest miller. The crisis unfolded in classic fashion. The first alarming sign came in the winter of 1621 or 1622, in some areas even earlier, when the crops failed.[14] In Langenburg district prices for spelt had doubled from three to six *gulden* per *malter* by 1622–3.[15] Wheat prices also doubled. Reports from every corner of the territory complained of shortages of grain, meat, and other commodities.

Grain prices would have soared anyway, but the sudden debasement of the coinage in 1621–2 made the inflation more difficult to check than in other times.[16] This made the economic crisis a serious problem for wealthy tenant farmers, millers, bakers, and petty merchants as well, many of whom lost, at one blow, substantial fortunes invested in movable goods, cash, and loans. The only solution for these villagers, to raise new sums of money by exporting large quantities of grain, cattle, and wine, only made matters worse for the territory.[17] Grain supplies all but disappeared. Like many other villagers unable to buy grain on the open market in 1623, Fritz Schelhemmer complained bitterly that he "could neither buy nor borrow grain and bread in these extremely difficult

---

[12] Ibid. 196–214. [13] Fischer, *Geschichte des Hauses Hohenlohe*, vol. 1, 54.
[14] See Table 6.2. [15] See Table 6.1 for the general price trends of this period.
[16] See Wilhelm Abel, *Agrarkrisen und Agrarkonjunktur: Eine Geschichte der Land- und Ernährungs-swirtschaft Mitteleuropas seit dem hohen Mittelalter*, 2d ed. (Hamburg: Paul Parey, 1966), 144–5.
[17] ALAL 338, July 7, 1625; 338, October 13, 1625.

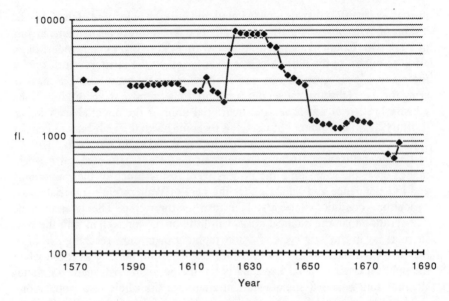

Graph 8.1. Counts' loans to villagers of Langenburg district, 1570–1683. *Source:* ALARL 1570–1 to 1683–4.

times."[18] All of these factors – the crop failures, the soaring prices for grain, the extraordinary inflation – began to turn a cyclical subsistence crisis into an economic crisis that stretched well into 1626.

The severity of the problem can be seen by looking at the way debts shot up in uncontrolled fashion between 1622 and 1628. As at every other time in the past, villagers responded to the subsistence crisis by taking out loans from a variety of sources, assuming new debt in complex ways. Some of these debts, those incurred to kinsmen, other villagers, petty merchants in particular, cannot be traced. But one important measure of the debt problems, the sum of interest-bearing loans made by the counts of Hohenlohe to their tenants, can be followed in detail and shows just how fast the crisis began to get out of hand. Between 1600 and 1620 loans of this type fluctuated consistently between 2,400 and 2,800 fl. for Langenburg district. But in six short years, beginning in 1622, the total rose dramatically to about 8,000 fl. (see Graph 8.1), and stayed at this level right into the late 1630s. Petitioners approached the stewards for loans of this type out of a variety of reasons. Hanns Prentsch, a proud tenant farmer from Billingsbach who found himself suddenly and unexpectedly short of cash, took

[18] ALARL 1623–4/B88, May 7, 1623.

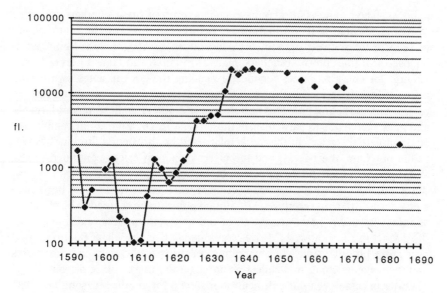

Graph 8.2. Debts of villagers from Langenburg district to the state, 1591–1683. *Source:* ALARL 1591–2 to 1683–4.

out a 30-fl. loan because he needed to hire a team of oxen to plough his fields.[19] But most, like Georg Köhler, took out loans to stave off hunger: "so that I will not come to harm and can better support my wife and children."[20]

The most ominous sign of the depth of the economic crisis was the total indebtedness of villagers to the state. Even in comparatively normal times, on the eve of the war, for example, the majority of Hohenlohers met the fiscal burdens of the state only with difficulty. Now total indebtedness rose dramatically. In 1622–3 the total sum of uncollected taxes, rents, and dues from Langenburg district stood at 1,300 fl., not an unusually high level when compared with other years in the past two decades. But in five years the sum nearly quadrupled, to 5,000 fl. (see Graph 8.2). Forty years earlier the refusal to pay taxes might have been a sign of calculated defiance of authority. But in the mid- to late 1620s it was a sign of sheer desperation. As Mathes Seuter, only one of the hundreds of petitioners from the district who put off their taxes, pleaded: "[I] do not know where I could get the means to rid myself of my debts, so unavoidable poverty forces me to plead with Your Gracious Lord for further postponement [of my taxes]."[21]

As the crisis deepened, old social cleavages and rivalries in the village inev-

[19] ALARL 1623–4/B195. [20] ALAL 1079, April 1, 1625. [21] ALKI 102/12, July 10, 1624.

itably surfaced. The state may have tamed some of these conflicts and even manipulated them to its own advantage before, but this time the state's power to keep order showed signs of breaking down. In 1624 Count Philip Ernst imposed stiff fines on two butchers, Hans Birndipfell and Hans Ebert of Langenburg, for charging prices for meat exceeding the government's own posted prices.[22] But these measures, harsh though they were at the time, did little to reform the marketing practices of butchers and others, millers, tenant farmers, and petty merchants in particular, in these years. In 1625 the count complained of "complete disorder" in the marketplace and he threatened dire punishment to the butchers, the bakers, and the tavernkeepers if prices continued to rise and supplies of food did not appear in their shops. Why, he demanded to know, did the district now have shortages of meat when cattle raising had been such a prosperous trade in recent years?[23] But no punishment seemed to be effective, as measures taken again against all of the important millers and butchers of the district in 1627 showed.[24] Prices continued to rise, the village poor protested ever more bitterly against the marketing practices of the rich, and the counts and their agents stood by helpless as order on the marketplace dissolved.

Order became even more difficult to maintain for another reason: The state had begun to concentrate all of its resources on the collection of war taxes. Precisely in the critical year of 1625, when the agrarian crisis deepened and the state's ability to impose order weakened, a crushing burden of war taxes fell on the territory and its increasingly desperate population.

The timing, the extraordinary amounts demanded, and the manner of collecting these taxes hastened the slide into chaos between 1625 and 1627. Up to this time no truly modern tax state had yet replaced the older, weaker, and more flexible forms of dominance of the late Middle Ages. Even when the small South German princes had earlier introduced a regular burden of imperial taxes, the actual amounts extracted from peasant households varied considerably from year to year, moving up and down roughly in a rhythm set by fluctuations in the agrarian economy. At critical moments in the 1580s and 1590s, when harvests failed and peasant incomes plummeted, the state suspended or postponed tax collection. When the counts replaced the imperial taxes with a *Landsteuer* in 1609, giving the state the appearance of a more modern tax state with a fixed yearly burden of taxes, the state continued to relax its demands in times of famine. Even in 1620 and 1623, when Philip Ernst felt compelled to levy an extraordinary tax to pay for the heavy cost of keeping imperial troops on their through marches, he redistributed the funds to villagers who bore the brunt of the burden, explaining that "other of our subjects, who did not suffer from constant quartering of troops, could help them up by the arm and carry

[22] Ibid. [23] ALAL 338, October 13, 1625. [24] ALAL 338, December 3, 1627.

the same burden with them."[25] Up to 1625 the small patrimonial state, as a claimant of peasant resources, could not and did not seek to extract surpluses in a way ruinous for the agrarian economy.[26]

The imperial army exploited peasant communities in a harsher and far more destructive manner. Wallenstein's system of war taxes, the hated *Kontribution*, bore the ugly mark of a modern and ruthlessly efficient tax state, backed with the full force of arms. Where petty rulers often relaxed taxes, the imperial army pushed forcefully ahead, imposing extraordinary demands regardless of economic conditions and then sending in commissars and troops to collect them, at bayonet point if necessary. The system was of Wallenstein's own design. In 1625 he contracted with the emperor to raise and command a hugh imperial army, a force of one hundred thousand men, and his own financial resources, vast though they were, hardly sufficed to pay the costs for keeping such a massive army in the field. His solution involved levying war taxes direct on subject territories and, if resistance were encountered, to occupy the territory, collect the tax himself (or confiscate property), and then execute townsmen and villagers who refused to cooperate.[27]

The transformation of Hohenlohe into a tributary state in this system occurred in two short, bitter years. The pattern varied from land to land in South Germany, but here the quartering of troops came before the levying of the *Kontribution* itself. The documents leave little doubt that princes and peasants, however pressed their resources were, preferred to shoulder the taxes rather than to take the soldiers. The reason is obvious: Soldiers took whatever they wanted and left nothing but disorder, destruction, famine, and disease in their wake. The first shock from this experience came late in the summer of 1625. Shortly after Wallenstein promised the counts, on July 30, 1625, that he would spare Hohenlohe from quartering his new imperial army, he sent in several regiments of soldiers anyway, there to live off the land while Wallenstein prepared his army for a campaign. The next year imperial soldiers left even more damage in their wake. In Öhringen, Ingelfingen, and Weikersheim the plague

---

[25] ALGAL 746/2, November 3, 1623.

[26] For a theoretical discussion of the early modern tax state see Gabriel Ardant, *Théorie sociologique de l'impôt* (Paris: SEVPN, 1965); and his "Financial Policy and Economic Infrastructure of Modern States and Nations," in Charles Tilly, ed., *The Formation of National States in Western Europe* (Princeton, N.J.: Princeton University Press, 1975), 164–242. See also the discussions by James Scott and Michael Adas on the particular effects of taxation on peasant economies. Scott, *The Moral Economy of the Peasant: Rebellion and Subsistence in Southeast Asia* (New Haven, Conn.: Yale University Press, 1976), 91–113; and Adas, "Moral Economy or 'Contest State'? Elite Demands and the Origins of Peasant Protest in Southeast Asia," *Journal of Social History* 13 (1980), 521–46.

[27] For a detailed discussion of Wallenstein's financial system see Redlich, *The German Military Enterpriser*, 223–57, 283–4, 322–7, 359–61 passim.

raged.[28] When Billingsbach, a village on the plain not far from the Emperor's Highway, quartered troops in January of 1626, the community was ruined. In this case no one complained of physical destruction: The troops simply bled the community of all of its reserves of money and grain, leaving even the wealthiest tenant farmer begging for help from the state.[29]

Then came the *Kontribution* itself, a cash tax assessed on every household. The counts themselves often laid out these sums from their own treasury between 1624 and 1626. But they soon exhausted their reserves. Count Philip Ernst, fully aware of the desperate plight of his subjects by this time, tried to keep his territory free of both troops and levies, but he had eventually to pass on these extraordinary burdens or face the unpleasant consequences of the troops collecting the taxes themselves. In October of 1627 he wrote to his stewards that the Imperial War Commissary "demands every week a large sum of money in addition to other provisions, regardless of the costs. We had to pay this from our own purse for a time so that our poor people would not be driven from their houses and estates, but we can no longer manage it."[30] At weekly and monthly intervals from this moment on, the state assessed and collected the taxes imposed on it by the imperial army. By the end of 1627 the state had, for all practical purposes, lost its autonomy and become an extension of Wallenstein's tax state.

Turning point

Between 1627 and 1634 a turning point was reached. From this point on, the insatiable demands for war taxes, raised to extraordinary levels, dominated political events, weakened the administrative structures of the state, and drove on the agrarian crisis to a catastrophic conclusion. Once the small German state came under military rule, once old practices of domination gave way to the savage exploitation of the imperial army's fiscal system, the prewar agrarian order came quickly and disastrously to an end. Feudal authority, the agricultural economy, and the social order all broke down with remarkable speed.

This turn for the worse came abruptly in 1627–8. Before this date the war levies fell at irregular intervals; after it they came yearly, monthly, even weekly. The actual burden of the levies varied considerably from land to land and depended on a territory's location, its perceived usefulness to the imperial army, and its rulers' political weakness in the eyes of Wallenstein and his commanders. Hohenlohe was easy to exploit for all of these reasons. One can follow the

[28] Fischer, *Geschichte des Hauses Hohenlohe*, vol. 2, 55.
[29] ALARL 1625–6/B101, January 13, 1626. [30] ALGAL 747/8, October 1, 1627.

Table 8.1. *War levies in Langenburg district, 1620-51*

Year	Amount (fl.)	Year	Amount (fl.)
1620	?	1636-7	6,500
1623-4	899	1637-8	?
1624-5	0	1638-9	2,181
1625-6	0	1639-40	5,272
1626-7	295	1640-1	2,855
1627-8	918	1641-2	4,080
1628-9	7,726	1642-3	3,270
1629-30	2,921	1643-4	3,500
1630-1	2,214	1644-4	5,021
1631-2	1,587	1645-6	3,226
1632-3	363[a]	1646-7	?
1633-4	281[a]	1647-8	5,420
1634-5	8,512	1648-9	10,380
1635-6	13,465	1650-1	1,059

Sources: ALARL 1620-1 to 1650-1; ALCRAL 1638-9 to 1648-9.

[a] The state increased the territorial taxes to make up for lower war levies in these years.

sharp increase in war taxes in some detail for Langenburg district, where the records of the war taxes somehow survived the confusion and destruction of this period. What stands out in the accounts of the taxes is the abruptness of the change in 1628–9 (see Table 8.1). In that year Wallenstein levied an extremely heavy *Kontribution* – the burden for Langenburg district alone amounted to 7,726 fl. – and then continued to impose taxes, at lower levels, into the early 1630s. Between 1634 and 1636 the levies shot up again, this time to crushing levels. In 1634–5 the taxes amounted to 8,512 fl.; the next year, the year the imperial army occupied Hohenlohe, a staggering 13,465 fl. From then to the end of the war the commissars generally extracted between 3,000 fl. and 6,500 fl., and never less than 2,100 fl., every year in war taxes. If one keeps in mind that before the war the two cash taxes, the labor service tax and the territorial tax, together brought in only 2,500 fl. a year, the extraordinary burden of these war taxes comes more sharply into focus.

One reason for the increase in war taxes was the new power of Emperor Ferdinand II over the German princes by 1629. As in the Bohemian–Palatine phase of the war earlier, the Lower Saxon–Danish phase had also ended in the triumph of the imperial and Catholic forces. Protestant resitance in Lower Saxony collapsed in 1626, and, with no serious opposition before him, Wallenstein and the imperial army stood unchallenged on the shores of the Baltic Sea in 1629. For a few years Ferdinand II could dream of reducing the German princes to pawns in his fantastic imperial plans.[31] For the weak Protestant princes in the south of Germany, already hard put to maintain their position before these new triumphs, the political situation grew desperate, for now the emperor and the imperial army felt fewer restraints in their dealings with them. Wallenstein exploited the lands of Hohenlohe mercilessly after 1626, for example, imposing at will one exceptionally burdensome war tax after another in 1628, 1629, and 1630.[32] Even worse, the emperor planned to strip the House of Hohenlohe of some lands that fell under the provisions of the Edict of Restitution in 1629. The decree came as a severe blow to all of Germany's Protestant princes, for it called for the return to the Catholic church of all ecclesiastical properties secularized since 1552.[33] Should the emperor have his way with Hohenlohe, the bishops of Würzburg and Bamberg would seize the properties attached to the church at Öhringen and lands once belonging to the monastery at Scheftersheim.[34]

The heavy burden of taxes came, then, as one painful sign of the weakness of the state in the face of Habsburg absolutism. But the burden of taxes rose for military and financial reasons as well. The massive size of the armies – both Wallenstein and Gustavus Adolfus commanded armies of a hundred thousand men after 1630 – and the continuous difficulties in financing them meant sharp increases in the fiscal burdens imposed on German territories. For an unfortunate land like Hohenlohe, situated at a strategic crossroads between the Rhineland, Franconia, and South Germany, this meant that the years between 1630 and 1634 brought a crushing burden of war taxes and troop quarterings. Once Gustavus Adolfus entered the war and moved swiftly into Franconia and South Germany in the fall of 1631, control over this small state passed back and forth between the Swedes and the Catholics.[35] The fact that the counts declared openly for Gustavus Adolfus did not save their lands from the harsh Swedish levies and troop quarterings. Monthly war taxes, introduced in May of 1630 to pay the imperial army, continued on into 1631 and 1632 and went into the coffers of the Swedes.[36] In addition, Swedish infantry and cavalry encamped repeatedly in the territory in 1631, 1632, and 1633.

The plight of Bächlingen, one of the poorest and most densely populated winegrowing villages of the Jagst valley, was typical. From the moment the first Swedish cavalry rode into the village in December of 1631, the winegrowers

---

[31] For a discussion of these plans see Evans, *The Making of the Habsburg Monarchy*, 67–79; and Heckel, *Deutschland im konfessionellen Zeitalter*, 142–6.

[32] ALGAL 747/2, April 19, 1627; 727/1, 1629.

[33] For a discussion of the decree see Heckel, *Deutschland im konfessionellen Zeitalter*, 145–50.

[34] Fischer, *Geschichte des Hauses Hohenlohe*, vol. 2, 56–8.

[35] On the course of the war in this period see Heckel, *Deutschland im konfessionellen Zeitalter*, 151–68; or Pagès, *The Thirty Years' War*, 89–172. The course of the war in Hohenlohe is discussed in Fischer, *Geschichte des Hauses Hohenlohe*, vol. 2, 58–62.

[36] ALARL 1630–1/B; 1631–2/B22a; 1632–3/B22a; 1632–3/B24.

played reluctant host to one troop of soldiers after another until 1650.[37] From this point on, in other words, this region suffered under a continuous burden of war taxes and troop quarterings, more than many other parts of Germany.

These burdens made the agrarian crisis immeasurably worse. Right when the small patrimonial state traditionally relaxed its efforts to extract taxes, thus helping villagers recover from a subsistence crisis, the ruthless agents of the imperial and Swedish armies bore down savagely on peasant householders. Forced to pay taxes in cash if at all possible, villagers began to sell off their assets. Parcels of land, the last reserve stocks of grain, most of the local herds of cattle, all were sold off at a dizzy rate. Wealthy tenant farmers, once prosperous rural capitalists in their own right, had sold virtually all of their livestock by 1630.[38] This step shows the desperation of the times, for now, with no oxen, horses, or even cattle to pull the ploughs, the tenant farmers could no longer work their fields or enrich the soil with fertilizer. Supplies of seed grain vanished.

All of these measures had a calamitous effect on the agricultural economy. In 1632 the peasants of Langenburg district explained their plight this way:

We have not only suffered more than other areas. We have also, because of the war, suffered several very bad harvests. Many of the common men can no longer get their daily bread. No one knows this better than we do with our huge losses from the dreadful and accursed troop quarterings and other marches. If you save a *batzen* and were supposed to pay the state with it now you are forced to give it to the soldiers (and in some places they take flesh!). So (woe be to God!) we have been driven into debt and many have fallen into such wretched proverty that debtors are no longer able to pay the state.[39]

By the spring of 1634 many fields had returned to waste or pasture. Vineyards went untended. Houses, barns, the brickworks in Liebesdorf, even the mills along the Jagst River, fell into disrepair. What little income came in from the fields and from the last of the cattle herds went mostly into the coffers of the imperial and Swedish armies. Villagers starved, emigrated, or eked out an uncertain and wretched existence at bayonet point.

Worse still, local officials of the small state itself bore down on villagers with unaccustomed harshness. From the 1560s on, the German Southwest became as densely populated as it did partly because small and weak states like Hohenlohe never became efficient and modern tax states. By relaxing their efforts to collect rents, dues, and taxes in times of crisis and by extending loans to tenants in time of need, these states supported a vast population of impoverished householders. The heavy demands of the imperial and Swedish armies after

[37] Gustav Bossert, "Bächlinger Ortschronik," HZAN, unpublished manuscript.
[38] ALKI 370/14, December 29, 1630. [39] ALGAL 747/17, January 20, 1632.

1627 changed all that. In a desperate effort to raise the war taxes the princes suddenly began to drive in all of the debts owed by villagers. And they refused to extend new credit. Langenburg district again illustrates the trend in Hohenlohe. During the famine of 1611–12 the state reduced rents and dues amounting to 125 fl.; in 1623–4, when the first part of the new crisis began, the state reduced a total of 400 fl. in taxes. But at the height of the crisis, in 1631–2 and again in the following year, the state relaxed its claims by only 50 fl. and 25 fl.[40]

These figures reflect an important shift in the day-to-day practice of domination in the territory. Gone were the restraint and the patience of the past when paternalistic rulers extracted in time of crisis less revenue in the hope that, when tenants' incomes recovered, state income too would rise. This shift coincided with a change in rulers. When Count Philip Ernst died in 1628 and his two brothers, Kraft and Georg Friedrich, left to fight for the Protestant cause, the practical administration of Hohenlohe-Neuenstein fell to Philip Ernst's widow, Countess Anna Maria. She soon showed Hohenlohers the hard face of a state bending all efforts to meet the extortionate demands of the armies. Pleading with the imperial war commissary for patience in 1631, she wrote that "poverty among our subjects, who have been bled to the bone, is so great that it is inhuman and impossible to hold them to the monthly war tax."[41] Still, she pressed on her stewards and village officials the importance of collecting the taxes at all costs. By the summer of 1634, when agricultural production had come to a halt and famine and disease spread through the villages, she continued to warn her stewards "to press earnestly on with the district's business and allow no revenues to go uncollected unnecessarily, ... for to put off the rents, as the old saying goes, means the ruin of the rentpayer."[42]

The small patrimonial state could not bear such a fiscal burden and drastically reform its practices of domination at the same time. The power and the force of a bureaucratic state simply were not at hand to do so. Inexorably the apparatus of the state began to break down, so that by 1630 the structures of authority became dangerously weakened.

First to show the strains were the stewards and the village officials, those officials who bore the brunt of day-to-day administration in the villages. These officials had difficulty bending villagers to their will in normal times; now their hold on the village weakened noticeably. By 1629 many local officials, overwhelmed with their fiscal duties, had simply stopped making their normal rounds to collect petitions, and the chancellery and the treasury, as a result, began to lose their hold on the administration of the state.[43] But even greater confusion spread soon after that. Harassed, overworked, and dishonest local officials began

[40] ALARL 1611–12; 1623–4; 1630–1; 1631–2. [41] ALKL II/10/4, January 12, 1631.
[42] ALGAL 181/17, August 1, 1634. [43] ALKI 31/3, November 17, 1629.

falsifying their account books and sending on reports deliberately misleading the court about the local state of affairs. The court, at first not fully informed about the problems, did not guess the scale of the calamity. The countess and the chancellor made their usual exhortations to the stewards to carry out their rounds faithfully, hold regular assemblies, and submit written reports.[44] But what local officials hid for a while was the fact that the collection of normal revenues was breaking down completely. Putting the story together as best as possible, one can see the inexorable collapse of the everyday fiscal power of the state at work in Langenburg district between 1630 and 1636. In 1630 and 1632 uncollected rents, dues, and taxes totaled between 5,000 fl. and 5,500 fl. Not long after, in 1634, the figure doubled. And by 1636 outstanding debts rose to over 20,000 fl. (see Graph 8.2). By the time the court learned the extent of the fiscal disaster, in 1634, it was too late. The normal fiscal resources of the state had collapsed.

The breakdown of the state became apparent in other ways as well. In the early 1630s the decline of the agricultural economy became irreversible, the state being without the customary power and resources to help the territory recover from the worst agrarian crisis since the fourteenth century. No subsistence crisis of the sixteenth century had ever quite reached this stage, partly because of the state's role in helping an economic recovery. In normal years the state kept on hand large supplies of grain for resale or distribution to villagers when crops failed.[45] In this way an elaborate system of redistribution, a kind of pump priming, went to work to help pull the agricultural economy out of a subsistence crisis. Tenant farmers and millers sold their surplus to the state; the state stored it and then released it, a bit at a time, to smallholders and the village poor, even wealthy tenant farmers if necessary, to help them through a crisis. This time, however, the mechanism failed. Between 1629 and 1632 the state purchased much less grain on the market in Langenburg than in the past; supplies simply were not available.[46] In the spring of 1634, as officials of the state struggled in vain to find a solution, one steward after another reported grave shortages of grain in the districts.[47] The steward from Langenburg summed up the miserable state of affairs by reporting that little or no grain was to be had in his villages, that for lack of supplies he had to turn away almost everyone who showed up at the mills for help.[48]

The market economy could not make up for this loss. Where once the state had brought some order to market relationships, preventing food riots and supporting the village poor in times of need, officials now stood helpless to

---

[44] ALKI 31/6, [1633?].
[45] Account books from the early seventeenth century report this activity on a yearly basis. ALARL 1618–19/B174; 1619–20/B170.
[46] ALARL 1628–9/B221; 1631–2.
[47] ALKL II/6/6, April 17, 1634; II/6/6, August 15, 1634.   [48] ALKL II/6/6, March 3, 1634.

stop the slide into economic chaos. For here, on the marketplaces of Hohenlohe, order was breaking down quickly, spreading panic and fear as it did. Millers, tenant farmers, and petty merchants, in desperate need of cash, sold whatever food they could to the armies or to nearby towns, communities that felt the pinch of hunger and famine as well. Supplies of grain disappeared completely; bread, a rare commodity, no longer appeard in the bakers' shops.[49] In May of 1634 Hanns Metz of Eberbach, his fortune gone and his family caught up in famine, begged and pleaded with the steward of Langenburg for grain "because we do not have the means to buy our dear daily ration of bread for our children and servants." On that day he was one of the few fortunate ones in the district. The steward granted him two *malter* of spelt.[50] Others went away hungry.

No decrees could stop the wild and desperate export of food out of the territory. Not even a series of extremely harsh fines, the heaviest ever imposed on villagers for flouting the laws on market activities, could correct the situation. In a village like Bächlingen, long dependent on the state for loans and supplies of grain, the effects of this economic crisis were nothing short of catastrophic. From May of 1633 on, mortality rates in the village rose sharply, some persons taken away by the plague, others by famine. By July of 1634 no food could be found anywhere, and one chronicler commented on the astonishing number of beggars found dead in the fields or on the streets. Those who survived did so by eating cats, dogs, the bark of trees, and stubble off the field.[51] In 1630 this village boasted fifty-six households, most of them winegrowers and laborers. When the state next surveyed the village after the war, in 1653, thirty-eight remained, most of them recent immigrants to replace the families who had perished from famine and plague between 1633 and 1635.[52] The worst part of the crisis, however, was yet to come.

End of the old order

All of the conditions described above – the war taxes and harsh measures to drive them in, the decay of public order, religious oppression, and the agrarian crisis – contributed to the rapid decay of authority after 1626. How one views this problem matters a great deal. From one point of view the peasant revolts of this period – first in Upper Austria (1626, 1632–6), then in Swabia, the Breisgau, and the Sundgau (1632), and finally in Bavaria (1633–4), to name only the important ones – shared the essential features of the classic "tax revolts"

---

[49] ALKI 16/2, October 2, 1632; 16/2.5, January 15, 1634; ALKL II/11/6, March 28, 1634; II/6/6, April 17, 1634; II/6/6, August 15, 1634; ALKI 16/3, May 30, 1635.
[50] ALARL 1634–5/B29, May 17, 1634.
[51] Bossert, "Bächlinger Ortschronik."   [52] L/L "Schatzungsanlage Amt Langenburg 1653."

of the early modern period.[53] But the savage desperation of these movements suggests a meaning beyond the usual resistance to taxes. For those who took part in these movements saw the order of things, the proper exercise of authority, the fortunes of the rural elite, and the secure place of the village poor in the community – in short, the whole prewar world as they knew it – rapidly falling apart. In Hohenlohe this collapse of the old order was felt no less keenly than elsewhere, and in 1630 and 1632 villagers tried in vain to put things aright.

One should not be surprised that the movement that gathered momentum in the winter of 1630–1 failed miserably to achieve its goals. The wonder was that villagers organized any movement at all, for the alarm went out while units of Wallenstein's imperial army stood at the ready in their winter quarters. Whatever action Hohenlohers planned therefore had to take place under the cover of secrecy, as much as was possible under the watchful eyes of the soldiers and the state's officials and spies. On December 20 Wendel Schum, the burgermeister of Langenburg, sent round to the villages of the district a note: "Send your representatives to Ober Regenbach on the morning of Thoma, and do so in a hurry, so that you can make your grievance or concern known."[54]

In quick order village leaders called on all of the complex ties that linked villagers – communal loyalty, class ties, common grievances against the state, and the war taxes – and sent delegates, two for every village, to the tavern at Oberregenbach. The choice of this tavern in the Jagst valley was both a logical and a significant one. By virtue of their trade, village tavernkeepers stood at the center of elaborate networks of contacts to villages throughout a territory; in times of crisis the tavern acted as a clearinghouse of information, a center for hatching a conspiracy, even a point for assembly when the alarm sounded. In this case Hans Haffner placed his centrally located tavern at the disposal of the conspiracy's leaders, and soon after Christmas fifty-two delegates gathered here from the districts of Langenburg, Ingelfingen, Döttingen, and Kirchberg.[55]

The leaders of this movement came from those who had the most to lose as the old order began to give way: the village elite. In this regard the social composition of the movement had much in common with the revolt in Upper

---

[53] Few of these movements have received the careful attention they deserve. For an overview see Günther Franz, *Geschichte des deutschen Bauernstandes vom frühen Mittelalter bis zum 19. Jahrhundert*, Deutsche Agrargeschichte, vol. 4 (Stuttgart: Eugen Ulmer, 1970), 179–90 passim; and, for a penetrating analysis from a Marxist perspective, Herbert Langer, "Der Dreissigjährige Krieg – endgültiger Abschluss der deutschen Revolution des 16. Jahrhunderts?" in Manfred Kossok, ed., *Rolle und Formen der Volksbewegung im bürgerlichen Revolutionzyklus* (Taunus: Detlev Auvermann KG Glasshütten, 1976), 16–36. For the best study of one of the Upper Austrian rebellions see Herman Rebel, *Peasant Classes: The Bureaucratization of Property and Family Relations Under Early Habsburg Absolutism 1511–1636* (Princeton, N.J.: Princeton University Press, 1983), 230–84.

[54] ALKI 370/3, December 20, 1630. "Thoma" is St. Thomas's Day, December 21.

[55] ALKI 370/5, December 27, 1630.

Table 8.2. *Oberregenbach assembly I: Participants from Langenburg district, 1630 (Thoma)*

Name	Village	Status	Wealth (fl.)	Decile
Hans Haffner	Oberregenbach	*Bauer*	2391	10
Michl Preider	Oberregenbach	*Bauer*	1695	10
Bartl Pfleüger	Raboldshausen	*Bauer*	1570	10
Peter Muntz	Bächlingen	*Bauer*	1338	10
Hans Eckard	Brüchlingen	*Bauer*	1280	10
Stoffl Bauer	Langenburg	*Bauer*	1144	10
Jörg Weinman	Nesselbach	*Bauer*	993	9
Hans Müller	Nesselbach	*Bauer*	970	9
Hans Lüllich	Billingsbach	*Köbler*	850	9
Jörg Köhn, d. A.	Raboldshausen	*Köbler*	810	9
Endres Vagt	Sölboth	*Bauer*	765	9
Hans Schum	Atzenrod	*Bauer*	714	9
Hans Mörrward	Bächlingen	*Köbler*	700	9
Wendl Schum	Langenburg	*Köbler*	658	9
Jörg Frankh	Eberbach	*Bauer*	600	8
Martin Köler	Unterregenbach	*Köbler*	463	8
Jörg Katzell	Billingsbach	*Köbler*	450	8
Weiten Hans	Unterregenbach	*Köbler*	155	5
Mathes Veninger	Atzenrod	*Köbler*	150	5
Hans Huetman	Hürden	*Köbler*	150	5
Gall Mola	Langenburg	*Köbler*	75	3
Jörg Schneider	Sölboth	*Bauer*	?	?
?	Eberbach	*Schultheiss*	?	?

Sources: ALKI 370/5, December 27, 1630; and L/L "Schatzungsanlage Amt Langenburg 1630."

Austria in 1626, and ones in Swabia and Bavaria.[56] The documents leave little doubt about this, since a list of the delegates from Langenburg district, one perhaps made by a spy planted in the tavern on that day, soon fell into the hands of state officials. The list reads like a roll of honor of men from the wealthiest and most influential families of the district, the tenant farmer and wealthier smallholder families who had consolidated their position at the top of the village hierarchy in the late sixteenth century (see Table 8.2). Of the twenty-three men on the list, thirteen came from tenant-farmer (*Bauern*) families, a number disproportionately larger than their actual number in the territory; ten came from smallholder (*Köbler*) families. But even this first glimpse does not tell the whole story. If one traces the names of these men in the tax assessments for the district in 1630, the full picture of their position becomes clearer. Fully fourteen of the twenty-three came from households whose total wealth lay in the top two deciles of all the households in the district.

In a second meeting a few days later, the leadership of the movement con-

[56] Rebel, *Peasant Classes*, 249–57.

Table 8.3. *Oberregenbach assembly II: Participants from Langenburg district, 1630 (Johannis)*

Name	Village	Status	Wealth (fl.)	Decile
Michl Preider	Oberregenbach	*Bauer*	1695	10
Michl Schneider, Stachlbauer	Brüchlingen	*Bauer*	1314	10
Michl Schneider, d. A.	Brüchlingen	*Bauer*	1300	10
Hans Preünger	Binselberg	*Bauer*	1216	10
Jörg Weinman	Nesselbach	*Bauer*	993	9
Hans Müller	Nesselbach	*Bauer*	970	9
Hans Lüllich	Billingsbach	*Köbler*	850	9
Jörg Köhn, d. A.	Raboldshausen	*Köbler*	810	9
Hans Schum	Atzenrod	*Bauer*	714	9
Hans Mörrward	Bächlingen	*Köbler*	700	9
Hans Weissmüller	Sölboth	*Bauer*	655	9
Jörg Frankh	Eberbach	*Bauer*	600	8
Peter Wagner	Billingsbach	*Bauer*	575	8
Hans Kutroff, d. A.	Billingsbach	*Köbler*	470	8
Martin Köler	Unterregenbach	*Köbler*	463	8
Anthoni Glockh	Langenburg	*Köbler*	425	7
Lienhard Flerer	Raboldshausen	*Köbler*	300	7
Hans Schappert	Oberregenbach	*Köbler*	275	6
Weiten Hans	Unterregenbach	*Köbler*	155	5
Mathes Veninger	Atzenrod	*Köbler*	150	5
Hans Huetman	Hürden	*Köbler*	150	5
Caspar Hanslman	Langenburg	*Köbler*	100	4
Jacob Prümmer	Bächlingen	*Köbler*	50	2
?	Eberbach	*Schultheiss*	?	?

Source: ALKI 370/5, December 27, 1630; and L/L "Schatzungsanlage Amt Langenburg 1630."

tinued to draw heavily from the ranks of wealthy tenant farmers and well-to-do smallholders. Of these twenty-four men present at this meeting in Oberregenbach, eleven came from the tenant farmers of the district, thirteen from the smallholders (see Table 8.3). The roster of names included the heads of some of the oldest and most influential tenant-farmer families in the area: Stoffl Bauer, Hans Schum, Hans Haffner (the tavernkeeper), Michl Preider, Hans Weissmüller (of the powerful miller clan), Michl Schneider d.A., and Hans Preünger. The smallholders too hardly came from among the district's poorest households. If one breaks down the group by wealth, one can see more clearly how men of substantial wealth continued to dominate the leadership of the movement. Eleven headed households that came from the ninth and tenth deciles; six more came from the seventh and eighth. As in the first meeting, householders of middling or comparatively little wealth – those whose total wealth fell in the fifth decile or below – formed only a small part of the group: four in the first meeting, five in the second. These were men, then, who not only dominated the village assemblies politically, but who also came from families that had built their fortunes during the agrarian expansion of the sixteenth century. Now as the crisis threatened to ruin their families' fortunes, to force them and their children into beggary, they turned out in force.

The goals or programs of peasant movements in these critical years tell us a great deal about how closely villagers identified themselves and their families' fortunes with the prewar agrarian order. In no way did the calls for a return to old laws or custom show rebels' ignorance, naivete, or, as some Marxists would have it, "false consciousness" about the structure of agrarian society. For, as we saw in the last chapter, old practices of domination in South Germany favored villagers more than modern scholars often assume. So it comes as no true surprise that the Oberregenbach assembly, after blaming their miserable condition on the war taxes, denounced the authorities for breaking with the old order, an order protected in this case by the terms of the Treaty of 1609:

As obedient subjects we trust that we have done our part according to our means in delivering the *Dienstgeld*, taxes, performing the prescribed labor services, and whatever else the often discussed *Assecuration* required. In addition, we bore for a number of years a heavy burden on account of the war and the weekly war taxes, despite the fact that the Lord Counts of Hohenlohe, our territorial lords and authorities, should take upon themselves all of the imperial, circle, and other general or special levies when decreed by the Empire, regardless if these were small or large, and pay them out of their income and purse without the help of the subjects.... These weekly war taxes are nothing more than one of the above-mentioned general or special imperial taxes that, according to the letter (of the *Assecuration*), your gracious counts would be obligated to pay.... We, as loyal, obedient subjects, do not wish to get a reputation for rebelliousness (God protect us from that!) ... but to pay such a heavy war tax along with the normal taxes and daily quarterings of troops is totally impossible for us.[57]

In this appeal the delegates did not hold up a dream of freedom from oppressive lords. Nor did they look upon the past as a golden age. Instead they called, in the clearest language possible, for a return to the rule of law – this when the state had cast restraint to the winds and exploited peasant households in the cruelest possible way.

But the small state, now locked firmly into the new fiscal system of the imperial army, could hardly turn back the clock and restore the old order. Even had its rulers and officials wished to do so, the military commanders of the imperial army, their purses constantly pinched by the costs of keeping their regiments in the field, would have made certain that the war taxes continued. The documents do not tell us all that the state did to crush this

[57] ALKI 370/7, December 29, 1630. The imperial circle, a regional administrative unit of the empire, levied its own taxes. Hohenlohe fell under the administration of the Franconian Circle.

movement, but what one can reconstruct of its response is noteworthy, for it showed the extent to which it had broken with former practices of domination. Some lower officials like Johann Hohenbuch, the steward of Langenburg who first told the court of the assembly's goals, sympathized openly with the movement and recommended that the state treat their demands respectfully. But Countess Anna Maria and officials at the court did not agree and may have arrested some of the leaders. One of those closely examined, Georgius Speltacher, the assembly's scribe, distanced himself quickly from the villagers, pleading that they had coerced him to write their peitition even though he personally considered their actions rebellious.[58] In any case the state pressed ahead with its war taxes, the next one announced a few days later, on January 22, with stern admonitions to collect the money regardless of local conditions.[59]

The same pattern of events repeated itself in February 1632, this time the denunciations and the recriminations coming more harshly than before. Even in the midst of an agrarian crisis as severe as the one gripping the territory at this time, the old networks of contacts remained intact and came into play to bring together another assembly at Hans Haffner's tavern at Oberregenbach on February 2. This assembly gathered for a longer time than the last one, at least two weeks, and, in words harsher and more vehement than in 1630, denounced the war levies, blamed them for "bleeding the common man to the bone," and called for the state to return to the old terms of taxation.[60] The state's response came swiftly. Orders went out from the court to round up the leaders, the burgermeisters, the scribe, and the town-council members of Langenburg in particular, and to put them in prision for eight days: "so that their punishment would be an example to the others, forcing them to recognize their wrong and crushing them into respect and obedience."[61]But that was not enough. Well into March the court carried out its repressive measures, collecting information on the participants and their connections with each other and eyeing the depth of their support in the territory.[62] Nothing came then of these movements. Little time or opportunity remained now for leaders to organize a successful revolt, even though fears of a violent rebellion lingered well into 1633.[63]

Far more effective than the state's repressive measures in suppressing the movement was the demographic collapse that now cut severely into the

[58] ALKI 370/9, January 19, 1631.   [59] ALKL II/10/4, January 22, 1631.
[60] ALKI 370/17, February 17, 1632.   [61] ALKI 370/12, February 16, 1632.
[62] ALKI 370/19, March 3, 1632; 370/20, March 5, 1632.
[63] In March and April of 1633, when the counts assembled with other Protestant princes at Heilbronn, they expressed their fears of an uprising. Fischer, *Geschichte des Hauses Hohenlohe*, vol. 2, 63–4.

ranks of the peasantry. The occasional plagues of the 1620s, the accelerated pace of economic collapse after 1630, and chronic famine had already
reduced the population of the territory. But now a devastating epidemic of
plague, one that began to spread in 1633 and reached its peak in 1634–5,
took a frightful toll on the population. For nearby Württemberg, Günther
Franz estimates, the prewar population of 450,000 fell to 100,000 by
1639.[64] One cannot estimate the losses in Hohenlohe in 1633–5 with such
precision, but they must have been severe. In 1630 the number of households in Langenburg district totalled 421; in the next survey, in 1653,
shortly after the war, only 283 remained, a loss of roughly 33 percent (see
Chapter 3). But even these grim numbers do not tell the whole story. For
the full effect of the demographic collapse becomes evident only when one
begins to compare the names of householders in the two lists. In the 1653
survey very few names from the old prewar families remained; the vast majority had fallen victim to plague or famine in 1633–5. Others fled the region, the largest number in the fall of 1634 after Catholic troops, fast on
the heels of the Swedish army after their defeat at Nördlingen, sacked the
towns and villages of the territory and took Langenburg by siege.

With the families that perished or fled went the last supports of the old agrarian
order. The collapse of traditional feudal dominance of the land, so essential to
order and stability on the eve of the war, could not have been more dramatic.
In the fall of 1634, shortly before the imperial army seized control of Hohenlohe,
Countess Anna Maria and her court fled. In the following year the emperor,
taking his revenge, sequestered Weikersheim and awarded control of it to the
Teutonic Order.[65] For the duration of the war, what remained of the local state
apparatus – the district officials and stewards – fell under the direct control of
whatever army occupied the land. But that was not all. Much of the land
reclaimed in the great agrarian advance of the sixteenth century returned to
waste; fields, pastures, and vineyards turned back into forests and swamps.
Those who survived the disaster saw all this as the calamitous end of the social
order as they knew it. "The war levies in recent years," commented Apolonia
Schüeler prophetically, "have so exhausted us that our children and our children's children will overcome it only with great trouble and effort."[66] Surveying
the countryside in 1637, one official reported, coldly but accurately, that the
economy had been "cruelly ruined," the survivors living "in the most wretched
conditions."[67]

---

[64] Günther Franz, *Der dreissigjährige Krieg und das deutsche Volk: Untersuchungen zur Bevölkerungs-
und Agrargeschichte*, 3d ed., Quellen und Forschungen zur Agrargeschichte, vol. 7 (Stuttgart:
Gustav Fischer, 1962), 42–4.
[65] Fischer, *Geschichte des Hauses Hohenlohe*, vol. 1, 66–9.
[66] ALARL 1632–3/B151, April 23, 1632.
[67] ALKL II/11/6, June 28, 1637.

The rule of troops

In the years that immediately followed, none of the important and troubling issues of the early 1630s could be resolved. The limits to Habsburg absolutism, the authority of the German princes in the empire, the terms of feudal domination, the structure of the agrarian social order, and the recovery of the agricultural economy, all remained in suspense. With hindsight one can now say that a recovery began, very slowly to be sure, after 1640. But even then much remained unclear until 1660 or so.

In the meantime many lands, like Hohenlohe, fell under the rule of the troops. How villagers structured their relationships to the armies mattered a great deal, for these relationships would influence legitimate practices of domination once order began to return in the 1640s. Too often one looks at the years between 1634 and 1648 as a period of unrelieved destruction, confusion, and disorder. In some places at certain times this was no doubt true. But it was not the rule. The remarkable feature of this period was, in fact, the way the warlords, state officials, and villagers, each in their own way, forced, prodded, and helped rural communities to accept extraordinary tax burdens in a time of economic crisis. What the small German state accomplished only with difficulty before the war, and then with only ambiguous results, the tax state after 1634 achieved with ease, but at a brutal cost.

Looking at the confusion of events in these years, this does not seem likely, or even possible. For soon after the triumph of the imperial army at Nördlingen in 1634 France entered the war on the Protestant side, and for the next fourteen years control over many parts of Germany passed repeatedly back and forth between the two sides.[68] The fate of Hohenlohe was perhaps typical in this regard. The imperial commander after Wallenstein, General Gallas, ruled the territory with an iron fist between 1634 and 1636, only to give way to Swedish troops who returned to the territory in 1637. But the Swedes did not stay long. Imperial forces came swift on the heels of the Swedish army, and in 1639–40 settled into winter quarters. The war taxes for that year were extremely heavy (see Table 8.1). In the 1640s troop movements and quarterings became even more confusing, and at times one cannot say with certainty who actually controlled the territory. In 1644–5, for example, Bavarian and French troops marched repeatedly through the region. The final Swedish and French campaigns in 1646–8 brought a harsh burden of war taxes and troop quarterings to Hohenlohe, since columns of the French army advanced right through the region on their way to and from Bavaria.[69] If the armies brought nothing but

---

[68] For treatments of the war in these years see Pagès, *The Thirty Years' War*, 116–204; and Heckel, *Deutschland im konfessionellen Zeitalter*, 175–80.

[69] For accounts of the war in Hohenlohe after 1634 see Bossert, "Bächlinger Ortschronik"; and Fischer, *Geschichte des Hauses Hohenlohe*, vol. 1, 66–80.

destruction and chaos in their wake, then Hohenlohe should have borne the marks of it.

But this was not the case. The new masters – the ruthless and greedy military entrepreneurs, their commissars and troops – ruled the countryside in a more orderly and systematic fashion than one is often led to believe. For, though they sometimes extracted war taxes with violence and force, they found it essential, if the extractions were to go on, to keep intact some structure of authority at the local level. If one looks back on the fourteen years of this period, four years – 1634–5, 1639–40, 1644–5, and 1648–9 – stand out as times of unusually destructive violence. One should not underestimate the effects of the brutal exploitation of these years. As one chronicler of the war in Hohenlohe commented, the commander of one of General Gallas's regiments in 1634–5, Johann Hülper, "seemed to be there only to drive in the harsh *Kontribution* for the Gallas Regiment."[70] But by 1637–8 local officials carried out the collection of the taxes in an orderly and largely peaceful manner.[71] One sees this transition even in Langenburg district, an area that suffered severely after the town fell to imperial troops in 1634. Here the steward began to interpose himself between the commissars and the villages. Then he began to keep accurate records of the war taxes and other revenues and debts. Finally, by 1639, he was in regular touch with the court in exile. For Count Heinrich Friedrich the rationale for helping the armies collect the war taxes was simple and clear: to protect the interests of the state until a settlement to the conflict came.[72]

Local officials became the key agents of the war-tax system, with much more coercive power over villagers than in the prewar years. Their power came primarily from their fiscal responsibilities, for they drew up tax assessments, distributed the burden among communities, and then collected the taxes, either in cash or kind. For those under their authority these decisions were matters of life and death. To the villagers of Crispach the local official, Georg Glockh, came across as a petty tyrant who unfairly burdened their village with additional levies when others, so they argued, should have borne the burden.[73] In Langenburg the steward used his power to excuse members of the town council, the Twelve, from certain types of services for the troops, an act that won their loyalty but that also created resentment among the town's citizens.[74] Still, villagers bore these burdens, since the force of arms stood behind the local officials. In 1640 villagers from Langenburg were cruelly reminded of this when a young lieutenant from the imperial army threatened the whole population of

---

[70] Bossert, "Bächlinger Ortschronik." [71] ALKL II/6/11, July 14, 1638; II/10/3/1, 1639–40.
[72] ALKL II/10/3/12/B2, December 23, 1645; II/10/3/12/B3, January 3, 1646; II/10/3/12/BG, September 1645; II/10/3/12/BH, October 30, 1646; II/10/3/12/BK, November 16, 1645.
[73] ALGAL 749/34, April 8, 1637. [74] ALAL 359, 1639–47.

the district, warning that if they did not deliver up supplies for his troops "the quartermaster accompanied by the entire artillery, a terrifying column with all its men and horses, will camp among you, as long as is necessary, until he is handsomely paid."[75]

The power of local officials over villagers was nowhere more evident than in the measures taken for self-defense after 1634. Repeatedly freebooters, bandits, and ill-disciplined troops threatened villages. The threat to villagers lay not so much against their lives, though this occurred often enough, but against local property, food, cattle, and supplies of grain. In response to this problem, all through South Germany local officials helped organize havens, usually fortified towns, safe from the soldiers.[76] When the alarm went out, villagers brought their families, supplies, and cattle into the fortified town and there waited until the danger had passed. Langenburg developed into one such retreat. In 1639, as French soldiers marched through Hohenlohe, the officials spread the alarm, and peasants, their families, and their cattle quickly fled into town, safe behind the town gates and the fortified walls.[77] So successful did this fortress become that villagers from nearby Ansbach sought safety there as well.[78] With such measures officials protected at least some important recources – cattle and oxen in particular – and made it possible for the agricultural economy to recover sooner than otherwise would have been possible (see Chapter 9).

For a small South German state the fiscal burdens of these years, and the harsh methods of collecting them, marked a sharp break with the past. As late as the 1620s local officials carried out the day-to-day practice of domination by getting villagers to share in their own exploitation, by relaxing the burdens when crops failed or by letting debts pile up. Now the fiscal demands of the armies made these practices impossible. This shifted the terms of dominance decisively against villagers.

If one reads carefully petitions from the 1640s one detects a shift in peasant attitudes toward authority. The evidence comes primarily from tenant farmers, millers, tavernkeepers, and others who held substantial farms and landed wealth, for these groups, not the smallholders, winegrowers, or laborers, had the resources to survive the crushing burden of taxes. Where on the eve of the war this elite flaunted their independence and freedom, they now showed a striking degree of deference. The pleas of Hans Hanselmann, heir of a veritable dynasty

---

[75] ALKL II/10/3/1/B30, June 1, 1640.
[76] See Ingomar Bog, *Die bäuerliche Wirtschaft im Zeitalter des Dreissigjährigen Krieges: Die Bewegungsvorgänge in der Kriegswirtschaft nach den Quellen des Klosterverwalteramtes Heilsbronn*, Schriften des Instituts für fränkische Landesforschung an der Universität Erlangen, Historical Series, vol. 4 (Coburg: Vest, 1952), 124–31.
[77] ALGAL 201/1, 1639. [78] ALGAL 201/14, February 6, 1641.

of wealthy tenant farmers before the war, sound more like the pathetic appeals of a prewar laborer than those of a Hohenlohe tenant farmer. All of his cattle were gone, his fields uncultivated, and debts unpaid, he said, "so that in my household, with my many children, we have eaten for two years only oat bread, and soup and vegetables without fat." Only with the sufferance of the authorities could he hope to overcome the "bitter suffering" of his family.[79] In the 1640s refugees in particular, those who fled Hohenlohe and then returned to reclaim their farms and properties, showed a degree of deference once rare for tenant farmers. Georg Streckher, one refugee who came back to Nesselbach in 1642, pledged absolute obedience and hard work if he could settle his farm again.[80]

This shift in attitudes toward authority was born of extreme physical want and powerlessness. Intense fractiousness within the village commune played its part as well. Behind the scenes of communal life all of the bitter differences between the elite and the village poor remained very much alive, perhaps even more so, in the 1630s and 1640s. Now those ancient feuds often became life-and-death struggles over who would shoulder the largest burden of taxes. One can see all of these factors at work in the case of the miller of Unterregenbach. To hear the plea of Michael Hohbach, the miller, the commune would have utterly ruined him in 1640 if it had had its way. Right from his start at the mill in 1639 this young man had struggled to make the barest of livings. When the imperial army settled into winter quarters the commune, so its representatives argued to the steward, thought that the wealthy miller should shoulder the largest share of the burden. But Hohbach protested. Out of desperation he turned to the steward, begging for help. "Grant me the helping hand of authority against the commune," he pleaded, "and let me go my way that I can bear my own and be left with my house's honor."[81]

In this particular case the miller, his wife, and child seem to have lost the struggle. But a pattern was emerging. If the village elite were ever to recover their position, if the agrarian order were to be restored and become stable once again, the state would have to restore its authority.

[79] ALAL 1079, December 23, 1639.
[80] ALAL 481, April 6, 1642. [81] ALAL 1080, January 10, 1640.

9

~~~~~~

Agrarian order restored

The significance of the crisis of the seventeenth century for the whole of Central Europe is not easily summed up. In some rural areas the years between 1620 and 1660 marked a decisive turning point, a watershed, a final break with the past that confirmed radical changes in the agrarian order. East of the Elbe River a new agrarian order took hold. Powerful landed noble families consolidated their hold on lands laid waste in the war, confiscated freehold properties, built up large estates, or latifundia, and forced peasants into a humiliating form of servitude, often called the second serfdom. In other regions, in the German West particularly, the structures of order, authority, and social control, built up slowly in the sixteenth century, proved far more resilient than one might at first suppose. The demographic crisis may have ended the expansion of population, contributed to a reversal in agricultural prices and wages, and altered the commercial climate for agriculture. But old systems of heritable land tenure, the seigneurial rights of lords, and the village social structure changed little, if at all.[1] In the reconstructed agrarian world of the German West the essential structures of property survived the crisis intact.

Scholars have often commented on the remarkable political and social stability that settled over Europe in the late seventeenth century. The roots of this stability are not fully understood, and the best explanations focus on important changes evident after 1660: the new power of the centralized state, the nature of warfare, the stable international political settlements, the new role of aristocracies in public and private life.[2] Stability in the political order, however, rested in the end on practices of domination in the countryside, now more certain and stable than in the 1620s, which underpinned authority and the power of the nobility. And these relationships, in the German West at least, continued practices well established by the eve of the Thirty Years' War. No-

---

[1] For a general introduction to agrarian development in Europe in this period see the Bibliographical Essay.

[2] This argument is put forward by Theodore K. Rabb in *The Struggle for Stability in Early Modern Europe* (New York: Oxford University Press, 1975).

where was this more evident than in the tiny hamlets, villages, and small towns of Hohenlohe.

Lords who practiced traditional methods of domination helped the agricultural economy recover relatively quickly from the depression of the 1630s and 1640s. Where large and powerful bureaucratic states continued to bear down on peasant households, extracting a heavy burden of taxes despite depressed economic conditions, recovery was delayed. But in the small German states, where old patterns of domination outlasted the crisis and set strict limits to the fiscal power of the state, tenant farmers accumulated capital resources more easily and, when these were invested in agricultural improvements, recovery came quickly. By the 1680s the tenant farmers of Hohenlohe were prospering once again, this time as cattle farmers selling their livestock on far-flung markets in Germany, Switzerland, and France. In the boom of the eighteenth century Hohenlohers became celebrated for their surprising wealth, their skill in commerce, and the stability of their rural communities. It is often argued that new crops and improved commercial conditions played a key role in the agrarian expansion of this period.[3] But it is also true that the prosperity of Hohenlohe's peasant capitalists depended upon an agrarian class structure that had taken shape in the sixteenth century.

Weakness of the patrimonial state

In looking at the resolution of the political crisis in the empire in the middle of the century attention falls far too often on the rise of Germany's few powerful centralized states. What is often overlooked is the resilience of Germany's small patrimonial states. The trappings of absolutism may have made rapid headway at the courts of many small rulers, but the changes remained just that: superficial cultural changes that left the traditional structures of the small state intact. We know far too little about how Germany's small princes, counts, and knights became forces for authority, order, and discipline in the late seventeenth century. The problem is all the more intriguing because these groups emerged from the crisis weakened, not strengthened, their autonomy protected by the balance of powers in Europe and the Holy Roman Empire. But if we look closer at this problem and examine the beginnings of a settlement of the political crisis in the small state in the early 1640s, one theme clearly emerges: a return to traditional methods of domination. These methods seem archaic now, at least when set beside the sure coercive power of a centralized state. But these

[3] For the eighteenth-century agrarian boom see Wilhelm Abel, *Geschichte der deutschen Landwirtschaft vom frühen Mittelalter bis zum 19. Jahrhundert*, Deutsche Agrargeschichte, vol. 2 (Stuttgart: Eugen Ulmer, 1962), 283–301; and Peter Kriedte, *Peasants, Landlords and Merchant Capitalists: Europe and the World Economy, 1500–1800* (Cambridge: Cambridge University Press, 1983), 101–57.

practices of domination brought order and authority to the countryside just as surely as did the dead weight of bureaucratic government or military force.

The long war, the agrarian crisis, and fiscal problems left many small German princes with their power shattered. Reasons for this collapse of state authority are not difficult to find. The small principalities and lordships lay in Central Germany, Franconia, the Rhineland, and the German Southwest, regions laid waste and heavily depopulated during the war.[4] Because their lands lay at the crossroads of strategically important roads in Franconia, the princes of Hohenlohe, as we noted in the last chapter, lost effective control of their lands, fled, and watched helpless from afar as one army after another exploited them right to the end of the war. The last troops pulled out of Hohenlohe in 1650.

But the war left the small state weakened in other ways as well. The ranks of the princes and nobles themselves were decimated. These losses threw the government of small states into confusion, for power quickly decayed in states ruled without the steadiness of bureaucratic institutions. Six princes of the House of Hohenlohe, the entire generation of rulers that began the war, had died by the time the troops left the territory in peace in 1650. Four of them – Georg Friedrich II of Waldenburg, Kraft, Philip Heinrich, and Georg Friedrich II of Neuenstein – died between 1635 and 1645 alone. Power then fell to the uncertain rule of widows and regents until Count Heinrich Friedrich (1625–99), the son of Philip Ernst (d. 1628), gradually assumed control of Hohenlohe-Neuenstein after 1640.[5] Centralized states could survive a succession of weak, uncertain rulers and emerge from the war even more powerful than before. But the rulers of small states faced the monumental task of rebuilding their authority with power diminished and uncertain.

In addition, the financial resources necessary to rebuild state authority could not be easily found, since the war left the princes with a deep fiscal crisis. The costs of the war were simply ruinous for the small state. In this regard Hohenlohe was not at all unusual. Officials who began to take stock of the fiscal crisis in the mid-1640s painted a nightmarish picture of the state's fiscal situation. The war taxes, it is true, had been heavy, but that was not what concerned officials the most. What appalled them was the complete collapse of state revenues. From 1634 on, local officials gave up completely on collecting taxes, rents, and dues.[6] Tithes too went uncollected. The granaries, well stocked in normal years, stood completely empty.[7] In 1641–2, when one can finally piece together an accurate picture of debts in Langenburg district, peasants owed the state the

---

[4] Günther Franz, *Der dreissigjährige Krieg und das deutsche Volk: Untersuchungen zur Bevölkerungs- und Agrargeschichte*, 3d ed., Quellen und Forschungen zur Agrargeschichte, vol. 7 (Stuttgart: Gustav Fischer, 1962), 47–8.

[5] Adolf Fischer, *Geschichte des Hauses Hohenlohe* (Stuttgart: Alfred Müller, 1866), vol. 2, 75.

[6] ALKL II/11/6, November 17, 1635; II/11/6, June 28, 1637; II/6/11, September 26, 1639.

[7] ALKL II/11/6, July 5, 1637.

staggering sum of 21,500 fl. in arrears in taxes, rents, and dues (see Graph 8.2). The princes, not surprisingly, had taken on a heavy load of external debt in these years, and creditors began to press their claims on the house's resources in the imperial court. One such case involved debts of 100,000 fl., a sum the house could never pay off.[8] Chancellor Assum, who surveyed the account books carefullly in 1643–4, concluded that the state's finances had taken on "a virtually desperate appearance."[9] Few small German states would ever pay off debts of this size, and the fiscal problems from these years would become a chronic source of weakness for decades to come.

The fiscal crisis inevitably dominated state–peasant relationships. But the extraction of additional revenues from peasant households still pressed by the military levies was problematic. How could a ruler with an uncertain hold on his own lands and a bankrupt treasury drive in overdue taxes, rents, and dues from an impoverished peasantry? Behind local officials empowered to collect the war taxes stood the full coercive force of Catholic and Protestant armies. No such threat stood behind officials whose task it was to squeeze tax arrears from the peasantry. Confusion in the district account books, inadequate information at the court's disposal, tenuous links with local officials, all added to the difficulty of restoring the fiscal power of the state. The task must have seemed overwhelming to the young Count Heinrich Friedrich. When he renewed contacts with his officials in 1640, he seemed eager to find out about local conditions back in the territory, but he hesitated to push his officials on with the collection of taxes.[10] A year later, in 1641, he gave reasons for his reluctance. He feared that any effort to collect taxes would drive villagers away: "For this reason hold the officials to their duties, that they are not to force subjects to pay off their eight years of debts."[11] Keeping peasants on the land, holding them with assurances of leniency, outweighed all other considerations at this time.

More than reluctance to drive off tenants lay behind the actions of the prince. A whole set of traditional attitudes about power and legitimacy, rooted in the culture of Germany paternalism, guided the prince's behavior in these years. The debate over taxes in 1642 shows these attitudes at work in some detail. In that year Heinrich Friedrich proposed to collect the labor-service tax once again. The entire discourse never moved beyond traditional assumptions about the fiscal power of the state. No one at the court proposed setting aside revenues from the tax to pay off state debts. No one even mentioned breaking the terms

[8] ALGAL 189/14 [1643 or 1644?]; 189/15 [1643 or 1644?].
[9] ALGAL 189/3, May 16, 1644; 189/9, July 6, 1644; 189/13, September 1643; 189/14, [1643 or 1644?]; 189/15, [1643 or 1644?].
[10] ALKL II /11/6, March 16, 1640; ALAL 341, June 26, 1641.
[11] ALGAL 880/10, September 5, 1641.

of the Treaty of 1609 by raising the assessments. Ruler and officials instead assumed that the key to the renewal of authority was renewed state control over the distribution, and redistribution, of the most important resource of the agricultural economy: grain. Officials were instructed to collect the tax in kind, to set aside the stocks of grain, and then lend it out "so that farmers can cultivate their fields and we can give out seed grain for planting."[12] Officials considered this use of the revenues essential for restoring respect for authority at the village level, since peasants would return this favor with gratitude and obedience. Others, though they agreed that the tax was needed, warned of resistance.[13] This was power understood in the traditional terms of paternalism and deference: the exchange of protection for loyalty and obedience.

Authority and power, however, never flowed simply from the top down in small German states. Villagers never offered up loyalty and obedience automatically, least of all in circumstances where the lord had abandoned his dependents to foreign armies. So the early efforts to renew old hierarchical ties inevitably met with resistance. "Down in the valley, in Oberregenbach and Bächlingen, as I began to start my rounds on Wednesday morning," the steward of Langenburg district reported, "I experienced in that hour the full mobilization of Döttingen and Langenburg districts." To a man the tenant farmers of the districts refused to pay the tax or even to perform labor services in their stead.[14] In Döttingen district, villagers rebuffed local officials more harshly, roughing up one who dared read the decree and taunting him: "And where will you get this money?!"[15] Similar incidents occurred throughout the territory.[16]

One does not have to look far to see the obvious reasons for resistance to state authority in the early 1640s. The war taxes remained at high levels, and most villagers, the once prosperous tenant farmers included, found themselves hard put to survive. But the steward's observations about the anger and the outrage of the villagers suggests another, deeper grievance at work: the idea that one returns deference and obedience only for protection. Though none mentioned bitter memories of 1630, 1632, or 1634, the year the court fled the territory, the lords of Hohenlohe had plainly not protected its villagers from the brutal exploitation and violence of the 1630s. Authority and power required legitimacy in the eyes of villagers. This meant the lord had to protect the peasantry, to spare them from unjust exploitation. The peasantry, in short, had to share once again in fruits of their own domination.

[12] ALARL 1642–3/B22, July 21, 1642.   [13] ALGAL 880/17, August 4, 1642.
[14] ALGAL 880/25, August 16, 1625.
[15] ALGAL 880/27, November 2, 1642; 880/30, January 30, 1645.
[16] ALGAL 880/26, August 16, 1642.

Domination restored

Whether the state, even a small and weak German patrimonial state, would actually overcome such resistance was an issue never seriously in doubt in the middle of the seventeenth century. German peasants could hardly resist the power and authority of their masters in the early 1640s as effectively as they once had, in 1525 or even in 1630. The makings of a revolution or even a concerted rebellion were simply not at hand. The village elite, the backbone of every major rising in the 1620s and early 1630s, had declined in numbers; plague, war, and famine had cut into the ranks of powerful tenant-farmer families just as surely as they had among the village poor. Social mobility and the movements of population had also broken families, changed the composition of local communities, disrupted class ties, and weakened loyalty to the village commune. Even if villagers had overcome these obstacles and thrown off local authority, Catholic or Protestant troops would quickly have suppressed a rising before it spread to other villages. A few small rebellions, and some drawn-out guerrilla wars in the Black Forest, did occur in the 1640s. But the time for Germany's peasant furies, rebellions that seriously tested the power of the state, had come and gone.

Rulers of small states, however, could not restore their domination of the countryside on whatever terms they wished. I have already mentioned three checks on the power of a small state over its subjects: weak administrative structures, the lack of fiscal resources, and cultural attitudes toward power and authority. In the mid-1640s and the 1650s other checks became apparent as well: the imperative to wield power legitimately, the endlessly imaginative tactics of peasants in resisting or evading taxes, and, finally, imperial and local law itself. Skillful rulers and officials could call upon a variety of well-tested methods to exploit weaknesses in the peasantry. But, even if submission was assured, the terms of domination did not necessarily favor the state.

Traditional practices of domination demanded that a lord continually establish the legitimacy of his authority. To evoke lawful obedience and deference was therefore a consuming process never to be taken as settled once and for all. This traditional axiom of lord–peasant relationships still held true in the 1640s, but was perhaps felt with a sense of immediacy one finds only in times when lordly power was uncertain or badly shaken. Count Heinrich Friedrich, for example, repeatedly urged on his subjects the legitimacy of his rule. In response to villagers who resisted the labor-service tax, he insisted to village assemblies that the state had never ceased to provide protection, even in the awful chaos of the 1630s. After the court fled, he argued, the state had protected its dependents, and had suffered for doing so. By refusing to drive in old debts, the state kept the peasantry on the land, sheltered them, freed them from burdens that otherwise would have driven them off, "and we did so for this reason alone, that you would be spared execution by the military forces, could keep your cattle and household goods, and then, when you had recovered, you could step into your old obligations, and therefore Authority and Subject could stay together."[17] His offer to redistribute resources (mostly grain) extracted by the stewards was also no idle promise. Petitioners who accepted their obligations but requested relief got most of what they wanted. Julius Renner, a young tenant farmer from Nesselbach, Ludwig Bauer of Raboldshausen, Johan Lepin, and others were freed from the tax in 1643.[18] Such benevolence fit the circumstances. The count avoided confrontations, protected his villagers in the traditional sense, and built up a fund of good will. The policy, however, cost the state dear: Badly needed revenues were written off.

A clear claim to legitimate authority opened the way for princely domination of the countryside. But by itself it added little to the actual power of officials to extract revenues from peasant householders. That could come about only by renewing carefully the everyday practices of domination. The opening of negotiations for a settlement of the war and the political problems of the empire in 1645 provided the first opportunity for many small princes to address this problem. For a political settlement would provide the political stability essential for small princes to bring order to their states. From this point on, rulers stepped up efforts to make the practice of domination possible once again. In Hohenlohe, Count Heinrich Friedrich instructed his officials to review systematically the state's finances and account books.[19] Officials engaged in these activities did not go over the books in quiet seclusion in the castles at Neuenstein, Weikersheim, and Langenburg. They walked every hamlet, village, and town of the territory, surveying each and every household, its attached properties, and its debts. Officials also brought new life to the petitioning process, the link between the court and the peasant household. After 1646 village assemblies began to meet again each week to air grievances before the steward and to send petitions on to the court for consideration.[20] Just as improved record keeping made the practice of domination more efficient in the sixteenth century, so the surveys of peasant indebtedness, account-book renewals, and a flood of petitions made domination possible again in the middle of the seventeenth century.

These surveys allowed rulers and officials to exploit the chief weakness of the peasantry in the 1640s: indebtedness to the state. Debts can be turned to many political purposes. Between equals they keep open the doors of influence. Between unequals they can serve as instruments of domination and exploitation.

---

[17] ALGAL 880/16, August 26, 1642.
[18] ALARL 1642–3/B163, February 23, 1642; 1642–3/B165, February 4, 1643; 1642–3/B164, March 3, 1643.
[19] ALGAL 880/3, May 16, 1644; 880/7, June 27, 1644.
[20] ALAL 347, March 9, 1646 and March 16, 1646.

Crisis and recovery

This the young prince of Hohenlohe and his stewards seemed to understand well. When the diligent new steward of Langenburg, Sigmund Knie, took over his job in 1646, the first task he completed was a systematic survey of indebtedness in his district. In his "Liquidation of Accounts," Knie gathered together all the old account books from his predecessor (most had miraculously survived the war) and surveyed the district's peasant households, each and every one of them, listing the debts of each as he went. He was familiar enough with the conditions of every propertyholder in his jurisdiction to divide them into five categories: surviving householders, the dead, those with debts outside the district, the winegrowers of Bächlingen, and those who owed past-due war taxes. For each household he listed the debts to the state, in every category, figured to the last penny. For the whole district, indebtedness amounted to 21,857 fl.[21] He was then ready to use his surveys to renew princely domination of the countryside.

As Sigmund Knie made his rounds, he reported on the condition of each petitioner's properties, past and present debts, and the likelihood that he would repay the state. He also received from each petitioner promises of loyalty and deference, pledges renewed each time the supplicant approached the steward for help. The obsequious deference of this period was one born of extreme want, of helplessness, of the urgent need for protection from soldiers in the brutal last years of the war. One finds scattered evidence of this attitude as early as 1640, as I mentioned in the last chapter. But now, in the hundreds of petitions that streamed into the chancellery after 1646, signs of it multiplied rapidly. The Bächlingen winegrowers, each of them heavily in debt to the state, gathered as a group together, pledged their obedience, and pleaded for a pardon from rents for a year, "so we can free overselves, bit by bit, from our debts, and not, after our deaths, pass them on, to the ruin of our children."[22] Tenant farmers, millers, butchers, bakers, craftsmen of every description approached the stewards with similar requests. Each pledged loyalty in return for protection, usually in the form of pardons from debts, rents, or dues.[23] In the everyday work of these stewards, in their routine rounds in the villages, in reports and meticulously kept account books, one can see the countless small steps taken to renew the ties of traditional paternalism and deference.

Princely domination of the village, however, did not become fully secure until after the war. The Treaty of Westphalia in 1648 was one important part in this process. The right to tax, after all, came from the empire, and the practical limits to that power depended upon the rights the empire granted the German princes. Under Charles V and Ferdinand II Germany's small princes had been constrained, vulnerable, uncertain of what they could practically ac-

[21] ALARL 1646-7. [22] ALAL 432, January 21, 1646. [23] ALARL 1645-6 to 1650-1.

234

complish within their own domains. The Treaty of Westphalia put an end to that uncertainty. The treaty restricted the power of the emperor over the princes, guaranteed the preeminence of the imperial diet, revoked the despised Edict of Restitution, and restored properties confiscated after 1624. The treaty essentially recognized the princes as separate sovereign rulers under the authority of the empire.[24] Imperial law remained fully in force, of course, and still constrained princes and lords – the imperial courts remained as busy as they were before the war, jammed with disputes between lords and peasants well into the eighteenth century. But the peace made it possible for the small princes to secure their authority and power over their own lands. For the counts of Hohenlohe this meant that Weikersheim and other ecclesiastical properties lost in 1634 returned to the house's control.[25] When Count Heinrich Friedrich took formal oaths of loyalty from his subjects in 1650, he enjoyed a stable political climate in the empire such as none of his predecessors had known.

Traditional practices of domination, however, still hemmed in the small prince and set strict limits to his power. This the treaty did not alter. The constraints came from three major sources, all by now quite familiar: weak administrative institutions, the peasantry itself, and imperial and local law. The first two, weak institutions of government and entrenched peasant resistance to authority, made it difficult for small princes to extract a larger share of peasant surpluses than was customary before the war. The effort to raise the *Landsteuer* in Hohenlohe, for example, ran quickly into insurmountable obstacles. The state had suspended collection of this tax in 1634, and Heinrich Friedrich pushed hard to restore the tax soon after the Peace of Westphalia had been signed. But his steward warned of resistance to the tax, since villagers were hard pressed to support the French and Swedish troops withdrawing through the region in 1648–9.[26] He was not far wrong in his assessment. Out of Döttingen district came reports of many peasants refusing to pay the tax. "The peasants cannot be brought to pay this tax," the steward stated matter-of-factly, "since they still owe 300 fl. of the peace taxes and the war levies." He went on to say that resistance was proving so stiff "that it was impossible for officials to carry out their duties."[27] As in the past, local officials relaxed their efforts to drive in taxes, rents, and dues. When they did not, villagers simply withdrew their cooperation, and the flow of revenues came to a halt.

Imperial and customary law constrained princes and lords as well. The learned jurist Samuel Pufendorf poked fun at the bizarre complexity of imperial

---

[24] For a discussion of the Treaty of Westphalia see Martin Heckel, *Deutschland im konfessionellen Zeitalter*, Deutsche Geschichte, vol. 5 (Göttingen: Vandenhoeck & Ruprecht, 1983), 195–8.
[25] Fischer, *Geschichte des Hauses Hohenlohe*, vol. 2, 75–80.
[26] ALAL 248, July 9, 1649.   [27] ALAL 248, July 15, 1649.

institutions and law codes, but these same institutions and laws made radical political change difficult in small territories. In a small and fragmented state this conservatism often favored the peasantry. The Treaty of 1609, designed to end resistance to imperial taxes and labor services and provide the state of Hohenlohe with secure sources of revenues, had never provided the state with adequate incomes, as we saw earlier. Yet, when Count Heinrich Friedrich finally reestablished the territorial tax, he did so strictly in accordance with the terms of the treaty.

The count waited until December of 1651 to try again, this time taking up the task with caution and with more attention than before to the task of cultivating villagers' cooperation. Teams of officials were ordered into the villages in 1652 and 1653 to reassess peasant property, the first time this had been done since 1630.[28] Sharp disputes broke out in village after village over the assessments. Some Hohenlohers protested their assessments and negotiated reductions in the value of their properties listed on the tax rolls. Others fell back on time-honored methods of deception, hiding property or wealth. Still others showed their defiance openly. All over Langenburg the alarm went out to assemble a committee to protest the assessments, an alarm not unlike ones that went out in 1630 and 1632. But this time the outcome was quite different. The count ordered his officials to punish the leaders, much as Countess Anna Maria had done in the earlier disturbances, but this time he quickly forgave them and restored them to grace.[29] Even more important, he abandoned plans to raise the rate of taxation and consented to set it at nine *batzen* per 100 fl. of assessed wealth – the same rate set by the Treaty of 1609.[30] The treaty remained the law of the land right to the formal end of the empire in 1806.

With this concession the terms of domination were fixed. The modern bureaucratic state, rapidly taking hold in other parts of Germany and Europe, never found stable roots in an early modern patrimonial state such as Hohenlohe. From the vantage point of the princes this may have been lamentable, but for the peasantry these checks on the development of the state came as a blessing. For the officials of the modern bureaucratic states of Europe extracted a heavy, unyielding, and sometimes ruinous burden of taxes from villagers. This accounts for the peasant furies that erupted in the middle of the seventeenth century in France, Spain, and Switzerland, for in these states officials imposed a heavy burden of taxes despite famine or economic decline in the countryside. But in a state like Hohenlohe that was never to be the case after 1650. Princes, officials, and peasants engaged in a continuous contest over the surpluses of the land, the prince yielding repeatedly to resistance to extracting

---

[28] ALKL II/11/6/, December 1, 1651 and January 3, 1652.
[29] ALKL II/11/6, February 1, 1653; ALARL 1652–3/B29, February 1, 1653.
[30] ALARL 1653–4.

revenues considered ruinous by the peasantry. The weakness of state institutions, traditions of successful resistance to taxes, the culture of German paternalism, and the weight of local and imperial laws reined in the fiscal power of the small German state.

Economic recovery

Traditional practices of domination, archaic as they seemed in the late seventeenth century, played an important role in bringing the economic crisis to an end. Practices that brought political order and stability to the state had practical consequences for the agricultural economy. Princes and peasants, as a rule, still made no distinction between politics and economics. The *Hausvaterliteratur* reached its peak only in the late seventeenth century, the most famous work of its genre, Wolf Helmhard von Hohberg's *Georgica curiosa*, appearing in 1682.[31] The moral imperative that the household should remain self-sufficient very much guided small German princes in the years of economic recovery. For this reason we should view the various state policies collectively known as "protection of the peasantry," or *Bauernschutzpolitik*, as nothing particularly new in state–peasant relations.[32] These policies simply continued practices of domination dating back to the sixteenth century. As was discussed in Chapter 6, after 1560 the small state assumed an important role in propping up the agrarian social order in times of crisis. Now, after the war, the state helped villagers recover from yet another agricultural crisis, only this time on a massive scale.

Several methods lay at hand to end the agricultural crisis. The first, propping up a class of tenant farmers with systems of heritable land tenure, was more an issue in northwestern Germany – in Brunswick, Calenberg, Hannover, Hildesheim, and western parts of Saxony – than in the German Southwest. Before the landed nobility could confiscate peasant properties on a massive scale – and create large estates on the Eastelbian model – the princes and prince-bishops of northwestern Germany established secure rights of heritable land tenure for their peasantries.[33] No comparable threat developed in the German Southwest. The lesser nobility and the imperial knights had long since withdrawn into their own small, fragmented enclaves separate from the domains of the princes, and so rarely stood between rulers and peasants as they did in

---

[31] See Otto Brunner, *Adeliges Landleben und europäischer Geist: Leben und Werk Wolf Helmhards von Hohberg 1612–1688* (Salzburg: Otto Müller, 1949), and "Das 'ganze Haus' und die alteuropäische 'Ökonomik,' " in Brunner, *Neue Wege der Verfassungs- und Sozialgeschichte*, 2d ed. (Göttingen: Vandenhoeck & Ruprecht, 1968), 103–27.

[32] See Franz, *Der dreissigjährige Krieg und das deutsche Volk*, 91–4; and Jan De Vries, *Economy of Europe in an Age of Crisis, 1600–1715* (Cambridge: Cambridge University Press, 1976), 61–3.

[33] For references to this problem see the Bibliographical Essay.

the Northeast. The nobles also wielded less power. Most important of all, heritable land tenure had been secured in the German Southwest at least since the middle of the sixteenth century. In Hohenlohe, after the war the state simply renewed its commitment to established customs of land tenure and inheritance.[34] The customs became one of the cornerstones of the law code of 1738.[35]

A second method, writing off peasant debts to the state, played an important role everywhere in the German West, allowing investment and capital formation to take place once again in the countryside. This practice freed villagers from debts that, had they been fully paid, would have siphoned off surpluses needed for the recovery of the agricultural economy. Like other practices of domination, this one too followed patterns well established before the crisis set in in the 1620s. But the massive scale on which states wrote off peasant debts dwarfed any comparable efforts from the sixteenth and early seventeenth centuries. As we noticed earlier for Langenburg district, total peasant indebtedness amounted to roughly 21,500 fl. in 1641–2. Stewards kept track of the debts in the account books, and one can follow the history of every single debt as it was pardoned, paid off in part, or assigned to heirs or to new propertyholders when the property changed hands.[36] Occasionally the state treated a tenant harshly and required full payment of the debts on the spot, a demand that drove a few tenants from their properties. The miller from Bächlingen came in for such treatment in 1651, and he and his family left the mill in humiliation.[37] Few tenants, however, were treated this way, and one suspects that, in this case, concerns other than the debts led to the expulsion.

On the whole, the state relaxed its claims to peasant debts or extended favorable terms to those who could not pay promptly. By 1655–6 the indebtedness from the war years had already fallen to 14,000 fl.; ten years later, it was under 11,000 fl. (see Graph 8.2). In the end, state officials made no public fuss over the mountain of debts that went unpaid. Chancellor Assum quietly ordered the steward to drop the remainder (a total of 9,910 fl.) from the books in 1674.[38]

Princes who wielded seigneurial powers over their villagers, as most petty princes did in Franconia and the German Southwest, stimulated investment in the agricultural economy in a third way. These lords reduced the burden of current rents, tithes, dues, and taxes and allowed villagers to invest the funds in new buildings, livestock, or improvements in the land. This prac-

---

[34] ALKI 33/7, 1663; 33/8, n.d.; 33/21, February 24, 1657; 33/22, May 19, 1707; 33/11, April 16, 1707; 33/14, December 29, 1709.

[35] See Eckart Schremmer, *Die Bauernbefreiung in Hohenlohe*, Quellen und Forschungen zur Agrargeschichte, vol. 9 (Stuttgart: Gustav Fischer, 1963), 23–4; and Peter Steinle, *Die Vermögensverhältnisse der Landbevölkerung in Hohenlohe im 17. und 18. Jahrhundert*, Forschungen aus Wüttembergisch Franken, vol. 5 (Schwäbisch Hall: Eppinger, 1971), 43–8.

[36] ALARL 1651–2 to 1673–4.

[37] ALAL 403, October 11, 1651. [38] ALARL 1673–4/B32, May 25, 1674.

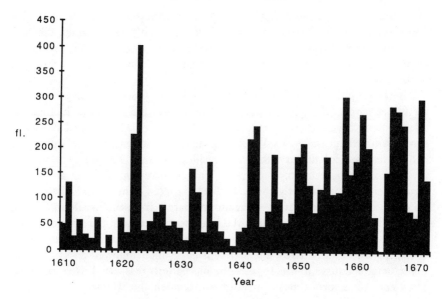

Graph 9.1. Yearly reductions of revenues in Langenburg district, 1606–71. *Source:* ALARL 1606–7 to 1671–2.

tice in effect continued the traditional practice of bargaining with peasants over the surpluses of the land. But lords approached this practice with a thoroughness, and a new zeal for record keeping, typical of the postwar years in Germany. The inventories of debtors compiled by the stewards aided in the task of driving in rents, or reducing them when called upon, in the 1650s and 1660s.[39] In one such case, when villagers from Unterregenbach petitioned for relief from rents in 1664, "to improve the times one bit at a time and bring up the village again," the count did not hesitate to meet their request.[40] Not always did such reductions in rents and tithes come about as a result of benevolence. Deceit and fraud at the village level still cost the state a percentage of its rents in kind every year, especially in the years immediately after the war. Repeatedly villagers concealed their crops, or local officials winked at deceptive practices.[41]

The significance of the state's response to the crisis after 1640 comes more sharply into focus once we examine the problem in the context of the whole seventeenth century. Graph 9.1 plots the revenues the state of Hohenlohe remitted in Langenburg district for almost every year in this period.

---

[39] ALKL II/6/6.   [40] ALARL 1664–5/B232, November 29, 1664.
[41] In 1668 the count discovered that the official responsible for collecting tithes and rents at the state granaries had not been earnestly doing his job. One encounters such complaints repeatedly in the documents of the late seventeenth century. ALKL II/6/6, February 12, 1668.

One should keep in mind that the graph refers only to those revenues *officially* entered in the account books in these years. We cannot track the revenues lost through fraudulent devices or oversight; those practices, so far as we can determine, prevailed on a large scale only in the 1630s, at the peak of the crisis.

The graph points to the early 1640s as a turning point of some importance for the economy. Early in the seventeenth century the counts of Hohenlohe relaxed their claims in a rhythm that closely followed the ups and downs of short-term agricultural cycles. When crops failed, agricultural incomes plunged, and famine spread through the countryside, the state relaxed its claims to revenues until the economy recovered. This occurred in 1611–12 and again, on a larger scale, in the early 1620s. In this last case, Count Philip Ernst relaxed claims to over 400 fl. in 1622–3, again up sharply from the usual amounts of 50 fl. or less. But after 1624, and well into the early 1640s, the state departed from the customary pattern. Instead of remitting more revenues as the crisis deepened in the late 1620s, the state cut back, then followed an erratic and unpredictable course in the 1630s. The old pattern reasserted itself briefly in 1632 and 1634, probably in an effort to dampen the widespread unrest in Hohenlohe's villages, but the reductions came too late to reverse the steep economic decline that had set in.

The state returned to a more regular pattern of remitting its revenues in the early 1640s. One can date the turnaround to 1642–3, the year Count Heinrich Friedrich and state officials began to restore traditional practices of domination. The graph points to two tendencies, however, that make the postwar practices stand out as different from those of the early seventeenth century. First, the amount of revenues the state gave up each year increased with each passing decade. Before 1620 reductions only once topped 100 fl. By the 1660s the yearly reductions amounted to between 100 and 200 fl. every year, sometimes a bit less. Second, the state fell into three- or four-year cycles of reductions, timed perhaps to offset short-term fluctuations in the agricultural economy or unusually heavy tax burdens on peasant households. The peaks between 1642 and 1655 all came at these times: 1642–3 (labor-service taxes); 1646–7 (heavy troop quarterings); 1651–3 (territorial taxes). Evidence is incomplete for the 1660s and 1670s, but here too one sometimes finds that the peaks corresponded to a time of crop losses or to the quartering of troops passing through Hohenlohe on their way to the French frontier. Regardless of the reasons, the benevolence of the state freed resources for investment in economic recovery and insured the peasantry once again against severe losses in times of crop failures.

To what specific uses did villagers put these resources? Petitioners mentioned a wide variety of needs, which varied from group to group. For the tenant farmers, millers, and tavernkeepers funds often went into rebuilding farms damaged in the war, hiring labor to clear fields once again, and replacing livestock sold off during the crisis. The steward, when looking over the condition of the Eberbach tenant farmer Jacob Dinckel, thought the state should look favorably on his request for relief so that he might rebuild his farm and barns for his cattle:

> It is not because one figures his costs as small, since he could well manage the costs of the house on his own; it is because he is in such deep debt that, if we don't show him some grace, if we don't grab him up by the arm, he will sink, and we will have to pass on his lands burdened with extreme debts to someone else.[42]

Other tenant farmers requested relief from taxes so they could more easily pass on their farms to an heir. The millers and tavernkeepers, whose establishments were the largest in the territory, needed considerable amounts of capital to rebuild their properties. Ludwig Casimir Ehrman, a tavernkeeper from one of the oldest and most prominent Langenburg families, asked for freedom from the wine tax so he could invest in capital improvements in his business and vineyards.[43]

Smallholders, winegrowers, craftsmen, and the village poor had smaller properties to tend to, and so their economic needs appear modest when set beside those of the tenant farmers. Many simply wanted relief from famine or aid to put their homes and small plots of land back in good repair. Some requested supplies of wood from the count's forests to help them with this work. Others asked for tax relief. Stoffel Schwab, returning to Billingsbach in 1646, petitioned to have his taxes deferred for a year "so that I can get my house and small plot of land back into shape and can have more capital."[44] For a brief time at the very end of the war, the state showed less favor toward petitioners, and many were brusquely turned away. Kilian Scheuerman of Atzenrod, recalling years of past service to the state and to the Protestant cause in the Netherlands, found his request for a new house denied in 1653.[45] But others in the years that followed usually received relief. The winegrowers of Bächlingen, a group set apart from all the others because of their special problems with viticulture, cleared their vineyards on the valley slopes, planted new vines, and made a modest recovery in the years after the war. Part of this came about because the state pardoned the group from such a large portion of its debts (see Graph 6.4) In 1650 and 1651 the steward wrote off about half of the total debts of the winegrowers, a sum that at the time amounted to over 500 fl.[46] Ten years later the steward wrote off most of the remainder.[47] But these efforts could not stop a slow and irreversible decline of viticulture in the Jagst valley that continued into the eighteenth century.

---

[42] ALAL 445, March 15, 1659. [43] ALAL 381, May 6, 1655. [44] ALAL 463, March 20, 1646.
[45] ALAL 384, February 7, 1653. [46] ALARL 1650–1. [47] ALARL 1660–1.

If petty German princes hoped that support for the peasantry would reverse the decay of state incomes, they were sorely disappointed. The two important sources of state revenues – seigneurial rents and dues, and taxes – hardly brought in sufficient incomes by the end of the century to make up the losses sustained in the crisis. Seigneurial rents and dues, in fact, declined in the long run, and rose only in the middle of the eighteenth century when population rose again. The income from entry fines, once the most important source of income from the land, declined steeply. From Langenburg district the counts collected between 735 fl. and 877 fl. every year in fines in the early seventeenth century, about 10 to 15 percent of the total income from the district. But income from this source fell precipitously in the 1630s. By the 1640s it averaged a mere 170 fl. per year and, though it rose slightly in the 1650s and 1660s, it averaged only 284 fl. per year (see Table 6.4). Income from rents could not make up for these losses. Because of the population losses and the lack of demand for land, incomes from this source stagnated or even fell. In Langenburg district they stagnated after 1640 at 522 fl. per year (see Table 6.3). In small states where seigneurial revenues remained fixed by custom and law, efforts to boost incomes could not pay off in the late seventeenth century.

Rulers of Germany's larger, more powerful bureaucratic states could make up such losses in revenues by raising taxes. Weaker princes, however, could not. "Absolute rule" never amounted to more than a superficial cultural change in the court life of the small states. The structures of authority, the limits on state power, remained essentially unchanged. For a state like Hohenlohe this meant that taxes never rose to compensate for the losses of revenues suffered after the 1630s. The terms of taxation remained rigidly defined by the terms of the Treaty of 1609, the methods of revenue collection still weak when compared with the coercive force of the larger tax states. On several occasions in the 1670s Count Heinrich Friedrich relaxed taxes when villagers assembled to protest them.[48] The incomes themselves proved a bitter disappointment to him. In the 1680s income from the two taxes barely covered the interest on state debt.[49] The count blamed the financial weakness of his state on lazy, ineffective officials who undermined his authority, complaining in 1686 that "the situation has become so serious that the reputation of the count could suffer."[50] But the coaxing and needling of lower officials to perform their duties in the 1680s could accomplish little more than did the same practices in the 1580s and 1590s. Old practices of domination may have helped economic recovery, but, once established, they made it impossible to create a truly modern tax state.

[48] ALARL 1675–6/B147, July 21, 1675.
[49] ALAL 1053, October 30, 1680. [50] ALAL 1052, September 8, 1686.

Agrarian class structure

Early in the seventeenth century, before the crisis set in, the elites of the countryside – princes, lords, district officials, pastors, peasant elders – worked to instill obedience, discipline, and a firm sense of social hierarchy among villagers of the German countryside. Each wielded power in some way for that purpose. Each also depended on the state, in some measure, for that power. In the late seventeenth century, the exercise of state power served the same end. For this reason the sharp fall in population in the 1630s and 1640s failed to weaken agrarian class structures in most lands of the German West. Social mobility increased as landlords and princes welcomed immigrants from other parts of Germany, Switzerland, and Austria into their lands. But this movement of population largely took place within social structures firmly fixed by the early seventeenth century.

Earlier we noted the extent to which village society became stratified in the sixteenth century, and the role that access to landed property played in the process of social stratification. Other factors – family status, commercial wealth, place in the market economy, occupation – complicated the social distinctions drawn among villagers. But the hierarchy rested, in the end, on control of land. By the time the massive new rent books were drawn up for Hohenlohe in the early seventeenth century, the hierarchy broke down, in its simplest terms, into three groups: tenant farmers, smallholders, and landless cotters.

In the late seventeenth century this social structure remained completely intact. The precise pattern varied, of course, from land to land in the German West, but the remarkable hold smallholders and tenant farmers had on the land set this part of rural Europe apart from France, Italy, and the German East.[51] A close look at the social structures of four rural communities in Hohenlohe at four points in the seventeenth century – 1605, 1630, 1663, and 1681 – illustrates this pattern clearly. The four all come from Langenburg district, and each was typical of a different kind of settlement in the region: Atzenrod, a large compact village on the Hohenlohe plain; Bächlingen, a large village of winegrowers and artisans in the valley of the Jagst River; Binselberg, a small hamlet on the plain; and Langenburg itself, a small market town. The number of households as a whole in this district fell by roughly one-third between 1630 and 1653. But those losses left the ranks of the tenant farmers and smallholders with middle-sized properties untouched.

One can see the pattern most clearly in the two compact villages, Atzenrod and Bächlingen. The rise and fall of population and the expansion and con-

---

[51] See De Vries, *Economy of Europe in an Age of Crisis*, 30–83 passim; and Eberhard Weiss, "Ergebnisse eines Vergleichs der grundherrschaftlichen Strukturen Deutschlands und Frankreichs vom 13. bis zum Ausgang des 18. Jahrhunderts," *Vierteljahrschrift für Sozial- und Wirtschaftsgeschichte* 57 (1970), 1–14.

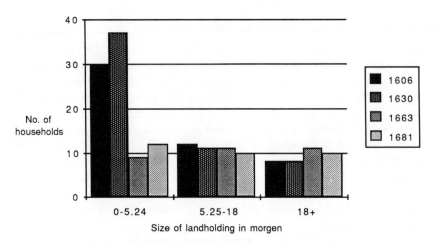

Graph 9.2. Landholders of Atzenrod, 1606–81. *Sources:* L/L 27, 1606; 28, 1606; "Schatzungsanlage Amt Langenburg," 1630, 1663, 1681.

traction of the agrarian economy never seriously reduced the solid hold middle-sized smallholders and tenant farmers had on the lands of the village. The number of propertyholders in these two categories showed a remarkable degree of stability. In Atzenrod the number of householders of middle-sized properties – those who remained marginally self-sufficient in grain production with landholdings between 5.24 and 18 *morgen* – remained consistent at ten to twelve (see Graph 9.2). The tenant farmers, those holding the compact farms, and other propertyholders with sizable properties (above 18 *morgen*) did even better. These propertyholders held their own as land became scarce in the first third of the century. Then, as the overall population of the village fell in the middle of the century and marginal lands reverted to waste, these villagers enlarged their landholdings somewhat, and their ranks even grew slightly, from eight in 1630 to twelve in 1663. The advance and fall in population came in a wholly separate category of households in the village: smallholders with under 5.24 *morgen* of land, cotters, poor craftsmen, and laborers. In 1630, at the peak of population density in the century, the village supported thirty-seven such households. In 1663 the number had fallen precipitously, to only nine. The overall pattern was the same in Bächlingen (see Graph 9.3).

Out in the hamlets of the Hohenlohe plain the permanent hold of the tenant farmers on the land was even more in evidence. Occasionally a family would divide a farm for a few years and then rejoin the two parts in the next generation. But, aside from this occasional practice, these hamlets remained secure islands, small worlds separate and apart from the great advance and decline of the sixteenth and seventeenth centuries. In Binselberg six, and sometimes seven,

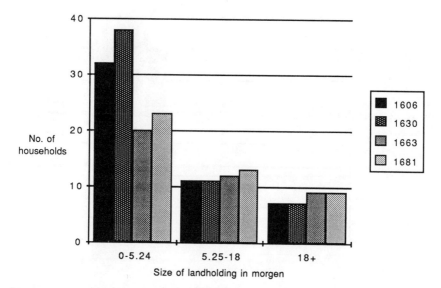

Graph 9.3. Landholders of Bächlingen, 1606–81. *Sources:* L/L 27, 1606; 28, 1606; "Schatzungsanlage Amt Langenburg," 1630, 1653, 1681.

tenant-farmer families held the land (see Graph 9.4). Some family lines on occasion died out or sold out to newcomers in the hamlet. The Hanselmans and the Otts, both families listed in the census of 1630, no longer appear in the lists of 1681. But the Preüngers and the Schums held sizable farms in Binselberg in every census of the century.

Some communities, of course, did not have social structures as stable, as enduring, as the compact villages and hamlets. Small market towns and towns dominated by a princely court tended to follow paths of social change quite different from the villages. The opportunities for small-commodity production for the market, occasional wage labor, or employment at the court continued to open up these communities to social change. The small town of Langenburg, nothing more than a walled village in 1500, for example, became increasingly complex in its social structure by late in the seventeenth century (see Graph 9.5). This town continued to house its own share of tenant farmers and large propertyholders, though the number dwindled significantly, from eleven in 1605 to a mere handful, four, in 1681. The smallholders and cotters, many of them winegrowers, tended to take their place, and quickly made up whatever losses in population the town suffered in the 1630s and 1640s. Among these groups one also finds a much higher proportion of craftsmen and shopkeepers than in the villages: tailors, weavers, smiths, leather workers, masons, cobblers, locksmiths, brickworkers, carpenters, bakers, butchers, and tavernkeepers. No

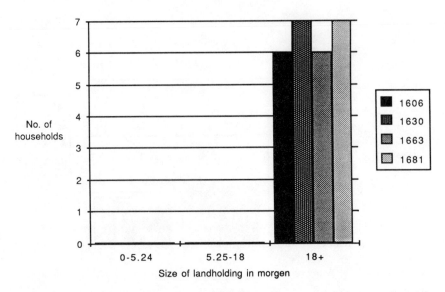

Graph 9.4. Landholders of Binselberg, 1606–81. *Sources:* L/L 27, 1606; 28, 1606; "Schatzungsanlage Amt Langenburg," 1630, 1653, 1681.

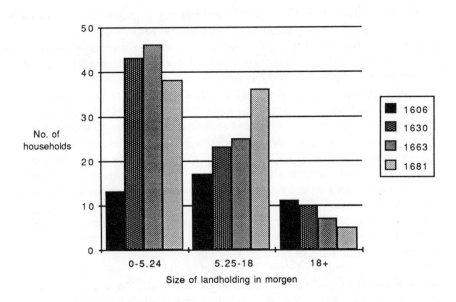

Graph 9.5. Landholders of Langenburg, 1606–81. *Sources:* L/L 27, 1606; 28, 1606; "Schatzungsanlage Amt Langenburg," 1630, 1653, 1681.

one of these occupations predominated. The town, like others in Hohenlohe, specialized in no particular industry. Craftsmen and shopkeepers tended to serve the local market and the court.

Peasant capitalism

Deep and powerful currents of change remained at work in the countryside despite, or perhaps because of, the social and political stability that came after 1650 and 1660. The impression lingers that dynamic change came to Germany only in those parts dominated by powerful centralized states. "Centralized" Germany, to use the term of the nineteenth-century sociologist Wilhelm Fried-rich Riehl, introduced Germans to life under a modern state. The other part of Germany, the "individualized" communities of Southwest and Central Germany where the land lay fragmented into numerous small principalities, small towns, and villages, seems, by contrast, to have been frozen into the archaic structures of political and social life of the past.[52] Up to now my discussion too has stressed the resilience of these structures in shaping the agrarian order of early modern Hohenlohe. But appearances sometimes deceive. For, if one looks not for political change but for social and economic change, the societies of "individualized" Germany appear quite different. Between 1660 and 1720 large stretches of the archaic, seemingly stagnant territories of the German West became the forcing houses for specialized commodity production on the land: the sure foundations for the commercial expansion of the eighteenth century.

The exact role and function of German landlords, tenant farmers, small-holders, and cotters in the world of commercial capitalism varied considerably from region to region in this period. Some areas became specialized producers of industrial products, others of various agricultural products. In rural areas scattered across Northwest Germany, parts of Thüringia and Württemberg, the Black Forest, Upper Swabia, southern Bavaria, and, of course, Hohenlohe, tenant farmers so dominated the local agricultural economy that a kind of peasant capitalism developed. Here the social and political order so favored the tenant farmers and smallholders that they could specialize in the production of agricultural commodities for the market, accumulate wealth, and prepare the way for deeper transformations of agriculture in the eighteenth century. I have

---

[52] Riehl, *Land und Leute*, 5th ed. (Stuttgart: J. G. Cotta, 1861), and *Die bürgerliche Gesellschaft* (Stuttgart: J. G. Cotta, 1851). The original insights of Riehl opened the small-town community of the eighteenth century to the incisive study by Mack Walker, *German Home Towns: Community, State, and General Estate, 1648–1871* (Ithaca, N.Y.: Cornell University Press, 1971). Even Walk-er's small towns, however, underwent profound changes as commercial capitalism caught up groups in almost every community by the end of the eighteenth century. See Christopher Friedrichs, "Capitalism, Mobility and Class Formation in the Early Modern German City," *Past and Present* no. 69 (1975), 24–49, and *Urban Society in an Age of War: Nördlingen, 1580–1720* (Princeton, N.J.: Princeton University Press, 1979), 239–87.

discussed the essential social and political preconditions for this to occur in Hohenlohe: political stability, limits on the fiscal power of the state, archaic practices of domination, capital investment, protection of the peasantry, the patriarchal family, impartible inheritance customs, a stable agrarian class structure. But the final push toward market specialization came from purely economic conditions: a long period of stable prices, wages, and market relationships between 1660 and 1720.

The push toward specialized agriculture came rather late to rural areas far from Germany's cities and towns. One chief factor accounts for this: the distance from market towns and high cost of transportion to reach them. The German economist Johann Friedrich von Thünen points out the implication of this fact for the development of specialized agriculture. Round about a town, in the catchment area of its market, the countryside divides naturally into separate agricultural zones. Because transportation costs rise steadily the farther out from the town one goes, each zone produces only those agricultural commodities that will bear the costs of transportation to the town. In the first zone, the one nearest the town, market gardens and dairy production develop. Farther from the town, in the second zone, farmers produce grains for the market. And in the zone farthest from the town rural producers specialize in the production of livestock for the market.[53] The model is static and does not take into account inequalities in social and political conditions, but nonetheless helps explain the patterns of specialization one finds in German agriculture in the early modern period. Hohenlohe, like some other rural areas far from the dense concentrations of population in the Low Countries, the Rhineland, and the Upper Rhine, fell naturally into Thünen's third zone. Here cattle farming developed and dominated specialized agriculture after 1660.

The reversal of key agricultural price trends encouraged the trend toward specialized agriculture. High grain prices discouraged specialization in cattle farming before the 1660s. Before Hohenlohe farmers would shift out of grain production, these high prices had to fall. This happened at the same time that economic recovery got under way. Wilhelm Abel once calculated the general movement of grain prices in the seventeenth and eighteenth centuries and showed how the decline began in Central European cities in the 1630s and then accelerated in the 1640s. Prices continued to fall at a steady rate in the 1650s and 1660s. When prices stabilized in the 1670s, they stood at 30 percent below the prices of the 1620s and remained at these depressed levels until the middle of the eighteenth century.[54] Outside of the large cities, where demand was less and supplies more readily available, prices fell even more steeply. The

---

[53] Thünen, *Der isolierte Staat in Beziehung auf Landwirtschaft und Nationalökonomie*, 3 vols. (Rostock: G. B. Leonard, 1842–63).
[54] Abel, *Geschichte der deutschen Landwirtschaft*, 247–50.

Agrarian order restored

price of spelt in Hohenlohe fell by 50 percent between the 1620s and the 1640s (see Table 6.1). The drop continued more gradually into the 1650s and 1660s and stabilized here, as elsewhere in Germany, in the 1670s. But prices were much lower than before, roughly one-third of the grain prices of the 1620s.

Reasons for the steep decline in grain prices are not hard to find. Prices of grain followed population trends. When population fell sharply in the 1630s and 1640s – 30 percent in Hohenlohe and up to 60 percent in Southwest Germany as a whole – the demand for grain dropped off sharply. The losses in population, coming as they did among consumers and not among producers of grain, gave further impetus to the fall in prices. Producers supplied markets with an abundance of grain unthinkable before 1640. Only once, in 1649–51, did serious shortages of grain and bread threaten the livelihood of villagers. After that date no subsistence crises comparable to the ones of the late sixteenth and early seventeenth centuries are recorded. Also regions like Hohenlohe, peripheral suppliers of grain to the cities and towns of South Germany, quickly lost their share if the urban market prices fell. Transportation costs always made grain from these areas more expensive than supplies from rural areas closer to the towns. Once prices fell, towns depended more on locally produced supplies of grain. Only the largest producers of grain, with access to cheap transport to urban markets, remained suppliers of grain on a large scale in the late seventeenth century. Such conditions favored the lords of Eastelbia, who could ship surpluses by river and sea to the cities of Northwest Europe. Small producers far from urban markets, who needed cash incomes to pay off their debts, were forced to turn to the production of other agricultural commodities.

The trade in cattle and oxen, on the other hand, still held out opportunities for small rural producers. What little we know about conditions in the cattle and ox trade in the late seventeenth and early eighteenth centuries suggests that small producers entered this trade profitably, at least on a small scale. Prices for cattle and meat in German cities remained stable throughout the whole period of low grain prices.[55] Demand remained high enough so that small producers of cattle could compete with the big exporters from Poland, Hungary, and other parts of eastern Europe. From the late sixteenth century farmers from Northwest Germany and Denmark, in fact, produced cattle for the markets of Nuremberg, Frankfurt, and Augsburg.[56] Hohenlohe farmers perhaps sold some cattle on the South German markets before 1620, but the cattle trade grew rapidly in the mid-1660s. On what scale it is difficult to know. In 1666 complaints came into the chancellery of shortages of meat and cattle in Langenburg.[57] But by the 1670s the trade had so increased that officials

---

[55] Wilhelm Abel, *Agrarkrisen und Agrarkonjunktur: Eine Geschichte der Land- und Ernährungswirtschaft Mitteleuropas seit dem hohen Mittelalter*, 2d ed. (Hamburg: Paul Parey, 1966), 153.
[56] Abel, *Geschichte der deutschen Landwirtschaft*, 158.
[57] ALKI 102/16, May 3, 1666; 102/17, May 8, 1666; 102/18, May 14, 1666.

commented on its importance for the eastern districts of Hohenlohe: Langenburg, Kirchberg, Schrotzberg, and Döttingen. The trade was still limited compared with the international trade of Hohenlohers in the eighteenth century. Merchants from Schwäbisch Hall and other towns of Franconia appear to have been the primary buyers of cattle in the late seventeenth century.[58] But stewards and other officials still considered the trade important enough to organize special cattle markets and fairs with care.[59]

Higher wages encouraged small producers to shift to cattle farming as well. This trend also established itself in the 1640s and reversed the erosion of wages in the sixteenth century. In every corner of Central Europe tenant farmers, millers, master craftsmen, and others who depended upon hired labor complained about wages they considered to be extortionately high.[60] In Hohenlohe, the counts and the tenant farmers, the two largest groups of employers of seasonal workers, at first lamented the increase in wages. The farmer who worked the count's estate at Lindenbronn, not far from Langenburg, complained bitterly in 1649 that his laborers threatened to leave unless he met their demands for prompt payment in kind, in bread and grain.[61] But by the 1660s the trend to higher agricultural wages was well established, and one reads in district reports of fewer complaints over wages. The answer for many tenant farmers lay in converting arable to pasture, raising cattle and sowing less grain. This trend was convenient since so many fields lay wasted after the Thirty Years' War. Shifting to cattle farming, at least on a small scale, also meant a real reduction in labor costs. A few permanent laborers, family members, or servants could tend the cattle. On small farms a family required hardly any additional labor at all to tend a few extra cows or calves to be sold on the market. With cereal agriculture, however, a farmer still needed to hire a great deal of seasonal labor to plant and harvest crops, all of this for smaller cash incomes from the sale of grain.

Cattle farming could not develop easily in every part of Germany. Few parts of the German Southwest, in fact, were suitable for raising cattle. Comparatively little land could be given over to pastures in the hilly lands of the Swabian Alb or in the small and winding valleys of the Neckar River and its tributaries. In addition, viticulture and garden farming remained profitable economic activities, and so the incentives for small producers to find new cash crops simply did not exist. On the Hohenlohe plain, comparatively open and easy to convert to pasturage, the story was quite different. The numbers of cattle and oxen tell the story here. For the village of Atzenrod the raising of cattle and oxen for the market marked a sharp departure from the past. In the tax survey of 1581

[58] ALKI 128/1, August 4, 1674; 128/9, July 8, 1675; 128/12, April 14, 1675.
[59] ALKI 50/2, August 1, 1667; 50/4, December 20, 1670.
[60] Abel, *Agrarkrisen und Agrarkonjunktur*, 150.   [61] ALARL 1649–50/B57, January 15, 1649.

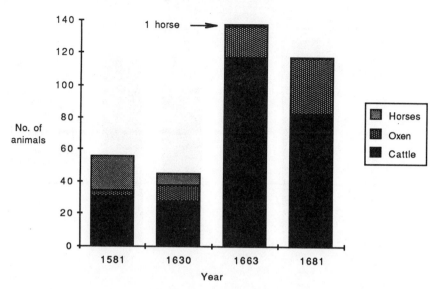

Graph 9.6. Livestock in Atzenrod, 1581–1681. *Sources:* LAN 42/16/10, 1581; L/L "Schatzungsanlage Amt Langenburg," 1630, 1663, 1681.

stewards counted about 30 cows in the village, and only a few pairs of oxen. In 1663 they found almost 120 head of cattle and 15 oxen. The number of cattle fell in the survey of 1681, but not enough to suggest that cattle farming had gone out of favor (see Graph 9.6). The pattern for Binselberg, a hamlet situated on the plain not far to the south of Atzenrod, was slightly different. Here the steady increases in numbers of cattle after the Thirty Years' War marked a rebuilding of its herds, sold off or lost in the crisis (see Graph 9.7). The same might be said of Bächlingen and, to a lesser extent, Langenburg (see Graphs 9.8 and 9.9).

Specialized commodity production did not yet penetrate every household and village and transform the entire landscape of a region as it would in the eighteenth century. In the early stages, communities and households of almost every description and means tried their hand at raising cash incomes from the new trade. The new trade, in short, fit in with subsistence agriculture, and only gradually did a division of labor develop to handle various specialized parts of the production process. In Hohenlohe, for example, villagers from almost every type of community – hamlet, compact village, small town – in every ecological niche tried their hand at cattle farming in the 1680s. Bächlingen, a village of winegrowers, raised cattle much as Atzenrod, Binselberg, and Langenburg did. The trade also engaged smallholders and tenant farmers alike, though tenant farmers clearly dominated cattle farming from the start. The survey of taxable

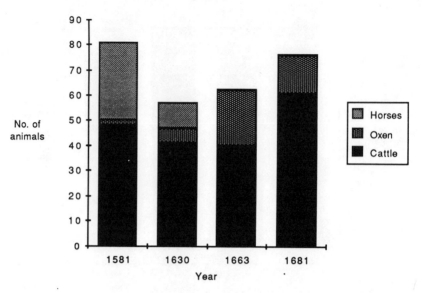

Graph 9.7. Livestock in Binselberg, 1581–1681. *Sources:* See Graph 9.6.

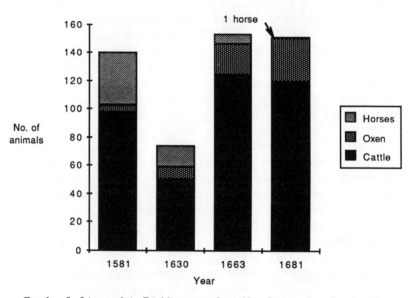

Graph 9.8. Livestock in Bächlingen, 1581–1681. *Sources:* See Graph 9.6.

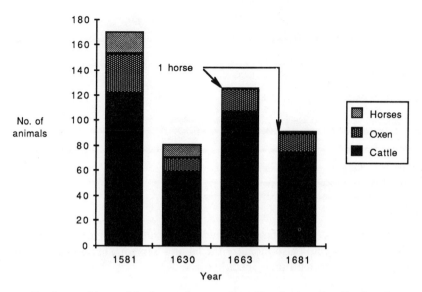

Graph 9.9. Livestock in Langenburg, 1581–1681. *Sources:* See Graph 9.6.

Table 9.1. *Livestock in Atzenrod, 1681*

Landholders	Cows	Bulls	Calves	Oxen
Cotters and smallholders[a]	10	0	4	0
Smallholders[b]	10	2	5	6
Tenant farmers	18	11	20	28
Total	38	13	29	34

Source: L/L "Schatzungsanlage Amt Langenburg 1681."

[a] Households with under 5.25 *morgen* of land.
[b] Households with between 5.25 and 18 *morgen* of land.

wealth in 1681 in two communities we have already looked at in some detail, Atzenrod and Bächlingen, shows this pattern clearly. In both of these villages the tenant farmers (those with landholdings of more than eighteen *morgen*) raised the lion's share of all livestock (see Tables 9.1 and 9.2). They held half the cows from the villages, two-thirds to three-fourths of the bulls and calves, and virtually all of the oxen. Their dominance of cattle farming should come

Table 9.2. *Livestock in Bächlingen,1681*

Landholders	Cows	Bulls	Calves	Oxen
Cotters and				
smallholders[a]	1 0	1	3	0
Smallholders[b]	1 6	1	9	0
Tenant farmers	2 6	2 1	2 9	3 0
Total	5 2	2 3	4 1	3 0

Source: L/L "Schatzungsanlage Amt Langenburg 1681."
[a] Households with under 5.25 *morgen* of land.
[b] Households with between 5.25 and 18 *morgen* of land.

as no real surprise. These farmers could afford to convert part of their lands to pasture. They could also mobilize the labor – servants, occasional seasonal labor, children – to tend their small herds.

Eighteenth-century epilogue

Where peasant capitalism of this kind flourished in the German West it depended upon a social hierarchy well established by the seventeenth century. The relationships of petty German princes to tenant farmers, smallholders, rural craftsmen, and laborers altered in subtle and important ways in the eighteenth century. But the basic patterns were long since set, and they made it possible for peasant entrepreneurs to dominate village property, to accumulate wealth and invest it in the rural economy, and to develop a flourishing trade in specialized commodities. These peasant capitalists were therefore well placed to prosper from the commercial boom of the eighteenth century. That boom grew out of a new wave of population growth after 1720, rising demand for agricultural products in the cities, an expansion in trade, improvements in transportation, specialized commodity production, and innovations in agriculture.[62] In Hohenlohe these improvements all favored the tenant farmers. New crops raised agricultural productivity; new techniques in stall feeding made specialization in cattle raising possible, and more profitable. Some farmers raised only certain breeds of prized cattle; others became petty traders, bypassing the hated middlemen and organizing their own trading companies. Great herds of Hohenlohe cattle (*boeuf d'Hohenlohe*) began to make their way on roads and highways to Heilbronn, Frankfurt, Strasbourg, and Basel and even as far as Paris. Travelers

---

[62] For an overview of this commercial expansion see Kriedte, *Peasants, Landlords and Merchant Capitalists.* For Germany see Hermann Kellenbenz, *Deutsche Wirtschaftsgeschichte*, vol. 1: *Von den Anfängen bis zum Ende des 18. Jahrhunderts* (Munich: C. H. Beck, 1977), 296–390.

marveled at Hohenlohe's enormous farmsteads, the ornately decorated houses and barns, the rustic peasant art of the region, and the wealth of the peasant households.[63]

But, though wealth flowed into the countryside, it was never destined to be distrubted equally and fairly. One of the consequences – indeed one of the primary functions of hierarchy in this archaic society – was the uneven distribution of material wealth and goods among households and groups. That little changed in this regard is best seen when one looks at the plight of smallholders, craftsmen, and the laboring poor by the middle of the century. A new wave of specialization certainly spread among the small towns and villages heavily populated by these rural groups. Some towns, in fact, developed a flourishing small-craft industry. Ingelfingen, Öhringen, and Weikersheim all became, more than ever before, centers of leather working and other trades.

But only where the social hierarchy was broken up, only where the tenant farmers lost their dominance of local landholding, could rural industry transform the face of a land. That process went ahead in some lands, in Swabia, Westphalia, parts of the Rhineland, the Erzgebirge, and Silesia. But that never happened in Hohenlohe or in other parts of the German Northwest, Bavaria, and Switzerland. The continued dominance of the village by tenant farmers, secure systems of heritable land tenure, the restricted roles of merchants in some of these territories, and the firm support of the state made these lands unlikely places for this to happen. Already by the 1770s in Hohenlohe one can talk about a new wave of rural poverty as many smallholders and cotters failed to profit from the commercial expansion of the eighteenth century. An old cycle began to repeat itself: Population continued to grow, wages eroded, the price of bread soared, and land became scarce. The compact villages and small towns of the region, those in the river valleys in particular, became densely crowded with the poor. Some left Hohenlohe for good in these years and moved to other towns and cities of South Germany. Later, in the terrible 1840s, others would follow. But many of these would leave Germany altogether and emigrate to the Americas.

Some of the prosperity, some of the ability to invest wealth in the agricultural economy and to profit from the commercial expansion, can be traced to the comparative weakness of Germany's small states. By the eighteenth century the structures of domination in these states appear even more archaic and outdated than in the middle of the seventeenth century. For by this time comparisons with the modern bureaucratic states of Württemberg, Bavaria, Austria, and Prussia are inescapable. But the obstacles that kept small states from becoming powerful centralized states were still too great to be easily overcome. The principality of Hohenlohe, if not entirely typical of the small German state in

---

[63] See Steinle, *Die Vermögensverhältnisse der Landbevölkerung in Hohenlohe.*

the eighteenth century, at least illustrates the limits set to state building in some corners of Germany until the end of the Old Regime. The structure of the empire, the continual political checks on small princes' power, a crippling burden of debts inherited from the past, the weakness of archaic structures of domination, the weight of customary law, and continued resistance of villagers to an expanded state: All frustrated the by now modest ambitions of the counts of Hohenlohe.[64] All of the checks that kept the petty princes from expanding the state by the seventeenth century remained firmly in place.

It was only fitting that the last major events in this principality's history, events played out in the shadow of the French Revolution, should have a ring of the familiar and archaic about them. In the early 1790s, as the small German states geared up for war with France, the princes tried to shoulder their share of the burden by raising a war levy. That villagers would resist the burden went without saying, but the resistance dragged on for ten years and could only be settled by a ruling of the imperial court. What arguments did villagers employ in their defense? As in the past, they invoked that ancient, and by now practically sacred, Treaty of 1609. They protested vehemently, in language reminiscent of 1630 and 1632, that the princes had no right to impose these extraordinary burdens! The treaty protected them from any such taxation! The counts prevailed, however, though the support of the magistrates on the court came too late.[65] For the end of this small land's autonomy was at hand, just as it was for all of the other small German states. Soon after, in 1806, Napoleon abolished the Holy Roman Empire, and the kings of Württemberg and Bavaria, eager to expand their states, split the small princes' lands between them. Only then did the peasants of Hohenlohe finally learn what it was to contend with the power of a centralized modern state.

---

[64] For a study of eighteenth-century Hohenlohe see Wolfram Fischer, *Das Fürstentum Hohenlohe im Zeitalter der Aufklärung* (Tübingen: J. C. B. Mohr, 1958).
[65] Ibid. 231–40.

~~~~~~

Village society and the practice of state power

In 1773 a newly published manual for rural householders drew public attention in Germany to the small land of Hohenlohe. The author of this manual, Johann Friedrich Mayer, a pastor from Kupferzell, was fast becoming known for his zealous efforts to reform agriculture and village society in his native land and in Germany. His voluminous correspondence and his treatises show a reformer who fought for numerous causes: improvements in fertilizer, the introduction of a more rational labor calendar, religious and moral instruction of young people, free trade, the planting of potatoes, the reform of the laws that governed inheritance and landholding, and the abolition of labor services. By the time he died he had accumulated five prizes for his works on agrarian reform, including coveted awards from the Elector Palatine of the Rhine, the Margrave of Ansbach, and Empress Maria Theresa.[1] But it was his *Lehrbuch für die Land- und Hauswirte* that earned him his fame as a quintessential agrarian reformer of the late eighteenth century.

What is striking about this work, what draws my attention to it as I conclude this study, is not the content of Mayer's ideas. It is instead the social drama that unfolded as Mayer tried to put his reforms into practice. For that drama, hidden from the view of those who simply read the manual, pointed up patterns of relationships typical in a small German patrimonial state of the early modern period. Try as he did, Mayer failed to convince his neighbors and other villagers from Hohenlohe to reform local custom. They refused his advice to plant new crops and alter the cycle of crop rotation. Sometimes they simply ignored his advice; at other times they openly resisted his schemes. On one occasion, a group of villagers bundled up copies of a calendar he had published, stormed into his house, and angrily threw them on the floor.[2] When he turned to the princes of Hohenlohe for help in this unhappy struggle, he met with disap-

---

[1] See Karl Schumm, "Pfarrer Johann Friedrich Mayer und die hohenlohische Landwirtschaft im 18. Jahrhundert," *Württembergisch Franken* N.S. 30 (1955), 138–67. See also Wolfram Fischer, *Das Fürstentum Hohenlohe, im Zeitalter der Aufklärung* (Tübingen: J.C.B. Mohr, 1958), 134–51.

[2] Fischer, *Das Fürstentum Hohenlohe*, 146.

pointment. A few embraced his ideas, but the power of the small patrimonial state was simply inadequate to push through all of the reforms Mayer called for.[3] He may have been, as some scholars have pointed out, a small example of the extension of the Enlightenment into the German countryside. But to stress this aspect of his reforms is to miss the more important point that the reform of village society and the exercise of state power rested on the complex relationships of power in village society in the early modern period. Village society itself left its imprint on the practice of state power almost as much as the state shaped the village.

In this study we have explored this theme in all of its complexity. The practice of state power did indeed come to underpin the social order in the early modern village, but the relationships upon which this power rested were never one-sided. Often one examines the development of the state and the practice of power from above and assumes that rulers, state officials, and ruling elites alone wielded the new powers of the early modern state to reshape village society, to make it conform to the needs of the state. The village is viewed as exploited, popular culture repressed, the villager cast in the role of the victim.[4] There is some truth to this view, of course, but we have stressed here the limits to state power, the ways in which villagers continued to share in the process of their own domination, the way in which village society shaped the structure of the early modern state. Power never flowed simply from the top down; and it did not rest solely on violence or coercion. Power remained more widely distributed within the village than is commonly understood. State power did not simply expand in the sixteenth and seventeenth centuries; it was very often drawn into the village by villagers themselves. State power was also checked, frustrated, often turned to purposes no ruler completely controlled. Unless this point is grasped the search for order in the sixteenth and seventeenth centuries cannot be seen in all of its complexity.

The first part of this study examined the agrarian expansion of the sixteenth century and its consequences for village society and the exercise of power at the local level. Steady population growth, the increasing shortage of land, the Peasants' War, and an increasingly stratified and complex village social structure clearly undermined late medieval patterns of domination and authority. Right from the beginning we discovered how important it is to understand not the theoretical rights of lords and villages but the *actual practice of domination* in the countryside. For theory and practice very often diverged. Once one examines the relationship of lords and peasants from this point of view, once one examines the actual practice of exercising power in the village, two important features of

---

[3] Ibid. 145–50 passim.
[4] For a statement of this view see Robert Muchembled, *Culture populaire et culture des élites dans la France moderne, XVe–XVIIIe siècles: essai* (Paris: Flammarion, 1978).

patrimonial domination around 1500 come sharply into focus. The rights of lordship or dominion, for one, did not translate into coercive rule in the countryside. The actual power of the lord or prince remained limited, and was sometimes tenuous at the village level. The reasons for this lay partly in the absence of centralized state control, the weakness of coercive power, the sometimes tenuous hold a thinly manned administrative hierarchy had on the countryside. But one also must grasp the significance of a second feature of the practice of power at the local level: the large extent to which villagers shared in the process of their own domination.

The Peasants' War hardly altered these fundamental relationships of power and authority in the countryside. The revolt itself therefore marked no decisive turning point in the development of the territorial state in early modern Germany. The progress in recent years in understanding the origins of the rebellion and the political programs that came out of the peasant armies has obscured our understanding of another, more important process at work: the wrenching long-term adjustments in the practice of domination over the course of the "long sixteenth century." The tendency has been to see the revolt as marking the triumph of the state and the nobility over villagers, a key event leading to "refeudalization" of the countryside or to the making of the early modern German state. From the vantage point developed here, this dramatic political event, this stunning but brief seizure of power by peasant armies, seems to have had less significance in shaping lord–peasant relationships than did the gradual social changes taking place within village society itself. One should certainly not view the rebellion as a hopeless peasant fury. The revolt was no typical early modern tax revolt. Yet the rebellion seems less important in preparing the way for an extension of state authority in the village than the steady growth in population and the gradual erosion of the social foundations of the village commune.

The strong traditions of communalism provided the organizational basis of the peasant armies in 1525. By 1600, however, communalism could no longer rally villagers' loyalties in the way it had in the early sixteenth century. The tendency is often attributed to Germany's rulers and state officials, the makers of Germany's territorial states. But the erosion of communalism was a complex social and economic process.

After the Peasants' War the development of other social ties tended to break up the solidarity of the village, to complicate social action. One cannot easily sum up all of the social, economic, political, and religious changes that contributed to this tendency; the variations from region to region, from village to village, were enormous. But one development played a particularly important role in this process: the process of social stratification within the village. By 1600 a wealthy class of tenant farmers tended to dominate landholding in many villages. The control of landed wealth therefore remained the primary deter minant of village social status in this period. But access to movable wealth, occupation, and place in the market economy became increasingly important as well. The market relationships studied here did not necessarily lead to a class society in the village, even though at times class relationships clearly drew together tenant farmers, the village poor, or specific occupational groups. This tendency toward class relationships never fully replaced communal loyalties. What complicated social action in the specific events analyzed here – the Reformation, the events surrounding the Treaty of 1609, the near-revolt of 1630–2 – were sets of social ties that cut vertically through the village commune and horizontally through the countryside. These included not only class relationships but also household and family ties and the complex bonds of paternalism and deference that bound villagers to their lords and rulers.

Partly because of the stratification within the village, rulers and lords could penetrate village society and redirect loyalties more effectively toward the emerging early modern state. The second part of this work looked in detail at the practice of state domination as it came to underpin social relationships on three different levels: within the family and household, in the marketplace, and directly with the state. In none of these areas was the early modern state able to dominate and control village life one-sidedly; in all of these areas villagers continued to share in the process of their own domination.

Small German princes, state officials, and Lutheran pastors certainly seized the initiative in these areas in order to impose a new sense of order, hierarchy, and discipline in the village. A number of scholars have recently stressed the role of these elites in the reform of popular culture and the family in the sixteenth and seventeenth centuries. But one can easily overestimate the part these elites played in shaping the cultural and social values – order, discipline, restraint, obedience, hierarchy – of this period so widely evident in rural Germany.[5] For villagers also sought to create order out of a world that seemed to them in flux, threatening, dangerously unstable and uncertain. Different groups of villagers therefore cooperated in the campaign to impose marital discipline in the village, and their support was essential in reforming the patriarchal family and the household, the cornerstones of social and political order by 1600. The appeal of marital discipline and stronger patriarchal authority cut through all ranks in the village: It worked to the advantage of any propertyholder seeking more effective control over family land and wealth. But the appeal seems to have been particularly strong for the village elite. Because of the work of the marriage courts, family elders acquired more power to arrange marriage alliances within the family; they terminated the undesirable courtships of their

---

[5] For Germany see especially Marc Raeff, *The Well-Ordered Police State: Social and Institutional Change through Law in the Germanies and Russia, 1600–1800* (New Haven, Conn.: Yale University Press, 1983).

children with greater ease and thereby tightened the controls on youths and family property.

Patriarchy, Protestantism, and the control of property and youths became inseparable from one another in a small land like Hohenlohe. The rituals of courtship and marriage therefore reflected the new importance of marital discipline and all the social strain it created in village society.

Clearly the new sense of social order, noticeable almost everywhere in the countryside of South Germany by the first decade of the seventeenth century, was achieved in part by princes and state officials improving the practice of state domination within the village. A bundle of tools of domination – new surveys of property and wealth; attempts to regulate inheritance practices, family disputes, the markets and market behavior; a heavy burden of taxes; and an extension of state power at the local level – gave the petty prince formidable power. But this shift, this expansion of state power, should not be viewed simply from the capital or the vantage point of the ruling elites of the early modern state; it should not be seen simply as the state forcing the village to conform to the fiscal needs of the early modern state.[6] One must place this change in the context of the process by which villagers continued to bargain, haggle, and negotiate over the precise terms on which they accepted state domination. For Germany's rulers and officials did not simply extract resources from the village; they remained bound up in and limited by villagers' demands for reciprocity and the expectations that the state would redistribute wealth within the society. In the land of Hohenlohe these demands grew as rural poverty and peasant indebtedness grew, as the market economy expanded and a brutal cycle of famine set in after 1560. The search for political and social order, for hierarchy and discipline, was partly a response to the instability created by the unequal distribution of wealth and the chronic economic instability of the late sixteenth century.

The power of the small patrimonial states of the Holy Roman Empire therefore remained limited, their rulers caught up in reciprocal relationships with their villagers that they were reluctant to break. The apparatus of the state certainly expanded their reach into new aspects of village life; state power underpinned the patriarchal family, supported the rural poor, and propped up wealthy tenant farmers. But the precise terms of domination on which villagers accepted this authority did not necessarily favor the state. This point becomes

[6] For approaches to state building that focus primarily on the elites see Gerhard Benecke, *Society and Politics in Germany 1500–1750* (London: Routledge & Kegan Paul, 1974); Volker Press, *Calvinismus und Territorialstaat: Regierung und Zentralbehörden der Kurpfalz 1559–1619*, Kieler Historische Studien, vol. 7 (Stuttgart: E. Klett, 1970); Heinz Schilling, *Konfessionskonflikt und Staatsbildung: Eine Fallstudie über das Verhältnis von religiösem und sozialem Wandel in der Frühneuzeit am Beispiel der Grafschaft Lippe*, Quellen und Forschungen zur Reformationsgeschichte, vol. 48 (Gütersloh: Gerd Mohn, 1981); and James Allen Vann, *The Making of a State: Württemberg 1598–1793* (Ithaca, N.Y.: Cornell University Press, 1984).

clear in examining the consequences of villagers' resistance to the heavy burden of taxes and labor services imposed in the late sixteenth and early seventeenth centuries. As the state began to extract a heavier burden of taxes and demand more labor services, rural disorders spread throughout South Germany and the empire and, at times, spilled over into revolts. The history of these disorders in the old County of Hohenlohe between 1577 and 1609 therefore confirms the view of Winfried Schulze that the order and the stability that came in the wake of taming rural unrest did not always strengthen the state. But in order to grasp the full extent of the complex relationships that limited state power one must also begin to grasp the importance of the vast web of social ties, continuously woven and rewoven, that bound a small prince with almost every peasant household in his domains. For these ties set limits on the actual fiscal burdens placed on the village.

These patterns of relationships proved so durable, so lasting, that they provided the basis for the political and social order in the small patrimonial state after the Thirty Years' War. The focus on the political and religious origins of the war, the military campaigns, and the diplomacy of the period has made it difficult to see the period between 1620 and 1660 as a wrenching crisis that called into question the social order built up before the war. A number of scholars have called attention to the consequences of the wage–price scissors in the countryside, the decline in population, and the series of peasant rebellions in this period, but it is only when one looks at the breakdown of social order and state power in the 1620s and 1630s that the dimensions of the social and political crisis become clear. As the crisis spread, questions were raised about political authority and the legitimacy of state power. It is helpful to see these decades as a "crisis of authority," as Theodore K. Rabb calls it.[7] But state power was so inseparable from the whole social order, it was so thoroughly identified with a whole bundle of specific social relationships, values, and social groups within the village, that questions were also raised about the legitimacy and the justice of the entire social order as well. When Hohenlohers questioned the right of their rulers to levy war taxes in 1630–2, it was only a part of a deeper social crisis for rich and poor alike in the villages of this small land.

Yet dramatic changes did not necessarily follow in the wake of the crisis. A number of scholars have noted the calm, the stability, that began to settle over most parts of Europe in the decades after 1660. Surely the early modern state provided a more stable setting for the reconstruction of the territorial state in Germany in the late seventeenth century. But the roots of this stability went deeper than this; they reached into the more settled social order that now underpinned, in complex ways, the practice of state power in the village. The patriarchal family, a fixed and secure property order, developing market rela-

---

[7] See *The Struggle for Stability in Early Modern Europe* (New York: Oxford University Press, 1975).

tionships, a more settled village social hierarchy: These were the stable social foundations of state power by the late seventeenth century. The fluid and shifting social patterns of the late sixteenth century hardened into a more rigid agrarian class structure in the decades after 1640. To an outside observer the rural society of Hohenlohe may have seemed archaic by 1720, its small state frail compared with a large territorial state. But the small patrimonial state also provided the basis for a sustained agrarian boom and unprecedented rural prosperity by the 1780s. If the extension of state power became such a troubling process in many parts of nineteenth-century Germany, it was not because small townsmen and villagers were unfamiliar with the practice of state power in underpinning the social order. It was because that power became more centralized, its practitioners less bound up in the subtle give-and-take of power within the village so typical of an earlier era.

Appendix A

Distribution of wealth in Langenburg district, 1528–1581

Table A.1. *Distribution of wealth in Langenburg district, 1528*

$CumP_1$	Wealth (fl.)	Cum. wealth (fl.)	% (W_1)	$CumW_1$	P_1CumW_1
10	198	198	1.4	1.4	.0014
20	408	606	2.9	4.3	.0043
30	642	1,248	4.5	8.8	.0088
40	948	2,096	6.0	14.8	.0148
50	1,202	3,298	8.4	23.2	.0232
60	1,400	4,698	9.8	33.0	.0330
70	1,558	6,256	10.9	43.9	.0439
80	1,792	8,048	18.6	56.5	.0565
90	2,426	10,474	17.0	73.5	.0735
100	3,780	14,254	26.5	100.0	.1000
Total					.3594

Source: L/L "Reichsteuer- und Schatzungsbuch Amt Langenburg 1525-68."

Note: Hence $G = 1 - 2(.3594) + .1 = .3812$.

Distribution of wealth in Langenburg district

Table A.2. *Distribution of wealth in Langenburg district, 1553*

CumP$_1$	Wealth (fl.)	Cum. wealth (fl.)	% (W$_1$)	CumW$_1$	P$_1$CumW$_1$
10	374	374	0.9	0.9	.0009
20	789	1,163	1.9	2.7	.0027
30	1,301	2,464	3.0	5.8	.0058
40	2,176	4,640	5.1	10.9	.0109
50	2,478	7,118	5.8	16.7	.0167
60	3,562	10,680	8.3	25.0	.0250
70	4,856	15,536	11.4	36.4	.0364
80	6,328	21,864	14.8	51.2	.0512
90	7,768	29,632	18.2	69.4	.0694
100	13,086	42,718	30.6	100.0	.1000
Total					.3190

Source: L/L "Reichsteuer- und Schatzungsbuch Amt Langenburg 1525-1568."

Note: Hence G = 1 - 2(.3190) + .1 = .4620.

Table A.3. *Distribution of wealth in Langenburg district, 1581*

CumP$_1$	Wealth (fl.)	Cum. wealth (fl.)	% (W$_1$)	CumW$_1$	P$_1$CumW$_1$
10	495	495	0.5	0.5	.0005
20	903	1,398	0.9	1.5	.0015
30	1,388	2,786	1.5	2.9	.0029
40	2,235	5,021	2.4	5.3	.0053
50	3,811	8,832	4.1	9.3	.0093
60	6,256	15,088	6.6	15.9	.0159
70	8,885	23,973	9.3	25.2	.0252
80	12,043	36,016	12.7	37.9	.0379
90	18,429	54,445	19.4	57.3	.0573
100	40,657	95,102	42.8	100.0	.1000
Total					.2558

Source: LAN 42/16/10, 1581.

Note: Hence G = 1 - 2(.2558) + .1 = .5884.

Appendix B

~~~~~~

Grain production and the peasant household

In order to understand the agrarian cycle and the great advance and fall of population that lay behind it, one must have a firm understanding of the productivity of the peasant household. Only with precise statistical data can one answer the pivotal questions that present themselves for any study of the sixteenth and seventeenth centuries. How much surplus grain could the rural economy actually produce? When did marginal returns on the land begin to set in, and in which parts of the countryside? Which households produced enough grain to feed its dependents, and which could not? As I point out in Chapters 6, 7, and 8, answers to these questions help us not simply to understand agricultural productivity, they guide us to other key issues in the making of the social hierarchy in the village as well. For one of the key functions of hierarchy in this society was control over the distribution of land, scarce material goods, and food. How villagers understood the polarization that took place in village society between wealthy and poor, the role food supplies and land scarcity played in conflict, the ability of villagers to pay taxes, and even popular attitudes toward state authority were all conditioned, to some degree, by access to land and agricultural productivity. Every study of these problems should therefore have a precise understanding of who controlled and produced such resources, and how far these resources met the material needs of the peasant household.

Accurate information about agricultural productivity, however, is not everywhere easily obtained. And, even where satisfactory records allow one to make statistical calculations, they do not always reveal the information one needs. One measure, discussed in Chapter 1, is the seed–yield ratio. But those figures only reveal overall productivity. For part of the arguments in Chapters 6, 7, and 8 what were needed were precise measurements of the variations in productivity from household to household. Fortunately some statistical measurements of precisely this problem could be undertaken based on a careful survey of household productivity made in September 1622. State officials obviously undertook this survey at harvest time, as villagers brought in their crops, and so it offers an empirical basis for understanding crop yields for that year. How

266

Grain production and the peasant household

Table B.1. *Peasant households and surplus grain production in Langenburg district, 1622*

Size of landholding (*morgen*)	No. producing surpluses	No. not producing surpluses
0-2.9	0	All
3.0-3.9	1	1
4.0-4.9	2	8
5.0-5.9	6	10
6.0-6.9	2	1
7.0-7.9	0	3
8.0-8.9	5	1
9.0-9.9	1	1
10.0-10.9	2	1
11.0-11.9	1	0
12.0-12.9	0	1
13.0-13.9	2	0
14.0-14.9	0	0
15.0-15.9	2	0

Source: ALKL II/6/13, September 26-27, 1622.

representative was the survey of productivity? Was this year a reliable guide in an agricultural economy in which variation was the norm? Obviously the study could not reveal the range of fluctuations in yields over time, and this limit must be kept in mind. But this much is certain about the sample: The overall seed–yield ratio of 1:3 to 1:5 matched the averages for Germany as a whole calculated by Slicher van Bath (Table 1.1). This survey is therefore the basis for more detailed measurements of the ability of households to produce surpluses of grain (Graphs 6.1 and 9.2–5).

The advantages of analyzing this sample lie in the precision of the surveyors' statistics, the care with which the surveyors noted actual consumption and production in the peasant household. After consulting the heads of each of the households in the villages, the surveyors divided the entire population into two groups: those who could produce no surpluses of grain and those who were known to have the potential to produce surpluses after meeting the immediate needs of the household. From the start, then, the surveyors excluded the majority of the households from the survey. As the surveyors of Bächlingen noted, "the other subjects, mostly poor leather workers and day laborers, have little in the fields and in the village and therefore have neither grain, fat, nor money in the house." The second part of the survey, while never fully completed, did bring in detailed information on fifty-one households from five villages (Brüchlingen, Raboldshausen, Billingsbach, Kupferhof, and Atzenrod). And for each of these households the surveyors recorded the amount of land in grain production (excluding fallow), the net yield at harvest, the yield of

267

threshed grain, seed requirements for the next year, and the household consumption of grain. The results showed, as one would expect, a wide variation in seed–yield ratios, from 1:2.7 to 1:8.5, and a complex picture of what a household needed to produce surpluses.

The results of an analysis of this survey suggest two overlapping, and sometimes confusing, views of peasant households and grain production. On the one hand, some of the data confirm that hard, crass distinction villagers drew between those who produced surpluses of grain and those who did not. Most peasant households in this region needed at least 18 *morgen* of land (12 assuming one-third of the land lay in fallow each year) in order to feed their families, store seed grain for next year's planting, and have a small surplus (see Table B.1). And this obviously only the tenant farmers, and a very few smallholders, could accomplish in 1622. But that simple subsistence calculus, on the other hand, obscures the importance of a third group: those households that tottered back and forth between the two groups. Some households with as little as 3 *morgen* could meet the subsistence needs of the family and its dependents and have a small surplus to sell on the market. Hans Kutroff disposed a mere 3.5 *morgen* in Billingsbach, but he and his wife had no dependents and produced a surplus of grain in 1622. But this was an extraordinary feat; his seed–yield ratio was 1:8.6. Others, like Bartel Pflüger of Raboldshausen, held as much as 13 *morgen* and failed to produce any surplus at all. Whether a household could meet its needs and produce a surplus therefore rested on a number of factors: the size of the landholding, seed–yield ratios, and the number of mouths to feed.

Manuscript sources

The following manuscript series are all to be found in the Hohenlohe-Zentralarchiv (Neuenstein) (HZAN):

Akten zum Bauernkrieg in Hohenlohe-Franken

5; 8–10; 12; 14–15; 28–9; 36; 38; 43; 47–58; 60–3; 66; 79–80; 82–7

Archiv Kirchberg (AK)

Kanzlei (AKK)

0/19/A/18; 0/19/A/28; 0/26/A/1; 0/26/A/2; 0/26/A/3; 0/26/A/4; 0/26/A/5

Archiv Langenburg (AL)

Almosenrechnungen Amt Langenburg (ALAlmAL)

Vol. 1 (1611–30); vol. 2 (1631–54); vol. 3 (1679–88)

Ältere Kammer Langenburg (vor 1700) (ALKL)

II/1/18; II/2/2/21; II/3/37/1–11 (1586–1602); II/10/3/1–17; II/6/3; II/6/5; II/6/6; II/6/13; II/7/2; II/10/4; II/11/6; II/11/7; II/11/16; II/11/17; II/11/66

Amt Langenburg (ALAL)

146; 152; 163; 169; 180; 187; 189; 205; 212–13; 217–18; 230; 236; 246; 248; 251–4; 257; 259; 267; 276; 317; 320; 325; 328–30; 332–3; 338; 340–1; 345–7; 357–60; 362; 365; 367–70; 372; 374; 377; 379–84; 386; 388; 390–1; 393; 395; 397–9; 401; 403–7; 409–12; 415–20; 422–4; 426–38; 441; 443–6; 448–50; 452–6; 459–60; 462–7; 469–84; 490; 494–500; 503–6; 508; 511–13; 517; 522–3; 531–2; 534–7; 541–4; 547; 552–8; 560–3; 565–7; 571; 574; 578; 581–7; 590; 592–4; 599; 601; 605; 611–12; 618; 621–6; 634; 637–8; 640; 643–50; 652–4; 655–6; 663; 667; 673–4; 676–83; 686; 691; 701;

Manuscript sources

711–12; 718; 720; 721–3; 725; 728; 737–40; 747–8; 751; 772–3; 782–3; 814; 817–18; 820–4; 863; 918; 920–5; 927–8; 931; 933–5; 943; 946; 948–50; 958–60; 965; 992–3; 999–1000; 1003–5; 1007; 1013; 1017–18; 1033; 1049; 1050; 1052–3; 1058; 1060; 1064; 1073; 1076; 1078–80; 1083; 1086–90; 1092; 1094; 1099; 1100; 1108–10; 1112; 1121; 1123; 1128; 1132; 1135; 1138–40; 1189; 1195

Amtsrechnungen Amt Langenburg (ALARL)

1504; 1514 to 1522; 1526; 1552–3 to 1555–6; 1557–8; 1572–3; 1577–8; 1583–4; 1590–1 to 1592–3; 1594–5; 1597–8; 1599–1600 to 1602–3; 1604–5 to 1607–8; 1608; 1610–11 to 1616–17; 1618–19; 1620–1 to 1641–2; 1643–4 to 1662–3; 1664–5 to 1669–70; 1670; 1670–1 to 1675–6; 1677–8 to 1683–4

Contributionsrechnungen Amt Langenburg (ALCRAL)

1638–9; 1 (1639–40); 2 (1640–1); 3 (1641–2); 4 (1642); 5 (1642); 6 (1643); 7 (1643); 8 (1643–4); 9 (1644); 10 (1645); 11 (1645); 12 (1645–6); 1648–9

Döttingen Spital Rechtnungen (ALDSR)

1621; 1622; 1626; 1636; 1639–40; 1649–50; 1661–2; 1662–3

Gemeinschaftliches Archiv Langenburg (ALGAL)

U/12; U/13; U/14; U/15; U/16; 1; 3; 7; 175; 178–9; 181; 184–5; 188–92; 201; 204–6; 209–10; 376; 386; 398; 406; 416; 418; 421; 426–8; 435; 446; 450; 453; 460; 470; 473; 485; 492; 503; 505; 518; 520; 522; 524–7; 529–30; 537–9; 542: 546; 548–9; 551; 553–5; 557; 570; 578; 584; 588; 616–712; 733–5; 738; 740–1; 743; 746–7; 749; 751–2; 756; 764; 876–8; 880

Kanzlei I (ALKI)

1; 2; 4–6; 10; 16; 18; 21–5; 28; 31–4; 37–40; 44–5; 48–50; 56; 98; 100–3; 105–8; 110; 115; 117; 123–5; 128; 130–1; 133; 164–5; 171–4; 210–71; 275; 277; 279; 281; 283–4; 286–7; 289; 291; 293; 295–6; 299–300; 303–5; 351–2; 356; 358; 360; 365; 370; 372; 378–9

Supplikenprotokolle Amt Langenburg, 1592–1602 (ALSPL)

Bibliothek C24

Dorfordnungen Amt Langenburg

Atzenrod (1604); Bächlingen (1654); Oberregenbach (1687); Nesselbach (1687); Allgemeines (1577); Unterregenbach (1627?); Raboldshausen (1683); Billingsbach (1688)

Manuscript sources

Gemeinschaftliches Hausarchiv (GHA)

Vol. 50 Lagerbuch 1490; 15/4; 15/8

Kirchenbuch I: Langenburg, 1587–1696

Lager-, Gült- and Schatzungsbücher (L/L)

"Gültbuch Amt Langenburg," 1470; "Reichssteuer-und Schatzungsbuch Amt Langen-burg 1525–1568"; 1528; 4, 1562; 5, 1553; 7, 1573; 17, 1581; 20, 1585–7; 24, 1595; 27, 1606; 28, 1606; 34, 1663; 37, 1681; 45, 1630; 63a, 1653; "Schatzungsanlage Amt Langenburg," 1630, 1653, 1663, 1681

Linienarchiv Neuenstein (LAN)

13/1 Lagerbuch 1357; 42/2; 42/5; 42/7; 42/10; 42/12; 42/13; 42/14; 42/16/1, 1554; 42/16/3, 1557; 42/16/4, 1562; 42/16/5, 1566; 42/16/6, 1567; 42/16/7, 1577; 42/16/8, 1578; 42/16/9, 1580; 42/16/10, 1581; 42/16/11, 1582; 42/16/12, 1583

Partikulararchiv Öhringen (PAÖ)

93/3/7, 1556; 93/3/8; 93/4/8, 1608; 93/4/11; 93/5/10; 167/1/1

Bibliographical essay

This study draws on a wide range of works on early modern Europe and Germany, the old County of Hohenlohe, comparative peasant studies, and social anthropology. The notes that follow serve as a guide to the most important works that have shaped the views developed in this book.

Introduction and chapter 1

General surveys of Germany in the sixteenth and seventeenth centuries abound, although most concentrate on the political and religious developments of the period. Some recent surveys include Bernd Moeller, *Deutschland im Zeitalter der Reformation*, Deutsche Geschichte, vol. 4. 2d ed. (Göttingen: Vandenhoeck & Ruprecht, 1981); Martin Heckel, *Deutschland im konfessionellen Zeitalter*, Deutsche Geschichte, vol. 5 (Göttingen: Vandenhoeck & Ruprecht, 1983); Heinrich Lutz, *Reformation und Gegenreformation* (Munich: Oldenbourg, 1982); and Winfried Schulze, *Deutsche Geschichte im 16. Jahrhundert, 1500– 1618* (Frankfurt: Suhrkamp, 1987). For Marxist surveys of this same period see Max Steinmetz, *Deutschland von 1476 bis 1648: Von der frühbürgerlichen Revolution bis zum Westfälischen Frieden* (Berlin: Deutscher Verlag der Wissenschaften, 1965); and Adolf Laube, Max Steinmetz, and Günter Vogler, *Illustrierte Geschichte der deutschen frühbürgerlichen Revolution* (Berlin: Verlag Das Europäische Buch, 1982). One can still profitably read Leopold von Ranke, *Deutsche Geschichte im Zeitalter der Reformation*, 6 vols., ed. P. Joachimsen (Munich: Drei Masken Verlag, 1925–6); and Karl Brandi, *Reformation und Gegenreformation*, 5th ed. (Frankfurt a. M.: Societäts-Verlag, 1979). No recent surveys of this period of German history exist in English; Hajo Holborn's *A History of Modern Germany: The Reformation* (Princeton, N.J.: Princeton University Press, 1959), the only such survey, has become dated. Gerhard Benecke's *Society and Politics in Germany 1500– 1750* (London: Routledge & Kegan Paul, 1974) and F. L. Carsten's *Princes and Parliaments in Germany from the Fifteenth to the Eighteenth Century* (Oxford: Clarendon Press, 1959) provide two views on the making of Germany's territorial states. An extremely helpful and concise introduction to the recent literature on the German Reformation is R. W. Scribner. *The German Reformation* (Atlantic Highlands, N. J.: Humanities Press, 1986).

The pioneering work of Wilhelm Abel on the agrarian cycle, *Agrarkrisen und Agrarkonjunktur: Eine Geschichte der Land- und Ernährungswirtschaft Mitteleuropas seit dem hohen Mittelalter,* 2d ed. (Hamburg: Paul Parey, 1966), remains the best introduction to rural society, population, and economy in Central Europe in the early modern period. It is available in English as *Agricultural Fluctuations in Europe: From the Thirteenth to the Twentieth Centuries,* trans. Olive Ordish (New York: St. Martin's Press, 1980). Also important is his overview of German agricultural history, *Geschichte der deutschen Landwirtschaft vom frühen Mittelalter bis zum 19. Jahrhundert,* Deutsche Agrargeschichte, vol. 2 (Stuttgart: Eugen Ulmer, 1962). Works complementing these studies include Friedrich Lütge, *Geschichte der deutschen Agrarverfassung vom frühen Mittelalter bis zum 19. Jahrhundert,* Deutsche Agrargeschichte, vol. 3 (Stuttgart: Eugen Ulmer, 1963); and Günther Franz's *Geschichte des deutschen Bauernstandes vom frühen Mittelalter bis zum 19. Jahrhundert,* Deutsche Agrargeschichte, vol. 4 (Stuttgart: Eugen Ulmer, 1970). Eberhard Weiss, "Ergebnisse eines Vergleichs der grundherrschaftlichen Strukturen Deutschlands und Frankreichs vom 13. bis zum Ausgang des 18. Jahrhunderts, *"Vierteljahrschrift für Sozial- und Wirtschaftsgeschichte* 57 (1970), 1–14, gives a remarkably concise comparative perspective. The best survey of agricultural technology and productivity for the premodern period remains B. H. Slicher van Bath's *The Agrarian History of Western Europe, A.D. 500–1850,* trans. Olive Ordish (London: Edward Arnold, 1963).

The recent literature on the old County of Hohenlohe has focused on the extraordinary prosperity of the territory's peasantry in the eighteenth century. The best general descriptions of the territory include Wolfgang Saenger, *Die bäuerliche Kulturlandschaft der Hohenloher Ebene und ihre Entwicklung seit dem 16. Jahrhundert,* Forschungen zur deutschen Landeskunde, no. 101 (Remagen: Bundesanstalt für Landeskunde, 1957); and Heinrich Renner, *Wandel der Dorfkultur: Zur Entwicklung des dörflichen Lebens in Hohenlohe,* Veröffentlichungen des staatlichen Amtes für Denkmalpflege Stuttgart, ser. C, vol. 3 (Stuttgart: Silberburg, 1965). The most useful historical analyses of the eighteenth-century peasantry include Eckart Schremmer, *Die Bauernbefreiung in Hohenlohe,* Quellen und Forschungen zur Agrargeschichte, vol. 9 (Stuttgart: Gustav Fischer, 1963); and Peter Steinle, *Die Vermögensverhältnisse der Landbevölkerung in Hohenlohe im 17. und 18. Jahrhundert,* Forschungen aus Württembergisch Franken, vol. 5 (Schwäbisch Hall: Eppinger-Verlag, 1971). The only work to attempt a broader picture of the territory's history in this period is Wolfram Fischer, *Das Fürstentum Hohenlohe im Zeitalter der Aufklärung,* Tübinger Studien zur Geschichte und Politik, no. 10 (Tübingen: J. C. B. Mohr, 1958). For a modern anthropological view of Hohenlohe see the work of Gunter Golde, *Catholics and Protestants: Agricultural Modernization in Two German Villages* (New York: Academic Press, 1975).

A number of works now provide a detailed understanding of agrarian conditions in Germany in the century before the Peasants' War. The best general introduction to this problem in English is Peter Blickle, *The Revolution of 1525: The German Peasants' War from a New Perspective,* trans. Thomas A. Brady, Jr., and H. C. Erik Midelfort (Baltimore: Johns Hopkins University Press, 1981). The argument for a late medieval "agrarian crisis," however, remains problematic; see Wilhelm Abel, *Strukturen und Krisen der spätmittelalterlichen Wirtschaft,* Quellen und Forschungen zur Agrargeschichte, vol. 32 (Stuttgart: Gustav Fischer, 1980).

Our understanding of regional social and economic patterns in the German countryside around 1500 remains very uneven. The best works are David Sabean's studies

Bibliographical essay

of the Upper Swabian peasantry, *Landbesitz und Gesellschaft am Vorabend des Bauernkrieges: Eine Studie der sozialen Verhältnisse im südlichen Oberschwaben in den Jahren vor 1525,* Quellen und Forschungen zur Agrargeschichte, vol. 26 (Stuttgart: Gustav Fischer, 1972); "Family and Land Tenure: A Case Study of Conflict in the German Peasants' War (1525)," *Peasant Studies Newsletter* 3 (1974), 1–15; and "Probleme der deutschen Agrarverfassung zu Beginn des 16. Jahrhunderts: Oberschwaben als Beispiel," in Peter Blickle, ed., *Revolte und Revolution in Europa: Referate und Protokolle des Internationalen Symposiums zur Erinnerung an den Bauernkrieg 1525* (Munich: Oldenbourg, 1975), 132–50. For a stimulating examination of town–country relations see Tom Scott, *Freiburg and the Breisgau: Town–Country Relations in the Age of the Reformation and Peasants' War* (Oxford: Clarendon Press, 1986); and Neithard Bulst, Jochen Hoock, and Franz Irsigler, eds., *Bevölkerung, Wirtschaft und Gesellschaft: Stadt-Land-Beziehungen in Deutschland und Frankreich 14. bis 19. Jahrhundert* (Trier: Auenthal, 1983). On agrarian conditions in Franconia see Klaus Arnold, *Niklaushausen 1476: Quellen und Untersuchungen zur sozial-religiösen Bewegung des Hans Behem und zur Agrarstruktur eines spätmittelalterlichen Dorfes,* Saecula spiritalia, vol. 3 (Baden-Baden: Valentin Koerner, 1980); and Heinrich Heerwagen, *Die Lage der Bauern zur Zeit des Bauernkrieges in den Taubergegenden* (Nuremberg: J. L. Stich, 1899). Of the older studies the most useful is Hermann Wopfner, *Die Lage Tirols zu Ausgang des Mittelalters und die Ursachen des Bauernkrieges* (Berlin: Walther Rothschild, 1908).

A number of scholars have discussed *Herrschaft* as a historical, political, and sociological concept. For a helpful overview of the terminological and conceptual problems see Dietrich Hilger, "Herrschaft," in Otto Brunner, Werner Conze, and Reinhart Kosseleck, eds., *Geschichtliche Grundbegriffe: Historisches Lexikon zur politisch-sozialen Sprache in Deutschland* (Stuttgart: Klett-Cotta, 1982), vol. 3, 1–102. From a sociological and anthropological point of view the work of Max Weber on the exercise of power remains extremely helpful; see his *Wirtschaft und Gesellschaft: Grundriss der verstehenden Soziologie,* 5th ed. (Tübingen: J. C. B. Mohr, 1985). On the practice of domination see Pierre Bourdieu, *Outline of a Theory of Practice,* trans. Richard Nice, Cambridge Studies in Social Anthropology, no. 16 (Cambridge: Cambridge University Press, 1977); and especially David Sabean, *Power in the Blood: Popular Culture and Village Discourse in Early Modern Germany* (Cambridge: Cambridge University Press, 1984). Still fundamental contributions from the vantage point of German constitutional history (*Verfassungsgeschichte*) are Otto Brunner's *Land und Herrschaft: Grundfragen der territorialen Verfassungsgeschichte Österreichs im Mittelalter,* 5th ed. (Darmstadt: Wissenschaftliche Buchgesellschaft, 1973), and Gerhard Oestreich, *Geist und Gestalt des frühmodernen Staates* (Berlin: Duncker & Humblot, 1969). These last two works, like most studies in German constitutional history, offer views of *Herrschaft* from the vantage point of the lords and the state.

The understanding of *Herrschaft* from the vantage point of the village has not received the attention it deserves. The work of Peter Blickle is therefore particularly important in this regard: *The Revolution of 1525; Landschaften im Alten Reich: Die staatliche Funktion des gemeinen Mannes in Oberdeutschland* (Munich: C. H. Beck, 1973); *Deutsche Untertanen: Ein Widerspruch* (Munich: C. H. Beck, 1981); and "Herrschaft und Landschaft im Südwesten," in Günther Franz, ed., *Bauernschaft und Bauernstand 1500–1970: Büdinger Vorträge 1971–72,* Deutsche Führungsschichten in der Neuzeit, vol. 8 (Limburg–Lahn:

C. A. Starke, 1975), 17–42. See also the important critique of Blickle's work by Volker Press, "Herrschaft, Landschaft und 'Gemeiner Mann' in Oberdeutschland vom 15. bis zum 19. Jahrhundert, *"Zeitschrift für die Geschichte des Oberrheins* 123 (1975), 169–214. For Franconia, with some insights about the County of Hohenlohe, see Hans Hubert Hofmann, "Bauer und Herrschaft in Franken," in Günther Franz, ed., *Deutsches Bauerntum im Mittelalter*, Wege der Forschung, vol. 16 (Darmstadt: Wissenschaftliche Buchgesellschaft, 1976), 424–67.

Ever since the great debates over state and community in the nineteenth century, German scholars have dedicated a great deal of attention to the medieval and late medieval village commune. The best introduction to the problems and the vast literature on this topic is the remarkably concise overview by Heide Wunder, *Die bäuerliche Gemeinde in Deutschland* (Göttingen: Vandenhoeck & Ruprecht, 1986). Still fundamental is K. S. Bader, *Dorfgenossenschaft und Dorfgemeinde: Studien zur Rechtsgeschichte des mittelalterlichen Dorfes*, 3 vols. (Vienna: Böhlau, 1957–73). One should naturally consult the works of Peter Blickle cited above as well as the work edited by the Konstanzer Arbeitskreis für mittelalterliche Geschichte, *Die Anfänge der Landgemeinde und ihr Wesen*, 2 vols., Vorträge und Forschungen, vols. 7–8 (Constance: J. Thorbecke, 1964); and Franz, *Geschichte des deutschen Bauernstandes*. For the best study of serfdom on the eve of the Peasants' War see Claudia Ulbrich, *Leibeigenschaft am Oberrhein im Spätmittelalter*, Veröffentlichungen des Max-Planck-Instituts für Geschichte, vol. 58 (Göttingen: Vandenhoeck & Ruprecht, 1979). On the late medieval cycle of peasant revolts in Germany see Günther Franz, *Der deutsche Bauernkrieg*, 11th ed. (Darmstadt: Wissenschaftliche Buchgesellschaft, 1977); and Peter Blickle, "Peasant Revolts in the German Empire in the Late Middle Ages," *Social History* 4 (1979), 223–39.

Chapter 2

The consensus of scholarly opinion on the Peasants' War that once centered on Günther Franz's *Der deutsche Bauernkrieg* has broken apart in the last fifteen years, and so no single work can introduce scholars and students to the complicated problems related to the events of 1525. Peter Blickle has offered the most compelling new interpretation of the risings in *The Revolution of 1525*, but many scholars still doubt that one can characterize all of the events as a "revolution of the common man." Recent views on the regional complexity of the revolt have been summarized in a helpful volume edited by Horst Buszello, Peter Blickle, and Rudolf Endres, *Der deutsche Bauernkrieg* (Paderborn: Ferdinand Schöningh, 1984). The Marxist view has been elegantly put forward by Adolf Laube, Max Steinmetz, and Günter Vogler in their *Illustrierte Geschichte der frühbürgerlichen Revolution*. The diversity of scholarly opinion can be seen in published collections of articles on the war: Janos Bak, ed., *The German Peasant War of 1525*, Library of Peasant Studies, no. 3 (London: Frank Cass, 1975); Peter Blickle, ed., *Revolte und Revolution in Europa: Referate und Protokolle des Internationalen Symposiums zur Erinnerung an den Bauernkrieg 1525 (Memmingen, 24.–27. März 1975)*, Historische Zeitschrift, N.S. Supplement no. 4 (Munich: R. Oldenbourg, 1975); Bernd Moeller, ed., *Bauernkrieg-Studien*, Schriften des Vereins für Reformationsgeschichte, no. 189 (Gütersloh: Gerd Mohn, 1975); Heiko A. Oberman, ed., *Deutscher Bauernkrieg*, Zeitschrift für Kirchengeschichte, vol. 85, no. 2 (Stuttgart: W. Kohlhammer, 1974); Hans-Ulrich Wehler, ed.,

Bibliographical essay

Der Deutsche Bauernkrieg 1524–26, Geschichte und Gesellschaft, Special Issue no. 1 (Göttingen: Vandenhoeck & Ruprecht, 1975); and Rainer Wohlfeil, ed., *Der Bauernkrieg 1524–26* (Munich: Nymphenburger Verlag, 1975).

For a critical overview of the recent literature on the Peasants' War three review articles in English are very helpful: H. C. E. Midelfort, "The Revolution of 1525? Recent Studies of the Peasants' War," *Central European History* 11 (1978), 189–206; Tom Scott, "The Peasants' War: A Historiographical Review," *Historical Journal* 22 (1979), 693–720, 953–74; and Robert W. Scribner, "The German Peasants' War," in Steven Ozment, ed., *Reformation Europe: A Guide to Research* (St. Louis: Center for Reformation Research, 1982), 107–33.

A number of specific issues must be examined in any survey of the Peasants' War. David Sabean's *Landbesitz und Gesellschaft am Vorabend des Bauernkrieges* still stands as the best modern study of the socioeconomic origins of the revolt in Upper Swabia. The role of anticlericalism in the revolt, a particularly important cause of the revolt in Franconia, has been cogently analyzed by Henry J. Cohn, "Anticlericalism in the German Peasants' War 1525," *Past and Present* no. 83 (1979), 3–31. Blickle was perhaps the first to address the issue of the alliances of peasants and townsmen in *The Revolution of 1525*, but his views have been successfully questioned by Scott in *Freiburg and the Breisgau*. The best place to begin any study of the Twelve Articles and the other peasant political programs is Blickle. The most extensive analysis of the peasants' political programs is Horst Buszello, *Der deutsche Bauernkrieg von 1525 als politische Bewegung mit besonderer Berücksichtigung der anonymen Flugschrift an die Versamlung gemayner Pawerschaft*, Studien zur europäischen Geschichte, vol. 8 (Berlin: Verlag Otto H. Hess, 1969). Much more work is needed examining the links between the revolts and the Reformation. The pioneering work on this problem is Francisca Conrad's *Reformation in der bäuerlichen Gesellschaft: Zur Rezeption reformatorischer Theologie in Elsass*, Veröffentlichungen des Instituts für Europäische Geschichte Mainz, Abteilung für abendländische Religionsgeschichte, vol. 116 (Stuttgart: Franz Steiner, 1984). For a broader view see Peter Blickle *Gemeindereformation: Die Menschen des 16. Jahrhunderts auf dem Weg zum Heil* (Munich: Oldenbourg, 1985).

The revolt in Upper Swabia has received the most attention in recent years. The literature on Franconia, thanks largely to the work of Rudolf Endres, has not lagged far behind. His views are summed up in "Franken," in Buszello, Blickle, and Endres, eds., *Der deutsche Bauernkrieg*, 134–53; "Probleme des Bauernkrieges in Franken," in Wohlfeil, ed., *Der Bauernkrieg 1524–26*, 90–115; and "Probleme des Bauernkriegs im Hochstift Bamberg," *Jahrbuch für fränkische Landesforschung* 31 (1971), 91–138. Other important works on the rising in Franconia include: F. L. Baumann, ed., *Quellen zur Geschichte des Bauernkriegs aus Rothenburg ob der Tauber* (Tübingen: Litterarischer Verein in Stuttgart, 1878); Paul Eilentrop, *Verfassung, Recht und Wirtschaft in Rothenburg o/T. z. Z. des Bauernkrieges* (Marburg: Spannagel & Caesar, 1909); Heinrich Heerwagen, *Die Lage der Bauern zur Zeit des Bauernkrieges in den Taubergegenden* (Nuremberg: J. L. Stich, 1899); and Ferdinand Oechsle, *Beiträge zur Geschichte des Bauernkrieges in den schwäbisch-fränkischen Grenzlandern* (Heilbronn: Carl Drechsler, 1838). The only works in English on the Franconian risings treat small parts of the region. See Lawrence P. Buck, "Civil Insurrection in a Reformation City: The *Versicherungsbrief* of Windesheim, March, 1525," *Archiv für Reformationsgeschichte* 67 (1976), 100–17; and "The Containment of Civil

Insurrection: Nürnberg and the Peasants' Revolt 1524–1525" (Ph.D. diss., Ohio State University, 1971).

The consequences of the revolt remain poorly understood. For an introduction to this problem the essay by Helmut Gabel and Winfried Schulze, "Folgen und Wirkungen," in Buszello, Blickle, and Endres, eds., *Der deutsche Bauernkrieg*, 322–49, is informative. Also helpful are Thomas Sea, "The Economic Impact of the German Peasants' War: The Question of Reparations," *Sixteenth Century Journal* 8 (1977), 75–97; and Thomas Klein, "Die Folgen des Bauernkrieges von 1525: Thesen und Antithesen zu einem vernachlässigten Thema," *Hessisches Jahrbuch für Landesgeschichte* 25 (1975), 65–116. The full implications of Winfried Schulze's view concerning the transformation of social conflict in his path-breaking essay "Die veränderte Bedeutung sozialer Konflikte im 16. und 17. Jahrhundert," in Wehler, ed., *Der deutsche Bauernkrieg*, 277–302, have not been fully realized.

Chapter 3

The demographic patterns of the sixteenth century remain much more poorly understood than those of the seventeenth and eighteenth centuries. Michael W. Flinn sums up recent work on this problem for all of early modern Europe in *The European Demographic System, 1500–1820* (Baltimore: Johns Hopkins University Press, 1981). The links between population growth and economic stagnation are best explored in the classic studies of the French countryside by Emmanuel Le Roy Ladurie, *The Peasants of Languedoc*, trans. John Day (Urbana: University of Illinois Press, 1976); Jean Jacquart, *La crise rurale en Ile-de-France 1550–1670* (Paris: Armand Colin, 1974); Pierre Goubert, *Cent mille provinciaux au XVIIe siècle: Beauvais et le beauvaisis de 1600 à 1730* (Paris: Flammarion, 1968); and Guy Bois, *Crise de féodalisme: économie rurale et démographie en Normandie orientale due début du XIVe siècle au milieu du XVIe siècle*, Cahiers de la fondation nationale des sciences politiques, no. 202 (Paris: Presses de la fondation des sciences politiques, 1976).

Our understanding of the patterns for Central Europe remains sketchy by comparison, but two recent works make important contributions: Herman Rebel's excellent study of the Upper Austrian peasantry, *Peasant Classes: The Bureaucratization of Property and Family Relations Under Early Habsburg Absolutism 1511–1636* (Princeton, N.J.: Princeton University Press, 1983); and Arthur Imhof's micro-study of the Hessian village of Laimbach, *Die verlorenen Welten: Alltagsbewältigung und unsere Vorfahren – und weshalb wir uns heute so schwer damit tun* (Munich: C. H. Beck, 1984). One can find also useful information on population patterns in Karlheinz Blaschke's *Bevölkerungsgeschichte von Sachsen bis zur Industriellen Revolution* (Weimar: Böhlau, 1967); F. Koerner's "Die Bevölkerungsverteilung in Thüringen am Ausgang des 16. Jahrhunderts," *Wissenschaftliche Veröffentlichungen des deutschen Instituts für Länderkunde* 15–16 (1958), 178–315; Erich Keyser's *Bevölkerungsgeschichte Deutschlands*, 2d ed. (Leipzig: S. Hirzel, 1941); Wilhelm Abel's *Massenarmut und Hungerkrisen im vorindustriellen Europa: Versuch einer Synopsis* (Hamburg: Paul Parey, 1974); and Abel's other works cited above.

Chapter 4

The literature on popular culture in early modern Europe has grown considerably in recent years. Peter Burke's *Popular Culture in Early Modern Europe* (New York: Harper & Row, 1978) and Robert Muchembled's *Popular Culture and Elite Culture in France 1400–1750* (Baton Rouge: University of Louisiana Press, 1985) stress the role of elites in transforming popular culture. Marc Raeff develops a similar view for Germany in his *The Well-Ordered Police State: Social and Institutional Change through Law in the Germanies and Russia, 1600–1800* (New Haven, Conn.: Yale University Press, 1983).

My own views have been influenced by recent works that stress the role of villagers in shaping their own culture. Particularly important in developing this perspective are the works of Natalie Davis, *Society and Culture in Early Modern France* (Stanford, Calif.: Stanford University Press, 1965); Carlo Ginzburg, *The Cheese and the Worms: The Cosmos of a Sixteenth-Century Miller,* trans. John and Ann Tedeschi (Baltimore: Johns Hopkins University Press, 1980); and especially the innovative and challenging study by David Sabean, *Power in the Blood.* Giovanni Levi's *Inheriting Power: The Story of an Exorcist,* trans. Lydia G. Cochrane (Chicago: University of Chicago Press, 1988), approaches this problem with conceptual and methodological sophistication. For a perspective on the literature from the vantage point of a German historian see Norbert Schindler, "Spuren in die Geschichte der 'anderen' Zivilisation: Probleme und Perspektiven einer historischen Volkskulturforschung," in Richard van Dülmen and Norbert Schindler, eds., *Volkskultur: Zur Wiederentdeckung des vergessenen Alltags (16.–20. Jahrhundert)* (Frankfurt: Fisher, 1984), 13–77. An important set of case studies for Germany is Richard van Dülmen, ed., *Kultur der einfachen Leute: Bayerisches Volksleben vom 16. bis zum 19. Jahrhundert* (Munich: C. H. Beck, 1983).

Most of the work on the religious culture of Germany after 1555 has focused on the role of the elites in creating confessional cultures. This literature has successfully demonstrated the close links between politics and religion for Germany's elites, but has not yet found ways of examining the role of non-elites in shaping the process of confessionalization. Ernst Walter Zeeden's *Die Entstehung der Konfessionen: Grundlagen und Formen der Konfessionsbildung im Zeitalter der Glaubenskämpfe* (Munich: Oldenbourg, 1965) is typical of this approach to the problem. The strongest argument for confessionalization as a process is Heinz Schilling's *Konfessionskonflikt und Staatsbildung: Eine Fallstudie über das Verhältnis von religiösem und sozialem Wandel in der Frühneuzeit am Beispiel der Grafschaft Lippe,* Quellen und Forschungen zur Reformationsgeschichte, vol. 48 (Gütersloh: Gerd Mohn, 1981).

The few recent attempts to explore the religious culture of common people in this period include the important and stimulating book of Gerald Strauss, *Luther's House of Learning: Indoctrination of the Young in the German Reformation* (Baltimore: Johns Hopkins University Press, 1978). Two excellent studies of the city are L. J. Abray's *The People's Reformation: Magistrates, Clergy, and Commons in Strasbourg, 1500–1598* (Ithaca, N.Y.: Cornell University Press, 1985) and R. Po-Chia Hsia's *Society and Religion in Münster 1535–1618* (New Haven, Conn.: Yale University Press, 1984). About the response of German peasants to the Reformation little is known beyond the handful of studies that include Conrad, *Reformation in der bäuerlichen Gesellschaft*; Thomas Robisheaux, "Peasants and Pastors: Rural Youth Control and the Reformation in Hohenlohe, 1540–1680," *Social History* 6 (1981), 281–300; Gerald Strauss, "Success and Failure in the German Reformation," *Past and Present* no. 67 (1975), 30–63; and Bernard Vogler, "Die Entstehung der protestantischen Volksfrömmigkeit in der rheinischen Pfalz zwischen 1555 und 1619," *Archiv für Reformationsgeschichte* 72 (1981), 158–96. No comparable studies yet exist on peasant responses to the Catholic Reformation in Germany. More references to the literature can be found in the bibliographies by Heckel, Lutz, Moeller, and Schulze cited at the beginning of this essay.

The works of Gunther Franz on Hohenlohe are essential for any study of the small territorial state and the Protestant Reformation; see *Die Kirchenleitung in Hohenlohe in den Jahrzehnten nach der Reformation* (Stuttgart: Calwer, 1971); and "Reformation und landesherrliches Kirchenregiment in Hohenlohe," *Württembergisch Franken* 58 (1974), 120–52. For printed sources on the Reformation in the territory see Gunther Franz, ed., *Die evangelischen Kirchenordnungen des XVI. Jahrhunderts*, vol. 15: *Württemberg* pt. 1: *Grafschaft Hohenlohe* (Tübingen: J. C. B. Mohr, 1977); and Johann Christian Wibel, *Hohenlohische Kyrchen- und Reformations- Historie*, 4 vols. (Onolzbach: Jacob Christoph Poschens, 1752–5).

On the response of Hohenlohe's peasants to the Reformation see Robisheaux, "Peasants and Pastors"; and G. Bossert, "Die kirchlichen Zustände der Grafschaft Hohenlohe-Neuenstein im Jahr 1571," *Blätter für württembergische Kirchengeschichte* N.S. 30 (1926), 2–42. A wealth of information can be found on the folk culture of Franconia in this period in Karl–Sigismund Kramer, *Bauern und Bürger im nachmittelalterlichen Unterfranken: Eine Volkskunde auf Grund archivalischer Quellen*, Beiträge zur Volkstumsforschung herausgegeben von der bayerischen Landesstelle für Volkskunde, vol. 11 (Würzburg: Ferdinand Schöningh, 1957); and *Volksleben im Fürstentum Ansbach und seinen Nachbargebieten (1500–1800): Eine Volkskunde auf Grund archivalischer Quellen*, Beiträge zur Volkstumsforschung herausgegeben von der bayerischen Landesstelle für Volkskunde, vol. 12 (Würzburg: Ferdinand Schöningh, 1961).

Of the recent general works on the history of the family in the early modern period the ones I have most profited from include: Jean-Louis Flandrin, *Families in Former Times: Kinship, Household and Sexuality*, trans. Richard Southern (Cambridge: Cambridge University Press, 1979); Ralph A. Houlbrooke, *The English Family 1450–1700* (London: Longman, 1984); Michael Mitterauer and Reinhard Sieder, *The European Family: Patriarchy to Partnership 1400 to the Present* (Chicago: University of Chicago Press, 1982); Andrejs Plakans, *Kinship in the Past: An Anthropology of European Family Life, 1500–1900* (Oxford: Basil Blackwell, 1984); and Lawrence Stone, *The Family, Sex and Marriage in England 1500–1800* (London: Weidenfeld & Nicolson, 1977). Hans Medick, David Sabean, and others in David Sabean and Hans Medick, eds., *Emotion and Material Interest: Essays on the Study of the Family and Kinship* (Cambridge: Cambridge University Press, 1984) stress the importance of placing family history within the broader context of the whole social, economic, and political structure. Steven Ozment in *When Fathers Ruled: Family Life in Reformation Europe* (Cambridge, Mass.: Harvard University Press, 1983) offers a controversial view of the reform of the patriarchal family in German-speaking Central Europe.

Until recently most scholarly studies of marriage have focused on the changing framework of ecclesiastical and secular law. For a superb overview of theological attitudes and church laws on marriage since the Middle Ages see Gabriel Le Bras, "La doctrine du mariage chez les théologiens et les canonistes depuis l'an mille," in *Dictionnaire de théologie catholique* (Paris: Librarie Letouzey et Ané, 1927), vol. 9, pt. 2, cols. 2123–317. A helpful look at the problem of clandestine marriage is Beatrice Gottlieb, "The Meaning of Clandestine Marriage," in Robert Wheaton and Tamara K. Harevens, eds., *Family and Sexuality in French History* (Philadelphia: University of Pennsylvania Press, 1980), 49–83. For Germany, Hartwig Dieterich's *Das protestantische Eherecht in Deutschland bis zur Mitte des 17. Jahrhunderts*, Jus ecclesiasticum, vol. 10 (Munich: Claudius, 1970), and Ingeborg Schwarz's *Die Bedeutung der Sippe für die Öffentlichkeit der Eheschliessung im 15. und 16. Jahrhundert*, Schriften zur Kirchen- und Rechtsgeschichte, vol. 13 (Tübingen: Ekehart Fabian, 1959), provide the best starting points. On the functioning of Protestant and Catholic marriage courts Thomas M. Safley, *Let No Man Put Asunder: The Control of Marriage in the German Southwest: A Comparative Study 1550–1600* (Kirksville, Mo.: Sixteenth Century Journal Publishers, 1984), is useful.

My interpretation of the marriage ritual rests on insights gained from the anthropological literature on the ritual process. Clifford Geertz in his *The Interpretation of Cultures* (New York: Basic Books, 1973) suggests viewing ritual as a window on the whole society. Victor Turner in *Dramas, Fields, and Metaphors: Symbolic Action in Human Society* (Ithaca, N.Y.: Cornell University Press, 1974) and *The Ritual Process: Structure and Anti-Structure* (Chicago: Aldine, 1969) and Mary Douglas in her *Natural Symbols: Explorations in Cosmology* (New York: Pantheon, 1982) focus explicitly on the inner dynamics and symbolic meaning of rituals. Still helpful is the classic study of Arnold van Gennep, *The Rites of Passage*, trans. Monika B. Vizedom and Gabrielle L. Caffee (Chicago: University of Chicago Press, 1960). The most stimulating studies of marriage rituals in early modern Europe are those of André Burguière, "Le rituel du mariage en France: pratiques ecclésiastiques et pratiques populaires (XVe–XVIIe siècle)," *Annales E. S. C.* 33 (1978), 637–49; and Christiane Klapisch-Zuber, "Zacharias, or the Ousted Father: Nuptial Rites in Tuscany between Giotto and the Council of Trent," in her *Women, Family, and Ritual in Renaissance Italy* (Chicago: University of Chicago Press, 1985), 178–212, and "An Ethnology of Marriage in the Age of Humanism," also in *Women, Family, and Ritual*, 247–60. For Reformation Germany the best case study is for a Protestant city, Lyndal Roper's " 'Going to Church and Street': Weddings in Reformation Augsburg," *Past and Present* no. 106 (1985), 62–101. Studies on the countryside and Catholic territories are completely lacking.

Chapter 5

My views on family, inheritance, and power evolved in response to the ideas of a number of social anthropologists, especially those of Jack Goody and Pierre Bourdieu. Goody's *Production and Reproduction: A Comparative Study of the Domestic Domain* (Cambridge University Press, 1976) is an essential place to begin any study of the peasant family and property. Bourdieu's *Outline of a Theory of Practice* explores the relationship of kinship, property, and power. Of the large number of anthropological case studies on kinship and property, the following are particularly insightful: Maurice Bloch, *Placing the Dead: Tombs, Ancestral Villages, and Kinship Organization in Madagascar* (London:

Bibliographical essay

Seminar Press, 1971); J. K. Campbell, *Honour, Family and Patronage: A Study of Institutions and Moral Values in a Greek Mountain Community* (Oxford: Clarendon Press, 1964); John W. Cole, *Estate Inheritance in the Italian Alps*, University of Massachusetts, Department of Anthropology, Research Report no. 10 (Amherst: University of Massachusetts, 1971); John W. Cole and Eric R. Wolf, *The Hidden Frontier: Ecology and Ethnicity in an Alpine Valley* (New York: Academic Press, 1974); Jack Goody and S. J. Tambiah, *Bridewealth and Dowry*, Cambridge Papers in Social Anthropology, no. 7 (Cambridge: Cambridge University Press, 1973); E. R. Leach, *Pul Eliya: A Village in Ceylon: A Study of Land Tenure and Kinship* (Cambridge: Cambridge University Press, 1961); and J. A. Pitt-Rivers, *The People of the Sierra* (London: Weidenfeld & Nicolson, 1955).

Most scholarly work on early modern Europe has focused on family structure and inheritance customs divorced from their broader social and political context. The pioneering work in this field is Jean Yver's *Egalité entre héritiers et exclusion des enfants dotés: essai de géographie coutumière* (Paris: Sirey, 1966). A number of the questions raised by Yver are explored in a set of broad-ranging articles and case studies edited by Jack Goody, Joan Thirsk, and E. P. Thompson, *Family and Inheritance: Rural Society in Western Europe, 1200–1800* (Cambridge: Cambridge University Press, 1976). Lutz K. Berkner and Franklin F. Mendels discuss the gap between theory and practice in "Inheritance Systems, Family Structure, and Demographic Patterns in Western Europe, 1700–1900," in Charles Tilly, ed., *Historical Studies of Changing Fertility* (Princeton, N.J.: Princeton University Press, 1978), 209–23. Other important studies include Lutz Berkner, "Rural Family Organization in Europe: A Problem in Comparative History," *Peasant Studies Newsletter* 1 (1972), 145–55; and Christiane Klapisch and Michel Demonet, " 'A uno pane e uno vino': The Rural Tuscan Family at the Beginning of the Fifteenth Century," in Robert Forster and Orest Ranum, eds., *Family and Society* (Baltimore: Johns Hopkins University Press, 1976), 41–69. There is now a need for broader studies that examine the interrelationship of family form, class structure, and state power. Giovanni Levi's study of Lombardy (see above) is unusual and important in this regard.

For Germany, in addition to the works of Imhof, Rebel, and Sabean, the best studies are those of Lutz K. Berkner, "Inheritance, Land Tenure and Peasant Family Structure: A German Regional Comparison," in Goody, Thirsk, and Thompson eds., *Inheritance and Family*, 71–95; and "The Stem Family and the Developmental Cycle of the Peasant Household: An Eighteenth-Century Austrian Example," *American Historical Review* 77 (1972), 398–418. A social and political history of the reform of inheritance practices in sixteenth- and seventeenth-century Germany remains to be written. The only works that examine this vital problem do so from the vantage point of legal history, as, for example, Rolf-Dieter Hess, *Familien- und Erbrecht im württembergischen Landrecht von 1555 unter besonderer Berücksichtigung des älteren württembergischen Rechts*, Veröffentlichungen der Kommission für geschichtliche Landeskunde in Baden-Württemberg, ser. B, vol. 44 (Stuttgart: W. Kohlhammer, 1968). For a discussion of inheritance customs practiced in the German Southwest two studies are very helpful: Helmut Röhm, *Die Vererbung des landwirtschaftlichen Grundeigentums in Baden-Württemberg*, Forschungen zur deutschen Landeskunde, vol. 102

(Remagen: Bundesanstalt für Landeskunde, 1957); and Albert Ilien and Utz Jeggle, *Leben auf dem Dorf: Zur Sozialgeschichte des Dorfes und zur Sozialpsychologie seiner Bewohner* (Opladen: Wesdeutscher Verlag, 1978).

Chapter 6

No studies provide a satisfying view of Central Europe's agrarian economies in the context of the developing European market economies. Fernand Braudel, *Civilization and Capitalism, 15th–18th Century*, 3 vols., trans. Siân Reynolds (New York: Harper & Row, 1981–4), contains some useful insights into German agriculture and commercial development, but the focus remains on the world economy. More problematic, but still provocative conceptually, are two books by Immanuel Wallerstein, *The Modern World System: Capitalist Agriculture and the Origins of the European World-Economy in the Sixteenth Century* (New York: Academic Press, 1974); and *The Modern World System II: Mercantilism and the Consolidation of the European World-Economy, 1600–1750* (New York: Academic Press, 1980). Also helpful from a theoretical perspective are Peter Kriedte, *Peasants, Landlords and Merchant Capitalists: Europe and the World Economy, 1500–1800* (Cambridge: Cambridge University Press, 1983); and Witwold Kula, *An Economic Theory of the Feudal System: Towards a Model of the Polish Economy, 1500–1800*, trans. Lawrence Garner (London: NLB, 1976).

Other works that discuss the overall patterns of agrarian and commercial expansion in Europe include *The Cambridge Economic History of Europe*, vol. 5: *The Economic Organization of Early Modern Europe*, ed. E. E. Rich and C. H. Wilson (Cambridge: Cambridge University Press, 1978); and Carlo Cipolla, ed., *Fontana Economic History of Europe*, vol. 2: *The Sixteenth and Seventeenth Centuries* (London: Collins, 1974). The comparative perspective of Jan De Vries, *Economy of Europe in an Age of Crisis 1600–1715* (Cambridge: Cambridge University Press, 1976), is sound and stimulating. For a survey of the general economic development of Germany in this period Hermann Kellenbenz's *Deutsche Wirtschaftsgeschichte*, vol. 1: *Von den Anfängen bis zum Ende des 18. Jahrhunderts* (Munich: C. H. Beck, 1977), is the best book to turn to. Hektor Ammann's study of Nuremberg, *Nürnbergs wirtschaftliche Stellung im Spätmittelalter*, Nürnberger Forschungen, vol. 13 (Nuremberg: Verein für Geschichte der Stadt Nürnberg, 1970), is a model study of how a South German city expanded its market area in this period. Heinrich Bechtel's *Wirtschaftsgeschichte Deutschlands vom Beginn des 16. bis zum Ende des 18. Jahrhunderts* (Munich: Georg D. W. Callway, 1952) examines the influence of the territorial state on German economic development, organization, and values. Abel's *Agrarkrisen und Agrarkonjunktur* and *Geschichte der deutschen Landwirtschaft* are excellent surveys of general population trends, wages, and prices for German-speaking Central Europe. M. J. Elsas, *Umriss einer Geschichte der Preise und Löhne in Deutschland vom ausgehenden Mittelalter bis zum Beginn des neunzehnten Jahrhunderts*, 2 vols. (Leiden: A. W. Sythoff's, 1936–49), remains the standard work on German prices and wages. On German viticulture see Friedrich Bassermann-Jordan, *Geschichte des Weinbaus*, 2d ed., 3 vols. (Frankfurt: Frankfurter Verlag-Anstalt, 1923).

Explanations of peasant responses to the market economy have created a great deal of controversy among rural sociologists, economic anthropologists, and historians in recent years. One can still benefit from A. V. Chayanov's *The Theory of Peasant Economy*

(Homewood, Ill.: American Economic Association, 1966), although his theory has been sharply criticized in recent years. His ideas are summed up by Teodor Shanin, "The Nature and Logic of the Peasant Economy," *Journal of Peasant Studies* 1 (1973–4), 63–80, 186–206. Mark Harrison cautions against the romantic assumptions in Chayanov's theory in "Chayanov and the Economics of the Russian Peasantry," *Journal of Peasant Studies* 2 (1975), 389–417, and "The Peasant Mode of Production in the Work of A. V. Chayanov," *Journal of Peasant Studies* 4 (1977), 323–36. The most important recent work that builds on Chayanov's model is James C. Scott, *The Moral Economy of the Peasant: Rebellion and Subsistence in Southeast Asia* (New Haven, Conn.: Yale University Press, 1976). The following works offer penetrating Marxist views on production for the market in a peasant society: Maurice Godelier, *Rationality and Irrationality in Economics*, trans. Brian Pearce (New York: Monthly Review Press, 1972); Claude Meillassoux, *Maidens, Meals and Money: Capitalism and the Domestic Community* (Cambridge: Cambridge University Press, 1981); Marshall Sahlins, *Stone Age Economics* (Chicago: Aldine, 1972); and Michael Taussig, *The Devil and Commodity Fetishism in South America* (Chapel Hill: University of North Carolina Press, 1980).

Views that stress the flexibility of the peasant economy and peasants' willingness to adapt to market opportunities include Michael Lipton, "The Theory of the Optimising Peasant," *Journal of Development Studies* 4 (1968), 327–51; Sutti Reisig Ortiz, *Uncertainties in Peasant Farming: A Colombian Case*, London School of Economics, Monographs on Social Anthropology, no. 46 (London: Athlone, 1973); and Samuel Popkin, *The Rational Peasant: The Political Economy of Rural Society in Vietnam* (Berkeley and Los Angeles: University of California Press, 1979).

Debate about Europe's peasant economies during the commercial expansion of the sixteenth and seventeenth centuries has recently taken its focus from the controversial views of Robert Brenner. The pivotal work in the controversy is Brenner's "Agrarian Class Structure and Economic Development in Pre-Industrial Europe," *Past and Present* no. 70 (1976), 30–75. Criticisms of his thesis, and Brenner's response, have recently been published together in T. H. Aston and C. H. E. Philpin, eds., *The Brenner Debate: Agrarian Class Structure and Economic Development in Pre-Industrial Europe* (Cambridge: Cambridge University Press, 1985). The work edited by William Parker and Eric Jones, *European Peasants and Their Markets: Essays in Agrarian Economic History* (Princeton, N.J.: Princeton University Press, 1975), offers diverse points of view on the peasant economy and several important case studies. The best study of how villagers adapted responsively to market opportunities in this period is Jan De Vries's study of the Dutch countryside, *The Dutch Rural Economy in the Golden Age, 1500–1700* (New Haven, Conn.: Yale University Press, 1974). Among the monographs on village society in early modern Europe three are noteworthy for their parallels with the themes discussed in this book: Cicely Howell, *Land, Family and Inheritance in Transition: Kibworth Harcourt 1280–1700* (Cambridge: Cambridge University Press, 1983); Margaret Spufford, *Contrasting Communities: English Villagers in the Sixteenth and Seventeenth Centuries* (Cambridge: Cambridge University Press, 1974); and especially Keith Wrightson and David Levine, *Poverty and Piety in an English Village: Terling, 1525–1700* (New York: Academic Press, 1979).

Few comparable studies exist for early modern Central Europe. The questions tend to focus instead on the emergence of second serfdom and large latifundia in East Elbian

Bibliographical essay

Germany. Rebel's *Peasant Classes* is the best sustained regional analysis of a peasant economy for this period. Helpful insights can also be found in Willi A. Boelcke, "Bäuerlicher Wohlstand in Württemberg am Ende des 16. Jahrhunderts," *Jahrbücher für Nationalökonomie und Statistik* 176 (1964), 241–80, and "Wandlungen der dörflichen Sozialstruktur während Mittelalter und Neuzeit," in Boelcke, ed., *Wege und Forschungen der Agrargeschichte*, Festschrift Günther Franz (Frankfurt a. M.: DLG, 1967), 80–103; and Rudolf Endres, "Zur wirtschaftlichen und sozialen Lage Franken vor dem Dreissigjährigen Krieg," *Jahrbuch für fränkische Landesforschung* 28 (1968), 5–52. On the problem of the second serfdom see Jan De Vries, *Economy of Europe in an Age of Crisis*, 55–7; F. L. Carsten, *The Origins of Prussia* (Oxford, 1954); Hans Rosenberg, "The Rise of the Junkers in Brandenburg-Prussia, 1410–1653," *American Historical Review* 49 (1943–4), 1–22, 228–42; Arnost Klíma, "Agrarian Class Structure and Economic Development in Pre-Industrial Bohemia," *Past and Present* no. 85 (1979), 49–67; and Kula, *An Economic Theory of the Feudal System*.

One place to begin to understand the links between the peasant economy and the development of rural industry is Myron P. Gutman, *Toward the Modern Economy: Early Industry in Europe, 1500–1800* (New York: Alfred A. Knopf, 1988). See also Franklin Mendels, "Proto-Industrialization, the First Stage of Industrialization," *Journal of Economic History* 32 (1972), 241–61. A challenging theoretical view about the interrelationship of agriculture, population growth, family patterns, and rural industry also appears in Peter Kriedte, Hans Medick, and Jürgen Schlumbohm, *Industrialization before Industrialization: Rural Industry in the Genesis of Capitalism* (Cambridge: Cambridge University Press, 1981). Other useful studies include Hermann Kellenbenz, "Rural Industries in the West from the End of the Middle Ages to the Eighteenth Century," in Peter Earle, ed., *Essays in European Economic History* (Oxford: Oxford University Press, 1974), 45–88; Wolfram Fischer, "Rural Industrialization and Population Change," *Comparative Studies in Society and History* 15 (1973), 158–70; E. L. Jones, "The Agricultural Origins of Industry," *Past and Present* no. 40 (1968), 58–71; and Hermann Kellenbenz, *Deutsche Wirtschaftsgeschichte*, vol. 1, 241–58, 327–40.

The important role of the state in shaping industrial development in early modern Germany is emphasized in Max Barkhausen, "Government Control and Free Enterprise in Western Germany and the Low Countries in the Eighteenth Century," in Earle, ed., *Essays in European Economic History*, 212–73; Bechtel, *Wirtschafts- und Sozialgeschichte Deutschlands*; and Hans-Joachim Kraschewski, *Wirtschaftspolitik im deutschen Territorialstaat des 16. Jahrhunderts: Herzog Julius von Braunschweig-Wölfenbüttel (1528–1589)*, Neue Wirtschaftsgeschichte, vol. 15 (Cologne: Böhlau, 1978). The development of the metals industries has naturally received the most attention for sixteenth-century Germany; see, for example, Adolf Laube, *Studien über den erzgebirgischen Silberbau von 1470 bis 1546: Seine Geschichte, seine Produktionsverhältnisse, seine Bedeutung für die gesellschaftlichen Veränderungen und Klassenkämpfe in Sachsen am Beginn der Übergangsepoche vom Feudalismus zum Kapitalismus*, 2d ed. (Berlin: Akademie Verlag, 1976). Also helpful is the excellent case study of rural industry in eastern Swabia by Rolf Kiessling, "Stadt und Land im Textilgewerbe Ostschwabens vom 14. bis zur Mitte des 16. Jahrhunderts," in Bulst, Hoock, and Irsigler, eds., *Bevölkerung, Wirtschaft und Gesellschaft*, 115–37. Rudolf Braun's *Industrialisierung und Volksleben: Die Veränderungen der Lebensformen unter Einwirkung der verlagsindustriellen Heimarbeit in einem ländlichen Industriegebiet (Züricher*

Bibliographical essay

Oberland) vor 1800, 2d ed. (Göttingen: Vandenhoeck & Ruprecht, 1979), has become the classic study of rural industry for German-speaking Central Europe. On rural poverty and poor relief see Abel, *Massenarmut und Hungerkrisen*.

My thinking about the fierce debates and conflicts over market relationships in rural Hohenlohe has been most influenced by E. P. Thompson, "The Moral Economy of the English Crowd in the Eighteenth Century," *Past and Present* no. 50 (1971), 76–136; Scott, *The Moral Economy of the Peasant*; and Otto Brunner, " 'Das ganze Haus' und die alteuropäische 'Ökonomik,' " in his *Neue Wege der Verfassungs- und Sozialgeschichte*, 2d ed. (Göttingen: Vandenhoeck & Ruprecht, 1968), 103–27. Some useful comments on the changes in social values in Germany in this period can be found in Heinrich Lutz, "Normen und gesellschaftlicher Wandel zwischen Renaissance und Revolution – Differenzierung und Säkularisierung," *Saec* 26 (1975), 166–80; and especially Winfried Schulze, "Vom Gemeinnutz zum Eigennutz: Über den Normenwandel in der ständischen Gesellschaft der frühen Neuzeit," *Historische Zeitschrift* 243 (1986), 591–622; and Renate Blickle, "Subsistence and Property in the German Society of Orders" (paper delivered at the 102d Annual Meeting of the American Historical Association, Washington, D. C., December 27–30, 1987). For a romanticized view of the social and economic attitudes of the nobility see Otto Brunner, *Adeliges Landleben und europäischer Geist: Leben und Werk Wolf Helmhards von Hohbergs 1612–1688* (Salzburg: Otto Müller, 1949).

Modern social histories of Germany's nobilities between 1550 and 1700 are lacking; for overviews of the problems see H. Rössler, ed., *Deutscher Adel*, 2 vols., Deutsche Führungsschichten in der Neuzeit, vols. 1–2 (Darmstadt: Wissenschaftliche Buchgesellschaft, 1965). On the economic conditions of the nobility see Hermann Kellenbenz, "Die unternehmerische Betätigung der verschiedenen Stände während des Übergangs zur Neuzeit," *Vierteljahrschrift für Sozial- und Wirtschaftsgeschichte* 44 (1957), 1–25; Rudolf Endres, "Die wirtschaftlichen Grundlagen des niederen Adels in der frühen Neuzeit," *Jahrbuch für fränkische Landesforschung* 36 (1976), 215–37; and Karl-Georg Faber, "Mitteleuropäischer Adel im Wandel der Neuzeit," *Geschichte und Gesellschaft* 7 (1981), 276–96.

Chapter 7

The literature on peasant rebellions has become vast in the last twenty years. Eric Wolf's *Peasants* (Englewood Cliffs, N. J. : Prentice-Hall, 1966) and *Peasant Wars of the Twentieth Century* (New York: Harper & Row, 1969) remain the classic anthropological works on the problem. James Scott's *The Moral Economy of the Peasant* (see above) builds upon Wolf's approach. Of the large number of works on the peasant "tax revolt" in early modern Europe, the most important ones are by Yves-Marie Bercé, *Croquants et Nupieds: les soulèvements paysans en France du XVIe au XIXe siècle* (Paris: Gallimard, 1974), and *Fête et révolte: des mentalités populaires du XVIe au XVIIIe siècle* (Paris: Hachette, 1976). Also insightful is Emmanuel Le Roy Ladurie's *Carnival in Romans*, trans. Mary Feeney (New York: George Braziller, 1979). On the interrelationship of state power, capitalism, and agrarian class structure the following works of Charles Tilly are particularly insightful: *The Contentious French* (Cambridge, Mass.: Belknap Press, 1986); "Proletarianization and Rural Collective Action in East Anglia and Elsewhere, 1500–1900,"

Peasant Studies 10 (1982), 5–34, and "War and Peasant Rebellion in Seventeenth-Century France," in *As Sociology Meets History* (New York: Academic Press, 1981), 109–44. On the waning power of the village commune Clifford S. Davies, "Die bäuerliche Gemeinde in England (1400–1800)," in Winfried Schulze, ed., *Aufstände, Revolten, Prozesse: Beiträge zu bäuerlichen Widerstandsbewegungen im frühneuzeitlichen Europa*, Bochumer Historische Studien, vol. 27 (Stuttgart: Klett-Cotta, 1983), 41–59, is very suggestive. For a sociological approach to taxes and state power see Gabriel Ardant, *Théorie sociologique de l'impôt* (Paris: SEVPN, 1965).

Winfried Schulze and Peter Blickle have opened up a whole new field of inquiry on the peasant rebellion in Germany after the Peasants' War. Schulze's "Die veränderte Bedeutung sozialer Konflikte" (above) first looked at the legal mechanisms in the empire for resolving disputes between peasants and lords, a thesis fully developed in *Bäuerlicher Widerstand und feudale Herrschaft in der frühen Neuzeit*, Neuzeit im Aufbau, no. 6 (Stuttgart–Bad Cannstatt: Frommann-Holzboog, 1980). On the growing importance of imperial taxes and the "tax revolt" see his *Reich und Türkengefahr im späten 16. Jahrhundert: Studien zu den politischen und gesellschaftlichen Auswirkungen einer äusseren Bedrohung* (Munich: C. H. Beck, 1978) and "Oberdeutsche Untertanenrevolte zwischen 1580 und 1620: Reichssteuern und bäuerlichen Widerstand," in Peter Blickle, ed., *Bauer, Reich und Reformation: Festschrift für Günther Franz zum 80. Geburtstag am 23. Mai 1982* (Stuttgart: Eugen Ulmer, 1982), 120–47. Schulze places the German revolts in a comparative context in "Peasant Resistance in Sixteenth- and Seventeenth-Century Germany in a European Context," in Kaspar von Greyerz, ed., *Religion, Politics and Social Protest: Three Studies on Early Modern Germany* (London: Allen & Unwin, 1984), 61–98. Peter Blickle views the role of the village commune and the dynamics of rebellion in his far-ranging essay *Deutsche Untertanen*. Still helpful as an overview is Otto Schiff, "Die deutschen Bauernaufstände von 1525 bis 1789," *Historische Zeitschrift* 130 (1924), 189–209.

Helga Schultz looks at peasant revolts from a Marxist perspective in "Bäuerliche Klassenkämpfe zwischen frühbürgerlichen Revolution und Dreissigjährigen Krieg," *Zeitschrift für Geschichtswissenschaft* 20 (1972), 156–73. Peasant views toward authority in the late sixteenth century are explored by Thomas Robisheaux, "Peasant Unrest and the Moral Economy in the German Southwest 1560–1620," *Archiv für Reformationsgeschichte* 78 (1987), 174–86; and Winfried Schulze, "Herrschaft und Widerstand in der Sicht des 'gemeinen Mannes' im 16./17. Jahrhundert," in Hans Mommsen and Winfried Schulze, eds., *Vom Elend der Handarbeit* (Stuttgart: Klett-Cotta, 1981), 182–98. Eberhard Elbs shows the political complexity and the tenacity of one peasant movement in "Owingen 1584: Der erste Aufstand in der Grafschaft Zollern," *Zeitschrift für Hohenzollerische Geschichte* 17 (1981), 11–127. The long-term political and constitutional implications of a peasant revolt are explored by Volker Press, "Von den Bauernrevolten des 16. zur konstitutionellen Verfassung des 19. Jahrhunderts: Die Untertanenkonflikte in Hohenzollern-Hechingen und ihre Lösungen," in Hermann Weber, ed., *Politische Ordnungen und soziale Kräfte im Alten Reich*, Veröffentlichungen des Instituts für Europäische Geschichte, Abteilung Universalgeschichte, Beiträge zur Sozial- und Verfassungsgeschichte des Alten Reiches, no. 2. (Wiesbaden: Franz Steiner, 1980), 85–112. The best study of the sociological foundations of a revolt is Rebel's *Peasant Classes*.

Other important collections of case studies can be found in Peter Blickle, ed., *Aufruhr und Empörung? Studien zum bäuerlichen Widerstand im Alten Reich* (Munich: C. H. Beck, 1980); Schulze, ed., *Aufstände, Revolten, Prozesse*; and Gerhard Heitz et al., eds., *Der Bauer im Klassenkampf: Studien zur Geschichte des deutschen Bauernkrieges und der bäuerlichen Klassenkämpfe im Spätfeudalismus* (Berlin: Akademie, 1975). For a full discussion of the literature and the problems of research on German peasant rebellions see Thomas Barnett–Robisheaux, "Peasant Revolts in Germany and Central Europe after the Peasants' War: Comments on the Literature," *Central European History* 17 (1984), 384–403; and Peter Bierbauer, "Bäuerliche Revolten im Alten Reich: Ein Forschungsbericht," in Blickle, ed., *Aufruhr und Empörung?* 1–68.

Chapter 8

My views on the agrarian crisis developed in response to the extensive literature on the crisis of the seventeenth century. The place to begin a study of this issue is Trevor Aston, ed., *Crisis in Europe 1560–1660* (Garden City, N.Y.: Doubleday, 1967). Other views can be found in Geoffrey Parker and Lesley M. Smith, eds., *The General Crisis of the Seventeenth Century* (London: Methuen, 1985). Theodore K. Rabb defends the concept of a crisis, reviews the literature, and offers a helpful view of the political dimensions of the crisis in his essay *The Struggle for Stability in Early Modern Europe* (New York: Oxford University Press, 1975). Some of the most penetrating views on the political upheavals of the period can be found in Robert Forster and Jack P. Green, eds., *Preconditions of Revolution in Early Modern Europe* (Baltimore: Johns Hopkins University Press, 1970); J. H. Hexter, "Trevor-Roper's 'General Crisis,' " *Past and Present* no. 18 (1960), 12–18; J. I. Israel, "Mexico and the 'General Crisis' of the Seventeenth Century," *Past and Present* no. 63 (1974), 33–57; and A. L. Moote, "The Preconditions of Revolution in Early Modern Europe: Did They Really Exist?" *Canadian Journal of History* 8 (1973), 208–34. Geoffrey Parker helps put the political events of the Thirty Years' War into the broader context of seventeenth-century politics in *Europe in Crisis 1598–1648* (London: Fontana, 1979). The most searching new interpretation of the political and social meaning of the war itself is J. V. Polišenský's *The Thirty Years' War*, trans. Robert Evans (Berkeley and Los Angeles: University of California Press, 1971). The traditional accounts of the war by Georges Pagès, *The Thirty Years' War, 1618–1648*, trans. David Maland and John Hooper (New York: Harper, 1970), and C. V. Wedgwood, *The Thirty Years' War* (Garden City, N.Y.: Doubleday, 1961) also remain helpful.

   The most concise recent treatment of the complicated political and constitutional issues raised for the Holy Roman Empire by the Thirty Years' War is the survey by Heckel (see above). Hartmut Lehman's *Das Zeitalter des Absolutismus: Gottesgnadentum und Kriegsnot, Christentum und Gesellschaft*, vol. 9 (Stuttgart: W. Kohlhammer, 1980), is noteworthy for its treatment of the links between the political crisis and the religious mentality of the age. On the expansionism of the Habsburg monarchy, by far the best treatment is R. J. W. Evans, *The Making of the Habsburg Monarchy, 1550–1700: An Interpretation* (Oxford: Clarendon Press, 1979). The political crisis of the small German territorial state during the 1620s, 1630s, and 1640s does not receive much attention in most accounts of the war. An exception is Ferdinand Magen, who looks at the politics of the House of Hohenlohe at the beginning of the war in his *Reichsgräfliche Politik in*

Bibliographical essay

Franken: Zur Reichspolitik der Grafen von Hohenlohe am Vorabend und zu Beginn des Dreissigjährigen Krieges, Forschungen aus Württembergisch Franken, vol. 10 (Schwäbisch Hall: Historischer Verein für Württembergisch Franken, 1975). The bibliographies on the war and the crisis in Heckel's *Deutschland im konfessionellen Zeitalter*, Lehmann's *Das Zeitalter des Absolutismus*, and Rabb's *Struggle for Stability* are also indispensable guides to the literature.

My views on the economic and demographic dimensions of the crisis have been partly shaped by E. J. Hobsbawm, "The Crisis of the Seventeenth Century," in Aston, ed., *Crisis in Europe*, 5–62; De Vries, *Economy of Europe in an Age of Crisis*; J. V. Polišenský, "The Thirty Years' War and the Crises and Revolutions of Seventeenth-Century Europe," *Past and Present* no. 39 (1968), 34–43; and Henry Kamen, "The Economic and Social Consequences of the Thirty Years' War," *Past and Present* no. 39 (1968), 44–61. The classic study cited above by Goubert, *Cent mille provinciaux au XVIIe siècle*, provides insights about the demographic reversal.

Studies of the economic and demographic crisis in Germany lag behind those for other parts of Europe. A rough overall view is sketched out by Günther Franz in *Der dreissigjährige Krieg und das deutsche Volk: Untersuchungen zur Bevölkerungs- und Agrargeschichte*, 3d ed., Quellen und Forschungen zur Agrargeschichte, vol. 7 (Stuttgart: Gustav Fischer, 1962). The best case study of demography and economy to date for this period is Christopher Friedrichs, *Urban Society in an Age of War: Nördlingen, 1580–1720* (Princeton, N.J.: Princeton University Press, 1979). Other than Imhof's work on Laimbach in *Die verlorenen Welten*, modern studies of the demographic crisis in the countryside are wholly lacking. Other useful studies on the economic crisis include Ingomar Bog, *Die bäuerliche Wirtschaft im Zeitalter des Dreissigjährigen Krieges: Die Bewegungsvorgänge in der Kriegswirtschaft nach den Quellen des Klosterverwalteramtes Heilsbronn*, Schriften des Instituts für fränkische Landesforschung an der Universität Erlangen, Historical Series, vol. 4 (Coburg: Vest Verlag, 1952); W. von Hippel, "Bevölkerung und Wirtschaft im Zeitalter des Dreissigjährigen Krieges," *Zeitschrift für Historische Forschung* 5 (1978), 413–48; Rebel's *Peasant Classes*; and Abel's *Agrarkrisen und Agrarkonjunktur*.

Herbert Langer calls attention to the special meaning of the Central European peasant revolts between 1618 and 1648 in "Der Dreissigjährige Krieg – endgültiger Abschluss der deutschen Revolution des 16. Jahrhunderts?" in Manfred Kossok, ed., *Rolle und Formen der Volksbewegung im bürgerlichen Revolutionszyklus* (Taunus: Detlev Auvermann KG Glashütten, 1976), 16–36. Also helpful is K. Gerteis, "Regionale Bauernrevolten zwischen Bauernkrieg und Französischer Revolution: Eine Bestandsaufnahme," *Zeitschrift für Historische Forschung* 6 (1979), 37–62.

Chapter 9

On the recovery of Germany and the territorial state after the Thirty Years' War, Rudolf Vierhaus, *Deutschland im Zeitalter des Absolutismuss (1648–1763)*, 2d ed., Deutsche Geschichte, vol. 6 (Göttingen: Vandenhoeck & Ruprecht, 1984) provides a comprehensive overview. Günther Franz's *Der dreissigjährige Krieg und das deutsche Volk* briefly examines the agrarian order after the war. In addition to the works of Abel, De Vries, and Kriedte cited above, Friedrich-Wilhelm Henning, *Landwirtschaft und ländliche Gesellschaft in*

Bibliographical essay

Deutschland, vol. 1: *800–1750* (Paderborn: Ferdinand Schöningh, 1978), and Diedrich Saalfeld, *Bauernwirtschaft und Gutsbetrieb in der vorindustriellen Zeit*, Quellen und Forschungen zur Agrargeschichte, vol. 6 (Stuttgart: Gustav Fischer, 1960), survey the agricultural trends of the late seventeenth and eighteenth centuries. Klaus Winkler examines the role of the state in propping up the agararian order in *Landwirtschaft und Agrarverfassung im Fürstentum Osnabrück nach dem Dreissigjährigen Kriege: Eine wirtschaftsgeschichtliche Untersuchung staatlicher Eingriffe in die Agrarwirtschaft*, Quellen und Forschungen zur Agrargeschichte, vol. 5 (Stuttgart: Gustav Fischer, 1959).

Most of the scholarly work on peasant economy and society in Germany in this period focuses on the narrow problems of income, state taxation, and the end of seigneurial burdens. Some of the studies in this genre include Walter Achilles, *Die steuerliche Belastung der braunschweigischen Landwirtschaft und ihr Beitrag zu den Staatseinnahmen im 17. und 18. Jahrhundert*, Quellen und Darstellungen zur Geschichte Niedersachsens, vol. 82 (Hildesheim: A. Lax, 1972); Friedrich-Wilhelm Henning, *Bauernwirtschaft und Bauerneinkommen im Fürstentum Paderborn im 18. Jahrhundert*, Schriften zur Wirtschafts- und Sozialgeschichte, vol. 18 (Berlin: Duncker & Humblot, 1970); Christoph Dippel, *Die Bauernbefreiung in Deutschland, 1590–1850* (Stuttgart: W. Kohlhammer, 1980); Eckart Schremmer, *Die Bauernbefreiung in Hohenlohe*, Quellen und Forschungen zur Agrargeschichte, vol. 9 (Stuttgart: Gustav Fischer, 1963); and Peter Steinle, *Die Vermögensverhältnisse der Landbevölkerung in Hohenlohe im 17. und 18. Jahrhundert*, Forschungen aus Württembergisch Franken, vol. 5 (Schwäbisch Hall: Hans P. Eppinger, 1971).

On the continuing importance of peasant rebellions in Germany into the eighteenth century see the collections of articles in Schulze, ed., *Aufstände, Revolten, Prozesse*. The role of peasant movements in shaping state power is explored by Gerhard Heitz, "Der Zusammenhang zwischen den Bauernbewegungen und der Entwicklung des Absolutismus in Mitteleuropa," *Zeitschrift für Geschichtswissenschaft* 13 (1965), 71–83. The best case study of one such movement is Werner Trossbach's study of Hesse, *Soziale Bewegung und politische Erfahrung: Bäuerlicher Protest in hessischen Territorien 1648–1806* (Weingarten: Drumlin, 1987). For a contrast between the small patrimonial state and the large territorial state at the end of the Old Regime, Hans Hubert Hofmann's *Adelige Herrschaft und souveräner Staat: Studien über Staat und Gesellschaft in Franken und Bayern im 18. und 19. Jahrhundert*, Studien zur bayerischen Verfassungs- und Sozialgeschichte, vol. 2 (Munich: Kommission für bayerische Landesgeschichte, 1962), is insightful.

Index

Index

ture, 28, 29, 37, 49, 191; Thirty Years' War, 203, 204, 212, 229
Frankfurt, 17, 249, 254
Franz, Günther, 49n, 79, 222
Frederick V, Elector, 203
Frederick the Wise, Elector, 100
Friedrich, Count, 179

Gallas, General, 223, 224
Georg I, Count: and Peasants' War, 58, 59; reign, 30, 32, 100, 179, 183
Georg Friedrich, Count, 204, 214, 229
Georg von Wertheim, Count, 63
Gerabronn, 22, 74, 75
Gerichtsherrschaft, 9; *see also* domination
Germany: 16, 23, 256; economy and population, 25, 27–8, 79, 123, 148, 149, 159, 161, 163, 164, 166, 170, 227, 228, 237, 238, 239, 243, 247, 248, 249, 250, 255; peasant rebellions, 72, 194, 232; Peasants' War, 42, 49, 68, 258; social structure, 12, 39, 69, 70, 90–1, 95, 99–100, 187, 227, 243, 247, 258, 259; state structures, 29, 30, 37, 180, 186, 228–9, 236, 242, 255–6, 260, 261–2; Thirty Years' War, 212, 213, 223, 229, 234–5; *see also* South Germany
Geyer, Florian, 62
Goody, Jack, 6, 127n
Gottfried, Count, 20, 34–5
Grimmelshausen, H. J. C. von, 202
Grosser, Martin, 163

Habsburg, House of, 175, 178, 202, 204, 205, 212, 223; *see also* Charles V; Ferdinand II; Maximilian I; Rudolf II
Hartmann, Gallus, 124–5
Hartmann, Johann, 95, 103–4
Hausvaterliteratur, 84, 237
Hegau, 81
Heilbronn, 22, 100; economy, 27, 57, 151, 153, 254; and Peasants' War, 54, 60, 64, 65
Heinrich Friedrich, Count: and peasants, 81–2, 230, 239, 240, 242; reign, 224, 229, 232–7 passim
Heresbach, Conrad, 163
Hergot, Johann, 47
Hipler, Wendel, 26–7, 32–3, 57, 63–5
Hohenlohe (land): economy and population, 9, 75, 79, 149–51, 156, 201, 216, 222, 238, 247–54; marriage and inheritance, 81–3, 111, 115, 116–20, 121, 122, 127–31; land and settlement patterns, 5, 7, 17–25, 80, 183; Peasants' War, 42, 45, 52, 53, 53–61, 64; social conditions, 8, 74, 95, 161–2, 203, 217, 243–7, 257–8

Hohenlohe, County of, 6; church and Reformation, 36–40, 100–5; state and society, 70–1, 72–9, 110, 164–6; state structure, 123–6, 179, 209–10, 223–6, 228, 233, 236, 255–6, 261; taxes, 177–86, 210, 212, 235–6, 240, 242, 262
Hohenlohe, House of, 22; authority and power, 7, 20, 28–36, 51, 56, 104–5, 119, 167, 170, 178, 191–4, 235, 256; and economy, 23, 34, 72, 77, 78, 148, 152, 160, 171, 174, 250; Hohenlohe-Langenburg, 81, 108, 110, 161–2; Hohenlohe-Neuenstein, 179–81, 186, 187, 214–22 passim, 229; Hohenlohe-Schillingsfürst, 29, 30; Hohenlohe-Waldenburg, 179; Hohenlohe-Weikersheim, 104; and peasant revolts, 44, 52, 57, 58, 59–60, 65–6, 190, 231; taxes, 177, 180, 193–4, 195, 201, 209–10, 242; and Thirty Years' War, 202, 204, 206, 212, 220, 229
Holy Roman Empire, 4; imperial taxes, 176–8, 182, 186, 220, 234, 262; institutions, 36, 178, 210, 214; and peasant revolts, 39, 60, 61, 64, 195; political structure, 11, 29, 35, 36–7, 90, 95, 124, 201, 235, 256, 261; and Thirty Years' War, 197, 202, 223, 228, 233
Huberinus, Caspar, 100–3, 124
Hungary, 204, 249
Hürden, 23, 78, 80, 89

immigrants, 78, 82, 83, 197, 216, 243
Ingelfingen: economy and population, 74, 152, 166, 255; marriage and inheritance, 104, 107, 114, 124, 126, 128–9, 133–6 passim; and the state, 34–5, 209, 217
inheritance customs, 3, 11; and economy, 147, 248; impartible, 80–3, 127–8, 143, 144, 145; partible, 81, 128–9, 143, 144; state regulation, 36, 122, 123–6, 131, 148, 261; strategies, 129–32, 133–5, 140–1, 142, 143–5
Isherwood, Baron, 83n

Jagstberg, 20
Jagst River: description, 6, 18, 24, 213; and economy, 137, 138, 151, 153, 156, 157
Jagst River valley: description, 19–20, 22, 29; economy, 73, 75, 241; social conditions, 73, 188, 212, 217, 243–4
John of Saxony, Duke, 65

Kappel, 57
Kirchberg (district), 151–2, 179, 217, 250
Kirchberg (town), 20, 74, 170
Kirchensall, 184

293

Index

Kocher River, 18, 20, 24, 27, 57, 133
Kocher River valley: princes' estates, 29, 77; social conditions, 26, 27, 28, 75, 183, 188
Kraft, Count, 204, 214, 229
Kraft VI, Count, 30; authority and power, 32, 34–6, 37–8, 171; reforms, 81, 97, 123–4
Künzelsau, 17, 20, 140, 181
Kupferhof, 23, 78, 80, 111–12, 153, 267–8
Kupferzell, 257

laborers: and economy, 78, 153, 156, 160–1, 165, 205, 216, 250, 267; and inheritance customs, 122, 130, 141, 146; and Peasants' War, 27, 43, 44, 46; and social structure, 80, 87, 106, 244, 254; and the state, 183, 184, 194, 225, 226
labor services, *see under* seigneurial burdens
Landsteuer, see taxes: territorial
Langenburg (district): debts, 229–30, 234, 238–41; description, 6, 7–8, 24; economy, 24–5, 149–52, 154, 161, 162, 205, 206, 213, 250; population, 26, 70–1, 74, 78–9, 222; property distribution, 81, 82–3, 129, 132, 137; social conditions, 73–9, 80, 113, 188, 217–21, 224, 243–7 passim; and state burdens, 168–70, 184, 189, 207, 211, 214, 215, 231, 236, 242; structures of authority, 26, 104, 171–3, 179, 221, 233
Langenburg (town), 29; description, 6, 20, 22–3, 30, 170; economy and population, 76, 79, 115, 148, 152, 153, 156, 157, 161, 162, 164, 166, 208, 215, 241, 249–50, 251; social conditions, 130, 142, 217, 221, 243, 244–6; Thirty Years' War, 222, 224, 225
Liebesdorf, 213
Lindenbronn, 161, 250
Löwenstein, County of, 29, 60
Ludwig Casimir, Count: 81, 103, 131; and economy, 164, 166; and taxes, 177, 179, 180
Luther, Martin, 46, 96–9 passim, 116

Main River, 17, 27
Main River valley, 48, 75
Mainz, archbishopric of, 29, 54, 61
Marienberg, 50, 65
Markbreit, 151
marriage, 6, 35, 96, 115–16; alliances, 106, 108, 109, 111, 112, 117, 122, 133, 137, 260; contracts, 131, 134, 144; courts, 7, 102, 104–5, 106, 108, 109, 110, 114, 115, 123, 125, 260; engagement, 83, 98–9, 102, 103, 108–15 passim; and inheritance practices, 83, 122, 123, 130, 134, 145; law, 103, 108–16 passim, 125, 131;

rituals, 99, 102, 107, 114, 116–20, 261; secret, 98, 102, 103, 106; state regulation, 36, 38, 97, 98, 99–100, 110, 123
Maximilian, Duke of Bavaria, 204
Maximilian I, Emperor, 29
Mayer, Johann Friedrich, 18, 23, 257–8
merchants: 82, 183, 188; and market expansion, 44, 148, 152, 153, 157, 164, 165, 205, 208, 216, 250; status and wealth, 90, 122, 197, 206
Mergentheim, 17, 19, 22, 29; economy, 133, 151, 152, 160; and Peasants' War, 45, 51, 53, 54, 60, 62
Michelbach, 57
millers: and economy, 153, 164, 165, 205, 208, 215–16, 238, 250; property and wealth, 87, 89, 122, 133, 137–40, 145, 195–6, 197; and the state, 183, 188, 219, 225–6, 234, 240–1
Mittelbach, 138
Müntzer, Thomas, 47

Neckar River, 27, 57, 133, 250
Neckar River valley, 26, 75, 81; and Peasants' War, 42, 48, 50, 52, 60
Neckar Valley–Odenwald Army, 65; organization, 49, 52, 53–61; and Reformation, 56, 60, 63–5
Nesselbach, 23; economy and population, 73, 74, 78, 152; property and wealth, 90, 154; and the state, 226, 233
Neuenstein, 133; administrative center, 20, 30, 33, 104, 125, 179, 233; Peasants' War, 59, 60; social conditions, 74, 124, 183
Nördlingen, 78, 223
Nuremberg, 50, 70, 99, 249

Oberregenbach, 23; economy and population, 73, 74, 78, 80, 155, 161; property and wealth, 89, 137, 138; and the state, 196, 217, 220, 221, 231
Ochsenfurt Field Ordinance, 53
Odenwald, 42, 48, 52, 54, 60
Öhringen, 37, 212; church and Reformation, 22, 56, 95, 100, 101; description, 17, 19, 20–2; economy and population, 26–7, 72, 74, 151, 152, 255; marriage and inheritance, 97, 102, 104, 124; and Peasants' War, 44, 55–9, 60, 62, 65; and the state, 30, 32, 33, 34–5, 35–6, 38, 119, 179, 183, 189, 209

Peace of Augsburg, 100, 124, 178
peasant revolts, 2, 11; early modern, 176, 194, 197, 221, 232, 236; Thirty Years' War, 216, 262

294

Index

Peasants' War, 1, 8, 24, 26, 27; consequences, 68, 70, 95; leaders, 56–7, 61–2,
63, 65; and Reformation, 10, 41, 61–5,
100; and the state, 41–2, 168, 174, 175,
182, 189–90, 258, 259
Pfedelbach, 30, 57
Philip, Landgrave of Hesse, 100
Philip Ernst, Count, 204, 214, 229; government, 119, 131, 179, 201, 208; taxes,
208, 210, 240
Poland, 249
Polišenský, J. V., 12
poor, 11; growth in numbers, 3, 10, 69–79,
81, 95, 106, 161, 261; and economy, 72,
75–7, 147, 155–62 passim, 165, 166,
167, 208, 215; marriage and inheritance,
112, 130, 131, 133, 135, 141; and social
structure, 69, 77–8, 79–80, 86, 96, 197,
255, 260; and the state, 69–70, 161–2,
173, 190, 193, 196–7, 232, 241, 261; see
also cottagers; laborers
population, 9, 43, 79, 227; decline, 12, 78–9,
151, 162, 166, 222, 243, 249, 262;
growth, 3, 10, 26–7, 70–9 passim, 80,
81, 95, 96, 106, 110, 124, 133–4, 146,
149, 205, 242, 243, 254, 255, 258, 259
Prague, 90, 178
prices: agricultural products, 153, 156, 166,
190, 196, 227, 249; grain, 44, 71, 148,
149, 154, 155, 161, 162, 173, 205, 206,
248–9, 255; and related trends, 82–3,
156, 162, 164, 190, 208, 248–9
princes: authority and power, 28–36 passim,
65, 66, 67, 69, 122, 124, 148, 164–5,
166, 170, 175, 191, 223, 228, 229, 235,
236–7, 242, 254–6, 260; and Holy Roman Empire, 204–5, 209, 211–12, 233,
234–5; and peasant rebellions, 39, 42,
45, 49, 51, 60, 64, 72, 176; society and
economy, 81, 90–1, 95–6, 100, 123, 237,
238–9, 243, 259; state burdens, 147,
176–80, 181–5, 187–8, 208; see also
domination; Hohenlohe, House of; state
Protestantism: imperial politics, 100, 178,
201, 203, 204, 211, 212, 214, 230, 232;
and patriarchal family, 103, 104–5, 106,
114, 261
Prussia, 255
Pufendorf, Samuel, 235–6

Rabb, Theodore K., 262
Raboldshausen, 23, 137; economy and popu-
lation, 25, 73, 74, 75, 78, 233, 267–8
Ranke, Leopold von, 1
Reformation, 1–3, 9, 178; and marriage re-
form, 96–105, 109, 110, 117–20, 121,

124; and Peasants' War, 46, 56, 59, 60,
61–5, 66; and society, 83, 95, 124, 130,
135, 260; and the state, 36, 38, 148
"Reformatio Sigismundi," 38–9
rents, see under seigneurial burdens
Rhineland, 75, 203, 212, 229, 248, 255
Rot am See, 22, 75
Rothenberg o.d.T.: 29, 78, 100; economy, 27,
151, 152, 153, 160; and Peasants' War,
44, 45, 47, 48, 51, 52, 62, 63
Rublack, Hans-Christoph, 50n
Rudolf II, Emperor, 177
Rupershausen, 173

Saxony, 64, 99, 105, 123, 237
Scheftersheim, 212
Schmalkaldic League, 100
Schöntal, 29, 52, 54, 55, 57, 59
Schrotzberg, 20, 203, 250
Schultheiss, see under state
Schulze, Winfried, 262
Schutz und Schirm, 9, 34–5; see also
domination
Schwäbisch Gmünd, 48
Schwäbisch Hall, 17, 22, 29, 78, 100; economy
and trade, 27, 151, 152, 153, 160, 250
Scribner, Robert, 1
seigneurial burdens, 35, 168–70, 179, 184,
186–7, 242; death duties, 52, 57, 63, 64,
168, 170, 173; dues, 47, 48, 51, 66, 161,
167, 172, 179, 180, 207, 213, 214, 215,
229, 230, 234, 235, 238–9, 242; entry
fines, 34, 57, 168–9, 173, 242; labor services, 34, 44, 46, 57, 63, 171, 176, 186–
90, 193, 195, 231, 236, 257, 262; and
Peasants' War, 45, 51, 52, 58, 63–4;
rents, 34, 46, 48, 51, 52, 161, 167, 168–
9, 170, 172, 179, 180, 207, 213, 214,
215, 229, 230, 234, 235, 238–9, 242;
serfdom, 28, 35–6, 52, 57, 63, 66, 187,
227; tithes, 27, 34, 46, 47, 48, 52, 57,
63, 64, 161, 167, 169, 229, 238–9; tolls,
52, 57, 66
serfdom, see under seigneurial burdens
servants: and economy, 80, 87, 250, 254;
marriage and inheritance, 101, 107, 133,
146, 250, 254
Silesia, 255
smallholders: economy, 76, 77, 83, 153, 155–
61 passim, 165, 166, 173, 215, 251; and
Peasants' War, 43, 44, 48; property and
wealth, 84–90, 122, 130, 133, 145,
145, 146; and the state, 183, 184, 187–
90 passim, 193, 194, 218, 219, 225, 241;
and social structure, 78, 243–7 passim,
254, 255

295

Index

Weber, Max, 6
wedding, *see* marriage: rituals
Weigandt, Friedrich, 63
Weikersheim, 20, 187; economy and society, 74, 152, 203, 204, 255; and the state, 29, 30, 77, 104, 179, 209, 222, 233, 235
Weinsbach, 57
Weinsberg, 50, 52, 60, 61, 65
Wertheim, 17
Westphalia, 255
widows, 11, 111, 162, 194, 229; and inheritance practices, 122, 129, 130, 132, 136, 138, 139, 140, 141, 145
Wimpfen, 17, 22, 57, 151, 203
winegrowers: economy, 24, 27–8, 44, 45, 153, 156, 157, 158–9, 212–13, 216, 234, 241, 251; and social structure, 24, 197, 243, 245; and the state, 46, 183, 189, 225
Wolfgang II, Count, 204; administrative reforms, 74, 170, 172, 173, 179; and economy, 157, 158, 166–7, 171; social reform, 72, 110, 131, 161–2; taxes, 186, 187–90 passim, 191–4, 196

women: inheritance practices, 128–9, 131, 132, 133, 134, 136, 138, 145; marriage, 97, 113–14, 115–16; social control of, 83, 96, 107, 114–15, 122, 197; *see also* widows
Württemberg, 29, 54, 60; economy and society, 123, 176, 222, 247; Reformation, 100, 103, 104, 105, 125; state structure, 255, 256
Würzburg (bishopric): authority and jurisdiction, 28, 29, 36, 37–40, 97, 102; Catholic Reformation, 178, 205, 212; and Peasants' War, 44, 46, 49, 51, 53
Würzburg (city), 19, 148, 149; and Peasants' War, 49, 50, 53, 65

youths, 11; marriage and inheritance, 107, 109, 118–19, 130, 131, 145; social control of, 96, 121, 122, 197, 261

Zürich, 99
Zweiflingen, 57

297